THE ILLUSTRATED
ENCYCLOPEDIA OF
FLY-FISHING

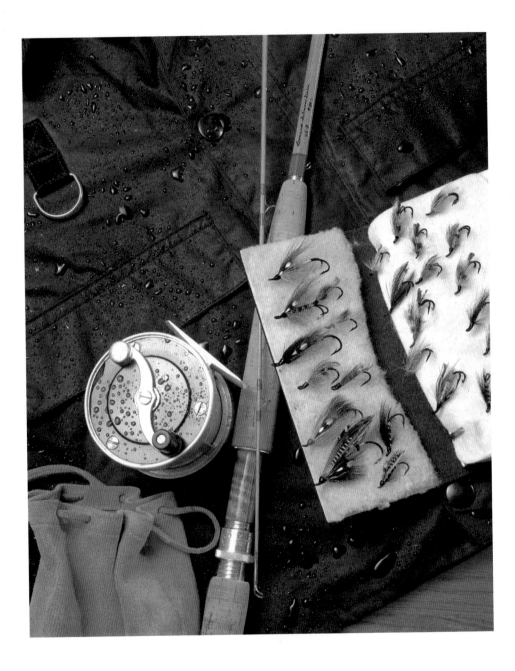

THE ILLUSTRATED
ENCYCLOPEDIA OF
FLY-FISHING

A COMPLETE A–Z OF TERMINOLOGY, TACKLE & TECHNIQUES

SILVIO CALABI

Henry Holt and Company
New York

Henry Holt and Company, Inc.
Publishers since 1866
115 West 18th Street
New York, New York 10011

Henry Holt ® is a registered trademark of
Henry Holt and Company, Inc.

Published in Canada by Fitzhenry & Whiteside Ltd.,
91 Granton Drive, Richmond Hill, Ontario L4B 2N5.

Library of Congress Cataloging-in-Publication Data

Calabi, Silvio.
    The illustrated encyclopedia of fly-fishing / Silvio Calabi—1st ed.
      p. cm.
    1. Fly fishing—Encyclopedias I. Title.
    SH456 . C28 1993   92-34565
    799 . 1 ' 2—dc20   CIP

ISBN 0-8050-1989-8

First Edition—1993

Produced by AM Publishing Services
227 Park Avenue, Hoboken, New Jersey 07030
and
Wieser & Wieser, Inc.
118 East 25th Street, New York, New York 10010

Design: Tony Meisel
Drawings: Patricia Shea
Origination: Regent Publishing Services Ltd.
Printing: Cronion SA

Printed in Spain

10 9 8 7 6 5 4 3 2 1

INTRODUCTION

Fly-fishing is the fastest-growing form of recreational fishing in North America. Every year more than 10 million people participate at all levels of the sport, drawn by its blend of contemporary sophistication and age-old technique.

Fly fishers, men and women alike, have gone far beyond the desire to catch a fish for the table; by choosing to fish with fly tackle, they stack the odds in favor of their quarry. Casting a specially weighted and tapered fly line is a rhythmic and even beautiful motion that is much more difficult to learn than conventional casting. The flies themselves—weightless bits of feathers and fur—often imitate tiny stream insects, whose behavior on or in the water is difficult to mimic with an artificial. And to succeed, the fly fisher must learn the behavior of his or her target species and the ecology of the stream—or lake or coral flat, etc.—in which it lives. These anglers delve into fisheries biology, the entomology of aquatic insects, even the politics of habitat conservation and restoration.

While many kinds of fishing have come to rely on large boats, electronic fish-finders and other artificial aids, fly-fishing is still the same one-on-one game it has been for centuries—a game that is often played out in chest waders on freestone streams around the world, from New England to Alaska and New Zealand to Patagonia. But high-tech has always been an element of the sport, although an 18th-Century angler would instantly recognize modern fly rods, reels, flies, waders, nets, gaffs and so on. Today Tonkin cane has been replaced as the rod material of choice by high-Modulus graphite fiber; leaders and lines are no longer gut and silk but specially formulated and coated nylons; today's waders deliver performance unknown even 15 years ago.

As the strength and durability of tackle has improved, the sport has expanded dramatically beyond the trout stream. Fly fishers, with their seemingly fragile tippets, insignificant hooks and long, willowy rods, now routinely take on tarpon, tuna, sharks and even billfish, and win—sometimes. But the chase is the thing.

Which leads to another important reason that fly-fishing has never been more popular: the catch-and-release ethic. In the 1970s the idea that "a good gamefish is too valuable to be caught only once" began to take firm hold across American fly-fishing. Today gamefish are played skilfully and released quickly, uninjured, to fight again and to spawn more gamefish. As a result, fly-fishing is significantly better across North America than it was in 1975. Although all sorts of fishermen are now beginning to release their catch, fly-fishing has become known as a non-consumptive and environmentally sensitive field sport. The angler who takes a big, difficult fish is a hero—but he's an even bigger hero if he lets it go again.

As fly-fishing grows, its spin-offs, notably fly-tying and tackle collecting, have become important pastimes themselves. Fly-tying is no longer a way to economize on the cost of flies; it is an end unto itself, with its own significant advances in materials, tools and techniques. And vintage fly tackle is an expression of art and craftsmanship even more refined than furniture-making.

Through the centuries fly-fishing has developed its own language: hundreds of terms, expressions and phrases—shorthand, slang and formal definitions alike—that convey this intricate sport to its devotees. Some are technical or scientific, some are emotional, political, illogical; some have come down to us from Old England, some were coined in a skiff last year. Like the sport, the language of fly-fishing is still growing and expanding. Language is the window to a soul; understanding this language opens up not only modern fly-fishing but also reveals its unique historic roots.

Silvio Calabi
Camden, Maine

THE ENCYCLOPEDIA

Abel Arm—A special offset and raised flyreel foot invented and patented in 1989 by San Francisco fly-casting authority Mel Krieger and reel maker Steve Abel, and subsequently put into production by Abel's company, Abel Automatics, of Camarillo, California.

The Abel Arm is made of machined aluminum and replaces the conventional foot on any Abel fly reel. When fastened to the reel seat of a rod, its L-shape moves the reel about an inch and a half away from the rod and the same distance up, away from the butt cap. Once the angler becomes used to reaching for the crank handle in a different place, the benefits of the Arm, though slight, become obvious (at least to the saltwater or salmon/steelhead fisherman): Prolonged, high-speed cranking is easier; and relocating the reel out from one's belly provides the advantages of a fighting butt, which include keeping the reel away from folds of clothing or chest waders. The inventors also claim an improvement in the casting balance of the whole rod/reel combo.

Abel Arm

ACA—The American Casting Association; see.

Advanced Composite Material—A substance made of two or more structurally different materials that, when combined, produce a substance with properties not found in its components. In fly-fishing, the most common advanced composite materials are boron, graphite and fiberglass (which see), along with the epoxy resins used to bind them together. Other examples, such as silicon carbide, have yet to find their way into fly rods.

Aftershaft—The aftershaft, or afterfeather, is the smaller, softer "accessory" feather directly underneath and attached to another feather; its purpose is to provide extra insulation for the bird. The soft aftershaft varies: In upland gamebirds such as grouse or quail it is long and narrow, with short barbs; a turkey aftershaft is often oval or elliptical, with long, fine barbs; ducks' afterfeathers are very short and have no stem.

AFTMA—The American Fishing Tackle Manufacturers Association; see.

Agate—Natural agate is usually chalcedony, one of a family of hard, very fine-grained, crystalline, quartz-like semi-precious minerals. Lumps of agate may have wavy bands of color running through them. The thin, highly polished bands of agate glued into some fishing-line guides are often a reddish, creamy or gray hue; if the bands are thick enough, swirls or clouds of another color may be visible inside. Because of its fine-grained hardness, smoothly finished agate is an excellent bearing surface for lines, and tackle manufacturers have been using it on the inner surfaces of stripping guides on rods and line guides on reels for more than a century. Its disadvantages are that it is relatively heavy (which was less of a problem on already-heavy bamboo and wooden rods) and, because of its crystallinity, it is also somewhat fragile, at least in thin-walled rings (heavy "aggie" marbles are anything but fragile). The round, thumb-diameter agate guides on vintage Hardy Perfect reels, for example, are often cracked; at least once in its long life, the reel was dropped. Agate guides are still available, but in pure performance they have been superseded by guides lined with manmade substances such as silicon carbide (see). See also Line Guide.

Albright Knot—Named for Captain Jimmy Albright, the dean of Florida Keys fishing guides, this is an excellent connector for monofilament lines of highly unequal diameter—which, in fly-fishing, usually means tying heavy saltwater shock tippets (see) to much lighter class tippets (also see). The Albright knot is also a good, if perhaps overly complicated, way to tie a leader butt to the tip of a fly line, and it can even serve to attach monofilament to a wire loop. See Knots.

Alder Fly—An unusual and somewhat rare (compared to midges, mayflies and caddis flies) aquatic insect, of the family *Sialidae*, of northern North America and Europe. The larvae look like beetles and the adults resemble caddis flies, with tented wings, long antennae and no tails. Alderfly larvae prefer cool lakes and slow-flowing streams whose bottoms are littered with leaves and other debris, for cover. The larval stage lasts eight to 10 months; then in the early spring the insect crawls out on land to dig a shallow burrow in which to pupate. A week or so later it emerges on the surface and metamorphoses into a winged adult. From here on, the lifespan is a week or less. The flies mate and the females lay their eggs on the underside of some structure that overhangs the water—anything from a leaf to a bridge or dock. In a few more days, the eggs hatch, the larvae drop into the water, and the cycle begins again. Alder flies are clumsy in the air and easily victimized by a breeze, and they are usually an easy meal for trout, smallmouth bass or other surface-feeding fish.

Alder Fly

Alevin—The youngest stage of a fish; the newly hatched fry with their yolk sacs not yet absorbed.

American Casting Association, The—The control organization for competitive casting in the USA. Its primary purpose is to sponsor and promote casting competition for distance and accuracy on the local, regional and national levels. Four kinds of tackle are covered: spinning, spin-casting, bait-casting and fly-casting; in all but some of the distance events, standard fishing tackle is used. See Casting Competition.

According to the ACA, the first casting tournaments in America were held at yearly meetings of the New York Sportsmen's Club in the early 1860s. When organization arrived, it was under the aegis of the National Rod and Reel Association from 1882 to 1889. Then in 1906 the National Association of Scientific Angling Clubs was organized in Kalamazoo, Michigan; its first national tournament took place in Racine, Wisconsin, a year later. National events have since taken place almost every year since. Two final organizational evolutions took place: In 1939 the NASAC was re-incorporated as the National Association of Angling and Casting Clubs, which in turn became the ACA in 1960.

In 1916, the Association became a member of the AAU, the American Athletic Union, and in 1954 it joined the US Olympic Committee. Casting has never become an Olympic event, but there are world championships every two years under the control of the International Casting Federation (which in turn was recognized by the International Olympic Committee in 1960).

The American Casting Association is headquartered at 7328 Maple Avenue, Cincinnati, Ohio 45231.

American Fishing Tackle Manufacturers Association, The—The trade group devoted to furthering the cause and the business of sport fishing in North America. It was established as the Associated Fishing Tackle Manufacturers in 1933 and adopted the present name in 1961. In 1958, the group launched its own trade exposition, now known simply as the AFTMA Show, which generally takes place in August. Some form of fisheries protection has always been a core plank in AFTMA's platform, and in 1949 it established the Sport Fishing Institute, now based in Washington, DC, to educate Americans (and their lawmakers) about fishing for fun. In the same vein, AFTMA is nearly unique among trade organizations in that it supported a tax upon its members— the 10% excise tax levied on fishing tackle under the 1952 Dingell-Johnson Act (see)— in order to support fisheries protection.

AFTMA has not been active in fly-fishing since the 1970s, when the use of fishing electronics and the bass and walleye tournament scene began to expand dramatically. At about the same time, fly fishers began to espouse the doctrine of catch-and-release more publicly, and the gap between the two camps seemed to widen and harden.

(The split became nearly complete in 1987, when the Fly Tackle Dealer Show was launched and when fly-fishing companies assembled to talk about forming what became NAFTA, the North American Fly Tackle Trade Association—see.)

However, AFTMA had at least one far-reaching and beneficial direct effect upon the sport of fly-fishing: In 1961, under the direction of member Leon Chandler, of the Cortland Line Company, AFTMA succeeded in establishing the numerical system of fly line sizes that is used today. Previously, fly lines were graded according to a complicated letter code that suited only silk lines. The new system, tailored to modern plastic-coated lines, expressed size (that is, weight) and type in a very simple, logical way that even beginners could understand and remember. The American Casting Association (see), which was still active then, endorsed the change; line companies embraced it; and fly fishers, particularly the newcomers, quickly made it the status quo. See Fly Line.

American Museum of Fly Fishing, The—Currently in a white clapboard building near the Equinox Hotel and the old Orvis Company headquarters on Historic Route 7 in the center of Manchester, Vermont. Both the hotel and the museum are closely linked with The Orvis Company, for the hotel was founded by Franklin Orvis, Charles F. Orvis's (see) brother, in 1853, and the museum was launched 110 years later by Charles' successor as head of the company, Leigh Perkins Sr.

Actually, it was the idea for such a museum that was born in 1963; exhibits opened to the public in 1967, in a rented wing of the Orvis headquarters store in Manchester Center.

Much credit for the museum goes to Hermann Kessler, who was then art director for *Field & Stream* Magazine. According to *The American Flyfisher* (since 1974 the official publication of the museum): "The idea of a museum was presented to Leigh Perkins by me [Kessler] in the bar of the Williams Club in New York City the night Wes Jordan [the renowned Orvis rod maker who perfected the impregnation process for bamboo rod blanks] presented for sale, for the first time, a limited edition of the Theodore Gordon Brushy Bank Fly Rod.

"After that meeting, down in the bar, I offered my idea for a museum to Perkins. Present at the table were Lee Wulff, Helen Shaw [the well-known fly tier, who was also Kessler's wife], Richard Grossenbach, Wes Jordan and some other members of Theodore Gordon Flyfishers.

"Six months or so later Leigh came back to me and showed an interest in me developing the museum idea. Months later, after much correspondence and many phone calls, a meeting was called, at which time a board of trustees was formed."

Other fly-fishing notables, including Arnold Gingrich, the founding editor of *Esquire*, offered support too, and Kessler, to his delight, was named the museum's first president.

The American Museum of Fly Fishing—an exhibit hall in Manchester, Vermont.

In its early days, much of the museum's collection was necessarily Orvis-related. That company dates back to 1856 and its relics are still piled up in attics from one end of Manchester (indeed, the entire Battenkill Valley) to the other. But as the museum grew in support, influence and stature, donations came in from around North America. In 1984, under the directorship of John Merwin (founding editor of *Fly Rod & Reel* Magazine, who left publishing in 1983), the museum was able to vacate the Orvis store block and move into its present, private building.

Given its large and growing collection of important, historic and merely interesting rods, reels, flies, memorabilia, books, catalogs, paintings, prints and so on—some of which tour the US in traveling exhibits—the museum has become a unique attraction and resource. It perfectly fulfills its charter, to preserve America's rich fly-fishing heritage. The public is welcome to tour the galleries, and annual membership dues are inexpensive. Contact The American Museum of Fly Fishing at P.O. Box 42, Manchester, VT 05254; 802-362-3300.

Anadromous—Sea-run; ascending rivers from the sea for reproduction; salmon and certain trout, such as steelhead and sea-trout, are anadromous because they migrate annually into fresh water from the ocean to spawn. Not only salmonids can be anadromous; shad and smelt are among various other anadromous species as well.

Many landlocked fish species exhibit similar behavior in that they too migrate to lay their eggs, often from lakes into streams.

Anti-Reverse Reel—A type of fly reel in which the crank handle does not turn backwards when line is pulled off the spool; the reel has a one-way clutch (as opposed to a direct-drive reel; see). The benefits are: First, when a hooked fish suddenly bores for the horizon, the internal drag comes into play immediately; the angler need not let go of the crank handle first. That has kept many a fish from breaking off. And second, the stationary handle is no threat to knuckles or loose clothing. The energy concentrated within a 10-pound bonefish or a 40-pound salmon or a 100-pound tarpon is difficult to comprehend. Under such impetus, a fly reel spool may briefly go berserk and render a fair imitation of a wood chipper.

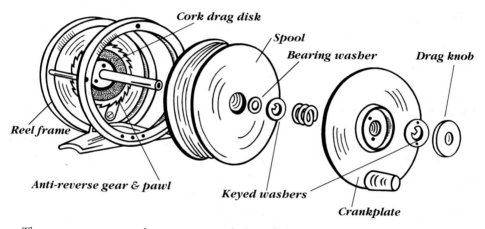

There are moments when one can only let a fish run. The internal drag should be operating then, whether the reel is direct-drive or anti-reverse. With the latter, the angler can rest his or her hand right on the reel handle, ready to crank instantly. (The time saving, however, is minimal.) The critical times in a big-fish confrontation are at the beginning and the end. The sudden shock of combat joined—the acceleration that terminal tackle and spool must endure—often ends fights before they are truly under way. And later, when both combatants are weary and the distance between them has shrunk to a boat or rod length, human error can play major a role. Many a tired, excited fisherman, fingers locked onto the reel, has broken his own tippet when a desperate fish turned one last time and he couldn't get his hand off the spool quickly enough. An anti-reverse reel is always ready—the spool can always turn, under drag, whether the crank handle is captive or not.

Some fishermen, however, contend that they need the positive control of a direct-drive reel in order to move a fish those last few feet to the net or gaff. Anti-reverse fans say that if the drag is set properly, it's no problem; or they even loosen the drag slightly (as a precaution against a final, wild lunge) and put finger pressure on the line (not the reel) to bring the fish to hand.

Generally speaking, anti-reverse reels are slightly heavier and more complex and thus more prone to failure, theoretically, than direct-drive. Expert big-game fly fishers are split about evenly between the two types. Deciding which to use is a personal matter that must be based upon experience and preference. However, the manufacturers of dual-mode reels (see) claim to offer the best of both worlds.

Aquaseal—a tough, effective trademarked adhesive sold in dive and fly-fishing specialty shops to repair tears and punctures in neoprene-rubber wet suits and waders. It is also useful for coating/protecting line splices and other rigging knots that have to pass repeatedly back and forth through the line guides on a fly rod. Aquaseal thinner is called Cotol. See also Cyanoacrylate Glue.

Arbor—The spindle, or axle, of a fly reel, on which the spool rotates. In most fly reels, the arbor is supported on only one side, where it is fastened to the reel backplate (see). This makes it easy to change spools; they can be slid off the free end of the arbor. However, many heavy-duty saltwater fly reels and some salmon reels (especially those that are patterned after early 20th-Century designs) have full cage frames and plates on both sides, and the center screw, which holds the crank handle, thus supports the outer end of the arbor. The trade-off here is strength for convenience—changing spools is difficult. See Fly Reel.

Arbor Knot—A slip knot often used to attach backing to the arbor of a reel spool. See Knots.

Arctic Charr—*Salvelinus alpinus*, a type of charr, an arctic salmonid found in high northern latitudes all around the world. Arctic charr are aggressive, highly predatory, fall-spawning gamefish and, in coastal zones, often sea-run; inland fish may live in lakes or in streams. To the native people of eastern Canada they were and still are an important food fish. In northwestern North America, arctic charr often overlap with Dolly Varden and rainbow trout, and in coastal rivers all three feed heavily on the eggs deposited by Pacific salmon in mid- to late summer.

Distinguishing arctic charr from Dolly Varden can be difficult. The rule of thumb is that if the spots on the fish are smaller than the iris of its eye, the fish is a Dolly. The Pacific-drainage arctic charr generally also has a more forked tail. However, as their ranges overlap only from west-central Canada westward, it's generally safe to say that an Atlantic-drainage charr—in Labrador, for example—is a not a Dolly, by default. Positive identification can be much harder in Alaska and western Canada. The author has found presumably cross-bred charr in British Columbia's remote Cassiar Mountains that shared the characteristics of Dolly Varden and arctic charr both. (The charrs have provoked discussion and disagreement among fisheries biologists ever since Carolus Linnaeus, the Swedish scientist who developed the modern system of taxonomy, mislabelled his own country's charr as a *Salmo* instead of a *Salvelinus* in 1758.)

In eastern Canada, arctic charr and brook trout (both *Salvelinus*) are often found in the same water, and fishermen who see only the spectacularly red-orange bellies and white-trimmed fins of both fish sometimes find them hard to tell apart. Arctic charr lack the worm-like black markings that brook trout carry on their backs. While charr may be spotted, the spots are not surrounded by lighter halos. See also Charr, Dolly Varden.

Arundinaria amabilis—The Latin taxonomic name for Tonkin cane, used in making fine split-cane fishing rods. See Bamboo.

Atlantic Salmon—Traditionally the "king of freshwater gamefish" for North American anglers. By law in the USA and Canada, these must be fly fishers, for it is illegal to take sea-run (as opposed to landlocked) Atlantic salmon on anything but flies—and often unweighted, single-hook flies, at that. In the rest of the Northern Hemisphere, the salmon is equally highly regarded, but angling is permitted with all sorts of tackle, even natural bait—large shrimp, called prawns, lashed to hooks.

The Atlantic salmon is *Salmo salar*, the leaper. In North America, this large, handsome fish was once so common from Ungava Bay down to about the Delaware River that colonists wrote of killing spawning salmon simply by riding a horse through a stream. In the same era, in the British Isles, Scandinavia and northwestern Europe, servants complained of being given salmon every day to eat. Early in the 20th Century, Atlantic salmon rivers in America were dammed and polluted and the fish stocks reduced by netting and disease to the point where salmon became a prized catch. The same process had taken place a century earlier in England; when wealthy British sportsmen began to buy up salmon rivers in Ireland and Scotland (and later in Scandinavia and Iceland)—where the locals had, until then, regarded their salmon merely as an occasional source of food—the elevation of the species to its prominent spot at the top of the fly fisher's pantheon began. The blueblood salmon-angling culture has since permeated the sport of fly-fishing. And in parts of the British Isles, poaching the landowner's salmon is still regarded as an honorable tradition—at least among certain classes. In North America taking an Atlantic salmon on fly tackle was regarded as virtually impossible up until about 1840, when visiting Brits began to prove that it could be done.

Atlantic Salmon—Aquaculture has removed much of the commercial netting pressure from wild fish stocks; these Atlantic salmon pens are moored in an estuary on Ireland's west coast.

River clean-up and ever-stricter regulation of all types of fishing on both sides of the Atlantic have halted the Atlantic salmon's long decline, but it will never be as common as it once was. And these efforts may be wasted if acid precipitation continues unabated.

Even non-angling city-dwellers know the Atlantic salmon is famous for its ability to return from the ocean to the very river it was born in. Upon entering its natal stream, usually between June and October, each salmon is a silver-bright, streamlined torpedo with a greenish-black back and small X-shaped black markings scattered across its shiny sides. If sea lice are still attached to the fish, it has been out of salt water only a few hours.

The salmon have returned to spawn, and *only* to spawn. They will not, and cannot, eat at all; their metabolisms have changed, diverting energy from the digestive to the sexual organs. This then is the question facing the salmon angler: How to catch a fish that won't eat? Theories are that salmon strike a fly out of curiosity; out of aggression, to defend themselves, their mate or the nest; or through a conditioned response to a sequence of events that weeks earlier meant food. The most successful salmon anglers are those who have learned a river well enough to pinpoint, even in high water, the lies where the migrating fish rest—the rocks, snags, ledges and shelves of the river bottom that break the current. Salmon consistently move into in the same spots on their way upstream, and a fly swum through there may bring a strike.

Lee Wulff, the greatest American salmon angler, likened the fish in fresh water to an electric battery: Charged with energy from its years at sea, it must survive without food for up to nine months. The angler who hooks one, plays it and releases it has drawn down that "charge" by forcing the fish to spend some of its vital strength. And so it is doubly important that the fisherman play the salmon well, to avoid injuring it directly (by hooking it elsewhere than in the mouth or by dragging it onto shore to land it) and to avoid playing it too long. Some experienced salmon fishermen use breakaway leaders (see) so they may release a fish that can't be landed within an acceptably short time.

Unlike the Pacific species, Atlantic salmon do not necessarily die after spawning (see). As water flow and temperatures permit, the returning salmon struggle "home," sometimes winning their way more than a hundred miles upstream until they reach a pool with the right combination of current and substrate. The hen fish selects a spot and, holding herself almost flat to the bottom, sends the gravel flying with powerful strokes of her broad tail. With the aid of the current she soon has scoured out a large, shallow redd, or nest, in which she deposits her eggs. The male fish, having driven off his rivals, takes his turn, fertilizing the eggs with a cloud of milt, and then the hen covers the eggs with new gravel she digs from just upstream. In doing so, she creates another redd and often uses that as well, eventually laying some 7,000 to 20,000 eggs.

The spawned-out salmon stay in the river through the subsequent winter and return to the sea, if at all, in spring. Then they are known as kelts, or black salmon. Thin, dark, nearly starved, still facing upriver, they allow the spring currents to push them back down to the sea. Something on this journey—perhaps the taste/smell of salt water—triggers their feeding and once again they begin to eat and grow, to regain their strength perhaps to return a year and a half later. It is estimated that only some five to ten percent of Atlantic salmon survive predation and injury to spawn a second time. A very, very few accomplish this three and even four times.

The salmon young, first called fingerlings and then parr, pass their first two or three years in the river until, as smolts of maybe eight inches in length, they too head for the sea. Like their parents, they are constantly attacked by predators on the way.

Atlantic salmon grow largest in Canada and Norway, where many rivers produce a few 40-plus-pound fish every season (and one or two that may exceed 60 pounds). Still, 10 to 25 pounds is the norm there, as it is in Iceland. In the USA's top native Atlantic salmon water, Maine's Penobscot River—where salmon are aggressively and some say fruitlessly re-stocked every year—10 to 15 pounds is a good fish. Every Atlantic salmon river also has an annual "run" of grilse, smaller salmon (variously defined as under twenty-four inches, or less than 10 pounds) that are thought to be sexually immature. Nevertheless, in rivers where it's legal, the guides often urge fishermen to kill their grilse, to prevent them from increasing and turning a "salmon river" into a "grilse river."

For centuries, the location of the offshore feeding grounds of the Atlantic salmon was a mystery, but inevitably Danish and Canadian netters found them, off Greenland and the Faroe Islands. This plunged politicians, fisheries biologists, sportsmen and commercial fishermen on all sides into yet another controversy between conservation and jobs.

The debate, however, appears to be ending well for the salmon. In the 1970s, the high price of table salmon spurred the development of pen-raising techniques; as "domesticated" salmon grew more common in markets, the price dropped—eventually to a point where fewer commercial fishermen were inclined to face the rigors of high-seas netting to catch wild salmon. And in the late 1980s and early '90s, groups of wealthy anglers in North America and Europe bought out more and more of the netters' annual catch quotas, from Labrador to the Faroes, to protect the wild stocks still more.

In addition, governments from Canada to Scandinavia began to ban the netting of salmon in estuaries and rivers (not just offshore) because of protests from anglers—protests backed up by the threat of losing the enormous sums of money injected into local economies by these anglers, who are often visitors who pay freely for the

Atlantic Salmon—A 24-pound hen fish killed on Norway's Gaula River.

privilege of casting to salmon.

(A 25-year lease on a single beat on a Scottish salmon river costs hundreds of thousands of pounds sterling—and the fishing is often frustrating. A week on the River Alta, in Norway, can exceed $10,000 US per rod. The Russian salmon rivers on the Kola Peninsula, with their tremendous catches of small to medium-size fish, cost about one third of that. And the excellent Crown, or public, water in New Brunswick or Nova Scotia costs a visiting angler no more than the price of a guide's day.)

Anglers themselves are contributing to the Atlantic salmon's long-term health by releasing more and more of their catch so they may spawn successfully. In New England and most of eastern Canada, strict regulations limit the kill—and even the fishing: On some waters, anglers must simply stop fishing after they've caught two salmon, even though they were released. And worldwide the old-line salmon fisherman, who used his fortune to buy his way onto private water where he felt entitled to kill as many fish as he could, is giving way to a new breed of sportsmen and women—those who fish mindful of the future.

Thus the Atlantic salmon may be less threatened today than ever. Worldwide, now only one Atlantic salmon in approximately 15 served at table is a wild, net-caught fish; the others were reared in pens anchored in salt water somewhere—Maine, New Brunswick, Iceland, Norway, Ireland or elsewhere (even Alaska, where the introduction of an exotic species, even in pens, has created its own controversy).

Some anglers suspect that pen-raised salmon may spread disease among wild fish or even damage the species' gene pool, but biologists tend to discount these fears. Overall, the spread of salmon aquaculture has contributed significantly to the great improvement in Atlantic salmon sport fishing throughout the world. And as never before, the salmon has become a "political" fish—an environmental bellwether whose presence in rivers is supported even by voters who wouldn't dream of wading into the water to try to catch one.

Runs of Atlantic salmon have been established in parts of the Great Lakes but, unlike other North American salmonids, the salmon have never been successfully transplanted into the Southern Hemisphere except in landlocked form. See also Black Salmon, Landlocked Salmon, Salmon.

Automatic Reel—A fly reel that retrieves line automatically; instead of a normal crank handle, it has a lever that extends up toward the angler's hand. Stripping line out winds up a circular spring inside the frame; triggering the lever releases the spring, which spins the spool and picks line up. The sole benefit is that such a reel needs no cranking. Its disadvantages, however, are many: It's relatively heavy and bulky. The retrieve action is sudden and difficult to control, especially if the spring is wound tight. And such reels are limited to very low line capacity. Although they are still available today, automatic fly reels were probably most popular in the 1940s and '50s. They are meant to be used on small streams and ponds for fish that can be played by hand (i.e., instead of off the reel). The auto-retrieve isn't meant to actually pull the fish in; it's to pick slack line up off the water or the bottom of a boat so it won't tangle while playing the fish.

A more modern and useful evolution of the spring-action reel is a lightweight electric fly reel made in France and sold in North America as the Electreel. It too has a finger lever but instead of a spring there is a small, silent, battery-powered, geared-down electric motor hidden inside. Triggering the lever starts the spool turning, smoothly and controllably, at a constant speed; and with no limiting spring, the reel can hold (and use) plenty of line and backing. Modern batteries last a long time, and the gasketed motor compartment is water-resistant. In addition, the reel even has a crank handle that can be screwed on as needed. The so-called Electreel fills a bona fide niche, particularly for handicapped anglers.

Avon—A British manufacturer of inflatable utility boats used all over the world for a wide variety of tasks, from dinghy duty on small Great Lakes cruising boats to high-speed fisheries patrol in the Falkland Islands. Generically speaking, however, in this context an "Avon" is a type of heavy-duty inflatable raft, powered by oars, favored by some fly-fishing guides on certain rivers (particularly rocky rivers), whether it is in fact

Avon—an inflatable raft set up as a drift boat.

Back Cast—The part of a fly cast that is in the air behind the caster. Fly-casting may loosely be described as whipping the line back and forth in the air; then, when enough line has been worked out through the tip of the rod in the right direction, the line (and of course the leader and fly it is carrying, which is the point of the whole exercise) is allowed to fall upon the water. It is an alternating rhythm of forward casts (see) and back casts, and in each segment the caster extends more line in the air and refines his or her aim until it is time to present the fly. Back cast and forward cast must flow seamlessly together; an incorrect back cast will inevitably lead to an incorrect forward cast.

Back casts are often more troublesome for the beginner because they are out of sight. Many instructors tell their students to turn their upper bodies enough to let them watch the back cast unfurl behind them, to help keep tension on the line and to keep the back cast from dropping too far (and hitting the ground) or fouling on trees or brush. See Fly-Casting.

Backing—The extra line on a reel between the fly line and the spool arbor. If fly line is for casting, backing is for fish-fighting. The fly line itself, specially tapered and weighted and treated to float or sink, is normally only 90 to 100 feet long; any gamefish beyond a couple of pounds could peel that off a reel. Thus backing.

Unlike plasticized fly line, backing is uncoated and of one diameter (much thinner than fly line); it is usually made of hollow-braided synthetic, usually Dacron, and there are no standards for backing except that it commonly comes in two tensile strengths: 20-pound-test, which is sometimes called freshwater backing, and 30-pound-test, or saltwater backing. (By way of comparison, fly lines usually have a breaking strength of between 14 and 20 pounds; a few specialty saltwater lines are reputedly built on cores of up to 45 pounds test.)

Backing is easy to knot and, since it is hollow, easy to splice too. A six-inch blind-spliced eye makes an clean loop, which can then be locked onto another loop in the end of the fly line for an elegant, strong (yet quickly undone) connection.

Backing can be attached to the reel with any number of slip knots; the most angler-esque of these is the uni-knot (universal knot) or the arbor knot. The link must only be tight enough to keep the line from slipping when you begin to crank in the first few turns—if a fish is strong enough to run away with an entire spool of line and backing, one final knot isn't going to hold it back. For more on these knots and connections, see Knots, Splice.

Backplate—That sideplate (see) of a fly reel that does not carry the crank handle(s). Many light- to medium-duty fly reels have only a backplate; the outer flange of the

Backing—High-speed machines at the Cortland Line Co. factory gather strands from the spools below and braid them into backing, stored on the drums at top.

spool is exposed. The backplate usually holds the drag adjuster and the reel spindle is permanently attached to it. See Fly Reel.

Badger—In fly-tying, a "badger" feather is white, creamy, ginger-colored or even silvery with a black or brown-black center or sometimes a black edge or tip. The term probably comes from the Old English *brock*, which refers to the light and dark fur of a badger.

Bailey, Dan—The man who brought the Eastern trout-fishing ethic to the Rocky Mountains and who founded the oldest fly shop in the West (and the oldest of all still in the same family), Dan Bailey was born in Kentucky in 1904 and died in Montana in 1982. After graduating from the Citadel in 1926, Bailey earned a master's Degree in physics at the University of Kentucky. Then he moved to the Ozarks and taught for a year at Jefferson City Junior College in Missouri. He'd been a serious fly fisherman and fly tier since boyhood, and his next step took him away from his beloved smallmouth bass to the trout waters of the Northeast: First he became an instructor at Lehigh University in Pennsylvania, and then in 1930 he moved again, to New York, to teach at Brooklyn Polytechnic Institute and to study for a doctorate in physics at New York University. Bailey found himself in the right place at the right time, for this was the Golden Age of Catskill (and Adirondack) fly-tying and fishing; the city was headquarters for many famous and not-yet-famous anglers, and innovations in fly design and fly-fishing technique came thick and fast. Bailey struck up what would be a lifelong friendship with another young and passionate fly fisher, a commercial artist and designer named Lee Wulff (see). In the depths of the Great Depression, the two of them launched a fly-fishing school in Wulff's apartment in Greenwich Village—but their first, and last, class had only three students. Both men found other ways to earn money, however little, from their avocation. Bailey concentrated on fly-tying; he even tied flies for Bergdorf Goodman, the department store, for ladies' hats. In 1936 he married Helen Hesslein, a public-health nurse in Greenwich Village, and she joined

Badger hackle, palmered on a hook.

her husband on his angling and hunting outings to the Catskills. From the beginning they had planned a camping honeymoon in Montana, which was still largely *terra incognita* in the East, and when they'd accumulated enough gear, funds and time, they went, by automobile. Bailey was enchanted from the first; Helen, less so. He spent days exploring the Madison and Gallatin rivers, and by the time they returned to New York it seems Bailey knew what he wanted to do with his life. That year he placed a small ad for his flies in *Outdoor Life* and in it he gave two addresses—New York in the winter and General Delivery, Ennis, Montana, for the summer. (Bailey was, after all, a professor; his summers were free.) In 1937 the couple returned to Montana and then again in 1938. That summer they had a minor accident that made fly-fishing history: With Helen at the wheel, the car went off the road on the Livingston side of Bozeman Hill and damaged an axle. They managed to nurse the car back down the hill and while they waited for several days in town for the repair Dan decided that was where he would set up his fly shop. He abandoned his PhD program and left Brooklyn Polytech.

He had already confided in Lee Wulff: He'd seen that Western dry fly-fishing was still primitive; most Westerners, if they fished dry at all (mostly they used snelled wet flies) used either a brown hackle or a gray hackle fly, which then cost 15¢. Bailey would "import" the much greater variety of hatch-matching Eastern flies to Montana; they would be so successful that he would be able to sell them for the New York price of 25¢ each and thereby make a living. And it wasn't just flies—all high-quality tackle was in short supply, and Dan had the contacts back East to fill the pipeline. He was correct. For the second time he found himself in the right place at the right time. And there was an additional bonus: many of his old customers in the East wrote to him for flies, which was the beginning of Bailey's large mail-order business; the first formal catalog was published in 1940.

More than 50 years later, the company Dan started is still in Livingston, still thriving, still producing American-made flies, still owned and managed by a Bailey—his and Helen's son, John. But now it is a multimillion-dollar enterprise that sells flies and tackle, at wholesale and retail, all over the world.

Bailey brought more than flies and angling technique to the Rockies; back East he'd seen what development could do to wild land. That Montana today is still one of the finest trout-fishing regions on earth is partly because of his lifelong dedication to conservation. His beliefs received a wide audience too, for—serving once again as a bridge between East and West—Bailey hosted outdoor writers who needed someone to guide them in this frontier of fly-fishing. His name appeared in print with ever-greater frequency, and this eventually brought "civilian" fly fishers to his store by the thousands. In the 1950s all these circumstances coalesced and the business, and Bailey's reputation, gained unstoppable momentum. At about this time Montana awoke to the value of tourism and the Chamber of Commerce instituted a significant program to introduce yet more travel and outdoor writers, photographers and TV crews to their state. Often they relied on Bailey for help. And Dan Bailey, that friendly, homespun-appearing yet articulate sportsman-entrepreneur, became a spokesman for his adopted state to millions of people everywhere.

When Bailey died, Ted Schwinden, the Governor of Montana, issued this proclamation:

WHEREAS, the Montana Fish and Game Commission with sorrow and regret observes the death of Dan Bailey of Livingston, Montana; and

WHEREAS, Dan's remarkable life includes many significant contributions to the preservation of trout waters, the conservation of trout and the art of angling; and

WHEREAS, the accomplishments of Dan Bailey were of such magnitude that the people of Montana can be assured for generations to come that Montana anglers will have a riffle for the flies, a trout for their efforts and flowing rivers for their souls; and

WHEREAS, the special relationship between Dan Bailey and the Yellowstone River ordains that his spirit will forever dwell in its waters, and that the river will run free as long as anglers share his love and respect for the river.

Now, Therefore I, Ted Schwinden, Governor of the State of Montana, do hereby proclaim August 14, 1982 as Dan Bailey Fishing Day in the State of Montana and urge all Montanans on that day to observe the contributions of Dan Bailey that are now recorded and remembered through sparkling riffles, still pools and wild trout.

No one knows what Dan himself would have thought of this, but he suffered the same conflicting emotions felt by nearly all who make their living from fly-fishing. According to his friend Charlie Waterman, after success was undeniably his and after son John had joined the business and things were going well, Dan expressed his reservations: "Too many people will come to Montana. And it's partly my fault."

Bamboo—For the period between the Civil War and about 1970, bamboo was widely accepted throughout the world as the material of choice for fine fly rods. Neither steel nor then fiberglass, which came into its heyday in the 1950s, '60s and '70s, could replace bamboo in the hearts of passionate anglers; not until graphite burst upon the rod-making scene was there a material that could provide the same lively, powerful casting action. Bamboo had displaced greenheart and lancewood (see) nearly a century before. Unlike those woods, which were used in solid form, bamboo must be split and shaped into strips that are then glued together. (A fishing rod made of a whole culm, or stalk, of bamboo is merely a cane pole, for farm boys dangling worms on bent safety pins.) More properly, then, a fine rod made of bamboo should be called a split-cane rod.

According to tackle historian Martin Keane, the first known American split-cane rods were made by a father-and-son team of Pennsylvania gunsmiths, Samuel and Solon Phillippe, some time between 1845 and 1860. These were of three- and four-strip construction (and paralleled work that had been done in Britain as much as 50 years or more earlier), which led eventually to the six-strip style that would dominate bamboo-rod building. The first known rod made entirely—each section, butt to tip—of six-strip cane was by Charles F. Murphy, of Newark, New Jersey, during the Civil War. He was a friend and admirer of the Phillippes and went on, in Keane's words, to build "the first commercial split-bamboo rods in sufficient numbers to influence American anglers to use American-made rods." This was the dawn of the Golden Age of Bamboo.

When split cane became the rod material of choice, the hunt began for the best and most suitable of earth's thousand-odd species of bamboo. Calcutta cane (see) from India was favored until the early 1900s, when Tonkin cane, with its high density of strong, resilient cellulose fibers near the outer skin, was discovered by Westerners. Besides being inordinately tough for its weight, Tonkin is also blessed with relatively unobtrusive nodes, which eases the rod builder's task considerably.

Classified scientifically in 1931 as *Arundinaria amabilis* ("the lovely bamboo"), it is known to grow only in China's Guangdong Province. Bamboo has been important in China for centuries; it is used for everything from sledgehammer handles (its flexibility increases the impact of the hammer) to bird cages to building scaffolding. Tonkin was known in China as *cha kon chuk*, or tea-stick bamboo.

For decades, tons of this bamboo were imported into North America by the New York firm of Harold Demarest. When the United States imposed a trade embargo against newly communist Red China shortly after World War II, rod companies hoped they had enough stockpiled to see them through. Some of the smaller shops did, for their production rates were fairly low. And as rod makers closed up shop (or died), the survivors bought up their remaining cane. (There is still pre-embargo bamboo stored away in certain barns and workshops—some of it nearly a century old by now, and well seasoned by any standard—if it was stored in a dry place.) Large rod companies such as Orvis went to fantastic lengths, ranging from personal diplomacy to near smuggling, to try to keep the cane coming in, while efforts to grow it outside of China failed.

The Bamboo Curtain was finally breached in 1973, following the famous bout of "ping-pong diplomacy," but the flow of high-quality, mature Tonkin cane to the West has never been dependable. The bamboo arrives in New York in hundred-plus-pound bundles wrapped in coarse burlap stencilled with exotic lettering. A good culm is six to 12 feet long and 1 1/2 to three inches in diameter, straight and reasonably free from slashes and insect holes. At a company such as Orvis or Thomas & Thomas, the initial inspection may junk half the shipment. It is, after all, a natural material, with all the imperfections to be expected from good and bad growth years, insects, disease, careless harvesting or shipping. It is also, however, an unusually hard natural material—though a "wood," it must be shaped with metal-working tools, and a machinist's file that is too dull to cut cane well will still file ordinary carbon steel. See also Cane Rod Building.

Barb—In fly-tying, the individual fiber of a hackle feather that projects laterally outward from the main stem.

Barbless Hook—A hook armed only with a point and lacking the kicked-up, rear-facing barb behind the point that is intended to keep the hook from sliding out of the fish's tissue. Because such a hook can be removed with comparatively little damage, it has become popular in no-kill fisheries.

Barbless hooks are often regarded as recent developments spurred by today's emphasis on catch and release, but in fact they were available at least before 1890, when Mary Orvis Marbury (see) was writing, in her book *Favorite Flies and Their Histories* (1892), "We would like to show some of the curiosities in novel-shaped hooks that have come to us: some with the barb on the outside of the hook; some with no barb at all . . . ."

Some barbless hooks have a slight bend, or bump, in the shank just behind the point; the maker means this to serve as a "benign" barb, an obstruction to keep the point from sliding back out. In fact it seems to act as an obstruction when the hook is going in as well. (Some anglers say that a conventional barb also works against a hook's driving home into tissue, and that better results come from barbless hooks, whether the fish is to be released or not.) Most fly fishers simply flatten the barbs of their hooks with a pair of fine-tip pliers.

With weightless flies, a limber fly rod and a stretchy fly line and leader, it is generally not difficult to hold a freshwater fish on a barbless hook. And without any doubt at all it is far easier and less painful to remove a barbless hook from one's fingers.

Barbule—In fly-tying, the webbing of a hackle feather, the material that projects laterally outward from each barb (above) and that interlocks to "marry" the feather's barbs together.

Barbour—Among Western fly fishers, gunners and other field-sports people, the name has become a generic label for any waxed-cotton waterproof garment, whether

Barracuda

in fact made by Barbour or any of its many competitors. The full name of the company is J. Barbour & Sons and it is headquartered in South Shields, England. Since the late 19th Century, the company has been solidifying its reputation as a maker of high-quality outerwear for fishermen, shooters, riders, farmers, gamekeepers and anyone else whose work or play demands rugged, warm, thorn- and waterproof garments. Barbour coats and jackets are made of heavy, long-staple cotton impregnated with a waxy dressing that keeps water from working its way in through the weave of the fabric, yet allows perspiration and condensation vapor to pass outward. The wax also lubricates the individual cotton fibers so they don't abrade one another; the result is a garment that may literally shrug off generations of hard use—so long as the dressing is renewed periodically.

Aware, perhaps, of the British heritage of their sport, upmarket American trout and salmon anglers took to "Barbours" willingly when the company's US distribution pipeline was finally improved in the middle 1980s. Barbour went on to establish itself as a fashion line as well when city-dwellers bought equally into this blend of British style and function.

Barracuda—*Scomberomorus commersonii*: A much-maligned tropical saltwater predator that should be better known as an excellent gamefish. Thanks to its undeserved reputation as a wanton killer, many inexperienced snorkelers have made dramatic exits from the water upon sight of even a small barracuda. But attacks on humans, even those wearing the mythical "flashing jewelry," are extremely rare.

Even a small barracuda has prominent teeth, and all barracuda are notably curious. The combination results in a deadly looking fish that may follow a diver—or a fly— a long way. But there are no recorded instances of a wading fisherman being struck by a barracuda. Any injuries usually come when the fish is being unhooked; gloves and pliers are recommended.

The bigger a barracuda is, the less likely it is to strike an artificial fly or lure. Fish up to about 20 pounds are relatively easy to take in shallow water. Fifty-pounders are sometimes caught by trolling along deeper reefs or wrecks. Barracuda of a hundred pounds—perhaps seven feet long—are known to exist, but are almost impossible to bring to a hook; the International Game Fish Association (see) lists the all-tackle world record as only 83 pounds. To escape a hook, or sometimes in pursuit of food, barracuda will make long, greyhounding leaps. Flats barracuda have been known to jump clear over mangrove bushes.

Fly fishers can find barracuda easily while stalking the inshore lagoons and flats that also teem with bonefish, snook, redfish and so on. Barracuda don't roam, as other flats gamefish do, so a slim shape holding position over the bottom near some sort of cover

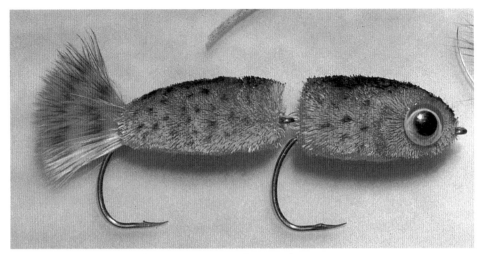

Bass Bug—a jointed-body deerhair minnow imitation.

is often a barracuda. Streamer patterns that imitate forage fish are most effective, and wire shock tippets are a virtual necessity. The fly has to land close enough to catch the fish's attention, but not so close as to drive it away. The strike, when it comes, is like lightning—one moment the fish is motionless; then, magically, the fly is gone.

Barrel Knot—Sometimes used as another name for the blood knot; see. See also Knots.

Bass Bug—A type of fly for bass fishing, usually largemouth bass. Bass bugs are normally large (tied on hooks that range from about size #6 to #1/0) and have bodies of hair, cork, balsawood or even plastic, and various assorted tails, eyes, legs, etc. They generally imitate frogs, baitfish, mice or other large and lively chunks of protein. As opposed to delicate trout flies, bass bugs are meant to be worked vigorously—slapped down hard, twitched with the rod tip, retrieved like a hard-body lure on a spinning rod; the disturbance in the water attracts the predator bass.

Being relatively heavy, bushy and air-resistant, bass bugs can be difficult to cast; fly line manufacturers often make special bass-bug lines that are tapered and weighted to help solve these problems. Rod companies also cater to this market, with rods long and stiff enough for these flies (and for the fish that eat them). See also Popper, Slider.

Bass-Bug Taper—A floating weight-forward fly line specially configured to cast a big, bushy fly; it has a short, steep front taper, or tip, and a thick belly that begins relatively far forward. The theory is that (with a short, properly tapered leader) the heavy front section of the line will muscle a bass bug or similar fly through the air better than a normal line. See Fly Line.

Belly—The thicker middle section of a fly line, between the head or tip and the running line. See Fly Line.

Bellyboat—A float tube; see.

Berners, Dame Juliana—The legendary noblewoman and/or nun known to fishermen as the author of the "Treatyse of Fysshynge wyth an Angle," a chapter of the second edition of *The Boke of St. Albans*, published at Westminster, England, by Wynkyn de Worde in 1496. She was reputedly the prioress or abbess of Sopwell, but whether she truly existed—or, if she did, she wrote the Treatyse—has been hotly debated for centuries. There is one fleeting reference in the fishing text to a "Julyans Bernes" and a good deal of what's in the Treatyse seems rather beyond the normal ken of a nun, even a practical-minded administrator nun/noblewoman of rural medieval times.

The first edition of the book, printed 10 years earlier, at St. Albans, was a compilation of current information on hunting, hawking and heraldry. A "Dam Julyans Barnes" or "Bernes" is credited as the author of the section on hunting, yet neither this text nor "Dam Julyans" had any influence on hunting through the centuries. The second, expanded edition of the book included the soon-to-be-famous chapter on fishing. John McDonald, author of *The Origins of Angling*, hypothesized that de Worde, the publisher, needed a name to attach to the anonymously written fishing treatise; since Dame Juliana's was the only byline in the first edition, de Worde simply tagged it onto the new fishing section. Her provenance as an abbess, says McDonald, stems not from anything in the two books but from assertions made a century and more later that the first edition had been printed in the Abbey of St. Albans and that the Dame was a prioress. McDonald is certain that she was a real person and that she contributed to the first *Boke*; that she was a nun and/or an angler he seems to doubt.

Regardless of its author, the Treatyse is a collection of wide-ranging how-to information that ranges from general advice—"Ye can not brynge an hoke into a fyssh mouth wythout a bayte"—to fairly specific instructions on fabricating rods and other tackle. Update the language and much of it sounds surprisingly modern and sensible. Many people mistakenly regard it as the oldest written work on sport fishing. However fishing for pure recreation—as opposed to fishing for the table or for the market— shows up in many earlier texts, some of which predate the Treatyse by four and five centuries; in fact the Treatyse itself refers to earlier sportfishing writers. (*The Boke of St. Albans* as a whole is the oldest known sporting book in English.)

The significance of Dame Juliana's text is that it is an excellent summary of most of what was known about hook-and-line fishing to date. Although older writings exist (see below), the Treatyse is far longer, more complete and more practical than any of them. It helped establish Britain as, if not the birthplace of sport fishing, at least the country where the sport matured, and it also helped spread the basic elements of fair chase and sportsmanship that predominate today. And whoever s/he may have been, the good Dame herself became the predecessor of many other famous British angling writers—from Izaak Walton on. (Incidentally, the Treatyse also appears to put women squarely into the fishing picture almost from the start.)

The Treatyse was hardly the first sportfishing text, however. In 1985 a Canadian scholar named Richard C. Hoffmann published the results of his research into historical fishing writing. He found a number of references to fishing as pure pastime in earlier writings from the British Isles, as well as from France, Germany, Austria and Spain. William Radcliffe's *Fishing From The Earliest Times* (Dutton, 1921) traces hook-and-line fishing much, much further back into history yet (to Macedonia and Ancient Egypt—see Fly-Tying) but without conclusive evidence that fishing was a sport per se.

According to Hoffmann, a German book describes a young prince wading barefoot in a stream in pursuit of trout and grayling with a *vederangel*, a feathered hook, while his lady companion waits on the steambank with their dog. The oldest fishing writer Hoffmann uncovered was a young 12th-Century French aristocrat named Gui des Bazoches, who was apparently free to enjoy a life of leisure. He was a canon of the church; he accompanied the Third Crusade to the Holy Land; he retreated to the country estate of a favorite uncle. In his letters he wrote of interspersing his studies with fowling, hunting, and with fishing—with nets and with hook and line for pike, barbel, eel, salmon, perch and other species.

Hoffmann's thesis is filled with other anglers—kings, emperors and assorted nobility—who all seemed to be passionate recreational fishermen. The concepts of fair play in fishing were so well established in medieval Europe that Hoffmann even found a British angling text that was apparently intended as a metaphor for proper sexual behavior, cautioning men against "poaching in others' waters" and other transgressions. It is a poem called "Piers of Fulham," and parts of it sound surprisingly modern. The unknown author, reported Hoffmann, "laments overfishing, especially by the unscrupulous fishers who take young fish before they reach their growth, and himself swears to keep only those of full size." (See Catch and Release.)

Another of Hoffmann's historical fishermen is William Wallace, an early hero of the Scottish struggle against English rule. According to his biographer, Blind Hary the Minstrel (writes Hoffmann), Wallace was taken unawares one day in 1296 by an armed band of Englishmen. Wallace not only failed to note their approach, he'd even left home without any weapons. His attention was entirely on his fishing. The marauders began to taunt him and took his catch. Words were exchanged and one of the Englishmen drew his sword. Wallace brained the man with his net, then grabbed the sword and killed three of his oppressors before making his getaway on one of their horses. (A seminal event in the development of Britain's rigorous angling etiquette?)

Beveler—A milling machine (see) for mass-producing precisely shaped cane strips for split-cane rods.

Big-Game Fishing—For fly fishers as for trollers, the big-game species are much the same: marlin, sailfish, tunas and large sharks (plus tarpon, the trophy that was "designed by fly fishermen"). However, while the conventional-tackle offshore fisherman armed with 130-lb-test tackle and gear-driven, 1,200-yard trolling reels may hunt "granders"—the 1,000-plus-pound fish—with some confidence, the fly fisher's big-game limit was until recently about 200 pounds. In 1991 the International Game Fish Association (see) expanded its world-record classes to include 20-lb-test (10kg) tippets (up from the previous maximum of 16-lb-test) and tackle companies followed suit with new, extra-heavy-duty fly rods, reels and lines. This has pushed—conjecturally, at least—the fly fisher's upper limits into the 300- to 500-pound range.

True big-game fishing in America dates back to the late 19th Century. According to Jack Samson, saltwater editor of *Fly Rod & Reel* Magazine, it began in earnest in California on June 1, 1898, when a Mr. Charles F. Holder boated a 183-pound bluefin tuna near Catalina Island. Within a few weeks there was a tuna club set up there, and two dozen members had already caught fish of a hundred pounds or more! On the East Coast, the Florida tarpon had already become the big-game fish of choice, after W.H. Wood took fish of 81 and 93 pounds on the same day, March 25, 1885. Big tarpon had been caught before, but this feat was heavily publicized and the rush was on. Later that year Wood took a tarpon of more than 100 pounds. In 1895, still in Florida, England's Lady Orford became the first recorded woman to take two large tarpon in one day; one of them weighed 128 pounds. Tackle and technique escalated quickly: On April 30, 1898, reel maker Edward Vom Hofe (see) boated a 210-pound tarpon at Captiva Pass, Florida.

(According to tackle historian Jim Brown, this was only the second tarpon over 200 pounds ever taken on rod and reel. It would be interesting to note that Edward Vom Hofe took the fish on one of his vaunted fly reels, but that is not the case; he used one of his equally fine level-wind saltwater reels. Outings like this helped him invent the star-drag clutch system still used on such reels.)

In 1913 a Mr. William Boschen, of New York City, became the first to record the capture on rod and line of a broadbill swordfish. And in 1924 the redoubtable Zane Grey set the sporting world on its ear by killing a 758-pound bluefin tuna off Yarmouth, Nova Scotia. The Golden Age of big-game angling was well under way.

Hundred-plus-pound catches for fly fishers, however, still are not commonplace today, and a "golden age" of big-game fly-fishing may only be starting in the 1990s, thanks to the 20-lb-class tippet. While trolling fishermen of the 19th Century could use solid bamboo or wood boat rods, going up in rod diameter as the quarry got bigger, fly fishers couldn't follow suit because their rods had to be flexible and light enough to cast with. The same was true for their lines. Small and mid-range tarpon, and a few other ocean fish, were taken often enough on heavy split-cane fly rods and then on fiberglass, but it took synthetic fly lines and ultimately graphite rods to really jump-start big-game fly-fishing. Lee Wulff caught a 148-pound striped marlin off Ecuador on 12-lb tippet in 1967; that it still stands as a world record for that species on that tippet is testimony to the difficulty of landing large fish on fly tackle. There was also a freak jewfish flyrod record set in 1967, when a man named Bart Froth caught a 356-pounder off Islamorada, Florida—also on 12-lb tippet.

All along, however, saltwater record-hunting fly fishers were frustrated by the 16-lb-tippet upper limit imposed by the IGFA. There was plenty of evidence that only a four-pound jump in tippet strength could open up a whole new world of big fish: In 1981, with conventional tackle, Gary Hoff caught a 907-pound tiger shark in Australia on 20-lb-test monofilament. And in 1957, a white shark weighing 1,068 pounds was taken on 20-lb line, also in Australian waters.

Now that the heavier tippet is in place and manufacturers have introduced rods, reels and lines to suit, it's just a matter of time.

Big-Game Reel—The largest of fly reel types, meant for marlin, sailfish, large sharks, tunas and other pelagic species. The adoption of the 20-lb-test class tippet by the International Game Fish Association (see) in 1991 opened up a new level of big-game fly-fishing and spurred the manufacture of "ultra" fly reels that could pick up where tarpon reels left off. Tarpon are usually caught in shallow water and they fight "horizontally"—on and near (if not above) the surface; by following a tarpon with the boat, the angler can nearly always stay within 300 yards of the fish. The pelagic gamefishes, however, may fight "vertically," sounding to tremendous depths where a boat can't follow; hence the need for reels that hold 300 to 600 or more yards of line and backing—and that can absorb the incredible punishment of long, hot runs punctuated by dead stops and sudden, brutal starts. See also Fly Reel, Saltwater Reel.

Big-Game Rod—Until the International Game Fish Association adopted the 20-lb/

Big-Game Reel—made by Angling Products, Inc.

10kg tippet class for saltwater fly-fishing records, big-game fly rods were generally meant for tarpon and designed to cast 12- or 13-weight lines. (There were a handful of semi-custom #14 or #15 rods available too, but these were often used for surf-casting, not big-game fishing.) However, the greater tensile strength of the new tippet class, along with the difficulties imposed by the species of gamefish it was intended for, demanded a new class of rod as well—fly rods that could pump large pelagic fish up from the depths.

In the early 1990s, manufacturers introduced fly rods for lines as heavy as 18-weight that had the backbone to dead-lift 25 pounds or more. By contrast, most tarpon rods couldn't exert more than five or six pounds of lift. The performance trade-offs were immediately evident: These ultra-stiff big-game rods might be able to pull a deep-swimming tuna to the surface, but they were hard-pressed to do what fly rods are supposed to—cast a tight, long, accurate loop of line. Billfishermen were more inclined to accept the compromise, as long casts usually aren't necessary to drop a huge streamer fly in front of a sailfish or marlin that has been teased almost to the transom of a boat.

Many all-around fly fishers and several prominent rod designers rebelled. They demanded 20-lb-class fly rods that could also cast, not just lift. Several pointed out that a rod that could exert more pull than the new tippet could stand was potentially self-defeating. Billy Pate, holder of world tarpon and billfish flyrod records, added that since the IGFA had not allowed a longer shock tippet (see) when it added the 20-lb class, the class tippet would abrade quickly because on these bigger fish the shock tippet was too short to protect the class tippet from rubbing against the fish's skin or pectoral fin. Few class tippets, he said, still tested at 20 pounds after landing such a fish, and a rod that could pull that much weight would simply let a fisherman snap his own tippet that much more easily.

True big-game fly rods, whether they can lift 10 or 25 pounds, should have reinforced ferrules, strong line guides and well-machined, extra-heavy-duty reel seats with secure locking rings; most have a fighting grip—an extra sleeve of cork or foam rubber on the rod blank just below the stripping guide—and a fighting butt, an extension that keeps the reel away from the angler's body and provides a bit more lifting leverage.

Billfish—Literally, fish with bills, or swords; that is, the various species of sailfish, marlin, swordfish and spearfish. Fly fishers regard the first two as among the most prized of trophies. Swordfish and spearfish are not not truly part of the gamefishing pantheon.

Billinghurst Reel—The Billinghurst "birdcage" reel, patented on August 9, 1859, and made in Rochester, New York, may be the rarest of all notable American fly reels. The first examples were made of brass wire, with soldered rib joints, and each had a single folding wooden crank handle. The unusual "birdcage" design allowed air to circulate through the reel and help dry rot-prone silk fly lines. The Billinghurst is a centermount reel; that is, instead of hanging off the end of the rod, it sits across the reel seat. It is historically significant in that it was only the fourth fishing reel to receive a US patent, and the first fly reel. Odd though it may look today, it marked the point at which fly reels began to diverge notably from other types of fishing reels: It ushered in the era of the American-made, narrow-frame (taller than it was wide), ventilated-spool fly reel,

Billinghurst—a rare "birdcage" reel with not only its folding handle but even its original box intact.

and it was a forerunner of the milestone Orvis 1874-patent reel. William Billinghurst was an eminent gunsmith whose large shop (in Rochester) also turned out fine target rifles and other long guns on a semi-production basis.

Bimini Twist—Sometimes also called the 20-times-around knot or the double-line loop, the Bimini Twist is most often used to create the loop that forms the long doubled-over part of a big-game trolling rig. In fly-fishing, it may used to make the six- to eight-inch loop in the end of the backing to which a smaller eye loop in a fly line is connected (although in reality a blind splice [see] is a better and easier connection to make in hollow-braided lines, be they backing or flyline core). Saltwater fly fishers also use the Bimini Twist in leader constructions that call for a doubled-over section. See Knots.

"Birdcage" Reel—An early fly reel named for its skeletal appearance; see Billinghurst.

Bivisible—A type of dry fly originated by Edward Ringwood Hewitt (see) in the early 1920s but soon adopted by everyone as the great advance that it was. Lee Wulff called it the most popular single pattern of the 1930s. Right behind the head of the fly Hewitt palmered (see) a single white or light-colored hackle that was easy for him to see on the water; from there on back he used whatever darker hackles the pattern called for, filling the hook shank so that it looked like a fuzzy ball. The result was a white-faced, highly visible fly that was still largely the color meant to attract fish. In rough water, poor light or for aging eyes, the bivisible is still a useful fly-tying variant.

Bivisible—a high-floating, contrasting-hackle dry fly (tied by Darrel Martin).

Black Salmon—Also known as kelts and spring salmon, black salmon are riverine adult Atlantic salmon that have survived the summer "run" in from the sea, the fall spawning season and the winter afterward. In the spring, when a black salmon returns to the sea, it does so not by swimming purposefully downstream but by maintaining its upstream heading and generally letting the current push it along. These fish may not have eaten for up to nine months, so black salmon are typically thin, sometimes almost snakey looking, and often somewhat dark (or at least more heavily spotted) from their months in river water. (A salmon fresh from the sea is called a "bright" fish, and may be almost chrome-plated by contrast.) Having spawned, spring salmon are beginning to feed again, and they sometimes strike flies voraciously; they are generally less selective than "fresh" salmon and usually easier to take.

Some Atlantic salmon watersheds have black salmon seasons in the spring. Many anglers refuse to fish for them, out of sympathy for a creature that has endured much and still has many miles and weeks to go before it can feed safely at sea again. Others dismiss this as Disneyesque anthropomorphizing and find that black salmon are, despite their somewhat gaunt build, still game fighters. See also Atlantic Salmon, Salmon.

Blank *or* **Rod Blank**—The rod alone, without any of its furnishings such as line guides, grip, hook keeper, etc., but usually with its ferrule in place. An un-ferruled rod blank is just two or more rod sections or segments. See Rod-Building.

Blind-Casting—Fishing not with eyes closed but where fish can't be seen; fishing by reading the water, which is to say casting to likely looking holding or feeding lies to see if fish are in fact present and will take the offering. The converse of blind-casting is sight-fishing (see).

Bloa—An arcane English fly-tying term for various shades of blue, usually a dark, purplish hue; the Scottish equivalent is *blae*, which means a dark blue or blue-gray.

Blood Knot—One of the most useful knots not just in fly-fishing but in any fishing that uses monofilament lines, the blood knot joins monofilament together smoothly and—at least if tied properly—it maintains 90%+ of the unknotted line's breaking strength. Thanks to its streamlined shape (the tag ends can be trimmed very close to the body of the knot), it casts well and if need be can be drawn through the line guides of the rod fairly well. In addition, the blood knot is unusual in that it can fasten together monofilaments of very different diameters. The sections of a multi-piece tapered leader—that is, a leader that is not one length of mono that has been chemically tapered—are tied together with blood knots. Even fly fishers who use one-piece leaders have to learn the blood knot, however—either that, or change the entire leader when it's time for a new tippet.

To tie together monos of vastly different diameters—a 50-lb.-test shock tippet to a 12-lb. leader section, for example—the *improved* blood knot can be used. See Knots.

Blow-Line Fishing—An ancient, pre-casting form of fly-fishing in which a short line was simply tied to the tip of a long rod and then swung out over the water so the wind could blow the fly (sometimes a live fly, at that) around on the water's surface. Dapping (see) is a form of blow-line fishing that is still popular in parts of Ireland and Scotland—for the famous mayfly hatch on Galway's Lough Corrib, for example.

Blue Dun—In fly-tying, a highly desirable hackle color that ranges from a light grey-blue to a deeper grey that is more properly called iron blue dun. Natural—that is, undyed—blue dun capes are uncommon and expensive; the lighter shades are generally easier to find.

Bluefish—Feeding bluefish, *Pomatomus saltatrix*, will strike literally anything, even bare hooks, if they are big and shiny enough to attract attention. Bluefish of any size— they occasionally reach 30 pounds or more, while five to 10 pounds is normal—are highly aggressive predators that sometimes beach themselves in pursuit of prey and that fight savagely when hooked. All this makes the blue a particularly attractive target for saltwater fly fishers in northeastern North America who otherwise could search for days for a fish to cast to. Sometimes the problem is catching too many fish; when a feeding frenzy is truly on, fishermen find it difficult to stop obliging these voracious predators. Often the result is a pile of dead fish and an appalling waste.

Blues are handsome, silvery to blue-black fish. They are streamlined, powerful swimmers with oversize, uptilted jaws armed with rows of large needle-sharp teeth. Biologists say that bluefish can see nearly as well out of the water as in, and many fishermen have seen large blues leap out of the water to take gulls. The implications for anyone who handles live bluefish are clear—and anyone who fishes for them more than casually soon bears the scars. Beside being fierce fighters on medium tackle, bluefish are first-rate table fare, at least when their dark, oily meat is eaten fresh, or smoked, or has been filleted and frozen properly. Bluefish are an increasingly important commercial catch too, particularly as more popular species of market fish are overharvested. Bluefish occur worldwide in temperate and warm waters, but the schools travel widely and often seem to disappear, even from their regular haunts. Regionally, their populations boom-and-bust in irregular cycles as well. In North America, bluefish occur on the Atlantic coast, migrating east to west and south to north and then back again each year as water temperatures climb and then dip: Blues may be plentiful in Florida in January and they may have reached Maine to Prince Edward Island by summer's end.

Small bluefish are called snappers; grown up, they're known as choppers. Other regional names include tailor, rock salmon and snapper blue. Most names reflect the fish's voracious appetite and feeding habits, and every year a few swimmers lose fingers or toes or wind up in coastal emergency rooms with bluefish slashes. Schools measuring 20 square miles have been seen in the Atlantic. When the bluefish are on top, finding them can be simple: From a distance, often the first clue is a flock of seabirds wheeling and diving at the surface. At close range, the angler may see myriad flashes of silver in the water—thousands of panicked baitfish jumping as the blues slash at them from below. Catching them in this case is just a matter of throwing a large, well-tied streamer on a shock tippet into their midst. Smaller pods of bluefish may

Bluefish

betray their presence by leaving slicks on the water's surface, created by the fish oil their feeding releases into the water. And often bluefish leave an olfactory trail—a distinctive smell that, in the sea breeze, reminds one of a fresh garden salad. When the school dives, sometimes for weeks, finding them again can be impossible.

Bobbin—A handheld, pen-like tool that holds and dispenses the thread used in fly-tying. See Fly-Tying Tools, Whip Finisher.

Bodkin—A needle; see Dubbing Needle, Fly-Tying Tools.

Bogdan—A brand of fly reel made in Nashua, New Hampshire, by machinist and angler Stanley Bogdan (b. 1917), assisted since 1973 by his son, Stephen. Always famous among salmon-fishing cognoscenti, by the middle 1980s their reels had become the most sought-after collector's items in fly-fishing. According to Stan, he made the first Bogdan reel in 1939 or '40. He took it to the sportsman's show in Boston and showed it to Herb Wellington, at the Ashaway Line booth, and to Ted Williams, the ballplayer who was already making a name for himself as an angler as well. "I'd been a fly fisherman," Stan recalled in an interview in 1988, "but never a salmon fisherman. Still, I had this idea I could make a pretty good reel." The experts proceeded

Stanley Bogdan (1990) in his shop in Nashua, New Hampshire.

Bogdan Trout and Steelhead reels.

to point out the shortcomings in his design and he returned to New Hampshire determined to do better.

In the 1950s, Bogdan made reels for The Orvis Company and for Abercrombie & Fitch; since then, however, Bogdans have been available at retail only direct from the maker and from a very few tackle shops such as Hunter's Angling Supplies, in nearby New Boston, New Hampshire. The best and most functional Bogdans—the reels he says he is most proud of—are the immensely strong salmon models, of which there are nine: In order of ascending size, they are the 00, 100, 50, 0, 150, 1, 2, 200M and 300M. Many are gear-drive multipliers; all are anti-reverse and have the famous twin-shoe drum brake; and all must be ordered in either right- or left-hand wind—they are not convertible and the spools are not easily changed. These reels are found on premier Atlantic salmon water the world around. They command top prices on the secondary market, from anglers (or vintage-tackle collectors or dealers) who don't want to wait years for a new one, and they often feature prominently in salmon fishermen's wills.

Around 1980 Bogdan began to produce trout and steelhead models as well—smaller, more delicate reels with the distinctive Bogdan look (which itself pays homage to Vom Hofe) but with ventilated spools and sideplates. Stan claimed that the smaller reels came about because he was "too cheap to throw away the ends of the tube left over after cutting out salmon-reel frames." To use up these undersize aluminum cylinders, he began making his Trout reels. At first they went mostly to salmon fishermen who wanted trout reels to match their heavier tackle, but eventually, spurred by huge demand in the Japanese market, the Trout models became almost purely collectibles and they are rarely seen on a stream.

Throughout Bogdan's production, output has varied from about 75 to 500 units annually. At present the two men turn out about one finished reel per working day. Except for the heavy-duty coil springs in the salmon drags and a few internal screws, every component is made in the shop, on old, manually controlled lathes and milling machines.

As with handmade British double guns or 12-cylinder Italian roadsters, ordering a Bogdan reel and having it actually arrive are events that may be separated by five years or more. Stories about Bogdan, and how difficult it can be to obtain a reel from him, abound; some have become fly-fishing legend. One of the best not only typifies this unique business, it also happens to be true—according to Bogdan confidant Bill Hunter: In the summer of 1989, while Bogdan was away fishing, the factory from which he rents his space did some renovation. Which included, among other niceties, a fresh coat of paint on walls and window trim and so on, to remove years of accumulated machine-shop grime. All well and good except that when they painted Bogdan's shop area they covered up some scribbled dimensions that Stan referred to when making certain reel parts. Not only that, they painted the ceiling post next to the telephone. But since Stan rarely had a clean sheet of paper handy when someone called to order a reel, he would simply jot it down on that post. How many orders were wiped out? It was never determined with any certainty, but Steve Bogdan reported, "We probably filled all the important orders that were on there anyway, sort of."

Boke of St. Albans, The—See Dame Juliana Berners.

Bomber—A rugged, high-floating surface fly developed in the late 1960s for Atlantic salmon (before Lee Wulff and others began doing it in the early 1930s, no one, in North America or Europe, fished anything but wet flies for Atlantic salmon). Usually dressed on a long-shank single hook, it is nothing more or less than a tapered cylindrical body of deer hair with palmered hackle (see) wound helically along its length—the hackle fibers protrude out through the deer hair—and a vestigial bucktail wing and tail. The most common size range is from a #10 up through #4 or so, and common colors are brown, brown-and-white and green. It can be dead-drifted or skated, or even pulled under and fished wet. Some say the fly imitates the apocryphal cigar butt that finicky salmon allegedly take when all else fails, but in fact the solid torpedo-shaped body riding on or buzzing across the surface film could resemble a number of real foods, especially a dragonfly. Bomber fans say the pattern gets a salmon's attention when all else fails—just like a cigar butt.

The Bomber itself spawned a series of smaller but very similar Atlantic-salmon flies called Bugs, of which the Buck Bug and the Green Machine are the best known.

Warren Duncan and other Canadian Maritime fly dressers say the first Bomber was tied by the fly-fishing priest Father Elmer J. Smith, of Doaktown, New Brunswick, and that it was most likely patterned after a deerhair mouse, a fly that is notably successful on the sea-run brown trout that also inhabit most Atlantic-salmon rivers.

Bonefish— The tropical and subtropical bonefish, *Albula vulpes,* "speedster of the flats," while a top flyrod gamefish, doesn't truly deserve its reputation. Yes, it is so wary that it must be stalked, and so silvery that it can hardly be seen against a sandy bottom; it can be finicky about what flies it will take, and it is powerful beyond its size. But bonefish readily take a natural bait left waiting on the bottom, and with 200 yards of 15-lb.-test mono on a spinning reel and an appropriate rod, simply catching a bonefish is little challenge.

The difficulty comes in fly-fishing, where bonefish habitat poses its own challenges. Often casting from the bow of a tiny, shallow-draft skiff over water that may be only knee-deep, the angler has to contend with brilliant sunlight, strong winds that always

Bomber—the classic pattern, tied by Darrel Martin.

Bonefish—an eight-pounder taken (and released) at Christmas Island.

seem to come from the wrong direction, and hours of staring at shifting patterns of sun and shadow on the water and the bottom. Since bonefish are slender and translucent—their fins may be actually transparent—and only two to 15 pounds or so, some capable casters say the hardest part of bonefishing is seeing the fish. In a week of bonefishing, the first two or three days will go simply to learning what to look for in that shifting kaleidoscope of light and dark. The guide will point and gesticulate and shout until suddenly the eyes and brain catch on.

Stalking bonefish on foot exercises the senses and skills even more. In less heavily pressured waters, such as Los Roques in Venezuela or Christmas Island, in the central Pacific, fly fishers are startled again and again by bones streaking away almost from underfoot—they didn't see the fish until then. (Bonefish are not always as shy as their reputations have it. At Christmas Island the author once "caught" a bonefish that took his fly while he was walking with his rod over his shoulder and the leader trailing in the water.)

Schools of bonefish advance with the tide up onto shallow, marly, coral-and-sand flats, feeding into the sun and the current with their heads down, scouring the bottom with their underslung mouths for mollusks. In very shallow water, their long, forked tails stick up into the air like waving seagrass. (Wading anglers sometimes squat to scan the horizon for tailing fish.) A school of "mudding" bonefish often leaves a cloud of disturbed sediment drifting in the water like smoke; when it clears, acres of bottom may be pockmarked where the fish rooted for crabs or snails.

A six-pound bonefish can take 100 yards of line in a few seconds; given its head, a larger fish can clean a saltwater reel completely. Fly fishers often hold their rods up overhead when a bone runs, to make the fish lift its head and keep the leader off the rough bottom, but surviving that first run is largely a matter of luck. Then, cranking the fish in may take many minutes. When the fish spots the angler or the boat it makes another, shorter dash—followed by more cranking. Eventually the fish will turn sideways and circle for a while before tiring enough to let itself be brought in. To date, the largest recorded bonefish caught on fly tackle weighed 15 pounds; the largest all-tackle fish recorded by the IGFA was 19 pounds. Sight-fishing for bones offers a level of excitement that is almost unique—many people compare it to upland hunting with a fly rod instead of a shotgun, the guide taking the place of the dog.

In the tropics, bonefish are commonly eaten—often marinated in lime juice or smoked—but preparing the fish for the table can take some time; they're not called bonefish for nothing.

Bonefish are common on the Gulf Coast of North America, the northern coast of South America, and in the Florida Keys and the Caribbean. Rare individuals have been found as far north as Long Island Sound and San Francisco Bay. In the tropical Atlantic, bonefish are found along the African coast. And seemingly every island in the Pacific Basin that has coral flats also has bonefish—sometimes in staggering numbers.

Bootfoot Waders—Waders with waterproof boots, usually made of vulcanized rubber or molded plastic, attached directly to the fabric uppers (as opposed to stockingfoot waders; see).

Boron—A basic element of the periodic Table, falling on the line between metals and non-metals. Boron is characterized by "outstanding lightness, stiffness, resistance to stretching, hardness and thermal stability," all qualities that have attracted flyrod designers. Pure boron is found naturally only in trace amounts; commercial boron is produced from borax, a hydrated boron salt often found in ancient inland sea beds. (Much of the world's borax, from the mineral kernite, is found in the Mojave Desert.) Because of its hardness—somewhere between tungsten carbide and diamond—and its chemical inertness and low electrical conductivity, boron powder is used in such diverse things as abrasives, phonograph needles, rocket-fuel compounds, lightning arrestors and nuclear-reactor control rods.

The boron fiber used in fly rods is formed when, in a reactor chamber, a gaseous mixture of boron trichloride and hydrogen is exposed to a filament of tungsten wire, which is heated by electrical induction to more than 2,000° F. In the ensuing chemical reaction, the vapor deposits boron on the filament, producing a fiber that is actually pure, elemental boron (over tungsten). Boron fibers are collected together, like graphite and fiberglass, onto narrow unidirectional "pre-preg" tape, so called because it is impregnated with thermosetting epoxy resin (see also Graphite Rods).

Unlike fiberglass or graphite, boron fibers are extremely abrasive; individual fibers must be precisely laid up on the pre-preg so that they do not touch each other and so potentially wear each other away in their final application. This characteristic, plus boron's extreme stiffness, eventually turned rod makers against the fiber. Boron proved difficult to "tame" and, though stiffer (but heavier) than graphite, produced no extra benefits for anglers.

What was probably the first boron fishing rod was made by Don Phillips (see also) in January 1972. Phillips, an avid angler, was then an engineer at United Technologies, Inc., in Hartford, Connecticut. His one-man company, FlyCraft Associates, Inc. eventually produced about 300 solid-boron rods, each made of narrow, tapered strips of boron tape hand-laid over wire or balsa cores.

In the late 1970s, the furor that swirled around the introductions of fiberglass and then graphite into rod-making was repeated, and intensified, with regard to boron. Rumors circulated that, for example, boron rods could shatter disastrously under load and spray a high-velocity shower of toxic boron flechettes into the skin and cause serious harm. No part of this tale, or any of the others, proved true in any way.

In the early 1980s, boron and boron-combination rods were offered in commercial quantities by Rodon, Fenwick, Browning, Composite Development Corp., Lake King, Phenix, Shakespeare, Orvis and probably others. Though Rodon and Fenwick enjoyed some success with these rods in the marketplace, the only boron rods to make anything approaching a lasting contribution to fly-fishing were the Orvis Powerflex series of boron/graphite hybrids, which won a Kudo award from *Fly Rod & Reel* Magazine in 1987 and lasted in the company's lineup until 1990. Boron breakage was contained by sheathing those fibers in an outer wrap of graphite, and the higher Modulus of Elasticity of the boron helped make these rods notably stiff and powerful for their time.

Bounce Cast—A form of slack-line cast; see.

Braided Leader—A leader that has a butt and mid-section (normally) of braided monofilament, with a conventional single-strand tippet. The leader is quite forgiving, as the braid is even more shock-absorbent than monofilament, and turns over well in casting. However, the braid also becomes waterlogged and thus sinks easily and is more difficult to pick up off the water. Braided leaders for dryfly fishing must be dressed frequently. The necessary taper in the leader is achieved simply by removing strands in the braiding process.

Hollow braid (as opposed to solid, or true braid) has two unusual benefits. First, it can be slid up over the tip of a fly line for a smooth, knotless connection that casts well and flows unhindered through the rod guides. It is anchored to the line either by a small sleeve of plastic tubing (which is removable) or with several drops of super glue (a permanent fix). Hollow braid also makes an excellent wet-fly leader, as high-density materials, usually lead or tungsten, can be put into it.

Knotting a tippet to the braid section causes some problems for anglers new to the material, but between the leader supplier's instructions and another dab of super glue, it's not difficult. Fishermen also wonder about the strength of such leaders, but every gamefish up to tarpon and marlin have been taken successfully on braid. See also Leader.

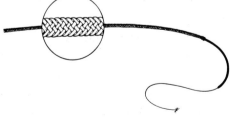

Breakaway Leader—A special, often custom-tied leader favored by some experienced tarpon and Atlantic salmon fishermen. A breakaway leader has a weak link in it—a section that the angler can snap at will (by pointing the rod directly at the fish and tugging sharply on the line with the other hand). This might be a piece of 5- to 8-lb.-test in a leader that might have a 12- or 16-lb. tippet, or it might be an ordinary leader that is simply lighter than what would normally be used on a particular fish.

The point is to be able to free the fish instantly, at any time, without having to bring it to hand. Atlantic salmon fishermen sometimes do this if a fish is unexpectedly strong and would have to be exhausted to near death in order to be landed (or if local rules demand they stop fishing after landing one salmon, whether it is released or not). Many tarpon anglers are also concerned with wearing their quarry down too far. Some say that a large tarpon needs eight hours or more to recover fully from being caught, even if it swims away with no apparent trouble, and in that time it is easy pickings for a shark. More directly, a breakaway leader lets them turn a tarpon loose to run for its life when a shark appears in mid-fight.

And finally, some experienced anglers admit they like a breakaway link for themselves, as a way to get out of an exhausting, bruising fight that could go on for hours. See also Leader.

Breaking Strength—The tensile strength of a section of line or leader, usually expressed as so-and-so many "pounds-test." The International Game Fish Association (see) has for decades tested the breaking strength of fishing lines in determining line-class record catches. See also Tensile Strength.

Bright Fish—Usually applied to anadromous species, the term refers to a fish that has not yet blossomed into its spawning colors. A "bright" salmon, for instance, is one that has just entered its spawning river from the ocean and is still a silver-sided sea creature; a "fresh" fish but not necessarily a "green" fish (see).

Bronzeback—A smallmouth bass; see.

Brook Trout—The brook trout, *Salvelinus fontinalis*, is in fact not a trout; it is a charr, an arctic salmonid native to clean and cold mountain streams, lakes and beaver ponds from Labrador to Minnesota and down to the Appalachians. Because of the east-west flow of colonization, the brookie was North America's "first" trout, the one that figures prominently in the early history of American fly-fishing. Until the brown trout arrived in North America in the 1880s, the brook—or speckled, or squaretail—trout was to most American fishing authorities (i.e. the Eastern writers) the *only* trout (although a

Brook Trout—a large male in spawning colors, caught and released in Quebec.

few had traveled to the Rockies and were familiar with "mountain trout," the cutthroat). The brookie was also the first American trout to be overfished and nearly wiped out— and the first to be "hatcheried" and subjected to experiments to breed a fish that could accommodate lower water quality. Modern as it sounds, the problem became apparent in the 19th Century. The famous fish culturist Seth Green opened the first commercial American fish hatchery in 1864, in New York State, to raise brook trout to release into the wild to augment those diminishing populations. Records from that era show brook trout of eight and nine pounds being taken every year in the States; but today, even in the remote streams and lakes of northern Maine or Wisconsin, a three-pounder is unusual. Bigger brook trout are found only farther north, in what is still true wilderness. The International Game Fish Association all-tackle record is a 14-pound 8-ounce brook trout caught in Ontario's Nipigon River in 1916.

As exotics, brook trout have been established in small numbers in the Rocky Mountain states and, intermittently, as far north on the West Coast as Alaska. Hatchery fish raised from captive wild stock have been used successfully to re-plant the species in northeastern waters where they had been fished or polluted out. (One type of brook trout that has not been well re-established is the "salter," the sea-run fish of the New England coast.) Of the salmonids, brook trout are among the most difficult to raise and relocate. The true native squaretail, the product of a wild gene pool culled, over hundreds of generations, by predators and climate, is a vibrant, slow-growing, sharply detailed and brightly colored fish that cannot be reproduced in a laboratory. Brook trout have very specific and narrowly defined needs in water temperature and chemistry and they do not tolerate the presence of man very well. Yet of some factors they are more tolerant than browns or rainbows; they can spawn successfully in lakes (which is why they were commonly used to replace the cutthroat trout that had vanished from many high Rocky Mountain lakes) and they can withstand greater alkalinity and acidity both.

Since the middle of the 19th Century, brook trout (mostly Maine stock) have been laboriously transplanted all over the world, from Australia to Spain, but the only place that suited them notably well is southern Patagonia, the lakes and rivers of Chile and Argentina. Brook trout there now grow to rival their Canadian cousins in size, if perhaps not in spawning colors.

Delicate and jewel-like in small sizes, awesome as large fish, brook trout are spectacularly colored, the aquatic version of the male wood duck. Their lower fins are red-gold, edged in black and white; in male fish, particularly in the fall at spawning time, this color extends up onto their bellies. Their green-black backs are decorated with wavy lighter markings, and scattered along their lateral lines are red or purple dots within blue halos.

The small brookies of northern ponds sometimes seem too easy to catch. The reason often is overpopulation—too much competition for too little food, brought on by the brook trout ability to spawn in still water. In severe cases, the fish may have thin bodies and disproportionately large heads and they will rush to strike at nearly any lure. However, even where the natural balance is proper, these fish rarely live longer than three or four years and rarely exceed a pound. Big brook trout need big water, from God's River in Manitoba to the famous Minipi watershed of Labrador, where most current world-record brook trout are caught (and released).

Brown Trout—*Salmo trutta*, the "salmon trout" or brown trout, the freshwater fly fisher's greatest challenge, is an exotic in North America. It is the native trout of Europe, Africa and the British Isles, so its introduction to the Americas was probably inevitable. On April 11, 1884, a certain J.F. Ellis and his assistant, using milk cans, transferred almost five thousand brown trout fry from a US Commission of Fish and Fisheries railroad car into the North Branch of the Pere Marquette River, near Baldwin, Michigan. These fish had been born from a second shipment of trout ova that Lucius von Behr, a German aristocrat, had sent across the Atlantic; the earlier batch hadn't survived the voyage. American trout fishing changed forever.

Not all American browns are descended from these German trout, however; the others were part of a small but significant "species dispersal" that took place long after earth's continents drifted apart and the Bering land bridge sank, a dispersal that had nothing to do with climate or glaciation. It came about because of the power of the

British Empire and the ethno- and egocentrism of its servants. The British did more to spread their field sports than perhaps any other group of people. They were in the right places at the right times to do so, when the Industrial Age was spilling out of western Europe, and they were convinced of the superiority of their way of life. Up through the Victorian era, British military men and commercial travelers and fortune-seekers transplanted "their" trout and salmon (and grouse and deer and ornamental shrubs and crops and more) all over the earth. Today, of course, the introduction of non-native species is illegal in most countries.

Thus America's second brown trout came from Britain—Scotland, actually. The descendants of those fish, which were brought to America in 1885, are still sometimes called Loch Leven browns.

As the name implies, the Loch Leven trout were a stillwater strain, as silvery as Atlantic salmon. Von Behr's stream-dwelling German fish bore the red and black spots and the saffron-yellow flanks that typify a brown trout to many fly fishers. Once transplanted, however, the two sub-subspecies eventually interbred (as all trout can, with varying degrees of ease) and present-day variations—mostly in color and markings—among North American browns are generally more due to environmental differences than to any original genetic traits.

Both types of browns are fall spawners. Like most salmonids, whenever possible they swim upstream into headwaters areas, or leave lakes for tributaries, to find the right gravel and flow conditions to dig their redds and lay their eggs.

Like many immigrants to North America, the brown trout eventually flourished. Also like many an immigrant race, it was vilified for some time after its arrival. Browns can tolerate a wider range of water conditions than brook trout and browns are also superior predators; in a stream where both fish came together, the browns often grew larger and more plentiful. Sportsmen of the northeastern US weren't happy to see "their" fish displaced by the newcomer. (In fact, the brook trout was hit much harder by steadily worsening pollution and habitat destruction—as development spread rapidly in the early 20th Century—than it was by the imported brown trout. Small brook trout, easier to catch than browns, fell victim to market-fishing too.)

As more time went by, however, fishermen began to appreciate the brown for its own qualities: It was a beautiful gamefish, more subtly colored than the brookie; it grows very large and strong; and it is more of an angling challenge than any native trout—brook, rainbow, laker or cutthroat. After the anti-German feelings of World War II dissipated, it became the premier American stream fish.

Brown trout occasionally reach 30 pounds or more, in clean, deep lakes, below large dams, or in stream pools where food is plentiful and competition is not. While trout are usually regarded as "northern fish," the current North American record brown trout,

Brown Trout—a male from the Madison River in Montana.

Brown Trout—a spec-tacularly marked eight-pound male from the South Island of New Zealand.

a 33-pounder, was caught in Arkansas, in the White River in 1977. The official all-tackle record is 35 pounds 5 ounces, taken in southern Argentina in 1952 (the brown trout emigrated very successfully to other countries too)—but fish of more than 40 pounds have been reported.

The consistently biggest wild brown trout on earth at the moment are probably the sea-trout of Tierra del Fuego, which commonly exceed 15 pounds. The best brown-trout fishery on earth—a high-quality angling experience that often yields at least one beautifully marked five- or six-pound fish each day—is probably New Zealand. But for sheer numbers—pounds, population, and even fishermen—the Salmon River and environs, where it flows into Lake Ontario north of Syracuse, New York, is probably "best." Thousands of browns between 5 and 20 pounds swim out of the lake every fall and winter into the rivers to try to spawn.

Sea-run browns—the sea-trout beloved by European anglers—or migratory lake-dwelling brown trout often resemble Atlantic salmon, at least until the spawning colors emerge; they are bright silver with black backs and black spots, and they may reach the size of salmon too. But brown trout spots are round while the salmon's markings are X-shaped. Trout usually have more spots as well, at least some of them within halos of lighter color. Another characteristic is their vomerine teeth, in the center of the roof of the mouth: Brown trout have a well-developed double row of these teeth and salmon only one row, and some teeth may be missing. Sea-trout and Atlantic salmon, despite their similarities, do not cross-breed in nature. The anal fin of a male brown trout has a rounded trailing edge; on a female the fin curves inward.

A riverine brown trout in fall spawning colors is spectacular: gold- and green-bodied, red- and black-spotted. Larger males develop kypes, hooked jaws that, with the well-fed brown's broad shoulders, humpback, and deep body, give the fish a bullish look that is often borne out by the way they fight a hook. Like all trout, stream- and lake-dwelling browns alike feed primarily on insects. Larger browns reach their size by hunting smaller trout as well as leeches, snails, crustaceans, shiners and other baitfish, and even frogs, mice and (reputedly) the occasional hapless small bird. Unusually large trout are very often browns, because they are harder to catch and because they are such successful predators. A big brown can crop the fish population of an entire pool singlehandedly, and killing such a fish—especially when it is past its spawning prime, at about eight or ten years—may benefit the fishery even more than releasing it.

Browns, especially the big fish, are caught less often than large rainbow, cutthroat or brook trout. However, brown trout are not necessarily more intelligent; but they are very wary and, unlike their three peers, they are generally nighttime feeders, while we are generally daytime anglers. Trophy browns are often caught by those who to learn to stalk, cast, strike and fight fish by feel rather than by sight.

Bucktail—In fly-tying, animal hair, often from a deer or calf tail. Also a broad classification of streamer flies (see) that are dressed with long hair wings—typically, but not only, hair from a deer's tail. Bucktails are generally simple, with a few strands of hair over a tinsel or floss body; the classic Mickey Finn is a good example. Like a streamer, a bucktail generally imitates a small foodfish, and the upper wing hairs may be dark or brightly colored, to represent the fish's back, and the lower hairs white, for its belly. Being hollow, hair inherently floats better than hackle, and bucktails can easily be "converted," with a bit of flotant dressing, to surface-riding flies. Bucktails are especially popular for large fish; not only are they effective, simple to tie, and streamlined enough to cast fairly easily even in large sizes, they also stand up better than featherwing flies to sharp teeth.

Bull Trout—For over a century, the bull trout, *Salvelinus confluentus*—sometimes known as the Western brook trout—was commonly identified as a Dolly Varden, even by fisheries biologists; the two are that similar in appearance and predatory feeding habits. But in 1978 a California scientist named Ted Cavender published his proof, based on "cranial characteristics," that the bull trout is a separate species. The fish is found throughout the Pacific Northwest as far south as northern California, generally in big water—heavy rivers, deep pools, cold lakes. Populations also exist in smaller waters as far east as western Montana. Positive identification of a bull trout versus a Dolly Varden generally requires dissection in a laboratory, but there is a rule of thumb: In Northwestern waters where both species might be found, any one that weighs much more than twelve pounds can safely be regarded as a bull trout.

Butt Action—A term used to describe the behavior of a fly rod that bends mostly in its butt section. See Rod Action.

Butt Cap—The disc or button at the end of a flyrod reel seat. The butt cap of many high-quality rods is machined aluminum or nickel silver; a presentation-grade rod may have a sterling-silver butt cap. In any event, the cap is often engraved with the specifications of the rod—"Orvis HLS 9'#6," for example—or the owner's initials, etc. Salmon, steelhead and saltwater fly rods often have removable butt caps; they hide a socket for a plug-in fighting butt (see).

Caddis Fly—There are thought to be nearly 1,000 species of caddis, or sedge, flies (*Trichoptera*) in North America alone, and they are one of the most important of the aquatic insects on which trout feed. Caddis are more resistant to pollution than mayflies, which fact alone may make them even more important to future trout fishers. They inhabit small streams, large rivers, ponds and lakes. The adults have a characteristic reverse-taper "tent-wing" shape (the two pairs of wings, when folded together, look like a long, narrow pup tent) and long, swept-back antennae and may be anywhere from a quarter of an inch or less in length (Ernest Schwiebert, in his *Nymphs* [1973] called them microcaddis) to about two inches. In the air, they resemble moths. The color range is wide, running from white through cream, brown, gray and black. Caddis flies usually hatch in spring or summer, but they can also appear virtually year-round almost anywhere in the US. Hatches can be very heavy, resembling summer snowstorms. The most popular caddis-based dry fly today is the Elkhair Caddis, developed by Al Troth, and its many variations, but flies that imitate the grub-shaped caddis larvae or pupae probably take many more trout.

Caddis differ from mayflies and stoneflies in their lifecycle, passing through an extra stage, the pupa, after transiting from egg to larva and before becoming a winged adult. Many caddis larvae build protective cases around themselves, from grains of sand or bits of vegetation lashed together with filaments secreted by the larvae. Different species of these "casemaker" caddis build highly distinctive shelters—some look like snail shells, others like free-form log huts or strange conglomerates of minerals, still others like long, fine tubes.

Caddis—green caddis larvae emerging from their casings.

Cage-Frame Reel—A type of fly reel in which the spool is fully enclosed by the frame; see Full-Frame Reel.

Calcutta Cane—*Dendrocalamus strictus*, a type of bamboo found in India (and shipped west largely from the port of Calcutta) that was favored for building split-cane fishing rods until about 1920, when so-called Tonkin cane (see), *Arundinaria amabilis*, from China, was discovered to surpass it in function. By comparison, rods made from Calcutta cane have a slower, more ponderous feel.

CalTrout—California Trout, Inc.; a highly influential non-profit state group dedicated to conservation and enhancement of salmonids, which splintered off from the national organization Trout Unlimited (see) in order to pursue its own more specific goals. The break came in 1971 when several officers and directors of California TU, frustrated by the cost of contributing to a national bureaucracy and by a "lack of sensitivity to distinct in-state needs," left the parent organization. California fly shop proprietor Peter Woolley wrote in *Fly Rod & Reel* Magazine (November/December 1989): "No national [group] of any sort could have understood California's problems or satisfied her anglers. Preserving fish habitat in this climate is too big a job for any organization not centered here." Virtually all California's hundreds of trout fisheries have enjoyed the benefit of CalTrout's involvement.

For its first 20 years, the head of CalTrout was Dick May, a strong-minded, persuasive and fearless activist who enraged many Californians—particularly farmers, ranchers, utility officials, loggers, meat fishermen, developers, and all their lawyers—while inspiring millions of others to support wild trout and their habitat. His fiery, full-time brand of environmentalism set the tone for CalTrout from the outset, and CalTrout's worldwide reputation has since inspired similar organizations in other places.

Not just California fish owe CalTrout a debt of gratitude. Catch-and-release (see) became doctrine among trout fishers across the US and in many other countries in the 1980s in part because of CalTrout's work. According to Dick May, the "seminal event that broke the logjam holding back C&R in the US and the world" was a two-day national symposium held in Arcata, California, in 1977. Called "Catch and Release as a Management Tool" and sponsored by the American Fisheries Society, Humboldt State University and CalTrout, it drew together fisheries managers, scientists, activists and interested citizens. The inescapable conclusion was that catch-and-release was indeed a potent benefit and a powerful management tool, and the published proceedings of the gathering spread this information rapidly around the world. In conjunction, CalTrout introduced its universal catch-and-release logo and put it into the public domain for all to use.

Cane—Bamboo; see.

Cane Rod Building—According to tackle historian Martin Keane, it was Samuel and Solon Phillippe, father and son, gunsmiths of Pennsylvania, who built the first known American split-cane rod sections, between about 1845 and 1860. These were of three- and four-strip construction (similar work had been done in Britain—and perhaps in America—50 or more years earlier) and then, finally and significantly, in the six-strip style that would eventually dominate cane rod building. The first known rod made entirely—each section, butt to tip—of six laminated strips of cane was by Charles F. Murphy, of Newark, New Jersey, during the Civil War. He was a friend and admirer of the Phillippes, and went on, in Keane's words, to build "the first commercial split-bamboo rods in sufficient numbers to influence American anglers to use American-made rods." This was the beginning of the golden age of bamboo rods.

It is difficult for the uninitiated to believe that even the wand-like tip of a slender bamboo trout rod, perhaps only a sixteenth of an inch thick, is made of six separate triangular strips glued together into a long, tapering hexagon. Each fine strip is cut to included angles of 60 degrees—or slightly less—so that their outside edges meet perfectly and there is room for the glue inside. Each strip also tapers precisely in thickness, to give the rod its final shape, strength and flex pattern, or rod action (see).

When split bamboo became the rod technology of choice, the hunt began for the best, most suitable of earth's 1,000-odd species of bamboo. Calcutta cane, from India, held sway until the early 1900s, when Tonkin cane, with its high density of strong, resilient fibers, took over. Classified scientifically in 1931 as *Arundinaria amabilis* (loosely, "the lovely bamboo"), it is thought to grow well only in the Guangdong Province of the People's Republic of China. For decades stocks were imported by the New York firm of Harold Demarest. When the US Government installed a trade embargo against newly Communist China shortly after World War II, rod companies thought they had enough stockpiled to see them through. The smaller shops did, for as they closed, put out of business by the new fiberglass rod, the survivors bought up their remaining cane. There is still pre-embargo bamboo out there, some of it nearly a century old, well-seasoned by any standard. Large bamboo-rod producers such as The Orvis Company went to fantastic lengths, ranging from personal diplomacy to near-smuggling, to try to keep the cane coming, while efforts to grow it elsewhere failed.

The Bamboo Curtain was breached in 1973, following the famous China tour of the US ping-pong team, but the flow of high-quality, mature Tonkin cane has never been dependable. It arrives in New York Harbor in 125-pound bundles wrapped in burlap that is stencilled with Chinese characters. A straight, strong 12-foot culm, with no

Cane Rod Building—Rod maker Walt Carpenter fitting a ferrule at his workbench.

machete slashes or insect boreholes, makes a rod craftsman smile in anticipation, for it is a remarkable material. Metal-working tools must be used to shape it, and a machinist's file that has become too dull to cut cane will still file ordinary carbon steel.

The initial inspection may junk half or more of a shipment of bamboo. It is, after all, a natural material, with all the imperfections to be expected from good and bad growth years, insects, disease and imperfect harvesting or seasoning. Select raw culms—often flame- or oven-tempered, which imparts a lovely honey-brown tone—are split apart: The maker bravely taps a froe into the end of a culm. Like good stovewood, it cracks apart again and again; the grain determines the splits, and the rod maker only initiates them. (Rodcrafters who cut their rough strips with table saws sometimes junk three-quarters of them because the saw teeth can rip through the valuable long fibers of the culm instead of separating them.) The rings on the outside of the cane are nodes, divisions between the cells of the stalk. The membrane inside is cut away, and the bumps outside are filed down or pressed flush. Particularly thick-walled strips may be fed through a power planer to mill away the useless inner pith. The strong fibers lie near the outside edge.

The next step is to shape the sticks. Many one-man rod shops still lay them into metal forms of exact depth and shape, and plane off the excess that protrudes above the slot. Naturally, every rod model requires a different set of forms. A few makers have bevelers, machines that cut a precise, tapered triangular segment out of each stick. When Hiram Leonard invented the power beveler, around 1876, it turned the rod business around, for suddenly it became possible to manufacture dozens of identical segments in minutes, and to within repeatable tolerances of a few ten-thousandths of an inch.

From the resultant pile of cane segments, six sound ones—free of splinters, cracks or other defects—must be "mis-matched" properly together, making sure no two nodes lie next to each other to produce a weak spot. The inner surfaces of the segments are liberally painted with a hide glue, which flows better than epoxy and remains slightly plastic when cured. The only drawback to such a glue is its water-solubility, potentially fatal in a fishing rod. Some rods are varnished for waterproofing, some are impregnated with an acrylic or other resin compound, which produces a near-perfect finish that can be rejuvenated, even years later, simply by buffing. Impregnation finishes were developed in the 1940s (by Wes Jordan—see) but the process is still regarded with suspicion in some circles. Done properly, it does not produce a "soggy" rod.

The glued-up rod blank is then wrapped back and forth with string, to hold everything in position while the glue sets up. Then the string is unraveled and the excess glue and any rough spots are scraped and sanded off. Now, if the blank doesn't flex properly, if it has a pronounced stiff spine along one axis, there's no point in continuing with the trimming, straightening, ferruling and furnishing with grip, reel seat, line guides and other fittings.

If all goes well, about a month may pass between the time the culm is split and when the rod is shipped, and many top rod makers are a year or more back-ordered. See also Bamboo.

Cape—In fly-tying, a section of the skin of a bird, usually a chicken, with the feathers still attached, extending from the neck down to the base of the back. Also called a neck or sometimes a saddle (although, strictly speaking, the saddle is a strip along the middle of a cape). Capes grown commercially for the fly-tying market are usually rated—#1, #2, #3, in descending order of overall quality—and priced accordingly. See Genetic Hackle.

Carapace—The hard, bony, protective case or shield over the back of a certain animals (such as a crab's shell) or insects. In tying fly patterns that imitate crustaceans or hard-shelled insects, the carapace is an important part of the dressing; clear, water-resistant, paintable synthetic materials such as epoxy have helped fly tiers make great strides in matching those particular hatches.

Cast—Verb: To deliver a fly to its target. Fly-fishing puts a premium on casting skill for, unlike other kinds of rod-and-reel fishing, in fly-fishing the lure (the fly) is effectively weightless and the line has to be heavy enough to cast itself. In spinning, spin-casting, bait-casting and so on, the momentum of the relatively heavy lure or bait pulls the essentially weightless line off its spool. See Fly-Casting.

Cast—Noun: In the United Kingdom and throughout much of the former British Empire (where fly-fishing, like cricket, bird-shooting and other upper-class British sports, flourished under the influence of the colonial managers), the cast is that part of the terminal tackle that a North American would call a tippet.

Casting Competition—The ACA, the American Casting Association (see), sanctions competitions in spinning, spin-casting, bait-casting and fly-casting, which may be held over water or land. There are three fly-casting accuracy events and three distance events, in men's, ladies', intermediate and junior classes.

The three accuracy contests are Dry Fly, Trout Fly and Bass Bug. The targets are 30-inch rings floating on water or wooden discs set on the ground, and an ACA-approved fly is provided. In the first two events, five targets are set at 20 to 50 feet from the casting box.

A Dry Fly rod cannot be longer than 9'6" and the leader must be at least six feet long; the line may be any weight or taper so long as it is not marked to show distance (or fastened to the reel at the 50-foot mark). An official Trout Fly competition rod can be no longer than 8'6"; the leader must be at least nine feet long, with an 18-inch tippet of no more than 0.008 inches thickness, and the line must be a standard DT6F (see Fly Line). It too may not be marked for distance or fastened to the reel at 50 feet. The Trout Fly event has a Wet Fly and Roll Cast round as well.

There are six Bass Bug targets—the five used above plus one more, set 65 to 70 feet away from the casting box. A Bass Bug rod may be no longer than nine feet, the leader no less than six feet with a tippet not less than 12 inches or more than 0.014 inches in diameter. The line has to be a standard WF9F.

The three distance fly-casting events are: Two-Hand Salmon Fly, One-Hand Trout Fly and Angler's Fly. The Two-Hand rod may be no more than 15 feet long, with a leader that is at least six feet and no more than two feet longer than the rod. There are no limits on the line or the reel—the caster need not use a reel at all, in fact—and the casting is, naturally, two-handed. The One-Hand rod can be no longer than 9'6" and the head, or casting part, of the line has to be at least 50 feet long and weigh no more than 1.5 ounces. The leader must be between six and 12 feet long, and again no reel is necessary. The Angler's Fly Distance rod must be no more than nine feet long and fitted with any standard fly reel. The casting line is a 31'6" shooting head of no more than 310 grains, and the leader has to be between nine and 12 feet long.

The ACA has developed a full suite of regulations—including time limits, stripping and false-casting rules, assistance, penalties, demerits and scoring—for all these events; they are available from the association at 7328 Maple Avenue, Cincinnati, Ohio 45231.

As a sport, competitive casting, with fly rods or any other kind, has nearly died out in North America, at least compared to the popularity it enjoyed through much of the 20th Century. In the 1970s, competitive casting went into a slump from which it shows no signs of recovering. American fly casters such as Steve Rajeff held world casting titles for years through the 1980s and into the '90s, but they received far more attention internationally than they did at home in the USA.

Part of the problem may be that in general fishing, the emphasis has shifted from developing personal skills to selling gear—fast boats, electronic fish-finders, etc.—and from casting to catching fish. Promotion-minded PR flacks and TV producers would rather sponsor and cover "professional" bass fishing and its large cash prizes than an event centered around a series of hoops floating on a pond.

Fly-fishing clubs still hold the occasional local casting events, but in keeping with most fly fishers' avowed dislike of competition in their sport, these are low-key and "non-threatening"—i.e., no significant prizes or other hoopla. Another influence in fly-fishing may be that in the 1970s and early '80s, for some unknown reason, a few tackle manufacturers drew a line in their advertising between tournament casters and "real" fly fishers. The implication that one was artificial and the other natural was all that many fly fishers needed—at a time when leather, wool and wood was "better" than vinyl, polyester and lexan—to steer them away from casting for anything other than fish. In truth, of course, casting skill is fully linked with fishing success; of two anglers of otherwise equal skills, the one who can cast farther and more accurately will catch more fish.

Casting Knot—See Wind Knot.

Cast & Blast—A colloquialism, probably spawned (as it were) in the Rocky Mountains, which refers to the unique pleasures available on many fly-fishing rivers in September or October, that being when the angling and gunning seasons overlap. In Alaska, that might mean rainbow trout fishing and caribou hunting on the same day; in Maritime Canada, Atlantic salmon and woodcock; in Montana, browns and grouse or cutthroats and geese. The variations are legion.

Catch and Release—The most important concept of present-day sport fishing, and the one that is chiefly responsible, directly and indirectly, for the great improvement in trout and salmon fishing in North America, is the idea of releasing a fish unharmed to spawn and even to fight again and to be caught another day. Much of the credit for publicizing the idea goes to Lee Wulff, who in *Lee Wulff's New Handbook of Freshwater Fishing* (Stokes, 1939) wrote, "Game fish are too valuable to be caught only once" and "The fish you release is your gift to another angler and, remember, it may have been someone's similar gift to you." He went on to preach that gospel at every opportunity until his death in 1991, and he was one of the most widely published, read, revered and influential outdoorsmen of all time.

The success of catch-and-release hinges upon a number of factors, not least of which is how the fish are played, landed, unhooked and released (see Mortality). Still, the idea that a fish can be unhooked and released uninjured is certainly nothing new; every small boy who has yanked a sunfish out of a pond instinctively realizes that. In 1936 John Alden Knight wrote, in *The Modern Angler*, "A fish, hooked with a fly and played to the net, is usually not materially hurt and may be returned to the water, slightly weary but otherwise as good as ever, to be caught again next year."

Almost 500 years before Wulff and Knight, the apocryphal Dame Juliana Berners (see), in her "Treatyse of Fysshynge wyth an Angle," cautioned anglers to "not be too greedy in catching your said game, as in taking too much at one time . . . could easily be the occasion of destroying your own sport and other men's also." And in fact the deeper one reads into angling literature—in America, England, even medieval Europe—the more similar statements turn up. Advice like that, however, is not unexpected from the sort of fisherman who is published: presumably an expert who, in thousands of hours on the water, has progressed from fishing for the table to fishing for numbers to fishing for pure enjoyment. He is no more likely to bring fish home than the man who has worked in the candy factory for years is to filch sweets. The turnaround for fisheries, at least in the US, came when even weekend anglers began to adopt the same attitude, a trend that became widespread only in the 1970s.

A few enlightened fisheries biologists helped too. Dr. Albert Hazzard, of the University of Michigan, proposed in 1952, in *Sports Afield* and elsewhere, a catch-and-release program to be called "Fishing for Fun." Possibly the time wasn't yet right; certainly the name was ambiguous. Scientists who early on believed in the idea (not all did, or even do today) had more success in forcing anglers to release their catch, by influencing state fish & game regulations. as far back as 1934 Pennsylvania stocked a section of Spring Creek, near Penn State, with large trout and restricted fishermen to killing but one each per day. To help sell the program to the public, that stretch was dubbed "Fisherman's Paradise." Soon, however, it was no mere snow job; it really *was* a fisherman's paradise, and a most valuable example was set. Other states, at first only in the East and upper Midwest, followed suit on a few experimental waters. All paid off. In the 1960s, similar management went in place in California, on Hat Creek, and in the Rockies, in Yellowstone National Park (where today it is not usual for cutthroat trout in heavily fished sections of the Yellowstone River to be caught—and released— a dozen times each every summer.) The groundswell was gathering.

According to Dick May, the influential first president of California Trout, Inc. (see; a state group that had splintered off from Trout Unlimited in order to pursue its own more specific and more aggressive conservation goals), the "seminal event that broke the logjam holding back C&R in the US and the world" was a two-day national symposium held in Arcata, California, in 1977. Called "Catch and Release as a Management Tool" and sponsored by the American Fisheries Society, Humboldt State University and CalTrout, it drew together fisheries managers, scientists, activists and interested citizens. The inescapable conclusion was that catch-and-release was indeed a very powerful benefit and management tool, and the published proceedings of the gathering spread this information rapidly around the world. In conjunction, CalTrout introduced its new universal catch-and-release logo and put it into the public domain for all to use.

Catch and Release—the international symbol for catch-and-release angling, developed by CalTrout in 1977.

Some of the strongest proponents of catch-and-release are anglers who live in exurban areas, where fishing pressure is great, and professionals—guides, outfitters, lodge owners—who operate in wilderness areas. The first group has seen first-hand what overfishing can do and may be enjoying the renewed fishing that catch-and-release or no-kill (not necessarily the same) regulations invariably produce. And the second group is well aware that their livelihoods depend on their clients' being able to catch many large fish each and every time they come to stay.

Opponents of catch-and-release often see it as an infringement of their "God-given" right to use up natural resources whenever and however they want to. Some who are capable of thinking more clearly sometimes argue that since rod-and-line sport fishermen take such a small percentage of the world's fish, asking them to release their catch is meaningless; better to go after the commercial harvesters or those who wreck fish habitat. However, anyone who has seen photographs of the huge hauls of fish taken by "sports" in the early 1900s from, for example, streams in Michigan or lakes in Maine knows that recreation can weaken a fishery as thoroughly as any gill net. And even in fisheries under pressure from commercial harvesters catch-and-release can play an important role: The sport fishing community's willingness to "give up" killing fish can be a valuable symbol in their fight for sane overall management.

Other, more credible opposition to catch-and-release exists in the United Kingdom, where much fishing is put-and-take (see) and natural reproduction either doesn't exist or isn't important to the fishery. On wild-trout streams, catch-and-release is making some headway, but even there many British anglers believe that a once-caught fish is an injured fish that will only die soon after release. And even if the fish survives, it may have picked up a skin infection from being handled, which could spread to other fish.

In parts of Europe there is a strong feeling that catch-and-release is cruel, that fishing simply to let the catch go again amounts to toying with a living creature for frivolous reasons. Better to land a fish quickly, the reasoning goes, and kill it humanely than to let it dance frantically about on the end of the line in mortal terror. In a famous case in Germany in 1990, a judge fined the organizers of a catch-and-release fishing competition for promoting cruelty to animals. Animal-rights groups in North America might agree, and perhaps someday even no-kill fly-fishing will come under attack by extremists.

Catch-and-release led to the spread of barbless hooks. Will the next evolution be hookless flies? Will anglers of the 21st Century find themselves fishing not to land a fish but just for the strike, like Plains Indians counting coup upon their enemies simply by touching them?

Fly tier and innovator Mike Tucker, inventor of the Liquid-Filled (see) line of flies, may have moved fly-fishing one step closer to that day already. In 1992 he introduced flies tied not with hooks in them but with small sections of fine mesh; the teeth of a fish tangled in the mesh and held it, unharmed, until it could be released—without a hole in its lip. (Unfortunately, if the fish breaks the tippet, it will not be able to remove or digest such a "hook.")

Accurately or not, catch-and-release has been closely identified with American fly-fishing since the 1930s, and to some extent it contributed to the "élitist" aura of the sport that grew up after spinfishing became popular in the '50s. After about 1985, however, when environmental concerns began to sweep the USA, the close association of the two has helped fly-fishing grow: It is seen as a field sport that the environmentally aware can enjoy without bruising their consciences—a "bloodless blood sport." From fly-fishing catch-and-release spread notably to offshore big-game fishing, where commercial netting and longlining has drastically reduced fish stocks in many areas of the world.

A corollary to catch-and-release was Lee Wulff's advice that if we were to kill any gamefish it should be the small ones, not the large, trophy fish. This flew directly in the face of the established "Bambi" school of game management, which applies human values, not biological science, to the predator-prey relationship. The notion of sparing the young, the weak, the small and the female has been around seemingly forever, but Wulff pointed out that sparing small fish (or deer or whatever) skewed natural selection their way; eventually, there would only be small fish or deer left. The fish to release, he said, were the large, strong, healthy super-predators, the individuals who had demonstrated in the clearest possible way that they could survive and prosper. The big, successful animals carry the strongest genes and must be allowed to reproduce. The logic is undeniable and examples that seem to prove it are everywhere, but as recently as January 1992, the *New York Times* carried a "news" story entitled "Throwing Back Undersize Fish Is Said To Encourage Smaller Fry."

How to release fish: First, bring the fish to hand as quickly as possible; don't exhaust it. Don't hesitate to put pressure on the terminal tackle—it is virtually impossible to break a tippet simply by pulling with the rod. And second, fish that are to be released should be handled as little as possible, if at all (see Slime).

Do not use a stomach pump (to see what the fish has been feeding on); doctors call that an "invasive procedure" and without proper training it often has fatal effects.

If the fish has been netted, keep the net in the water as much as possible. Don't let the fish struggle and tangle itself in the mesh; don't let it trash against the side of a boat or on the shore; keep its head facing into the current. To release a fish from a net, simply turn the net inside out in the water.

To weigh a netted fish, simply weigh it in the net; then weigh the net and subtract.

If the fish is to be gaffed, put the gaff into its mouth and hook it in the lower jaw, from the inside out. Then to release it, simply slide or twist the gaff out.

Photo fish should be lifted horizontally out of the water, cradled gently in both hands, and never kept in the air much longer than 15 seconds at a time.

Don't squeeze a thrashing fish; you may damage a vital organ.

Do not lift a fish by its tail, for fear of separating its vertebrae or, again, damaging soft organs. Turning a fish upside-down, to quiet it, may have the same effect.

Always hold a fish over water, so that if it struggles, it won't fall on rocks or sand, which may injure it or contaminate its gills.

Never touch a fish's gills (if the gills bleed at all, it will likely die).

Protect a fish's eyes and fins as well.

Bass may safely be "lipped," gripped by thumb and forefinger in the lower jaw.

Many fish—particularly small ones, with soft mouths, can release themselves, given some slack and the opportunity.

If the hook is well-lodged and accessible, use fingers, forceps or pliers to twist the hook out cleanly; barbless hooks come out easily.

A hook taken deeply should simply be left there; clip the tippet as close as possible and release the fish. Within hours it will have removed the hook itself, by rubbing it against the bottom, or within days the hook will have been dissolved by gastric juices or encapsulated by tissue. Don't use stainless-steel or nickel-plated hooks for catch-and-release fishing; bronzed steel hooks corrode much more quickly in a fish. The price of a fly fades to nothing when weighed against the time and energy it took to spawn and grow that fish to its present size.

Don't "release" larger fish by throwing them back into the water; lower them into the water in your hands.

If the fish must be revived, face it upstream in a quiet section of the current to let oxygenated water flow into its mouth and through its gills. In still water move the fish gently forward, never backward, to get the same effect. Watch to see if its gills begin to work.

Release fish in shallow water so that you can reach it if it sinks, exhausted, to the bottom.

Cradle the fish loosely in the water. When it is ready to go, it will.

Catskill Patterns—a classic Quill Gordon tied by Ted Niemeyer.

Catskill Fly Fishing Center and Museum, The—A non-profit educational organization founded in 1981 and dedicated to "Preserving the heritage, enhancing the present, and protecting the future" of fly-fishing, both nationally and in upstate New York. The Center is on 35 acres bordering the Willowemoc in the town of Livingston Manor. The small museum has an excellent collection of flies, tackle, books and memorabilia from past and present Catskills angling celebrities, but the Center is perhaps best known for its hands-on programs that teach stream ecology, entomology and habitat conservation and restoration as well as fly-tying and fly-fishing.

Catskill Patterns—These are not so much specific patterns as they are dry flies tied according to a particular style that developed along the banks of the famous trout streams of the Catskill Mountains, north of New York City. American fly-fishing did not begin in the Catskills—it began in Long Island, in Pennsylvania and in eastern Canada, among other places—but, beginning around 1840, the Catskills became the "laboratory" where fly-fishing took on a truly American style.

Catskill patterns look strangely proportioned and sparsely dressed to someone used to other things, but of course they are the fruits of their environment—impressionistic, high-riding, well-balanced, delicate flies that suited their narrow, tumbling mountain streams. The late Harry Darbee, Catskill fly shop proprietor and fly critic extraordinaire, credited (in *Catskill Flytier*, 1977) four famous anglers with developing this uniquely clean and practical Yankee style: Theodore Gordon, Herman Christian, Roy Steenrod and Edward Hewitt. Through them, the Catskill school of fly-dressing began at the time of the Civil War and hit its peak in about 1915, but dozens of well-known American fly tiers, from Rube Cross to Art Flick to Larry Duckwall and others, have inherited the tradition from those four and taken it intact into modern times.

Within the Catskill style, the best-known patterns are the Quill Gordon (named after Theodore), the Hendrickson, the Gray Fox Variant and the Cahill.

Fly-tying historian Darrel Martin, writing in *Fly Rod & Reel* in May/June 1992, catalogued the essential features of a Catskill dry: a lightweight model perfect hook (in the absence of the original Allcock 04991, the Mustad 94840 became the modern choice); a divided mottled or barred wing of wood-duck hackle, set about a third of the way back from the hook eye and often canted slightly forward; a clean, stiff, glassy hackle—with barbs fully as long as the hook shank—wrapped sparely before and behind the wings; an equally spare hackle tail that is also as long as (or longer than) the shank; a short, spare, tapered body of dubbed fur or stripped quill; and an all-but-nonexistent head of just a few wraps of thread set about three eye lengths behind the hook eye; and on a true classic Catskill fly, the front of the shank, ahead of these wraps, is simply left bare.

Various other historians have noted that even the "hallowed four" did not necessarily include each and every one of these features in their own Catskill flies.

The point of the unusual hackle placement and the "longneck" design was to balance the fly so well on its hackle tips that, according to Harry Darbee, a proper Catskill pattern rode "broken, turbulent waters like a coast guard lifeboat, so nearly balanced that often the tail . . . doesn't touch the water at all."

CFO reels

CFO—The initials are those of Charles F. Orvis, founder in 1856 of The Orvis Company (see) in Manchester, Vermont. Since about 1970, the company has applied those initials to its premier light- to medium-duty trout reel. The CFO series was the first mass-produced half-frame, palming-rim fly reel in America. It is more widely known today for its lightweight strength, its dependability, its classic good looks, and its harmonious, purring click when a fish takes line out.

CFS—Cubic Feet per Second, a measure of how much water is coming down a particular stream at a given moment. It is used widely primarily in western North America, where recreationists, ranchers, farmers and municipalities have for more than a century warred over water rights and so have learned to pay attention to such things. Many important Western rivers are dammed, and a dam operator (invariably a government agency) thus controls their flows. Anglers and fishing guides know at what flow levels their rivers fish well, not so well, or not at all. And at what flows their trout begin to die—if the volume is too low, summer water temperatures can climb too high; in winter, the river can freeze completely. In the late 1980s and early '90s, several landmark legal decisions were handed down (in California, for example) that stipulated flow minimums for certain rivers in order to maintain healthy fish populations—as opposed to keeping farmers' irrigation canals full.

Charr—A Dolly Varden from the Goodnews River in western Alaska.

Charr—In classifying and identifying the various charrs, genus *Salvelinus*, confusion has reigned ever since Linnaeus himself misnamed the Lapp charr of his native Sweden in 1758 (he called it a *Salmo*). Scientists agree that charrs are arctic trout, especially cold-adapted salmonids that originally were found everywhere in the high northern latitudes, but there is no agreement on which charr are species and which are subspecies; some biologists say that, with the addition of the Western bull trout, there are as many as a dozen recognizably different charrs in North America alone. The best known of these are the brook trout (*S. fontinalis*), the lake trout (*S. namaycush*), the arctic charr (*S. alpinus*) and the Dolly Varden (*S. malma* or *S. malma alpinus*, depending upon which school you favor)). The confusion extends even to the name: Is it char—or charr? And where does the word come from?

Worldwide, charrs are native occasionally as far south as about 40°N latitude and are found farther north than any other salmonid. In North America, native brook trout exist as far south as the southern Appalachian Mountains. They are generally fall spawners (given the variety of types, there may be exceptions to this). Charrs may be sea-run or landlocked—depending upon opportunity, genetic pre-disposition, and where the retreat of the last northern glaciation stranded them—and lake- or stream-dwelling. With the exception of the laker (called, accurately enough, gray trout in parts of Canada), charrs are often wildly colorful and such seemingly reckless predators that they may be easy pickings for fishermen. They may also grow to very large size—lake trout, for example, have been known to reach 100 pounds.

Distinguishing the charrs can be difficult. First, note that charrs may have light spots or red spots, while "true" trout—rainbows, browns, cutthroat—have black spots. In addition, trout have a complete set of vomerine teeth (the vomer is the bone that forms the front section of the roof of the fish's mouth) while charrs usually have only a few teeth on the front of the vomer.

In eastern Canada, arctic charr and brook trout (both *Salvelinus*) are often found in the same water, and fishermen who see only the spectacularly red-orange bellies and white-trimmed fins of both fish sometimes find them hard to tell apart. Arctic charr lack the worm-like black markings that brook trout carry on their backs; and while charr may be spotted, the spots are not surrounded by lighter halos.

The variety of charrs is impressive. In New England alone, for example, along with the brook trout there are the Sunapee and the blueback trout—charrs, in fact. Even more rare is a charr called the silver trout, which reputedly inhabits a single deep lake in the interior of Maine. A few specimens have been examined by biologists at the University of Maine. The last one seen was taken by an ice fisherman around 1980,

Chum Salmon—Netted fish drying on an Inuit rack on Alaska's Seward Peninsula.

but since the lake can only be reached by hikers and access is controlled by a utility company, the silver trout may be living on unmolested. These three fish are almost certainly descended from arctic charr populations that were isolated by glacial accidents (when the last Ice Age ended in New England, about 10,000 years ago) and went on to develop their own characteristics independently. In the rest of the world, biologists have named at least 16 species of charr and more distinct strains. There is even an Asian *Salvelinus fontinalis*, a subspecies that is distinct from the North American *S. fontinalis*, the brook trout.

Chenille—In French, a *chenille* is a caterpillar; and so, in the fabrics trade, chenille is fuzzy, thick-pile yarn. Chenille may be cotton, wool, silk or synthetics; in fly-tying, it makes excellent body dubbing for certain patterns.

Chinook—Another name for king salmon; see.

Chum Salmon—*Oncorhynchus keta*, also known as dog salmon because the native people of the northwestern North America netted them to feed their dogs. From July through December, depending on latitude, chum salmon are plentiful in the rivers of western Canada and southern Alaska and progressively less so down to the southern end of their range, northern California. When they return to fresh water to spawn they are generally eight to 15 pounds and silvery colored. Chums are the only Pacific salmon that do not turn bright red at spawning; instead they develop unique rusty streaks that extend irregularly up their greenish-gray sides like flames. In spite of their reputation as "dogs," they will take flies and fight hard, if sluggishly, at least while fresh. See also Pacific Salmon, Salmon.

Class Tippet—A leader tippet of a certain specified length and breaking strength; usually the specifications are those set by the IGFA, the International Game Fish Association, in its certification of record catches. In 1981 flyrod-record tippet classes were standardized at: 1kg/2-lb, 2kg/4-lb, 4kg/8-lb, 6kg/12-lb and 8kg/16-lb. And on April 1, 1991, the IGFA officially ratified a 10kg/20-pound tippet class. See also Tippet.

Clicker—In a fly reel, the small spring-loaded pawl that supplies the clicking sound when line is being stripped out and/or reeled in. Historically, a fly reel had a "poacher button," a sliding stud on the reel backplate that let the angler stop the click by moving the pawl away from the sprocket it was striking; that quieted the reel, ostensibly so that a game warden or water bailiff couldn't hear it. While no one calls them poacher buttons any more—in this age of catch-and-release and respect for game laws—many fly reels still have them because some fly fishers won't buy a reel without a click and others prefer their reels to be silent.

Some fly reels click only when line is going out, and some have two clicks—one sound for retrieving line, the other for stripping line. The idea is to give the angler an audible indication of how fast a fish is running, or whether the drag is engaged or the reel is in free-spool (see). The clicker may also do double-duty as an overrun check (see).

Though it may in fact be the same mechanism in many reels, a clicker is held to be different from a sprocket & pawl drag (see), and many reels with completely different drag systems still have pawl-type clickers. See also Fly Reel.

Clinch Knot—One of the fly-fishing's basic connections. The clinch knot is how most flies are tied to most tippets, and in most cases it suffices—at least for light- to medium-duty fishing. Its strengths are that it is easy to tie, it is not very bulky, and it leaves the tippet pulling straight off the hook eye, aligned with the hook shank. The tippet is simply passed through the hook eye, wrapped back around itself three, four or five times (depending on the thickness of the mono) and then the tag end is brought back and stuck through the loop at the eye, between the hook and the first turn. Lubricate the wraps (with water or saliva) and draw them tight by pulling on the hook and the standing part of the tippet. The tag end can be trimmed fairly closely.

The clinch knot is easy to tie and reasonably dependable, especially in non-demanding fishing situations. Anglers who may encounter larger fish (and who doesn't imagine him- or herself in that category?) often leave the tag extra long, for insurance, and on many flies this tag simply disappears into the dressing. Or they may prefer to use the *improved* clinch knot instead. The only difference is that after sticking the tag end through the loop at the eye, extend it a bit and then pass it back through the larger loop created by itself and the twisted section of the knot. The traps the tag under one more section of line, which helps considerably to keep it from slipping out and letting the whole knot unravel. An even stronger version of the clinch knot is called the two-times-around knot or the Berkley knot; see. See Knots.

Clutch—In a fly reel, a one-way power coupling that applies, for example, drag to the spool when line is running out but not when the angler is cranking line back in. Or, in an anti-reverse reel (see), that disengages the crank handle from the spool when line is running out. See Fly Reel.

Coachman—A dark-colored hackle feather or a fly pattern. The Coachman series of fly patterns are attributed to a famous British angler named Tom Bosworth, who was said to be a coach driver for England's royal family some time in the 18th Century. The "Royal" Coachman, however, has a different origin: Legend has it that when Mary Orvis Marbury (see) tied a red belly-band on a Coachman, her father, Charles Orvis, said "That's a beautiful fly, a regal fly. Let's call it a Royal Coachman." The Royal Coachman is one of the most enduringly popular dryfly patterns; while anglers argue over just what insect it may represent, they go on tying, buying and using them and catching fish with them. In its classic featherwing form the Royal Coachman is difficult to keep afloat in choppy water and it is also fairly fragile. As he did with so many other elements of modern fly-fishing, Lee Wulff (see) greatly improved the Royal Coachman. He substituted deer body hair for the tail and made the upright wings out of calf-tail hair. The result was dubbed the Royal Wulff (see Wulff Flies); the stiff, hollow hairs added the flotation and durability the original pattern lacked.

Coch y Bonddhu—A red-black color combination. A hackle feather with a black or very dark center and reddish-brown to brown outer fibers that darken to black at their tips. Except for this black outer edge, it is like a furnace (see) feather. Coch y bonddhu is also the Welsh name for the June bug, which is reddish-mahogany with a black belly.

Coho—See Silver Salmon.

Compression Drag—A type of disc drag; see.

Corks—The drilled-out cork rings that are glued together at the base of a fly rod's butt section to form the grip. See also Fly Rod, Rod Grips.

Counterbalance—The opposing mass, usually a knob or button, on the spool of a direct-drive fly reel that serves to balance the weight of the crank handle. Without a

Creels

counterbalance, the spool would not spin smoothly when a fleeing fish takes line out. A reel with twin crank handles doesn't need a counterbalance. See also Fly Reel.

Crank Handle—What one holds to turn the spool of a fly reel. Reels may have one or two crank handles. In most single-action direct-drive reels (see), handles are mounted right on the edge of the spool. Multiplying or anti-reverse (see) reel handles are generally on a bar that is attached, through the center of the sideplate, to a shaft that drives an internal clutch or gearset. See also Fly Reel.

Cree—A mottled-ginger color. Also a hackle feather with three colors: cream, red and gray or black, usually arranged as red and black barring across a light background.

Creel—A hackle feather with reddish bars on a white or light background. Sometimes called a ginger grizzly (see). Creel and cree (above)are both said to derive from an Old English bird.

Creel—In sport fishing, a basket or pouch in which to stash fish. Once considered part of every trout angler's tackle or attire (a creel was usually slung from a shoulder strap), creels lost favor rapidly with fly fishers in the US in the 1970s, when the doctrine of catch-and-release (see) became firmly established among them. Vintage creels were gracefully shaped wicker baskets, woven from whole or split laths (often willow), with hinged tops and holes through which to slide the fish; the bottom would have been lined with damp ferns or moss to help keep the catch fresh longer. In England in the 18th Century a gentleman's creel might have been made of leather. This sort of vintage creel can be a handsome artifact, and classic creels often change hands at antique-tackle sales for sums that their original owners would marvel at. Instead of being carried astream, they then take up pride of place on a mantel or shelf.

In America, a creel was particularly an eastern trout fisherman's gear; bass were usually kept on a stringer and western trout were often too large to fit a creel. Thus the Currier & Ives-type depiction of a gent in a tweed jacket, necktie, pipe, fly rod and creel.

Creels are still available for their original purpose, but they're usually made of some sort of coarse woven fabric, which can be wetted so that evaporation keeps the contents cooler, and even lined with plastic against fish slime. A few such pouches are available as accessories for fishing vests, with hooks or clips to hang the creel from, but they don't set any sales records.

Curing Oven—An industrial oven large enough to hold racks of rod mandrels

Cutthroat Trout—a Snake River fine-spot cutt from Wyoming.

wrapped with pre-preg (see) and hung vertically. A controlled bake cycle cures the thermosetting epoxy in the pre-preg and binds the fibers together into a hollow rod blank. See also Rod-Building.

Curve Cast—A specialized presentation cast that bends the end of the line to the right or the left in order to deliver the fly to a stretch of water that is otherwise blocked (by brush, for example). A curve cast can also be used to compensate for current, to obtain, for example, a drag-free float.

The curve cast is simply an overpowered sidearm cast—stopping the rod suddenly at the end of the cast lets the horizontal loop unroll past the straight-on position and carry the fly around into a curve. Right-handed casters make natural curves to the left, left-handers to the right.

To make a negative curve cast—that is, one to the other side—simply *under*power the cast and let it fall to the water before it can unroll completely.

Cuttbow—A rainbow trout-cutthroat trout hybrid. Cuttbows are not necessarily the product of an artificial hatchery program; they are naturally very common in western North America, in waters where the two species cohabit.

Cutthroat Trout—Sometimes called the mountain trout, *Salmo clarki*, the cutthroat, is a native of western North America, a trout that exists in perhaps dozens of different strains. Cutthroat trout, however, are not as plentiful individually as their native peer in the American West, the rainbow trout; certain strains of cutthroat are, like certain charrs, confined to only a few small mountain lakes. Biologist Robert Smith, author of *Native Trout of North America*, identifies 14 major subspecies of cutthroat—including the Snake River, Yellowstone, Westslope, Paiute, Bonneville, and Rio Grande—and there are likely to be more as well. Cutthroat are desert trout too, and distinctive strains were once found from arid inland Oregon as far south as northern New Mexico.

Cutthroats vary in color and size more than other salmonids, from yellowish-green to flaming red, with large or small, sparse or dense black spots. A pound may be large for some of the mountain-lake strains while the Lahontan cutthroat, native to Nevada's Pyramid and Tahoe lakes and once thought to have been commercial harvested to extinction, may grow to 40 pounds or more. Some West Coast cutts, from southern Alaska and British Columbia to northern California, are sea-run. Cutthroats build redds and spawn in winter or early spring, and their diet and feeding habits are the same as other trout.

The "cutthroat" name derives from a bright slash of red or orange along the fish's lower jaw. The jaw marking is present even in rainbow-cutthroat crosses—"cuttbows"—

which are very common in Western-US rivers where the two species mingle (they also share the red "rainbow" on their flanks). This easy hybridization frustrates purists, for some strains of cutthroat are among the most beautiful and rarest of trout. Like their Eastern counterpart, the brook trout, cutthroat are particularly susceptible to overfishing and degradation of their habitat, and they do not compete well with other, often hardier fish.

Several Western states have begun to breed and then re-stock their original native strains of cutthroat in remote, undisturbed watersheds. Ironically, this often requires poisoning out the other trout—commonly rainbows or even brook or lake trout—that were brought in to supplant the vanished natives in an earlier "hatcherification." Colorado's vivid greenback cutthroat are a good example: In the early 1970s, remnant wild populations were found in tiny mountain streams where they had been protected from hybridization by waterfalls or other natural barriers. (Another local strain, the yellowfin cutthroat, has apparently disappeared forever.) Two decades later, after much research into artificial breeding and trial releases into the wild, greenbacks are again spawning and wintering naturally in Rocky Mountain National Park and Roosevelt National Forest. Greenbacks are still a "threatened" species, but in 1987 Colorado opened a limited and supervised catch-and-release fishing season for them.

Utah has had equally impressive success in re-stocking the Bear Lake strain of the Bonneville cutthroat, another of the large, predacious big-lake cutts that had been netted nearly to extinction between the 1860s and about 1930. A 20-year program of trapping, selective breeding, and research, along with poisoning Strawberry Reservoir to make room for the "new" fish, has paid great dividends in restoring what once was.

Cyanoacrylate Glue—Widely known as superglue (which is in fact a brand trademark, like Krazy Glue), fast-setting, strong cyanoacrylate glues are used in everything from household repairs to surgery. Anglers may use them to reset loose inserts on line guides. In fly-fishing they are occasionally used to anchor tying materials on heavy-duty flies and to reinforce and slip-proof knots, especially knots tied in slippery, springy monofilament. A drop of super glue significantly improves the breaking strength of any connection. Most cyanoacrylate glues are long-term water-soluble, susceptible to ultraviolet radiation, and (like most adhesives) require dry, flush-fitting mating surfaces. However, a few, such as the kind sold under the names Zap-A-Gap and CA+, are none of the above and thus are ideally suited to fishing. (The head chemist at Pacer Tech, makers of CA+, told angling writer Bill Hunter that he tied leader sections together with simple overhand knots and then bound them together with his company's glue; he said he never had one break.)

CA+, Zap-A-Gap and similar formulations are hydrophobic (water-repellent) and gap-filling (mixed with baking soda, they will fill in and bond to even large cavities). In addition, according to the manufacturer, wet and also oily surfaces can be glued together almost instantly. The operating temperature range is typically -65° to +300°F, more than adequate for any fly-fishing on planet Earth. And, while such a glue bond is susceptible to shocking, in normal conditions it has a shear strength of more than 5,000 PSI; a warm saline bath reduces it to about 2,100 PSI, but even that is far more than enough for any Christmas Island flats angler. All cyanoacrylates brittle with age (but reportedly slower than epoxies), so change your glued connections every two years, just to be safe.

These glues should be applied as sparingly as possible. To reinforce a knot, apply a drop or two, quickly rotate the knot to let the glue flow, then snap it or blow on it to get rid of the excess. To glue a line splice, simply let the liquid soak in or press it into the braid between sheets of waxed paper (which will protect your fingers; if you do glue your fingers together, Acetone or Xylene will dissolve the bond quickly. These are hazardous substances, so follow the directions closely.) Cyanoacrylates can let us be lazy in our connections; not only does a drop of the glue improve any knot, it can take the place of many knots: Some anglers make loops in the ends of fly lines simply by doubling an inch of the tip (with its coating) back on itself and putting a drop of super glue into the valley between.

Any knot or connection should be tested right after it is made: Stretch it between your hands and apply an appropriate pull. A poor glued connection will fail right away, if it's going to fail at all.

For line connections that must slide repeatedly through the guides—such as flyline/backing splices—rigging experts recommend a coating of Aquaseal, the adhesive used to repair divers' neoprene wet suits. Cyanoacrylate glue is too brittle to bend and some of the other formulations sold specifically for this purpose peel off too readily.

Dacron—A trademarked name for a polyester fiber of great strength and toughness. In fly-fishing Dacron shows up primarily in hollow-braided form as backing (see), the thin, strong line tied between the plastic-coated fly line and the reel. Dacron is ideal for backing because it has no appreciable memory, it is rot-proof and can be put away wet, and it is very easy to knot and even to splice. See also Knots, Splice.

Dame, Stoddard—Today simply called Stoddard's, it is the oldest retailer of fly-fishing gear in the USA; the name Dame, Stoddard (or variations of it) appears on many vintage fly rods, reels and other tackle that shows up at tackle auctions and sales. The store, now at 50 Temple Place in Boston, has been continuously in business since 1800, when it opened under the name S. Bradler. It became known as Samuel Bradler in 1822, William L. Bradford in 1845, Bradford & Anthony in 1867, Dame, Stoddard and Kendall in 1880, was shortened to Dame, Stoddard around 1900 and finally, in about 1930, simply to Stoddard's. That's when it was bought by the father of Arthur Marks, the present owner.

The company worked with some of the most famous of American tackle makers, including Hiram Leonard, the Vom Hofe family and the F.E. Thomas Rod Company, and was one of the first American importers of Hardy Bros. tackle from England.

Damping—The ability of a fly rod tip section to come to rest after it has been flexed in casting. See Rod Action.

Danglies—The leader clippers, tippet straighteners, forceps, mini scissors, knot tiers, flashlights and myriad other small gadgets that fly fishers like to hang from their vests. See Pin-On Reel.

Danglies—A leader clipper with its pin-on retractor reel.

Dapping—Fishing by holding a fly out at the end of a rod, on a short line, and simply "tapping" it on the water's surface. This can be an effective way to fish a tiny brook with a conventional fly rod—the angler hidden behind a boulder or tree—or it can call for specialized tackle. Traditional dapping methods, on the lochs of Scotland and Ireland, require a rod 12 to 18 feet long with a very light silk-floss line tied to the tip. The flies are usually tied on extended-shank hooks and are thickly palmered (see) with stiff, long hackles, for good flotation and wind resistance (no casting is involved; the wind becomes an ally instead of something to overcome). The fisherman just drifts, letting the wind push both rowboat and fly, which is kept dancing lightly on the water. This is also known as blow-line fishing.

Dingell-Johnson Act—Its formal name is the Federal Aid in Sport Fish Restoration Act, and it was passed into law by the Congress, on August 9, 1950, after lobbying by various fishing groups. Its sponsors were Representative John Dingell Sr., of Michigan, and Senator Edwin Johnson of Colorado. In the words of the US Fish and Wildlife Service—in its pamphlet *Restoring America's Sport Fisheries*—the act "created the most ambitious program for fisheries improvement that the United States has ever known." (It should be noted that before 1950 there was no fisheries-improvement program in the US at all. And that a similar Federal Aid in Wildlife Restoration Act was passed in 1937.) The key to this was a 10-percent excise tax levied on fishing tackle sales.

As it became clear that sport fisheries were not being improved by the Restoration Act, fishermen—chiefly through the American league of Anglers and the Federation of Fly Fishers—again lobbied the Congress, in 1983, to expand the 10-percent tax to more fishing gear, to add a three-percent tax on electric trolling motors and fish sonars, to tag a duty onto imported fishing tackle and pleasure boats, and even to attach part of the federal tax on powerboat fuels. This was accomplished via the Wallop-Breaux Amendment to the 1950 Restoration Act, which was passed in 1984. The sponsors were Louisiana Representative John Breaux and Senator Malcolm Wallop of Wyoming. This expanded the funding available for nationwide sport-fish "restoration" to some $200 million annually.

A decade later, it was becoming clear again that sport fish were *not* being restored by these lavish funds—which must be spent every year or else they revert to the federal government—and observers began to question not the act but how the money was being spent. Environmentalists noted that state fisheries departments were still building hatcheries, still installing boat-access ramps and parking lots, still treating waters with chemicals, and still trying to create or introduce exotic gamefish species that could tolerate degraded habitat—instead of promoting wild, native species and biodiversity by restricting access, cleaning up habitat and preventing the implantation of exotics or hatchery hybrids.

Dinging—A little-used fly-tying term. In the *Roundtable*, the magazine of the American Museum of Fly Fishing, in January/February 1979 ("The Wulff Flies"), Lee Wulff wrote ". . . my first step is to pick up the hook and start the dinging with a piece of thread long enough to tie the fly."

Direct-Drive Fly Reel—A type of reel in which the crank handle is attached directly to the spool, at least to the extent that the handle revolves backward when line is stripped off the reel. In a single-action (see) direct-drive reel, which is by far the most common type in fly-fishing, the handle is nearly always part of the spool, screwed or riveted to the edge of the outer flange. (The exception are reels such as the venerable Hardy Perfect, with its full sideplate that screws down over the spool and carries the handle. Modern reel designers, concerned with saving weight —and cost—do away with that extraneous plate and put the handle right on the spool.) In a multiplying direct-drive reel, such as a Bogdan Salmon, the handle(s) also turn backward when line runs out; the gear train that supplies the multiplying effect has no one-way, anti-reverse clutch mechanism. See also Anti-Reverse Fly Reel.

Disc Drag—There are two distinct types of disc drags used in fly reels. Both employ discs, or washers, as frictive surfaces; what differs is the way in which this braking friction is applied. The **compression-type** disc drag has been around in one form or another for literally centuries (tightening the retaining nut on the spool of a 200-year-old Nottingham "winch" amounts more or less to adjusting a compression-type disc drag), but the modern era was probably ushered in by Fin-Nor in the 1930s. Those reels and the handful that followed—virtually all heavy-duty saltwater models, and quite expensive for their day—rely on a disc, or discs, stacked on the spindle next to the spool; tightening the external drag knob simply presses the discs more firmly against the spool, to retard its revolutions. To spread the workload, some reels have two or three discs, usually impregnated leather or cork, with a steel washer on top that was keyed to the spindle. The steel washer served as an "anvil" for a stiff coil spring that transmitted the pressure from the drag knob. Along with this thrust washer there might also be a thrust bearing, usually a sealed ball bearing. Such systems were, and still are, usually very smooth, reliable and long-lived—when a drag disc wears out, it can be replaced, just like the brake pads in a car.

In the 1980s, other reel makers (Abel, Pate, STH, et al.) entered the market with smaller fly reels bearing scaled-down versions of this compression-disc drag. These reels usually had only one drag disc—sometimes free-standing, sometimes glued to or integral with the clutch sprocket. For anglers using the new, super-strong tippets and light, high-Modulus (see) rods for steelhead, salmon, large trout, bonefish and the like, the benefits were immediately obvious: down-size fly reels that balanced the modern tackle yet offered big-reel drag performance.

Many older compression-type disc-drag reels are not easily convertible from one winding direction to the other, and spools don't interchange readily either. The mid-1980s Regal Engineering big-game reel, a more-or-less classic disc-drag type, is an exception: Its spool comes out quickly and without a lot of loose parts, and its cork disc is glued directly to the spool, so a fresh drag is only a spool change away.

In fact, using up a properly made and maintained drag disc is something most anglers will never accomplish. Discs today are usually made of a phenolic or cork impregnated with some sort of resin, for long life and smooth operation. As noted, discs can be replaced and the systems are easy to maintain—a periodic wash-and-wipe (especially after every saltwater use) and a drop of Neatsfoot Oil or the like annually is all it takes. In storage, the drag knob should be backed off all the way, to avoid compressing the disc needlessly.

A more recent evolution of the disc drag is the **caliper type**, which creates friction by squeezing a single disc from one or both sides with a pad, or pair of pads, like an automotive disc brake. And, as always, there is an external knob or lever to adjust the compression. The disc is fastened to the spool with a one-way clutch for free cranking. The thing drag disc, nearly always steel, tends to dissipate heat well, and if the caliper mechanism is up to snuff, the system works well and is also easy to maintain. When it wears out, instead of replacing the disc, the owner replaces the pads.

There are several variants on both these disc drags. In its top-shelf System 3 big-game reel, Scientific Anglers offers an **O-ring & disc** system: It is a steel disc (clutched to the spool) sandwiched between two rubber O-rings that are in turn clamped between a pair of aluminum plates. The external drag knob turns a threaded rod that draws the plates together, which compresses the O-rings for drag.

And The Orvis Company's heavy-duty DXR reel has a *offset* compression column of thrust washers and resin discs, which rides on a small spindle—actually a threaded bolt—of its own. Screwing down the drag knob squeezes the stack of discs and the resultant friction is passed on to the spool via a sprocket arrangement. This design saves some space, at the theoretical cost of potential sprocket problems. See also Drag.

Dog Salmon—Another name for chum salmon, one of the five species of Pacific salmon that are native to northwestern North America. (The steelhead was reclassified in 1989 as a Pacific salmon, so strictly speaking there are six species in North America. Few fishermen recognize the change, though, which was purely taxonomic; under their new name, steelhead did not suddenly begin to die after spawning, for example.) The dog salmon's name stems from the fact that it was commonly caught in huge numbers during the summer spawning run by Inuit and Aleuts as food to keep their dogs alive through the coming winter—when a team of a dozen huskies would eat four to five tons of dried fish. See Chum Salmon, Pacific Salmon, Salmon.

Dolly Varden—Dolly Varden, *Salvelinus malma* (or *S. malma alpinus*) are fall-spawning charr of western North America, occurring as far south as northern California and the northern Rockies. They are especially common in the salmon rivers of Alaska and the Pacific Northwest, where, like the rainbow trout of those rivers, they feed heavily on salmon eggs. They are very active predators, and commercial fishermen claim they make sizable inroads into the salmon fingerling populations as well. Like other salmonids, they are fine gamefish (Dollies of eight to ten pounds are common, at least in less-fished drainages) and they also feed on aquatic insects, mice, terrestrials and other "fly-fishing foods." Dolly Varden are as brightly and variously colored as any salmonid too, with white-edged fins, blazing red-orange bellies (in spawning season) and white-, lavender- or even yellow-spotted sides and bronze-green backs. Sea-run Dollies tend to a more monochrome silver.

The story goes that these fish are named after Dolly Varden, a character in Charles Dickens's *Barnaby Rudge* who supposedly also wore lavender spots. However, Dolly's dress is described in the book only as cherry-colored; another theory is that a northwestern gold-rush miner, who perhaps read Dickens by candlelight, romantically dubbed his claim "The Dolly Varden," Dolly being a popular Victorian name. If these fish were in the stream nearby, they might have picked up their name by association . . . .

Distinguishing arctic charr from Dolly Varden can be difficult. The rule of thumb is that if the spots on the fish are smaller than the iris of its eye, the fish is a Dolly. The Pacific-drainage arctic charr generally also has a more forked tail. However, as their ranges overlap only from west-central Canada westward, it's generally safe to say that an Atlantic-drainage charr—in Labrador, for example—is a not a Dolly, by default. Positive identification can be much harder in Alaska and western Canada. The author has found presumably cross-bred charr in British Columbia's remote Cassiar Mountains that shared the characteristics of both strains.

For decades the bull trout—occasionally referred to as the Western brook trout—was commonly identified as a Dolly Varden, even by fisheries biologists. However in 1978 a California scientist named Ted Cavender published his proof that the bull trout is a separate species. Positive differentiation generally requires dissection, but there is a rule of thumb: In waters where both species might be found, any individual that

Dolly Varden—A southwest-Alaska Dolly in spawning colors.

weighs much more than 12 pounds should be regarded as a bull trout.

The confusion among fishermen and disagreement among biologists over charrs worldwide began at the beginning. Carolus Linnaeus, the Swedish taxonomist who developed the modern way of classifying animals scientifically by genus, species, and subspecies, put his native Lapland charr into the wrong category right at the outset, in 1758. He called it a *Salmo*.

Double Haul—A modification of fly-casting technique that accelerates the line to a higher speed so it makes a tighter loop that can travel farther or punch through the wind better. The "haul" is a pull made by the line hand just as the rod hand begins to power-snap the next cast be it a false cast or the presentation cast, when the fly will be sent on its way. Double-hauling means to pull the line on both back and forward false casts; single-hauling is pulling only on the forward cast.

The rod propels the line forward; the caster hauls by pulling sharply on the line in his hand at the same time (instead of just holding it until it's time to let go for the final shoot). The line moves through the guides while the guides themselves are moving with the rod. The length of the haul varies from six inches on a medium cast to as much as four feet on an all-out heave across a coral flat or a competition casting pool.

Many fly fishers routinely double-haul throughout their false-casting, to help shoot more line on both the back and forward casts and thus reach their distance sooner. See also Fly-Casting.

Double-Line Loop—Another name for the Bimini Twist (see); see Knots.

Double-Taper Line—A type of floating fly line that has a casting taper on both ends and no running line; that is, the tip and forward taper (a section perhaps 10 or 12 feet long) and the thick belly are duplicated on the other end of the line, with no thinner-diameter line in between. Double-taper lines are used mostly on smaller trout streams. Some anglers also prefer them because when one end wears out, the line can be renewed simply by swapping it around on the reel. See Fly Line.

Downrunner—In East-Coast angling parlance, a downrunner is a shad (buck or hen, or roe fish) that has survived the spring/summer spawn and is returning downstream to the sea to begin another cycle of foraging and growth before returning to the river. Biologists on the Delaware River, for example, estimate that perhaps five percent of shad survive pollution, predation and other hazards to become downrunners (they also reckon that in pre-industrial times the survival rate may have been as high as 30 percent). With their sexual urges satisfied, downrunners have begun to feed normally again, and will strike a lure for "normal" reasons. See also Shad.

Downstream Mend—A way of repositioning a fly line on the water so that it "bellies" or curves below—that is, downstream of—the fly. If the current the fly is riding in is moving faster than the water where the belly of the line lies, a downstream mend will prolong the drag-free float of the fly by delaying the moment when the fly outpaces the line and uses up its slack. The mend lets the line catch up with the fly, at least briefly.

If the situation is reversed or if the current is the same everywhere along the line and leader, then a downstream mend will make the line drag the fly sooner than otherwise—a situation that is not necessarily bad; Atlantic salmon, for example, sometimes prefer a fast-moving fly that skates across the water. Continually mending line downstream will accelerate the fly even more.

A downstream mend may be made when the line is on the water—by flicking the line in the right direction with the rod tip—or it can be made while the cast is still in the air, by reaching downstream with the rod to make sure the belly of the line hits the water there. See also Mend.

Downstream Presentation—In dryfly or nymph fishing, a downstream presentation is just that—instead of facing and casting upstream, as is traditional, and letting the fly drift back down toward himself, the angler casts downstream. The angler uses a pile cast or an S-cast (see) to keep the fly from dragging as soon as it hits the water and the current begins to take it away from him instead of toward him. Obviously, the drag-free float is considerably shorter than in an upstream presentation, where good line control may keep a fly swimming naturally for 10 feet or more. A downstream presentation is used mostly when there is no good way to approach a particular lie from below. Success depends on the angler's ability to read the water well and to place the fly just right, so its abbreviated drift occurs right over or in the fish's feeding zone.

Drag—As it applies to fly reels, drag is a means to slow a fish. There are two basic ways of applying drag: externally, through friction applied by the angler's fingers to the spool or the line, or internally, by way of a mechanism built into the reel; a brake, usually adjustable. The importance of the drag system varies from minimal (in light-duty fly reels that are little more than line-storage drums) to crucial, in high-capacity reels built for saltwater big-game species. Regardless of type or cost or sophistication, a built-in drag should apply friction only when line is going out, so the angler is spared the inconvenience of reeling against it. The drag should also be smooth, to maintain an even tension on the line (and particularly on the tippet), and it should start up and then run at the same friction setting. Drags for powerful fish should also be impervious to heat build-up. And finally, the adjuster knob or lever ought to be fairly easy to find and operate.

Like the brakes of an automobile, fly reel drags eventually wear out, no matter how well they are maintained; one component or another is slowly worn away by friction and then has to be replaced. Practically speaking, however, few recreational fishermen ever spend enough time on the water to see this happen.

There are several different types of mechanical drags: See Disc Drag, Palming Rim, Sprocket & Pawl; see also Fly Reel.

Drag—As it applies to fly-fishing, drag is the force exerted on a fly by the current of the water it's in or on. Flies fished on a tight line down- or across-current—streamers, some wet flies, and skating dry flies—rely on drag; that is, the current gives them the lifelike action they were meant to have. Flies that should drift freely, such as dries and nymphs, must be shielded from drag. Otherwise, the telltale wake of the fly against the current tips the fish off that all is not as it should be—this food item that should be drifting rudderless is in fact something unnatural.

Note however that in nature movement is life, and live food is more attractive to predators than dead carrion. Sometimes a nymph that should drift freely in the water column is snapped up by a fish when the fly reaches the end of its swing and begins to climb toward the surface as the tippet comes taut. Or a dry fly that has been spurned is suddenly attacked when it too begins to drag slightly. To adopt a dogmatic approach to drag—that it is always bad, or always good—is to limit oneself severely as a fly fisher.

Drag-Free Float—The holy grail for dryfly fishers: A fly presentation that is, for a few inches or a few feet, wholly "natural," or free of the drag created when the pull of the tippet counters the pull of the current. See above. A drag-free float is usually the end result of a combination of factors that stem from the skill and experience of the angler. He or she must: position himself in the water to minimize the effects of current and to reach the fish's feeding zone; and then cast so that the tippet doesn't come tight until the fly is past the zone. Even before that, the angler must have tied on a leader that will unroll properly, with a tippet balanced (in length and thickness) with the size of the fly. And don't rule out just plain luck, either.

Drake—Any of a variety of large mayflies, such as the Brown Drake (*Ephemerella simulans*) and the Green Drake (*Ephemerella guttulata, E. grandis* and others). According to fly-tying historian Darrel Martin, the name most likely comes from the Old English word *draca*, meaning dragon, and it is also related to the Anglo-Saxon *duce*, meaning "to dive," from which we get the word duck; the first reported reference to mayflies as drakes was by Harold Hinsdill Smedley in 1658, and it derived from the fact that the imitations could be tied with feathers from the mallard drake.

Draper Hook—A type of fly hook meant for nymph imitations. It was originated by a New Zealand fly tier named Keith Draper and then put into production by Partridge of Redditch in 1980. A Draper hook has a double shank made of two wires, brazed together at the bend, which are bent outward to help create a flat-bodied nymph. Each wire is finely serrated at the "shoulder" to help hold the body material of the pattern in place.

Dressing—In fly-tying, the assorted materials that "dress" the hook and turn it into one or another particular fly pattern. The term dressing is also used to mean the various treatments applied to flies, leaders or lines to make them float or sink, or just to clean them of accumulated dirt and oils.

Drift Boat—What some call the "ultimate fly-fishing boat," a drift boat (also known as a McKenzie boat—see) is a flat-bottom, shallow-draft, oar-powered skiff that in silhouette resembles a classic Grand Banks cod dory. All its features are slanted toward providing an angler with a safe, dry, high and maneuverable perch from which to fish a river too big to wade easily. The boat slides over riffles and is very stable on its broad, flat bottom. The tall, sharp bow, generous freeboard and flared gunwales keep the boat riding high and dry through white water. The rocker, or longitudinal curve, of the flat, keel-less bottom lets the boat pivot easily around its center, yet the hard chines (sides) give the craft some "grip" on the water when it's needed.

The oarsman sits in the center and rows "backwards"—that is, facing forward, over the bow, to see what lies in wait downstream. The center seat is fixed and usually incorporates a gear locker or even a built-in cooler. The bow and stern seats have backrests that pivot so their occupants may cast to either side. Usually, however, at least the bow angler stands to fish most of the time, for built into the foredeck is a knee slot that he can brace against. (Some drift boats also have knee braces at the back.) The top of the foredeck is flat and smooth and serves as a stripping tray for fly line.

Where a true ocean dory is nearly as sharp at the stern as at the bow, a drift boat has a squared-off stern with an anchor davit extending off it. The anchor hangs off the transom, and the anchor line passes up over a pulley and, via a series of turning blocks, goes to a jam cleat at the rowing seat. The oarsman can stop or slow the boat at will simply by jerking the line out of the cleat and letting it slip. (The anchor itself, whether it is a commercially cast pyramid of lead or just a cluster of sash weights, relies on mass, not hooking ability, to hold the boat. A marine-style Danforth or kedge anchor would

Drift Boat, with knee braces bow and stern.

snag hopelessly in the rocky bottom of most trout rivers.)

Drift boats are commonly made of aluminum, fiberglass or wood and they are easily hauled on and launched from small flat-bed trailers. They are very popular throughout the Intermountain West of North America, where every fishing guide (if not every ardent fisherman) owns at least one. See also McKenzie Boat, South Fork Skiff.

Driftboat Fishing—Casting and fishing from a drift boat on a moving river is surprisingly different from fishing the same water in waders, and the transition may take some getting used to. The biggest change involves the float of the fly: While the wading angler may get five feet of drag-free float (see) in his presentation, the fly fisher drifting with the current in a boat may get 50 feet or more of clear float; his fly is simply riding along with him, a cast-length away. Until they get accustomed to this, anglers find themselves continually picking their flies up and re-positioning them when there's no need for it—which reduces the time their flies are working on the water. Getting the most out of such a long float also calls for some skill in mending the line, both during the cast and while the fly is riding on the water; inevitably, variations in current drag the line or the fly ahead of the other, and the angler should compensate.

When two anglers are casting from the same drift boat, it is common to work out a system of rotation before setting out—switching places every two hours, or at midday, or whatever; the bow spot, facing downriver, tends to deliver more fish, since the bow always arrives first. In casting, the person in the bow should stand facing almost directly downstream and work far forward of the boat, to give the stern position (which is the more restricted) as much fishing room as possible. The angler in the rear sits or stands facing more to one side or the other, and fishes quartering off in that direction. The oarsman should keep the boat angled slightly bow-in toward the run his anglers are fishing.

The bow angler has to be very cognizant of his back cast, the stern angler his forward cast. It is much simpler to do than to read about.

Two other things always surprise, even annoy, fishermen new to drift boats: They're not used to seeing so much good-looking water go by untouched—in waders, they could simply stay on a stretch of river until every pocket was picked; the boat simply slides by all but the one being fished. And the concentration required to fly-fish this way develops a sort of tunnel vision that keeps people from noticing much of the often impressive scenery all around.

To slow the pace, driftboat guides periodically pull over to the bank to let their people climb out and fish a few stretches on foot. Even so, it is common to cover anywhere from five to 10 miles of river in a day this way.

Drop—Atlantic salmon rivers in the Maritime provinces of Canada are often fished, by canoe, in "drops," the stretches where the anchor (or killick) is dropped over the side to stop or slow the boat for fishing. Like a wading angler who moves two steps downstream after every swing of his fly through the water, each "drop" of the boat may be only two or three feet.

To a whitewater boatman, a drop is a hole or falls in the river that the boat must avoid or somehow survive.

Dropper Fly—A second fly attached, on its own tippet, to the leader a little ways above the "point" fly. A common two-fly rig is a dry and a nymph; one may attract the fish's attention and the other draw a strike, or the dry may do double duty as a strike indicator (see) or float for the sunken nymph (see). In waters where it is illegal to attach weight to the leader, a common way to beat the rule is by fishing a heavily weighted dropper fly as a sinker.

Dry Fly—A fly that rides on top, or just within the surface film, of the water, whether it is actively retrieved ("skated," perhaps) or left to float drag-free. Interpreted broadly, the term could apply to any of thousands of fly patterns ranging from a Quill Gordon to a deerhair mouse, but to most anglers a dry fly is a small mayfly or caddis imitation used for trout.

When "dry fly" is used as an adjective, it conjures up strong cultural leanings. The foundation of modern fly-fishing is the imitation of an aquatic insect floating freely where it hatched, atop the currents of a trout stream. This was formalized by Frederic Halford in England in the late 1800s, but the use of dry flies dates back centuries before that, to dapping and blow-line fishing. According to The American Museum of Fly Fishing, the first known reference to dryfly-fishing in print in the USA was in *The American Turf Register and Sporting Magazine* in 1838—a long account of fishing floating flies on an English stream, which was apparently reprinted from elsewhere. A mystique grew up around casting dry flies to stream trout, and with it an informal code that seemed, to observers, to dictate much more than just a method of fishing.

Thus to label an angler as A Dryfly Fisherman is often to describe him or her as a purist who knows the Latin names of insects and fishes with a narrowly prescribed menu of tackle and techniques: classic flies (often, in the US and Canada, the so-called Catskill patterns—see), upstream presentations (see), floating lines, very fine tippets, perhaps a split-cane rod. Dryfly purists may scorn streamers as "bait" and nymphs as "bottom dredging." A certain lifestyle attaches to the term too: Saltwater and Rocky Mountain fly fishers might imagine a dryfly fisherman as an Easterner decked out in a tweed hat and canvas waders and smoking a pipe . . . . Cultural differences are nothing new to fly-fishing, however. In the 1890s Halford wrote, in his *Hints on Dry-Fly Fishing*: "For obvious reasons it is well not to enter on any controversy as to the comparative merits of the two schools of fly-fishing,— the wet, or North Country [of England] style, and the dry, or South Country style. Each is, beyond doubt, effective in its own particular streams and under circumstances favoring its use, and a considerable degree of science is attained by the earnest followers of both . . . ." See also Fly.

Dryfly Rod—According to master rod designer Tom Dorsey, of Thomas & Thomas, a dryfly rod must be capable of extreme accuracy and delicate presentation; dependable leader turn-over; and a quick roll pick-up (see) to dry the fly, extend line and present the fly again; all these things happen in the air. (The action of a wet-fly rod should be designed to focus on events underwater.) See also Rod Action.

Dual-Density Line—A fly line of two sections that behave differently on the water. Usually a dual-density line is a sinking-tip line (see), with a short front section that sinks and a floating belly or running line behind it.

Dual-Mode Reel—A fly reel that combines the best features of both anti-reverse and direct-drive design (see) without their disadvantages. When the angler reels line in, he or she has the full, drag-free control of a direct-drive reel. But when the fish runs, the reel automatically and instantly switches over to anti-reverse mode. Going back to direct-drive then should require only slight forward pressure on the crank handle.

Over the years, very few dual-mode reels have reached the market. They are usually relatively expensive, complicated and heavy, and they have not always worked as advertised. In fact, there is little demand for such a reel; fly fishers learn to cope with conventional reels as part of the challenge of fly-fishing.

Dubbing—The material, soft natural fur or synthetic fibers or a mixture of both, that makes up the fuzzy body of an artificial fly. Dubbed bodies are usually tied only on wet flies or nymph patterns; in the water the material takes on a translucent, lifelike (at least to the angler) look and it also helps the fly sink. Prepared loose dubbing may be bought bagged according to color and material; fly tiers also make their own by chopping fur or other fibers up with scissors or a small electric blender. To wrap it around a hook, the loose dubbing has to be put on a thread: The single strand of tying thread may be rubbed with dubbing wax, to which the dubbing will then stick (after rolling it between thumb and fingers); or a separate section of dubbed thread can be made up and then tied into the hook shank. Do this by making a loop of thread, waxing it, getting the dubbing to stick to both strands, and then twisting the loop. This makes a more durable (if slightly bulkier) body because the dubbing is captured between the twisted threads.

Thanks to electronic flocking and unusual synthetic fibers, prepared dubbing is now also available already on the thread, ready to be tied in and wound onto a hook shank.

The archaic meaning of dubbing—dating back at least to the 15th Century—was simply to dress a hook; that is, to tie a fly. And a "dub" itself was a tied fly. A famous sentence in Dame Juliana Berners' (see) "Treatyse of Fysshynge wyth an Angle" (1496) reads: "There ben the xii flies or dubbes wyth which ye shall angle." See also Fly-Tying.

Dubbing Needle—A tool used in fly-tying for a variety of tasks. Since it is nothing more than a steel pin set in some sort of a handle, it can be used to separate materials, to free hackles or hairs that have been trapped under the thread, to clear the eye of the hook or to apply a drop of head cement or paint precisely where it's needed. The name, however, comes from another use: picking at the fibers of the dubbing to give the fly body a fuzzier and presumably more lifelike look. Sometimes also called a bodkin. See Fly-Tying Tools.

Dubbing Wax—A slightly sticky, semi-hard paste that is smeared on tying thread to make dubbing material adhere to it so it can be wound around the shank of a hook to create the body of a wet fly or nymph pattern. Dubbing wax is usually sold in some kind of tube dispenser (like an oversize lipstick) for easier handling and it may come in different degrees of tackiness for different kinds of flies and dubbing materials. See Fly-Tying Tools.

Dun—An insect (here meaning a mayfly or most other aquatic insects) in the subimago stage of its life, or an artificial fly created to imitate it. The subimago is an adult stage when the insect develops the ability to fly but not yet to reproduce; it comes after the nymphal and before the imago, the sexually mature state of its life. Generally speaking, most "classic" dry flies—small, palmered hackle, sparse tails—are dun imitations.

The name comes from the old English *dunn*, which was a shade of gray—the shade of the insect's wings. And "dun" still today may mean simply "gray."

Ebonite—Hard rubber, which became the "plastic" of its day after Charles Goodyear invented the process of vulcanization (which cured, or stabilized, rubber and made it non-sticky) in 1839. Its first use in fishing reels apparently was Dr. Alonzo Fowler's "Gem" fly reel, patented in 1872. The Fowler reel relied on ebonite as a structural material—it resembled a flattened egg of hard rubber—and it failed in the market because it was too fragile. Hard rubber came into its own in reel manufacturing when Edward Vom Hofe (see) successfully introduced ebonite sideplates in his reels around 1880. Many of them survive today, often marred only by spiderweb cracks around the pillar screws, caused by overtightening.

Eclosion—For an aquatic insect, the act of emerging from its egg or its pupal case.

Entomologist—One who studies insects; a fly tier or fly fisher dedicated to "matching the hatch" (see).

Epoxy—a synthetic resin-based liquid glue, sometimes thermosetting and sometimes used with a catalyst, that is widely used in the manufacture of fly rods and rod components and even in fly-tying. The sheets of graphite fiber that are the raw material of flyrod blanks are said to be "pre-preg"; that is, pre-impregnated with epoxy, which binds the rod fibers solidly together after the assembly has been cured in an oven. (In its uncured state, the pre-preg is tacky to the touch.)

The resin adhesive used to fasten reel seats and grips to rod blanks, or to coat certain saltwater fly patterns, is two-part epoxy. The catalyst, which is mixed with the glue just before assembly, does away with the need for oven-curing. Two-part epoxies are available with cure times of from five minutes to 24 hours. In general, the longer the cycle, the stronger the bond. See also Graphite, Mother of Epoxy Flies.

False Cast—Aerial, preliminary fly-casting, which leads to the final presentation cast, when the fly is allowed to drop to the water. False-casting is often included as an important element in definitions of fly-fishing, which are relevant to record-catch classifications and to fishing regulations. See also Fly, Fly-Casting, Fly-Fishing.

Fanwing—A type of dry fly in which the wings are a matched pair of feathers tied to stand fully upright, with their tips curving away from each other. A real difficulty with dry flies is making sure they land upright on the water, and some tiers believe that fanwing-style hackle helps turn a fly over in the air and land it hook-down, as a parachute might.

Fanwing—an English mayfly imitation, by Darrel Martin, with an extended body as well as the wings.

Featherwing—A type of fly that is tied primarily with hackles; as opposed to a hairwing pattern, which is primarily dressed with fur. These two distinctions are most often applied to Atlantic salmon flies: A Green Highlander is a featherwing pattern while a Bomber is a hairwing.

The classic British salmon flies of the 19th Century defined the "featherwing" concept. For example, the eponymous Jock Scott (see), invented in 1845 or 1850, contained—among other things—hackles from no fewer than 18 birds: swan, teal, mallard, gamecock and "barred summer duck"; peacock and peahen (from Sri Lanka, then called Ceylon); Chinese golden pheasant; Madagascar guinea hen; toucan, macaw and blue chatterer (from Central or South America); North American turkey; bustard and black ostrich (Africa); and Indian crow, florican and jungle cock from India. (Ironically, according to legend the first Jock Scott did in fact have some hair in it—a few strands of Lady John Scott's celebrated "Titian" hair.)

Federation of Fly Fishers, The—An umbrella organization, founded in 1965 and based in Montana, that by 1992 had 191 member fly-fishing clubs and 9,770 individual associate members. Its motto is, "Conserving - Restoring - Educating Through Fly Fishing" and the FFF is active at every level, from teaching children to tie flies and cast to producing educational videotapes and pamphlets to lobbying in Washington DC for environmental programs. Although the organization's membership is international, most participants are in North America, which the Federation divides into 10 regional Councils. Most Councils sponsor an annual meeting called a Conclave, and the Federation itself holds a national Conclave each summer, usually in the Rocky Mountains. The chief organ is a quarterly magazine called *The Flyfisher*, a subscription is included with the annual membership dues. The Federation's address is Post Office Box 1088, West Yellowstone, Montana 59758.

FFF historians say that the idea of a national confederation of fly-fishing clubs sprang up more or less simultaneously in the early 1960s in different regions of the USA, but E.J. Strickland, the first secretary-treasurer, writing in *The Flyfisher* (Fall 1985), singled out the first overt move: In May 1964 the McKenzie Flyfishers organized in Eugene, Oregon; one of their expressed goals was specifically the promotion of a national group. Earlier discussions of the idea had taken place at the Everett Fly Fishing Club, in Washington, and among members of the Theodore Gordon Flyfishers, of New York, notably Lee Wulff, Ed Zern and Gene Anderegg. That club appointed Anderegg to speak with other groups around the country about the idea. In September 1964 he met with William Hilton, William Nelson, Webb Russell and Stanley Walters, of the McKenzie club, in Aspen, Colorado. They hammered out the basic plan for a national organization and the McKenzie Flyfishers offered to host its first meeting.

Working with a list gathered largely through the grapevine, the Mckenzie group invited every known fly-fishing club—and all individual anglers—to The Country Squire, in Eugene, Oregon, on June 18-20, 1965. Some 200 people and 11 clubs attended this first conclave. Most were from California—the Fly Fishermen for Conservation (Fresno), The California Fly Fishermen Unlimited (Sacramento), the Pasadena Casting Club, the Wilderness Fly Fishers (Santa Monica)—and the Northwest: the Cascade Fly Fishing Club (Sumner, WA), the Evergreen Fly Fishing Club (Everett, WA), the Inland Empire Fly Fishing Club (Spokane), the Fly Fishers' Club of Oregon (Portland), the Washington Fly Fishing Club (Seattle), and the McKenzie club. The East was represented by the Theodore Gordon Flyfishers.

The featured speakers at this first conclave included Lee Wulff, Polly Rosborough, Pete Hidy, Ted Trueblood, Enos Bradner, Ashley Hewitt, Cliff Wyatt, Roy Patrick and Kay Brodney. Jim Green, Fenwick's famous rod designer, also helped set the style of conclaves to come when he offered merchandise for a fund-raising auction. Other manufacturers, as well as retailers and artists, contributed enthusiastically also, and this first sale brought in some $800. When expenses had been deducted from this and other revenues, a conclave surplus of $972 remained, which became the bankroll with which the Federation of Fly Fishermen (as it was first called) was launched.

By the close of 1965, 12 clubs had formally affiliated with the Federation, and the resultant publicity attracted others. Tackle shops and writers provided mailing lists and press. At the second national conclave, at Jackson Lake, Wyoming, on September 2-4, 1966, the number of member clubs rose to 29. Individual associate memberships had been offered since January of that year, and by conclave time the total was 1,220. In addition to angling notables—such as casting champion Jon Tarantino, fly tier Helen Shaw, Wulff, Hermann Kessler (who was the art director of *Field & Stream* as well as Helen Shaw's husband, and was also, with Wulff, instrumental in launching the American Museum of Fly Fishing; see), publisher Arnold Gingrich and many others— the second gathering welcomed Idaho Senator Frank Church and Wyoming Governor Clifford Hansen. Gene Anderegg was elected the Federation's first president.

By the end of 1967 The FFF had adopted a conservation policy and was drawing up plans for an official publication and an audio-visual library for its member clubs to draw upon. Volume 1 #1 of *The Flyfisher* appeared in the spring of 1968; its first editor was the distinguished Arnold Gingrich, founding editor and publisher of *Esquire*.

The organization grew rapidly, in memberships, funds and activities. By 1974 there were 7,000 associate members and 120 member clubs. In 1981, recognizing the impact that women have had upon the sport of fly-fishing, the FFF officially changed its name to the Federation of Fly Fishers. In 1983 the dream of a permanent home base finally came true when the Board of Directors approved a plan to take over the 17,000-square-foot West Yellowstone Convention Center (formerly the Union-Pacific Railroad commissary). After a $150,000 renovation, the building re-opened as The International Fly Fishing Center in time for Conclave 1984.

Today the largest of the various FFF gatherings is the Southwest Council's spring conclave in Los Angeles, which draws about 2,000 attendees. However, as fly-fishing has expanded into warmwater and saltwater fisheries, smaller but no less enthusiastic conclaves have taken root in such possibly unexpected places as Mountain Home, Arkansas, and Asheville, South Carolina.

Felt Soles—No longer made of true wool felt, "felt" soles on waders or wading shoes are generally made of a longer-lasting synthetic. When new, the soles are often three-eighths of an inch thick. In use, they rapidly pack down, however, and a professional guide can wear out a pair in a matter of weeks on a rocky river. Felt, it was discovered long ago, provides better traction on wet, slippery rocks than about any other material, and wading fishermen quickly put the discovery to good and widespread use. Just about every wader or wading shoe sold to fly fishermen is available with felt soles, but accessory felts can be added to virtually any waders, at home or by a cobbler. Generally, the original rubber tread must be sanded down, to get a flat, clean surface, and then the felts (cut to size) are carefully glued in place. On wading shoes, which need not be watertight, the soles may also be riveted, for a better hold. Similarly, worn-out soles can be replaced.

Felt soles are not needed on sandy bottoms, and in mud they may load up. On metal surfaces such as boat decks or floatplane pontoons they can be unexpectedly slippery. In winter temperatures, soaked felts may freeze when they come out of the water and then perform a creditable imitation of ice skates. On mossy or algae-covered rocks, aluminum stream cleats (see) will give a better grip. See also Wading Shoes.

Ferrule—The connector between sections of a fishing rod. Ferrules are particularly critical to fly fishers because fly rods are often long (and must be broken down for travel or storage) and because their flexural profile, or action, is so important. A ferrule joint should be as strong as an uncut section of rod and should also flex the same way—seemingly impossible when you consider that an assembled ferrule always creates a short double-wall section in the rod, where the male and female sections overlap. Graphite rods usually have graphite ferrules, either sleeve type (in which a short tube of graphite glued over the end of an upper rod section simply slides over the tip of the lower section) or spigot type. Spigot ferrules are plugs that extend from within the lower rod section to nest up inside the hollow end of the next section. An assembled spigot-ferrule rod shows no "bump" at the joints. Both types have been perfected over time; while the spigot type is more demanding to make, it does not necessarily guarantee better performance. Both types must be closely fitted to begin with, or they will jam or let go in casting, and the wear of repeated assembly and disassembly will eventually make them fail. However, the wear is normally so slow that for most anglers this is only a theoretical problem.

Expensive split-cane rods and mass-merchandised "toy" rods alike usually have metal ferrules. The difference is that the cheap ferrules are mass-produced from drawn tube (you can tell by the one-piece construction of the male, which has a rounded end) and the former are machined, one at a time, by hand. Such ferrules, nearly always made of nickel silver, are the lineal descendants of rod joints that date back at least to the 15th Century.

Rods then were quite long (the rod had to reach, since casting—beyond flipping the line—wasn't yet possible) and made of two or three different woods and might have tips of whalebone. A drawing in "The Treatyse of Fysshnge wyth an Angle," a chapter in *The Boke of St. Albans*, which appeared in 1496, shows rod sections mated together with an iron reinforcing ring over the joint. It looks something like a metal sleeve ferrule, but on that rod likely only the tip flexed; the ferrule didn't have to.

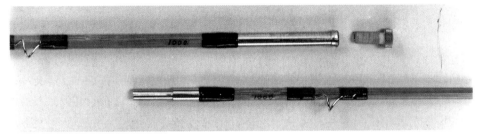

Ferrule—a modern, thin-wall, stepped-diameter, nickel-silver ferrule.

Other early rod joints were actually splines, or splices, rather than sleeves: The end of each rod section was cut flat on a long angle; two of these flats were mated up and lashed together as securely as possible with cords or leather thongs. Such a splice joint, ridiculous as it sounds, is in fact fairly strong, and some British rod makers still offer them today on large, two-handed salmon rods (even on graphite rods!). Devotees of spliced joints claim nothing else provides such a smooth, uninterrupted rod action.

Rod makers centuries ago also came up with hollow sleeve joints of brass, copper, silver and eventually German silver (nickel silver) tubing, which slide together. Crude ferrules often had no metal male section; the wooden end of the upper rod section was simply jammed down into a tube on the butt section. Next to appear were spike, or doweled, ferrules, which had tapered male pins. These probably didn't hold very well, so the next step was to add a lock-fast device. This was usually some sort of notch-and-pin arrangement or even an external screw thread.

For better flex and feel, ferrule walls were thinned and diameters reduced. For better holding power, the tapered male spikes were eventually replaced by straight sections. By 1878, American rod-building pioneer Hiram Leonard (see) had patented waterproof ferrules with split edges that allowed a smoother-flexing rod. By then, fly fishers were truly casting their lines, not merely flipping them, and rod action had become very important. By 1900 the modern metal ferrule had been perfected: a pair of precisely machined and matched, stepped-diameter, soldered nickel-silver tubes that fit exactly together and hold by friction.

Such ferrules are made in sizes that step up by a sixty-fourth of an inch (in outside diameter of the male plug). The size relates directly to weight and stiffness, and bamboo-rod craftsmen often describe their rods by length and ferrule. A 7 1/2-12, for example, is not a seven-foot six-inch rod for a #12 line (as it would be for graphite rod makers). It is a 7 1/2-footer with a #12 (12/64") ferrule. Since only one ferrule is mentioned, the rod must be a two-piece. A 7 1/2-11 would be a slightly finer and less powerful rod, a 7 1/2-13 a beefier rod for heavier use. See also Multi-Piece Rods, Nickel Silver.

Ferrule Cement—A low-grade thermosetting adhesive that usually comes in a paper tube like a crayon. The heat of a match will liquify it and it hardens rapidly at room temperature. Though it is little used today, and not at all in most high-grade fly rod ferrules, many anglers still have a stick of it in their tool kits. It is useful for replacing worn tiptops, the only line guide on a fly rod that need not be wound on with thread. Since ferrules usually wear out before rod sections, replacing them without harming the rest of the rod should be fairly easy. Therefore the epoxy that holds ferrules in place should melt at a lower temperature than the epoxy that binds the rod fibers (not to mention the graphite of the ferrule itself) together.

FFF—The Federation of Fly Fishers; see.

Fiberglass—Glass in fiber form. From some time in the early 1950s until about 1980, fiberglass was by far the most popular material for building fishing-rod blanks. Although the tendency is to regard fiberglass as some sort of plastic, in its raw form it is literally glass, heated and drawn (or blown) into flexible filaments. Technically speaking, however, a complete fiberglass rod blank, hollow or solid, is an example of FRP, or fiber-reinforced plastic: The glass filaments have been embedded in a thermosetting resin and then bonded together with pressure—by cellophane shrink-wrap tape—and heat, in a curing oven. (Fiberglass rod blanks are made the same way graphite rods are—see Graphite Rod Manufacturing.) The resultant laminate of parallel, longitudinal fibers is stronger for its weight than steel or aluminum. Fiber-reinforced plastics were developed as strategic materials in World War II; they were first used in aircraft and aboard naval vessels and as domes and shields for radar antennae. When the war ended and the markets for household, construction and recreational goods mushroomed in the USA, fiberglass was quickly put to use for everything from shower curtains to boats and fishing rods. The very first glass rods, in the late 1940s, were viewed with some suspicion, especially by traditionalists. There were instances where heavily stressed surf rods broke, allegedly impaling the fishermen with their own jagged, recoiling rod butts. In addition, said many conservative fly fishermen, fiberglass was ugly and would never replace bamboo. Much the same happened when graphite and boron made their debuts as rod-building fibers.

In reality, each rod-making material—cane, fiberglass, graphite, boron—was only another step along the same path. Bamboo is nothing more or less than a natural fiber laminate. Glass and graphite, with their progressively greater Modulus of Elasticity (see Rod Design), allowed designers to produce ever lighter, stiffer, stronger, faster-damping fly rods—once the manufacturers de-bugged each material and each process. Boron (see) proved too stiff and too difficult to use in manufacturing fishing rods, and is no longer popular. In hindsight, fiberglass was relatively easy to "tame" and to mass-produce fishing rods from. As sport fishing participation exploded in the 1950s, the traditionalists were left in the dust. Fiberglass put inexpensive, strong, light rods that could cast beautifully and tire fish quickly into the hands of millions of new fishermen.

Fighting Butt—An extension of the butt of a fly rod below the reel seat that's meant to aid in fighting large or strong gamefish. There are long fighting butts—extending six inches or so below the reel—and short fighting butts, of only an inch or two, but both serve to improve the leverage of the rod.

The best way to use a fighting butt is by gripping the rod well above the corks, up near the stripping guide, and jamming the butt end of the rod into one's belly; the upper hand pumps the rod, the other cranks the reel. Therefore, almost equally important is that a fighting butt also keeps the reel away from the angler's stomach and clothing, so it can turn and be cranked unimpeded.

Many medium- to heavyweight fly rods have detachable, accessory fighting butts that plug into the end of the reel seat, for use as needed. Several manufacturers—Thomas & Thomas today, Payne in the 1920s, for example—offer a reel seat with a screw-lock fighting butt that pulls down out of the seat when needed. Fighting butts should have large, comfortably rounded end caps or plugs; even so, it's common after a long battle with a large fish to develop a saucer-size bruise near the sternum.

Fighting Grip—A second rod grip, above the first, up on the rod blank near the stripping guide. Shifting the rod hand to this fighting grip (and tucking the rod butt, with or without an extension, into the chest or stomach) provides a considerable advantage in leverage in playing a strong fish. The disadvantages are that such a grip

Fighting Butt—The first and third are removable, plug-in types; the center rod is a Thomas & Thomas with a screw-lock butt extension that tucks away into the reel seat.

means extra weight, stiffness and wind resistance. Unless they are specifically going after big game, many anglers do without and just grab the bare rod blank when they need to pump a fish in.

Fingerling—A baby fish, about the size of a finger. More specifically, fingerlings are fish that have completely absorbed their yolk sacs; at about a year of age, a fingerling salmon becomes a parr.

Fin-Nor—Makers of one of the first fly reels designed and produced especially for saltwater fishing. The company name is actually Tycoon/Fin-Nor, and it started in south Florida in 1933 with heavy-duty trolling reels. The first Fin-Nor was built by a machinist named Fred Greiten, of the Finlay-Norwood (hence Fin-Nor) Garage & Machine Shop. The design was by Tom Gifford, a local boat captain who was looking for something better in big-game reels. Fittingly, given where they were made, the bearings in those early reels were from car generators. The rest of the name came within a decade, when Fin-Nor paired up with a rod-making company named Tycoon.

By 1950, Fin-Nor trolling reels were famous among offshore anglers around the world for their quality, features and durability (and their cost); by early 1992, Fin-Nors had been used to land 122 current IGFA (see) record fish.

The first Fin-Nor fly reels appeared in the late 1960s, when saltwater fly-fishing was a little-known curiosity, a tantalizing niche within another niche that was still devoted mostly to trout and salmon. The reels were large, rugged, single-action, direct-drive or anti-reverse models fitted with precision bearings. The mechanism clicked like a fine watch and the gold-anodizing drew the eye. A Fin-Nor became an ultimate status symbol among fly fishers, a badge and a trophy unto itself, like the tarpon and bonefish it was designed for. The early "wedding-cake" Fin-Nor fly reels—so named because the backplate was layered like a cake—have become collector's items. Fly reels eventually grew to about 20 percent of the company's dollar volume.

Fin-Nor also began to manufacture spinning reels, similarly gold-anodized and also regarded—by those few fishermen who knew of them—as the finest in the world.

But during the 1980s the company seemed to lose its way. Saltwater fly-fishing boomed, but without Fin-Nor. Other reel makers took over the big-game market, and Fin-Nor lost much of its mystique. The trolling-reel side of the business fared somewhat better.

Fin-Nor—An assortment of direct-drive (below) and anti-reverse Fin-Nor fly reels.

In 1990 Tycoon/Fin-Nor was acquired by Olympic Company, Ltd., one of the largest of the Oriental fishing-tackle manufacturers. Olympic installed new management, gave them an operating budget, issued marching orders, and then allowed Fin-Nor to operate independently. The result has been new machinery, new products, a cohesive business plan and a new lease on life.

Fishing Gloves—Self-explanatory as this term seems, there is a distinction between gloves for fishing (particularly fly-fishing) and ordinary coldweather protection for hands. The oldest and best-known "fishing gloves" are the British Millar Mitts—thick, close-fitting, loosely knit gloves with fingers that end at about the first knuckle. The fingertips are left bare, for better feel of the line. Though bare fingers still get plenty cold in raw weather, Millar Mitts are a big improvement over no gloves at all.

Attempts to improve on Millar Mitts have centered entirely upon newer materials and fabrics, mostly hydrophobic polypropylene types that don't soak water up and that dry rapidly. For truly cold weather, the best bet may be Glacier Gloves, which are made of neoprene and have removable fingertips.

Saltwater anglers may have a different take on the notion of fishing gloves: Particularly to gameboat deckhands who "bill" their clients' marlin and sailfish and to fishermen who handle spiny or sharp-toothed species, or who prepare baits or gut their catch, fishing gloves have studded, non-slip palms (for a good grip on a live fish) and backs and fingers reinforced with Kevlar or steel links, which even a fillet knife finds tough going.

Flag—In rod manufacturing, a section of graphite or fiberglass (or any other fiber) pre-preg that has been cut to shape for a particular rod section. When the leading edge of this piece is "tacked" (with a hot iron) to the mandrel it will be rolled around, then it looks like a flag on a staff—albeit an unusually tall and narrow flag with a bias-cut edge. See Graphite Rod Manufacturing.

Flats—To fly fishers, flats are hallowed ground, the shallow sand, mud or marl area near many tropical and semi-tropical land masses where bonefish, tarpon, redfish, permit, snook, sharks and other gamefish come to feed. Flats are . . . flat; the water depth across them is remarkably uniform and dependent on the tide. Flats may cover hundreds of acres and stretch as far as the eye can see—a shallow marine plain teeming with plant and animal life. Many flats fish well with only 18 inches of water over them; others may be under six feet of water. Flats fishing has led to the development of some unusual angling gear, from Kevlar-sole neoprene booties for wading comfortably and safely through sharp coral to highly effective and water-resistant sun-block creams.

Flats—Bonefishers on the flats of Christmas Island, in the center of the Pacific Basin.

Flats Skiff—A shallow-draft, center-console, open powerboat specially outfitted for light-tackle fishing on the flats. Although they would function equally well in other parts of the world, they are common only in Florida and the Gulf Coast, where the market can support their expense. The hulls are about 17 feet long with a sharp bow, low freeboard and a flattened-vee bottom; most are fiberglass but a few are made with Kevlar. The drive is a single outboard motor of about 100 horsepower; some flats boats also carry small trolling motors, gas or electric, for maneuvering. With a top speed of usually more than 40 knots and a draft of a foot or less, these craft are ideal for long, fast passages from one distant fishing ground to another. On site, the guide/captain cranks the motor out of the water, steps up onto the elevated platform at the stern, picks up the long fiberglass pole stowed in brackets along one gunwale, and begins pushing the boat along slowly and quietly. The angler stands in the foredeck, which is flat and free of obstructions that might catch his line, with rod in hand, ready to cast to a fish.

Flats Skiff—A typical Florida Keys fly-fishing boat with its poling platform aft and an open, uncluttered foredeck for coils of fly line.

Flick, Art—Born in New York City on August 3, 1904, Arthur B. Flick was the proverbial right man in the right place at the right time. He achieved lasting fame within American fly-fishing for putting information on aquatic insects into layman's language through his *Streamside Guide to Naturals and Their Imitations*, published by Putnam in 1947, and its later version, *Art Flick's New Streamside Guide* (Crown, 1969). The second edition is a vest-pocket, thoroughly illustrated basic guide to Catskills mayflies and their imitations. It was the culmination of a long study of aquatic flies: thousands of hours of collection, classification and categorization of naturals, followed by equal time at the tying bench, developing and modifying artificials to be effective imitations. The *Guide* was the first highly readable and "user-friendly" book that put this how-to information into the hands of fishermen—as opposed to quasi-scientific discourses meant for fishing entomologists. By 1990, about 100,000 copies of the *Guide* had been sold, a mark that very few fly-fishing books have reached.

Flick's chosen trade suited and mirrored his later fly-fishing achievements perfectly. His family had moved upstate, to Kingston, New York, in 1921 and from there to West Kill, on the banks of the Schoharie Creek, in 1941. His parents owned and ran a lodging called the Westkill Tavern, which he and his bride, Lita, eventually took over. Thereafter, Flick catered to and guided fly fishermen and upland gunners. Many of the greats of American fly-fishing passed through his hands; he knew, was influenced by, and influenced in turn, men like Preston Jennings, Ray Bergman, Sparse Grey Hackle, Lee Wulff, Ernest Schwiebert and many others. Like many top guides, he learned to be preternaturally observant and a quick study; he was also an uncritical and humble friend.

Art Flick was an extremely gifted fly tier as well, known for his work on the Red Quill, the Dun Variant and Preston Jenning's Gray Fox Variant, and for his book *Art Flick's Master Fly-Tying Guide*, published by Crown in 1972. A quiet, shy family man (who had to be prodded unmercifully—by Ray Camp, the *New York Times* outdoor columnist—to write the *Guide*), he contributed occasional articles to angling magazines and anthologies, but in reality Flick wrote far less than his fame suggests. Rather, organizations and other authors wrote about him. He was a dedicated conservationist decades before most people knew what "ecology" was. He advised five New York Conservation Commissioners and he was a force behind the first no-kill regulation in that state. In 1983 Flick was named Trout Unlimited's Conservationist of the Year.

In the fall of 1985 he was one of the first two people inducted into the Catskill Fly Fishing Center's Hall of Fame (the other was Theodore Gordon) and he was also chosen as *Rod & Reel* Magazine's first Angler of the Year. Flick learned of the first honor while he was dying quietly in Kingston's Benedictine Hospital—during a lucid moment, Leta read the letter to him; he smiled faintly and said his final coherent words:

"Isn't *that* nice!"—but he missed news of the second by only a day or two. He passed away on August 30.

Float—In fly-fishing, "float" is often a verb describing how a particular river is fished, as in, "we floated the Madison"—usually in drift boats, inflatable rafts or so-called "personal watercraft" (only the foolhardy travel a river in bellyboats). Also implied is that along the way the boat stopped so certain sections could be fished more thoroughly from the banks.

As a noun, a float can be a trip down a stretch of river or the short distance traveled by a dry fly, nymph or other pattern fished with the current before drag sets it.

Float Tube—Also known as a bellyboat, a float tube is a "personal watercraft" consisting of an inflated doughnut shape with a hammock-type seat slung in it for fishermen (or gunners, or birders) to paddle their way out to fish beyond the reach of chest waders or a long cast; in effect, a floating chair. Float tubes have dramatically added to fly-fishing, particularly in the American West. (In the East, the canoe still hangs on as the favorite fly-fishing "float.") Float tubes generally have a couple of zippered tackle pockets, along the "arms" of the chair, and a backrest, also inflated. Other features usually include several D-rings for attaching more gear, a fabric casting apron that keeps coiled fly line out of the angler's lap, various web handles and other straps to help carry the thing when it is inflated, and some sort of air pump. Some manufacturers offer a special backpack for toting a tube into a high-country lake. Most bellyboats are made a nylon form snugged around a truck-tire inner tube, but a few need no tube, having instead an integral bladder. These are often lighter and pack down to a more compact size.

Float tubes are often not truly round. Some have squared-off corners (in an attempt to provide a bit of directional stability when under way) and some squeeze more air to the back of the tube, where most of the angler's weight is suspended.

The angler wears swim fins to move the tube around, but maneuvering is slow, tiresome and backwards. To solve this problem, several innovative companies have introduced oversize bellyboats powered by electric trolling motors. The motor and its battery usually sit in a second, smaller inflated doughnut attached to the main tube. This is a much more practical, if more expensive, rig than the mini-motors sometimes sold for conventional tubes. Anglers can cover relatively great distances under electric power, then switch to foot fins for close-in maneuvering and fish-fighting.

Fly-fishing from a bellyboat is a learned art. newcomers may complain that stripping line is difficult because their arms hit the tube and their back casts slap the water because they are sitting quite low to the surface. But persistence pays off, and often

Float Tube—an array of "bellyboats."

spectacularly. Tubes can go virtually anywhere in complete silence, and fish seem to be much less disturbed by a human body hanging down in the water than one looming up above it. (Hunters report much the same success in approaching rafts of ducks or even shore-feeding deer and other game.) Surface-feeding fish sometimes come simply too close for casting. Expert tubers who spend many days on big lakes tell of encountering large salmon or trout eye-to-eye when a wave lifts the fish above their tube.

Float tubes should only be used on still water; in running rivers, bellyboaters have drowned when their feet caught in a snag and the current overcame the tube and dragged them under. Otherwise the chief danger is hypothermia because so much of the angler's body is immersed for long periods of time. Experienced tubers wear heavy neoprene waders or even wet suits. Note that since the US Coast Guard does not certify bellyboats as personal flotation devices, a tuber should, strictly speaking, wear an approved life vest. In fact high-quality tubes are extremely safe when used properly; the air pressure in them is typically so low that even in the rare event of a puncture, enough air stays inside to float the occupant for a long time.

Although bellyboats seem to be an invention of the 1980s, they are at least a century older than that. *The Fishing Gazette* of May 30, 1896, featured the Layman Pneumatic Boat—a float tube. It was a pair of bootfoot chest waders, complete with front pocket and suspenders, with a large inflatable rubber doughnut at the waist. It boasted grab handles, a secondary air chamber at the back for extra flotation, both foot and hand pumps, folding foot-fins for propulsion, and a compact backpack carrying case. It was meant for fishing and also for waterfowling—the tube had sockets spaced around it into which the hunter stuck poles that supported a blind. It differs from today's bellyboats only in that the tube and waders are apparently one piece; an illustration of a hunter wearing it in the woods shows the tube deflated and belted snugly around his waist.

Flue—From the French *velu*, meaning hairy or shaggy; the soft, fur-like down beneath a bird's feathers or the softer fibers at the base of a feather.

Fly—In this context, either an aquatic insect on which fish feed or an artificial imitation of an insect with which fly fishers try to fool those fish. The "fly" from which fly-fishing gets its name is most likely the mayfly (see), but whether the first artificial lure tied with feathers was meant to imitate an insect or a baitfish or something else of course isn't known. That famous Egyptian fresco—dated at 1500 BC and publicized by William Radcliffe in his *Fishing From The Earliest Times* in 1921—which shows a seated aristocrat plying fish-filled waters with what looks like a rod and line also depicts a flying insect at the center of the action. Fishing "flies" of course may imitate fish, frogs, mice, birds, snakes, crabs, shrimp, leeches and even garden worms and fish-food pellets as well as insects, so a fishing fly is simply an artificial lure that may be cast with fly-fishing tackle.

Note, however, that in the hunt for order, some anglers define fly-fishing tackle as equipment with which flies can be fished; others swap it around, defining flies simply as lures that can be fished with fly tackle. But is a hard-bodied fly a fly—or a lure? Is fishing a fly downstream on sinking line that can't be cast truly fly-fishing? Precise definitions, or at least definitions that satisfy most fly fishers, have never been arrived at. Some people would restrict the definition of a fly to a lure tied with fur or feathers; others would allow synthetic materials so long as they imitated fur or feathers; still others favor the first, broadest definition: a lure that can be false-cast with fly tackle.

In 1986 Wulff told the author: "A fly is a lure that doesn't move by itself, that has no diving lip or anything to give it an action; the action should come from the guy on the rod. And it must be something that can be cast on a fly rod with a fly line—cast and false-cast several times, not just heaved out there."

Wulff was trying to interest anglers in plastic-bodied flies (see Surface Stone Fly) as far back as 1950 and traditionalists have been squabbling about them ever since. Those who prefer the narrower definitions are often people who are put off by the thought of plastic flies.

Today, the three generally accepted elements of fly-fishing are aerial false-casting (see), a casting line with mass and differing dimensions, and a fly that is essentially weightless, regardless of what it is made of. A more precise definition would help governing bodies such as the IGFA (see) and state fish & game agencies tighten up their rules and regulations. See also Fly-Casting, Fly-Fishing, Fly-Tying.

Fly Box—A container for carrying, dispensing and protecting fishing flies. The ideal fly box is strong, yet light and compact enough to fit a fishing-vest pocket; hinged to open flat if need be; securely latched yet able to be opened easily with cold, wet fingers; fully gasketed to float and stay dry inside; corrosion- and rot-proof throughout; transparent enough to show its contents; and roomy enough not to mash the hackles of flies inside. Some fly boxes are lined with foam or wire clips or spirals, to stick hooks into; others are divided into compartments that hold loose flies. Moisture can be a problem—old-style boxes with steel clips or other components usually rust if wet flies are put away in them. Used flies should be allowed to dry on a fleece patch or the like before being stowed away.

Wet flies and streamers, which are often not as three-dimensional or as delicate as dry flies, may be carried in a fly wallet (see) instead.

Fly boxes

Fly-Casting—The art, or science, of delivering a fishing fly upon the water. Fly-casting may loosely be described as whipping the line back and forth in the air; then, when enough line has been worked out through the tip of the rod in the right direction, the line (and of course the leader and fly it is carrying, which is the point of the whole exercise) is allowed to fall upon the water. It is an alternating rhythm of forward casts and back casts (see), and in each segment the caster extends more line in the air and refines his or her aim until it is time to present the fly. Back cast and forward cast must flow seamlessly together; an incorrect back cast will inevitably lead to an incorrect forward cast.

Fly-casting differs most significantly from other kinds of casting in that the weight of the line, as opposed to the weight of the lure, helps generate the kinetic energy that powers the cast. A lure is heavy enough to pull its essentially weightless line off a spinning, spincasting or level-wind reel, but a fly has no effective mass; it is carried outward by the line. See Curve Cast, Double Haul, Rod Action, Single Haul, Slack-Line Cast, Steeple Cast.

Fly Dressing—The material of the fly body, as opposed to the hook; the assorted hackles, fur, hair, thread, tinsel, eyes, weights, adhesives and so on, whether natural or man-made, that are fastened to a hook to make it into a particular fly pattern. The term is archaic but still in use. However, in some cases (depending on context) the term may refer instead to the flotant or sink agent that is applied to a fly to help it perform better on the water. See also Fly-Tying, Fly Flotant.

Fly-Fishing—The art of fishing with an essentially weightless feathered lure, which often imitates a fly; i.e. a mayfly or caddis or other aquatic insect. Because of the delicacy of the tackle needed to fish such flies, for centuries fly-fishing was restricted to smaller gamefish, particularly trout, which predominated throughout Europe and which fed most obviously on hatching insects. As technology made the gear stronger and more versatile and as sport fishing expanded into Europe's colonies, other fish came into play, from Atlantic salmon and freshwater bass to, eventually, bonefish, tarpon and permit and then pelagic species ranging from smaller tuna and sharks to sailfish and marlin. The "flies" used on these larger fish generally imitate other fish, not fingernail-size insects, and may be a foot long.

To the occasional distress of fish & game regulatory agencies and record-keepers such as the IGFA, the International Game Fish Association (see), the precise definition of a fly (see) and thus of fly-fishing, has never been pinned down to everyone's satisfaction. In casual use, the definitions have a chicken-and-egg relationship: A fly is a lure that can be cast with fly-fishing gear; and fly-fishing is fishing with a fly. The definitions break down when fly rods are used with monofilament that is not cast but stripped off the reel and allowed to run downstream in the current (a technique sometimes used on steelhead in the Pacific Northwest, for example) or when hard-bodied, ultralight lures are cast on a fly rod.

The central element, however, that makes fly-fishing distinct is casting—false-casting the line back and forth in the air before laying it out across the water on the final, presentation cast. This in turn imposes some stipulations of its own: The rod must be long and flexible enough to keep line in the air; and the line itself must have enough mass (and shape, or taper) to be cast this way and to deliver its payload, the fly. All the other elements of fly-fishing tackle and technique stem from this.

By this definition, a "fly" may in fact be hard-bodied—carved wood, epoxy, molded plastic, whatever—and it may have a double or even a treble hook, so long as it can be false-cast in the air. And monofilament may be used—but only as running line or backing behind some kind of casting head. The definition also stipulates some sort of a leader, for clearly a small fly can't be tied directly to a thick line with any hope of fooling a fish.

Note that the fly reel doesn't enter into the definition at all (fly reels, at least smaller reels, are often dismissed as just convenient places to store line). In fact the reel too stems from this definition of fly-fishing: If you had never seen a fly reel, you could use a spinning reel with the sort of rod and line described above without deviating from the definition; but the inconvenience would eventually lead to the development of just what is now known as a fly reel, and it would hang just where it does, below the end of the rod, to contribute to the casting, that essential element of fly-fishing.

Fly Flotant—A dressing applied to a dry fly to help it float on (or in—see Surface Film) the surface of the water. Most commonly fly flotants come in a paste form, to be liquified by rubbing between the fingers and then to be applied sparingly to the hackle, body and tail of the fly, but some are sprayed directly onto the fly. Competing manufacturers sometimes dismiss each other's product as "re-packaged hand cream" (possibly true) but that doesn't mean they're no good. Fly flotant is meant to waterproof the dressing of the fly—the materials themselves, the hackles and hairs, may not be able to absorb water but the entire dressing can. Too much flotant, however, leaves the hackles clumped together and the fly as logy as if it were already waterlogged. Questions about longevity, odor, or damage to the fly (or even the water) have never been put to the test in a lab.

Fly Line—A line with enough mass and dimension to be used in fly-casting (see Fly-Fishing). For more than a century, fly lines have been generally 90 to 100 feet long, though now some entry-level lines may be only 60 feet and some saltwater lines may be slightly longer. They are made of a plastic, usually polyvinyl chloride, coating applied in differing thicknesses to a "stock," or core of braided Dacron or nylon. (The coating in its syrupy application state is called plastisol.) Some specialty lines have cores of thicker nylon or even Kevlar fiber (see Monocore). Although the core also affects the way a line handles, it is the coating that determines how the line will cast and whether it will float or sink. Floating fly lines do so because their coating is packed with microballoons, microscopic, thin-wall, hollow glass beads; by adjusting the size and the density of the microballoons, manufacturers vary the weight and specific gravity of the line. The coating of sinking fly lines may be impregnated with lead or tungsten. The outer surface of the coating determines how well the line slides through the rod guides; some manufacturers prefer smooth, others a pebbly finish. In either case, a clean, lubricated line will cast better and last longer.

For hundreds of years fly lines were, like leaders, laboriously made of braided horsetail. Some time in the early 1800s strands of silk were added to the braid. Then, from about 1870 until the 1950s, fly lines were generally made entirely of braided silk— a material with a supple feel and a thin diameter for its weight but with little else to recommend it. The tapers were created by adding or subtracting individual silk fibers. If not thoroughly dried after each use, a silk line would rot; it would sink if it wasn't oiled properly and even if it was it would sink soon enough anyway. To help them float and repel water, silk lines were made hollow and also enameled, but to little avail; water soon infiltrated. After WWII, when the great boom in synthetic materials occurred, fly lines were made of nylon. At least they were rotproof, but they also were difficult to float, with the further problem that they stretched too much. Then, in 1949, Leon Martuch Sr. and Clare Harris—who, along with Paul Rottiers, had founded the Scientific Anglers Company in 1945—found the first practical flyline coating, thermo-setting polyvinyl chloride.

In the early '50s the Cortland Line Company introduced the first commercial synthetic floating fly line as we know it now, called the 333. It had a plastic coating over a braided *and* tapered stock; the coating was uniform; the taper was in the core line. Not long afterward, Scientific Anglers moved fly-fishing along significantly again by perfecting its variable-die method of making fly lines. This patented process allows the taper to be applied over a level stock by passing the uncured line through a series of openings that determine the thickness of the coating. The stock emerges from a vat of plastisol and passes between a pair of large wheels that turn against each other; in the rims of the wheels are semicircular slits that, when they meet, form hollow tubes—molds, in effect, for the coating. The line then moves through heated tubes that bake the plastisol onto the core. This turned flyline manufacturing into an automated, high-speed, high-precision process.

Scientific Anglers also pioneered the use of microballoons (the first ones, in the '50s, were bakelite, not glass) in the coating for buoyancy, which was the derivation of the Air Cel trade name.

Flyline design and manufacture then evolved slowly until the middle 1980s, when a British company, known variously as Sue Burgess and FishTec, introduced its Airflo series, lines with non-stretch Kevlar cores and highly abrasion- and chemical-resistant urethane-based coatings. At first these unusual lines offered as many drawbacks as benefits, but their mere presence—and their claims—spurred the two American line manufacturers to new efforts. As Airflo slowly improved (early lines broke, did not float well and held their coil "memory" too tenaciously) the market became more sophisticated, and today it is difficult to buy a medium- to high-price fly line that does not perform its design task well.

According to Martuch, who was president of Scientific Anglers, double-taper and weight-forward lines were being used by 1885. Today fly lines come in a bewildering variety of weights, tapers, uses and even colors, but prior to 1961 the confusion centered mostly on size.

Before 1961 fly lines were designated by letter codes that indicated diameter: "A" (0.060") through "I" (0.20"). An HCH line, for example, was a double-taper with a thickness that built from 0.035" to 0.052" and back again. An HCF line, however, had a single taper; it was a weight-forward with the same tip and belly but in this case the "F" meant floating. Since nearly all fly lines were silk, diameter and weight were always in the same relation. Fly fishermen had to learn the code, but that was fairly simple and there weren't many choices anyway.

However, when synthetic lines appeared, with their different densities, diameter and weight were no longer in lockstep and the letter designations became obsolete. It was in 1961 that line companies, assisted by the American Fishing Tackle Manufacturers Association and the American Casting Association, replaced the diameter code with a new one that graded lines by weight. Instead of letters, lines were assigned numbers. The numbers indicated the weight, in grains, of the first 30 feet of the line, no matter what it was made of or how thick it was. (There are 7,000 grains in a pound, 15.385 grains in a gram; the unit comes from the average weight of a single grain of wheat.)

At first the scale only went from size 1 through 12; as saltwater fly-fishing expanded, so did the size scale.

Size numbers are used with letters that designate the type of line: WF = weight-forward, DT = double-taper, L = level, LB = long-belly, F = floating, S = sinking, I = intermediate, TT = Triangle Taper. The ST designation once meant single-taper, but as the weight-forward took its place, line companies began to use ST to mean sinking-

Line Size	Weight	Tolerance
1	60	54-66
2	80	74-86
3	100	94-106
4	120	114-126
5	140	134-146
6	160	152-168
7	185	177-193
8	210	202-218
9	240	230-250
10	280	270-290
11	330	318-342
12	380	368-392
13	450	435-466
14	480	500-520
15	550	529-569

tip.

An HCH line now would be described as a DT6F, a double-taper #6 floater. The HCF would be a WF6F, a weight-forward #6 floater. With this system rod makers and line companies can balance their products to each other's needs and the fly fisher can sort through the tackle jungle with some idea of what to look for.

TYPES OF FLY LINES

The design of a fly line, the thickness and length of each section—the front taper, belly, back taper and shooting or running line—are as important to fly-fishing as the choice of rod or fly. After determining the weight of the line that's needed on a particular rod, the type of fishing it will be used for sets the type of line. Fishing in quiet water with tiny, delicate flies calls for an unobtrusive presentation that would be impossible with a heavy shooting-head line; and a line suited to small flies and still water would be hard put to deliver big, bushy patterns through a stiff breeze. The basic types of fly lines are listed below; the chart indicates their approximate relative dimensions.

Double-Taper Line

A type of floating fly line that has a casting taper on both ends and no running line; that is, the tip and forward taper (a section perhaps 10 or 12 feet long) and the thick belly are duplicated on the other end of the line, with no thinner-diameter line in between. Because of this greater thickness, a double-taper line takes up more room

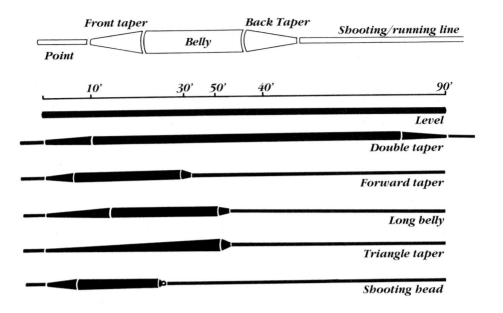

on a fly reel and is much more difficult to cast a long way. Double-taper lines often have a shallower (that is, longer) front taper than a weight-forward line and so can provide greater delicacy in presenting a fly.

These features limit a double-taper line to close-in fishing, and they are used mostly on smaller trout streams. Some anglers also prefer them because when one end wears out, the line can be renewed simply by swapping it around on the reel.

Intermediate Line

A versatile fly line designed for neutral buoyancy, with a density close to 1, the density of water. Dressed, an intermediate line will float for a time; cleaned, most I-lines (with PVC coatings their density is about 1.15; a few other lines dip as low as a density of 1.05) slowly sink. (A true neutral-density line would actually be less useful, or at least less convenient, since it would hover in the water column wherever it happened to be, and wouldn't sink *or* float unless it was forced to with a dressing.) Intermediates are thinner than floating lines and so they cut through wind and water better, in casting and fish-fighting, and they land more delicately on the water. In shallow water they are often favored for tarpon, bonefish, steelhead and Atlantic salmon, spooky species that may demand long, careful casts. Float-tube fishermen use them with great success over shallow weedbeds too. As more and more fly fishers discover them, I-lines are appearing in more and more colors and sizes.

Level Line

A fly line that has no changes in its diameter, no bulky casting head or tapered sections; although it has a plastic coating over a braided core, as most fly lines do, it is level, or constant, in its thickness from one end to the other. Inexpensive level lines are still occasionally found in cheap beginner outfits—even though they are difficult to cast and hardly appropriate for novice fly fishers—but they're best used in custom-building special-purpose lines: A high-density shooting head or fast-sinking head can be attached to a length of level running line that will handle and shoot through the rod guides better than uncoated line.

Long-Belly Line

A variant of the basic weight-forward fly line with a longer front taper and belly that comes close to being the front half of a double-taper line.

Shooting-Head Line

A highly specialized composite fly line that has a heavy casting section, or head, attached to a running line that may be level fly line or a length of monofilament. The head itself is usually about 30 feet long (though there are mini-heads of only 10 feet); it may float or sink, and it usually has small loops on both ends, to attach the running line and the leader butt. Such a connection, however, emphasizes the "hinge" effect in casting, so some anglers prefer a solid connection that turns over better and provides a smoother flow of casting energy. Shooting heads are easy to make, by cutting up old lines, but they are also available commercially in a wide range of weights and lengths. Effective fast-sinking heads can be made from sections of lead-core trolling line.

The idea of a separate shooting head came from the Golden Gate Casting Club in San Francisco around 1950, and it had a great impact on competitive distance casting and on fishing, particularly in the big steelhead rivers of the Pacific Northwest. Casting shooting heads takes some practice. The head provides extra punch and distance, but it also provides time; usually one back cast is all that's required—just enough to get the head and a few feet of line out beyond the tip of the rod—and then the forward cast launches the head so that it pulls the lighter line out behind it. Extra false-casting just gives the hinge effect time to build and the heavy head may hit the ground on a long back cast.

Sinking Line

A fly line that sinks along its full length; also called a full-sinking line. Sinking lines let the angler go deep with the fly, down to where gamefish feed most often. To do so, these lines come in a great variety of sink rates, from about one foot per second to as much as 10 feet per second. Line companies call their sink rates Type I or Class I and so on, but the numbers don't relate across the spectrum; a standard sink-rate nomenclature would be helpful.

Choosing the right type for any fishing situation means compromising between getting the fly down to the feeding zone quickest versus keeping it working there the longest. Full-sinking lines are most useful in still water, where line-mending is not so important and where the angler is usually in a tube or boat, so that the coils of stripped-in line can pile up without sinking away.

Sinking-Tip Line

Sometimes also called a dual-density line, the sinking-tip is a short (usually 10 to 30 feet) section of sinking line ahead of a floating belly and running line. In moving water a sinking-tip line lets the angler swim his or her fly well below the surface while still maintaining some line control by mending the topwater portion. Sinking-tip lines are made in a fairly wide range of line sizes and sink rates. Like shooting-head lines (see), sinking-tips can be somewhat difficult to cast because of the "hinge" effect where the two dissimilar line coatings meet.

Triangle Taper

A type of fly line invented and marketed in the mid-1980s by Lee Wulff. The name has caused some confusion among anglers, who often aren't sure just which part of the line is "triangular"; some are surprised to find the line is in fact round in cross-section, not three-cornered. The name derives from the profile of the casting head of the line: From its relatively fine tip, the line diameter increases continuously for the first 40 feet; at that point, then profile then reverses and the thickness tapers rapidly, in the next eight feet, down to the thin running line (see). By contrast, a typical weight-forward line (see) has a fatter tip that builds in thickness for the first 10 feet or so, then flattens out to a constant-diameter "belly" section for the next 20 feet, and finally drops gradually, over 10 or 12 feet, to the running line. The Triangle Taper line is a compromise between the delicacy of a double-taper and the casting capability of a weight-forward.

The Triangle Taper's continuously increasing diameter means that as the head unrolls in normal casting, thinner line is always being pushed (or pulled, depending on how you look at it) by heavier line. The same is true in roll-casting, where TTs also really shine: heavier line is always pulling lighter line from the water surface.

The benefit of the Triangle Taper is the ease with which it handles a wide variety of fishing situations. Should you need delicate presentations in close, the line can do it, since the point is so light. If you need a long reach, the line can be extended with minimal false-casting and used like a shooting head. And because of its head shape, the TT has no equal when it comes to roll-casting.

Weight-Forward Line
The weight-forward line has most of its casting weight (and thus its thickest diameter) in the belly, the 30 feet or so just behind the front taper. The rest of the WF profile is relatively fine-diameter running line. The weight-forward floater is today's basic fly line, the most popular line design of all. The rationale is that since most freshwater fish are caught within 40 feet or so of the rod, a longer tapered section is not necessary; and when it is necessary to cast farther, the heavy front section pulls the lighter running line out behind it like the tail of a kite. Line manufacturers experiment continually with their WF designs, changing the tips and bellies, the length and steepness of the tapers and so on. Bass-bug, "rocket" or saltwater tapers, and shooting-head lines are variations on the basic weight-forward theme.

Flymph—A soft-hackled fly (from "fly" and "nymph"); see.

Fly Reel—At one end of the angling spectrum, a fly reel is needed only to store line, since it does not affect casting. The small-stream or pond fisherman cranks line onto the reel so that it doesn't tangle in loops at his feet; when he catches a fish, he often plays it with his fingers rather than off the reel, feeding and retrieving line by hand. A true mechanical drag (as opposed to an overrun-protector—see) isn't needed, so fly reels are often very simple, light and even elegant.

However, since gamefish accelerate and stop, turn, run again and often jump, even a smaller fish may end up pulling line out of the reel. Line, leader and rod (and the angler's body) absorb some of these shocks, but the reel has to stop, start and accelerate right along with the fish. Even small reels must be able to cushion a tippet by reversing promptly and smoothly.

Since late in the 19th Century, fly reels have been: mounted below the hand grip on the rod (and also below the centerline of the rod itself); in line with the rod; made mostly of aluminum alloy; and of narrow-spool construction—that is, wider in diameter than in thickness. Though earlier reels such as the Nottingham (see) and the Fowler (see) showed the way, the first truly "modern" fly reel—which featured all these elements *and* was drilled, or ventilated, for lightness and to let the line dry—was Charles F. Orvis's famous 1874-patent model (see). More recent innovations have brought us graphite, plastic, magnesium or titanium frames and spools; synthetic internal components (gears, etc. made of nylon, Delrin and so on); ball or roller bearings; and a variety of sophisticated mechanical drags that employ Teflon or similar self-lubricating materials. The overall design hasn't changed, however.

See also Anti-Reverse Reel, Automatic Reel, Direct-Drive Reel, Dual-Mode Reel, Full-Frame Reel, Multiplying Reel, Salmon Reel, Saltwater Reel.

Fly Rod—A rod for fly-fishing; that is, for casting a weighted line with a more-or-less weightless fly at the end, and then playing and landing a fish. A fly rod may be six to 15 or so feet long, meant to be cast with one or both hands, and made in one to eight or more sections, fitted together with ferrules (see). Barring the presence of fighting butts or grips (see), the fly reel is fastened at the very end of the rod, below the primary grip, and it hangs below the rod in use. Thus the line guides are also on the underside of the rod. Fly rods are generally made of graphite (called carbon fiber in the UK and Europe), fiberglass, or split cane (bamboo); fly rods have been made of steel and boron fiber too, as well as, historically, of many different (and generally unsuitable) woods such as greenheart and lancewood.

For good casting, a fly rod should have a certain flexural profile, or "action," and the pursuit of perfection in this regard is to a large extent what drives the rod market. A springy, whippy strength also, however, makes a fly rod an excellent fish-fighting tool. The common perception that all fly-fishing is ultra-light fishing is a misconception; heavy-duty fly rods are as powerful in their way as any big-game tackle. See Rod Action.

Fly-Spin Combo—A term used to describe multi-purpose rods (usually light-duty 6-to 7 1/2-foot fiberglass pack rods) that their manufacturers claimed could serve as spinning or fly rods. Invariably they performed one task better than the other, but some models were in fact fine all-around rods. The concept peaked in the 1970s, just as graphite was coming on, when fiberglass rods reached the apogee of their development. The best fly-spin rod was probably The Orvis Company's Rocky Mountain combo rod, made of split cane, which came in a fitted walnut case that also held a spinning reel, a fly reel, and spools of the appropriate line.

Fly-Tying—The art and techniques of "dressing" a fishhook with feathers, fur, hair, tinsel, floss, wire and other materials to represent the body, tails, wings, eyes and other characteristics of whatever gamefish are likely to eat—such as insects, forage fish, crustaceans, frogs, eels and so on. The art is in the representation; manmade flies are either slavish imitations, faithful to the natural right down to its antennae, abdominal segments and claws, or impressionistic renderings that rely on overall color, size and silhouette (and then the angler's skill) to trigger a fish's feeding instinct. The techniques of fly-tying are many and varied, but they stem from the desire to tie each pattern with

Fly-Tying—a portable fly-tying kit, to be used in camp or streamside.

a single unbroken length of thread. From the foundation of thread wraps on the bare hook shank to the final whip-finish at the head of the fly, each material is used and each step is done in a sequence that keeps the tying thread moving continuously back and forth along the hook. Although Lee Wulff and perhaps others found ways to tie flies without thread already in the late 1940s (see Surface Stone Fly), glued flies came into their own only in the 1980s, with the advent of easy-to-use epoxy and cyanoacrylate adhesives. See Mother of Epoxy Fly.

Historians continue to pore over ancient records in search of "the antecedents of angling" (as William Radcliffe put it in his *Fishing From The Earliest Times*, Dutton, 1921) but by now it seems unlikely they will discover any older references to fishing flies than are already known—or supposed. The two most famous are a tomb fresco from ancient Thebes, in Upper Egypt, dated about 1500 BC, and a passage from Aelian , a scholar of classical Rome, who lived from 170-230 AD (and wrote in Greek, for some reason). The first shows an aristocrat seated in a chair, holding a short rod in one hand and apparently dangling, from its tip, a line in the water. There are representations of fish and one of a flying insect with two tails and two antennae; the connection isn't unmistakable but it is certainly suggestive. In regard to fly-tying, the question becomes: Is that an artificial fly? Or a natural put on the hook as bait? Or is it just an indication that upperclass Egyptian anglers too were bothered by bugs? In his famous *Natural History*, Aelian is clearer (from *Angling Literature in England*, Oliver Lambert, 1881):

"I have heard of a Macedonian way of catching fish, and it is this: between Beroea and Thessalonika runs a river called the Astraeus, and in it there are fish with speckled skins; what the natives of the country call them you had better ask the Macedonians. These fish feed on a fly peculiar to the country, which hovers on the river. It is not like flies found elsewhere, nor does it resemble a wasp in appearance, nor in shape would one justly describe it as a midge or a bee, yet it has something of each of these. . . . The natives generally call it the *Hippouros.*

"These flies seek their food over the river, but do not escape the observation of the fish swimming below. When then the fish observes a fly on the surface, it swims quietly up, afraid to stir the water above lest it scare away its prey; then coming up by its shadow, it opens its mouth gently and gulps down the fly, like a wolf carrying off a sheep from the fold or an eagle a goose from the farmyard; having done this it goes below the rippling water.

"Now although the fishermen know of this, they do not use these flies at all for bait for fish; for if a man's hand touch them, they lose all their natural color, their wings wither, and they become unfit food for the fish. For this reason they have nothing to do with them . . . but they have planned a snare for the fish, and get the better of them by their fisherman's craft.

"They fasten red wool around a hook and fit on the wool two feathers, which grow under a cock's wattles, and which in color are like wax. Their rod is six feet long and their line the same length. Then they throw their snare and the fish, attracted and maddened by the color, comes straight at it, thinking from the pretty sight to get a dainty mouthful. When however it opens its jaws, it is caught by the hook and enjoys a bitter repast, a captive." (For a continuation of the history of artificial flies from this point, see Berners, Dame Juliana.)

Fly-Tying Tools—For centuries fly tiers relied upon thread, bodkins, scissors and perhaps a crude vise to dress their flies. In the 1980s, when the fly-fishing market

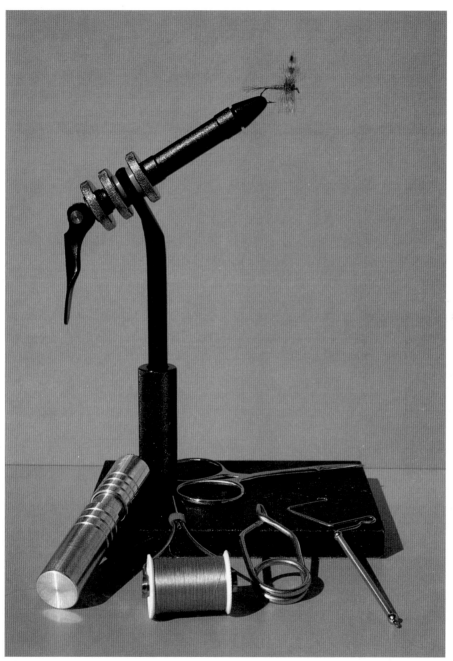

Fly-Tying Tools—the basics: vise and (from left) hair stacker, bobbin, scissors, hackle pliers and whip-finisher.

expanded dramatically and when fly-tying became an avocation unto itself (instead of just a way to beat the price of "store" flies) innovative fly tiers began designing and producing an ever-widening array of specialized tools. From the sublime—precision-machined vises that cost as much as big-game reels—to the unnecessary—such as a low-temperature steamer to rejuvenate tired hackles—it seemed every option and need was covered. Fly-fishing expanded from the trout stream and the salmon river to the bass pond to the tropical flats to the offshore big-game grounds, and fly-tying followed. In keeping with the traditions of the "parent" sport, much of this new tying gear is as esthetically pleasing as it is well-made and functional: Many new-generation vises look like industrial art; often the hand tools, from bobbins to hair stackers, are beautifully polished, knurled or otherwise set apart from the ordinary. In fly-tying as in fly-fishing, the manufacturers and vendors are avocationists first and business people second, highly focused upon the product instead of simply the return on investment.

Vise

A clamp for a hook, to hold it by the bend while the fly tier dresses its shank with hair, hackle, tinsel, floss and so on. A tying vise may have a clamp, to grip the edge of a table, or a pedestal, a flat, heavy base that sits on the table top. Vintage vises often had thumb loops, so they could be hand-held, or the standrod was coarsely threaded to be screwed into a tree stump or a wooden bench.

The critical part of any tying vise is its jaws, which hold the hook. These are usually one piece of high-quality steel; the opening for the hook is a milled slot, which closes as the jaws are pulled (by a cam lever or a screw thread) into a tapered collar; alternately, the jaws may be closed by a thumbscrew. The temper of the jaws is important: If the steel is too brittle, the jaws may break; if it is too soft, they won't hold well. A rough-edged set of jaws may mar or crush the hook. Compounding the difficulty is the fact that fly tiers now work with hooks ranging from #24 to about #4/0 in size, and few, if any, jaws can encompass such a wide range of wire diameters. The solution is interchangeable sets of jaws, with different slot widths.

A rotary vise is one that allows tying a fly by turning the hook, in the vise, and feeding thread, dubbing, tinsel, yarn, floss, etc. onto it from a stationary bobbin, instead of leaving the hook fixed and winding the material around it. Rotary tying requires a rotary vise, one with a head that can turn like the chuck of a lathe. Some high-production fly manufacturers use rotary vises powered by electric motors and controlled with foot pedals, but usually rotaries have some sort of small wheel or tiller to let the tier spin the jaws by hand. They also have a means to lock the head in one position for conventional tying. Many simple flies with wound bodies can be tied very quickly on a rotary vise. (Many conventional vises have a mechanism that unlocks the head so that the fly can be rotated—for trimming hackle underneath, painting eyes, etc.—but they simply index from one position to another instead of turning freely the way a true rotary does.)

Tying vises come in a wide variety of styles and prices, but in general they can be divided into home and travel types. Travel vises fold or disassemble into compact bundles; they are meant to be used in camp or even right at streamside, to match exactly whatever the fish are feeding on.

Bobbin

A hand-held, pen-like tool that dispenses and also holds the thread used in fly-tying. Often the thread is wound first on a small spool (from a sewing machine, for example) that clamps into the tying bobbin; other bobbins accept spools direct from the thread supplier. In either case, once in the bobbin, the thread comes off the spool, under tension, through a thin tube, which lets the fly tier apply thread with the precision of a draftsman's fine-tip pen. Equally important is that it also lets the tier stop in the middle of a fly to perform another operation—the weight of the bobbin hanging free under the hook (while the fly is clamped in the vise) keeps tension on the tying thread. Without a bobbin, it is far more difficult to tie a fly with one unbroken length of thread—but not impossible, for bobbins came into widespread use in fly-tying only in the 20th Century.

The tube is particularly important, for if it is burred or sharp it will fray or cut the thread passing through it. A commercial fly tier can wear a groove in a steel bobbin tube in a few weeks. Tubes can be replaced, but several manufacturers now offer bobbins with tubes made of, or lined with, a hard ceramic material, which is smooth and extremely abrasion-resistant. The length and strength of the tube are also important, for that (along with the tension on the spool itself) affects how much pull the tier exerts on the thread and the fly while tying—too much and the thread snaps easily; too little and tying becomes sloppy.

Dubbing Needle or Bodkin

A tool used in fly-tying for a variety of tasks. Since it is nothing more than a steel pin set in some sort of a handle, it can be used to separate materials, to free hackles or hairs that have been trapped under the tying thread, to clear the eye of the hook or to apply a drop of head cement or paint precisely where it's needed. The name, however, comes from another use: picking at the fibers of the dubbing to give the fly body a fuzzier and presumably more lifelike look.

Hackle Guard

A small disc of plastic or cardboard that can be slipped over a hook to protect a mounted hackle or other dressing from a subsequent tying operation.

Whip Finisher

A bent-wire tool used to tie a whip-finish onto the head of a completed fly. Flies can be whip-finished by hand but the tool makes the job easier and faster. Some whip-finishers even have internal bearings to let them spin around the fly head more smoothly.

Hackle Pliers

A tool used to grip the tip of a hackle feather in order to wind it around a hook. Hackle pliers have cushioned jaws, to prevent crushing or cutting the feather, and a locking mechanism (often just a spring) so they can be shifted from hand to hand—while being passed around the hook, for example—without losing their grip on the feather. Hackle pliers often have a loop in the handle so the tool can be spun around the hook on a finger tip. This makes for a smoother, uninterrupted winding and also leaves the other hand free to preen the hackle with a dubbing needle as it goes into place.

Scissors

Fly-tying scissors must have loops that fit the fingers comfortably—many tiers leave them in their hand as they tie—and fine tips capable of precise cutting. For specialized uses, some tiers prefer scissors with their tips curved one way or the other; and for trimming tough, abrasive materials such as deer hair some heavy-duty tying scissors may have serrated or scalloped edges, which prevent the material from squirting away in cutting. Many high-quality fly-tying scissors are in fact surgical instruments.

Hair Stacker

A short section of tube with one end closed off, used to even up a clump of hair that is to be tied into a fly pattern. The hair is clipped off and put in the tube; a couple of gentle raps against the table top and the ends are neatly aligned.

Dubbing Wax

A slightly sticky, semi-hard paste that is smeared on tying thread to make dubbing material adhere to it so it can be wound around the shank of a hook to create the body of a wet fly or nymph pattern. Dubbing wax is usually sold in some kind of tube dispenser (like an oversize lipstick) for easier handling and it may come in different degrees of tackiness for different kinds of flies and dubbing materials.

Flyweights—Durable urethane-coated nylon stockingfoot waders.

Head Cement

A lacquer-like liquid applied to the head of a finished fly to lock the tying thread in place and protect it from abrasion and wear.

Fly Wallet—An envelope, sometimes leather or vinyl, that is lined with sheepskin or some other soft, absorbent material and that closes with a zipper or Velcro, snaps, buttons, etc. It is meant for streamers, nymphs, wet flies and similar patterns that—unlike delicately hackled, three-dimensional dry flies—can be stored flat. Of course, streamers and so on are three-dimensional too, but their long, flat hackles are are brought back to life by the water, while the stiff hackle tips on which small dries float would be crushed and destroyed by a fly wallet.

A wallet can hold separately a great number of flies that in a box might get tangled up with each other. A wallet may also dry a used fly by absorbing the water from it.

Flyweights—A brand name that became a generic term for lightweight stockingfoot (see) chest waders after the Red Ball company introduced the first version in the late 1970s. They did as much for stockingfoot wading as nylon monofilament did for leaders. Early versions of the Flyweights were made from 70-denier nylon water-proofed with a coating of polyurethane inside and held together by electronically welded seams that, in the words of one field tester, "look ridiculously inadequate." In fact, crude as they looked, the seams were not inadequate at all—like a steel weld, the joint was stronger than the material around it. The thin, flexible fabric also proved far more durable than it looked or felt. Eventually, even tougher versions appeared, up to 200-denier or more, and such features as latex-rubber feet and such accessories as cut-down Flyweight hippers.

Flyweight and Flyweight-type waders fold into compact bundles for travel; mold themselves to one's legs underwater (thus providing the least resistance to the current); are very easy to get into and out of; and are loose and baggy enough to provide a cooling "bellows" effect when out of the water in hot weather and to fit over nearly any combination of longjohns and insulating pants for coldweather wading too. And any leaks that may come along can be repaired on the spot with duct tape or a variety of other stick-ons.

Foot—The base of a fly reel, usually about 21/2 inches long and always radiused on the bottom to conform to the round barrel of the fly rod reel seat that it fits into. A foot may be integral—that is, machined in one piece with the reel frame—or made separately and attached, usually by machine screws or, less often, rivets. For a stronger, wobble-proof fit, a separate foot may also be dovetailed to its reel. Obviously, a high-quality connection is important, particularly in a reel meant for strong fish.

Curiously, even in this age of standards and mass production, not all reel feet fit all reel seats, a problem that has plagued fly fishers for decades (if not centuries); the most common flaw in an otherwise more-valuable vintage fly reel is a foot that has been filed down to fit a particular rod. See Fly Reel, Reel Seat.

Forward Cast—That portion of fly casting that is in front, or forward, of the caster. Fly-casting may loosely be described as whipping the line back and forth in the air; then, when enough line has been worked out through the tip of the rod in the right direction, the line (and of course the leader and fly it is carrying, which is the point

Fowler—A center-mount Fowler Gem reel.

of the whole exercise) is allowed to fall upon the water. It is an alternating rhythm of forward casts and back casts (see), and in each segment the caster extends more line in the air and refines his or her aim until it is time to deliver the fly. Forward cast and back cast must flow seamlessly together; an incorrect forward cast will inevitably lead to an incorrect back cast. The final forward cast, the presentation of the fly, is the culmination of all the motions that preceded it. See Fly-Casting.

Fowler Reel—The design successor to the famous Billinghurst reel (see), the center-mount, half-frame Fowler "Gem" was awarded a patent on June 18, 1872. Its greatest significance is that it was made of hard rubber, then called Vulcanite. (Charles Goodyear had received the first of the rubber patents that made this possible in 1851.) Dr. Alonzo Fowler, the inventor, was a dentist, and by using the molding technology of his trade he became one of the first to make fishing reels of hard rubber, also known as ebonite. The little Gem was too eggshell-thin and fragile to be much of a success in the market, but it led American fly reels farther down the design path that the Billinghurst (see) had initiated: It had a modern-looking, exposed ratchet-and-pawl clicker and its spool was drilled; it was clever, light and innovative. The next step down that path was taken by Charles F. Orvis's 1874-patent reel (see). See Fly Reel.

Free-Spool—A fly reel is in free-spool mode when its drag or overrun check is disengaged and the spool can turn freely. Some reels have no free-spool setting. In certain types of downstream fly-fishing, free-spooling is useful to feed out extra line to prevent current drag on the fly. The Rogue steelhead reel even has a finger lever that instantly disconnects the drag to let the spool run.

Full-Dress—A term used to describe a fly, usually a classic Atlantic-salmon pattern, that has been tied to the original specifications, if not necessarily with the original—but now often illegal—materials, such as polar-bear hair and various jungle-bird plumages.

Full-Frame Reel—A full- (or cage-) frame fly reel is one in which the frame surrounds the spool, or at least one side and both rims of the spool, entirely. Such frames may be one-piece with integral pillars, or the pillars may be screwed to the frame. A one-piece frame may be machined from bar or tube stock, it may be investment-cast, or it may be stamped from sheet metal. Generally speaking, a full-frame reel is stronger and heavier than a half-frame type, but usually the gain in strength is only theoretical, at least as far as fishing performance is concerned. Where full-frame construction does offer an advantage is in protecting a reel from the shocks of travel or being dropped. And some large full-frame fly reels (usually saltwater or salmon models) have a sideplate that supports the outer end of the spool axle and so insulates it against the torque of big fish pulling against high drag settings. See Fly Reel, Saltwater Reel.

Gaff—Primarily a saltwater tool; a large hook, set on the end of a handle, used to land fish that are too large for a net. Fish to be kept and killed for the table may be gaffed anywhere through the body, while a tarpon that will be released alive is often lip-gaffed, pinned through the lower lip to the gunwale of the boat so that the fly can be removed. A flying gaff is a detachable hook with a line on it; if the fish pulls away from the handle, it can be landed with the heavy line instead. A still-strong fish with a gaff in it can be dangerous, pulling fishermen overboard or lacerating them with the sharp point if it thrashes unexpectedly.

Gaiters—Pull-on or zip-on coverings that go around the lower leg and over the tops of wading shoes (see), to keep out stream gravel and sand that could abrade the stockingfoot wader, causing leaks or blisters. Gaiters are usually made of stretchy neoprene. Some extend down over the front of the shoe and also prevent sticks from getting caught in the laces.

Gape—The gap, or "bite" of a hook; the opening between the point of the hook and the shank. See Hook.

Genetic Hackle—Feathers grown on chickens that have been bred specifically to produce fly-tying hackle of a certain quality: color, length, barb stiffness, barb density, etc. These qualities contribute to the appearance and performance of a fly—the way it floats or swims, its silhouette, how long it will last, even how easy it is to tie. In a business that has been compared to growing grapes and making wine, poultry breeders combine science and art to cultivate "better" chickens. They select, for breeding or harvesting, their birds according to standards. How many feathers per square inch does the cape hold? What is the size range of those feathers? Is each feather densely barbed? Are the barbs themselves of a useful and generally uniform length? Are they long and stiff enough for tying crisp, high-floating dry flies? Are the quills fine in diameter and soft enough to wrap tightly around a hook? Does the webbing extend only a short way up the quill? Color is one of the most difficult challenges for the hackle grower: Not only must the grizzly hackles be sharply barred, not only must the traditional colors be rich and true, but the grower must try to anticipate demand for unusual hues and variants. It takes a hackle farm usually two years to react to orders for new colors.

Genetic hackle, even high-priced, top-quality capes, may be dyed or bleached to achieve certain colors. Years of experimentation with handling techniques and chemicals has led to so-called "soft" dyes that do not harm the feathers. (Michigan hackle grower Ted Hebert dyes not simply the skin; he dyes the entire bird, to get what

Genetic Hackle—a prime grizzly rooster.
Below—closeup of hackle feathers.

he says is a more natural color.)

Genetic hackle capes are graded by the breeder—#1 is better than #2, which is better than #3. However these numbers are usually compromises that reflect an overall level of quality, and a given cape may be well suited for one type of fly but not for another, regardless of its rating. A #2 cape may have best-quality feathers yet it was graded down because the color was slightly off or streaked. Similarly, a cape that is luxuriantly hackled with a wide range of feather sizes, all in a desirable color, may be rated a #1 even if the individual feathers are not of top quality. In addition, there is no set grading standard; breeders rate their own product according to their own criteria. Some may value a full range of fly sizes, others may work to produce capes thick with smaller hackles for trout flies. Hackle growers often strive for prime dryfly feathers but as saltwater fly-fishing expands, so does the market for purpose-grown saltwater hackle, which must have other characteristics.

Experienced fly tiers often regard the quality rating as just a starting point and buy according to different criteria depending on what sorts of patterns they are tying. For example, large tarpon streamers call for feathers that are not only long but also wider, with thicker webbing and rounded, not sharply pointed, tips. (Although this too is a matter of personal preference.)

In 1992 it was estimated there were nearly a quarter of a million genetic-hackle chickens being raised in the US, in a dozen or more farms. (One, the Metz Hatchery in Pennsylvania, had 100,000 birds all by itself.) The business risks are great. Disease can wipe out an entire flock in a matter of days. Some of the larger farms split their stock, keeping a breeding nucleus in a location far from their production birds. Many of today's "name-brand" birds are descended from famous flocks, such as the legendary stock that Harry Darbee began to raise in the Catskills in the 1940s and then passed on to Andy Miner, who later sold a few birds to Ted Hebert. Darbee-Miner descendants are also being crossed with the famous Hoffman birds. The gene pools are protected at all costs, and the techniques of husbandry are jealously guarded. Since feathers are only as long as a chicken is tall, at least one grower is working to develop a bird with longer legs. Another found that in dry desert air his eggs were losing embryonic fluid; he solved the problem by breeding chickens with stronger, less porous shells.

German Silver—An obsolete name for nickel silver (see), a centuries-old alloy used in making fine split-bamboo rod ferrules.

Gillie—A Scottish fishing or hunting guide. In Ireland it is spelled "ghillie."

Goddard Knot—A variant of the nail knot, which is used on monocore fly lines. The coating of the fly line is stripped away for an inch or so at the tip, and then the end of the tip is melted into a ball with a match. The nail knot is tied around the fly line above the ball, which acts a stopper to prevent it from sliding off. (In a conventional coating-over-braid fly line, the nail knot bites deeply into the fly line for a good hold.) See Knots.

Graphite—Graphite made its public debut as a rod-making material when it was presented to the annual convention of AFTMA, the American Fishing Tackle Manufacturers Association, in 1974 by the Fenwick and Shakespeare companies. Don Green, founder of the Sage rod company, had begun experimenting with graphite as a rod material in 1968 when he was with Fenwick. As did fiberglass more than 20 years earlier, graphite caused an unhappy stir among angling traditionalists, who perhaps were more put off by its color—flat black—than by anything else. The black stems from graphite's high carbon content; natural graphite is a soft mineral that leaves black streaks behind and goes into pencil lead. Synthetic graphite, on the other hand, is an engineer's dream material. It has unusual physical characteristics that help answer structural, mechanical, electrical, aeronautical and even medical needs, and it is indisputably the best material yet discovered for making fishing rods, especially fly rods with their unusual performance demands. A graphite rod blank is a tapered laminate of hundreds of relatively fine (less than 0.010" diameter) fibers of graphite that are bound together by a heat-setting resin. (See Graphite Rod Manufacturing.) The result is a hollow tube that is extremely light in weight yet far stiffer than any similar structure built from aluminum, steel, magnesium or fiberglass; the fine diameter of the tube minimizes air resistance in casting, and its ability to damp out vibrations—to come to rest quickly after being flexed—makes casting inherently smoother regardless of the angler's skill. Graphite is also chemically and thermally inert. The performance characteristics of a graphite rod don't differ from an equatorial bonefish flat to a Michigan winter steelhead run; and no substances encountered while fishing can affect either the graphite or the resin content of a rod. (Compare this to the hide glues, used for decades to laminate split-bamboo rods, which were water-soluble!) Graphite is, however, an excellent conductor; anglers have been electrocuted when their rods struck high-tension lines overhead, especially in Britain, where two-handed rods of 15 to 17 feet are common.

Synthetic graphite fibers are made by charring, or carbonizing, strands of a polymer yarn, typically PAN, or polyacrylonitrile. The filaments are sometimes called graphite or carbon depending on whether the strands were produced at above or below about 4,500°F. Technically, the term carbon is more accurate since these fibers usually lack

An Irish gillie on the Castle Ballynahinch water.

the three-dimensional atomic structure of true graphite. In Britain and Europe, rods are said to be made of carbon; North American anglers use the word graphite. The material is the same.

Although one can't ignore the contributions made by modern teaching methods, fly lines and even leader monofilament, the introduction of graphite rods did more to improve casting than anything since the change from loose-footed to stand-up line guides. Just as composite skis led to the boom in downhill skiing in the 1960s, graphite rods helped popularize fly-fishing in the 1970s and '80s. Graphite rods added between 10 and 20 feet to the average fly fisher's casting range, which all by itself greatly improved his or her fishing success. Because of their springiness and light weight, graphite rods are also highly efficient fish-fighting tools—shock absorption, to cushion a fine tippet, and ultimate strength, to land a strong fish, can exist in the same rod. Graphite rods may break in use, because of a manufacturing flaw or after the blank has taken a sharp blow, but they do not wear out; one result is a secondary market that lets any angler eventually buy a high-quality used rod that he or she couldn't afford when it was new.

While graphite rod blanks do not wear out (the grips, guides and reel seat might, but they can be replaced), graphite rods do change. Rod tapers evolve and the graphite available to sporting-goods manufacturers has improved steadily. Together these factors make a 1990s fly rod perform as much better than a 1975 rod as that rod outperformed a 1950s glass rod.

One of the most important characteristics of a graphite fiber is its Modulus of Elasticity, or E. E is a measure of stiffness, expressed in millions of pounds of pressure per square inch.

(The E values sometimes given in rod manufacturers' literature are "pure"; that is, for the fiber alone. But when the fibers are built into a rod blank, within the epoxy resin that binds them together, the "effective E" is considerably less. The stiffness of a finished fly rod also depends on many other factors, including ferrules, line guides, finish and fiber direction.)

Since 1970 Modulus values for fishing-rod graphite have approximately doubled. Today, what is considered low-Modulus graphite has an E of about 32 to 34 million PSI; stiffer graphite such as IM-6 has a Modulus of 39 to 42 million PSI; and some rods are said to be made of graphite with a Modulus of 47 to 50 million. However, as Modulus increases the tensile strength of the fiber must also, or the rod blank would be stiffer yet weaker, more brittle. Low-Modulus graphite is a forgiving material for manufacturers to work with and it can make an excellent and very durable fly rod. High-Modulus graphite can drive up a rod builder's scrap rate and place extra demands on manufacturing tolerances and quality control, but it can also produce fly rods of almost exotically low weight and crisp stiffness. The difference is akin to that between a family car and a race car; one is no "better" than the other, just better suited to certain needs. Note also that a high-performance fiber by itself does not guarantee a high-performance fly rod; design and construction make a fine fly rod, not merely material. See also Rod Design.

Graphite Rod Manufacturing—A rod manufacturer's raw material is a spool of "pre-preg," or graphite "cloth": a large roll of thousands of individual graphite fibers laid down parallel to each other on a thin backing of scrim cloth and held together by uncured epoxy resin. Typically the fibers may be .010" thick; the cloth is tacky to the touch and stiff and unwieldy. Unlike true cloth, rod-making pre-preg typically has fibers running only longitudinally; there are no interwoven warp-and-woof strands. Since the resin is thermosetting, the spools of graphite are stored in a freezer to keep the layers from sticking to each other.

Because the graphite fibers are only unidirectional, the scrim backing is a necessity. With graphite, the scrim is usually fiberglass, and it is simply rolled onto a rod mandrel with the graphite layers. In fact, the scrim serves a critically important function: It adds the hoop strength that the epoxy and the longitudinal graphite fibers can't provide; without hoop strength the rod blank would collapse under load. Note then that many—probably most—"graphite" rods contain a small amount of fiberglass. However, there are other ways to provide hoop strength that don't necessarily require fiberglass, and a reputable rod company that claims its products are "100% graphite" may well be telling the truth (except for the resin fraction, of course).

To produce a rod section, the fiber cloth is cut into a trapezoidal shape with an ordinary industrial knife and a sheet-metal pattern. The long straight edge of this "flag" is attached—with a hot iron that spot-melts the epoxy—to a precisely ground tapered stainless-steel mandrel, or form, which determines the inside dimensions of the finished graphite tube. The flagged mandrel is then laid onto a hydraulic rolling table; the upper and lower plates of the table come together and, under pressure, smoothly roll the graphite flag onto the mandrel. From there the assembly passes through a machine that wraps it with heat-shrink cellophane tape, and then it is hung in an oven for curing. As the tape shrinks in the heat, it squeezes out excess epoxy, for a better fiber-to-resin ratio; the remaining glue sets and binds the graphite fibers together.

After curing, the graphite blank is separated from its mandrel in a hydraulic pulling tool and the tape, now crusted with expelled resin, is stripped off. After being trimmed to length, sanded and inspected, the hollow blank—which may become half of a two-piece rod, one quarter of a four-piece rod, etc.—is ready to be matched with its corresponding sections, then ferruled, furnished, finished and sold.

There are variations on this basic process, such as adding other layers with the graphite fibers running at an angle to the long axis of the tube (which provides hoop strength without a glass scrim) or even weaving fibers, through a complex series of guides that move around the mandrel, into a finished tube, but the basic process is the same. See also Rod Design.

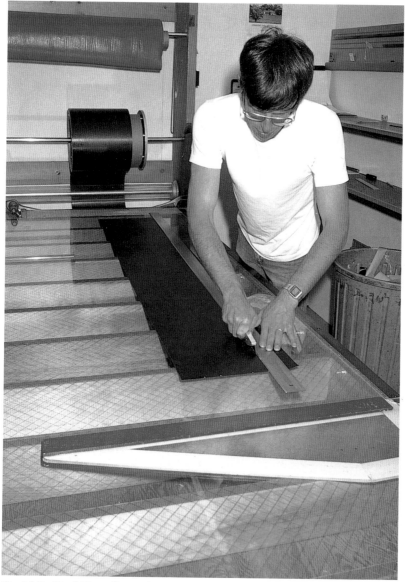

Graphite Rod Manufacturing—Cutting a flag of pre-preg graphite cloth.

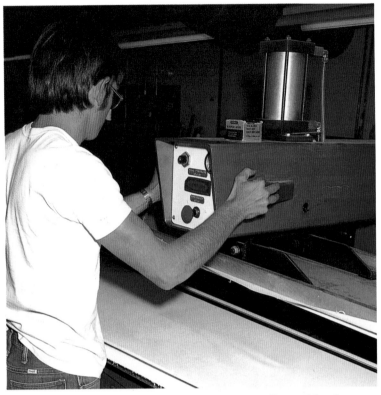

Graphite Rod Manufacturing—An hydraulic rolling table about to wrap a flag of graphite around a rod mandrel.

Grayling—*Thymallus arcticus*, a uniquely beautiful salmonid native to the clear, cold streams and lakes of northern North America, especially Alaska and Canada west of Hudson Bay, and eastern Siberia. Grayling have stricter environmental needs than most other salmonids and they have disappeared from many waters that still hold trout. Some remnant grayling populations exist in Montana, Wyoming, Idaho and perhaps elsewhere in the northern Intermountain West. Historically, grayling flourished in northern Michigan and the upper Midwest as well, but by the early 1900s those stocks had been wiped out (by market fishing and by habitat destruction due to heavy logging) as ruthlessly as the buffalo. Taxonomists once recognized at least four species of grayling in North America—the extinct Michigan fish was called *Thymallus tricolor*—but now they are all regarded as subspecies of *T. arcticus*.

In Europe the grayling, or lipan or umber, *Thymallus thymallus*, is an especially prized gamefish. Folklore has it that the grayling feeds on gold nuggets and that its fat can cure diseases. In central Europe, its status relative to trout is indicated by an ancient adage that if the Count of the Rhine eats trout, the Emperor of Germany eats grayling. Native to most of northern Europe as far east as the Ural Mountains, the range and numbers of *T. thymallus* are shrinking because of pollution, habitat loss and, in some places, overfishing.

Grayling are instantly identifiable by their large, sail-like, folding dorsal fin, decorated with stripes and spots, and by their iridescent olive-green-blue coloring (which may shade from gold through brown to silver-gray) and prominent scales. In the males, the dorsal fin may reach all the way back to the adipose fin; they flaunt it as a threat display in defending their territory. Grayling spawn in spring in shallow, fast streams. They are first-rate flyrod gamefish that feed actively on insects, crustaceans, the eggs of other fish and small forage fish. However, at usually no more than two or three pounds, in Alaskan waters grayling may seem inconsequential alongside eight-pound rainbows and 15-pound salmon. (Anglers traveling to Alaska often pack a three- or four-weight grayling rod too, to cast small dry flies for rising grayling as a break from slinging large wet flies to salmon and trout.) There is a belief that grayling are hard to hold because their mouths are soft; in fact their mouths are only small, not soft, and a well-hooked grayling is no more difficult to land than a comparable trout. Grayling have tender, subtly flavored white meat and in remote waters where they are still plentiful, they are a popular "lunch" fish.

Greased-Line Fishing—A form of topwater fly-fishing first ascribed to Arthur H.E. Wood, an expert British angler who used the method, between 1913 and 1934, to catch a total of 3,490 Atlantic salmon in Scotland, mostly on the lower Dee near Cairnton. He did this not with heavy tackle and large flies but with small, sparsely dressed wet flies (only three patterns, in fact—Blue Charm, Silver Blue and March Brown) fished on a braided silk line "greased" (dressed) to float. In his book, *Greased Line Fishing For Salmon* (1935), "Jock Scott" (Donald Rudd) wrote of Wood's method: "The basic idea is to use the line as a float for, and controlling agent of, the fly; to suspend the fly just beneath the surface of the water, and to control its path in such a way that it swims diagonally down and across the stream, entirely free from the slightest pull on the line." And later, "The greased line, if fished properly (and this is by no means the case every time) has no drag and often is all slack and crooked." (See Slack-Line Cast.) Wood's line "grease," in those days before silicones, was literally that: red-stag fat.

The secret in this then-revolutionary method of fly-fishing was that it allowed Wood to mend his line, upstream or down, to get or prolong a natural drag-free drift. It also lets the angler slow down or speed up the progress of the fly in the water. (This may seem basic, but even now many anglers simply let their wet flies drag helplessly in the current.) Greased-line fishing—with modern floating lines—has become a proven

Grayling—Thymallus arcticus from western Alaska.

technique for steelhead in the American Northwest as well as for Atlantic salmon in the Northeast, and it applies to wetfly fishing some of the art of controlling a dry fly.

Green Fish—Not a species; a "green" fish is one that is still too strong to be brought safely to the net or the gaff. The term is used most often in big-game trolling, where the possibility exists of boating a fairly large fish—on 80- or 130-pound-class tackle, for example—simply by overmuscling it with heavy gear and good boat handling. But only an inexperienced crew (a "green" crew, in fact) would bring such a fish aboard immediately; a fresh 100-pound tuna or shark can do an impressive amount of damage. Any gamefish that can be summarily hauled out of the water on fly tackle, even 20-pound-class (see) gear, is normally too small to pose much real threat. On the freshwater fly-fishing side, salmon anglers may speak of "green" fish; large spawning salmon are capable of behavior that seems inexplicable and every now and then a large fish lets itself be brought to hand too soon.

(As an aside: While wading an Alaskan coastal river, the author was once clipped at the knees by a bright king salmon that was too occupied in fighting another angler's hook to watch where it was going. More than any incident involving a landed fish, this brought the meaning of "green" fish home. Besides scaring him half to death—the water was waist-deep and too dark to see into—the fish nearly knocked him off his feet. When it was finally landed, the fish weighed only 17 pounds. Seventy-pounders were common in the same water.)

Greenheart—A tough and highly rot-resistant tropical hardwood that was widely used in Great Britain between about 1880 and 1920 for making high-quality fishing rods. It was less popular in America, where split cane quickly became dominant after the Civil War. Greenheart was brought from the West Indies to England principally to serve as a structural timber for building ships as well as piers and breakwaters, but its flexibility and straight, dense grain made it useful for fly rods as well. Its chief drawbacks were that it was heavy and that it could split lengthwise if the rod was seasoned badly or if it was allowed to dry out too much.

Unlike bamboo, greenheart was not split and glued; the rod sections were single pieces of wood. Greenheart is yellowy-brown, sometimes dark brown, and often looks at first glance like cane, but the rod sections are round, not flat-sided as a laminated split-bamboo rod would be. Still today, custom rod crafters in Britain will make greenheart rods to order.

Greenwell—A ginger hackle with a black center; a ginger-badger hackle. A Greenwell can have a pale red edge; however, if the edge is dark red, the hackle is often considered to be a furnace hackle, not a Greenwell. The name comes from the hackle used in the Greenwell's Glory salmon pattern first tied by the professional tier James Wright, of Sprouston, England, and (legend has it) christened and popularized by Canon William Greenwell of Durham. When the term is encountered in American fly-tying—which is seldom—it is often used to mean a "glorified Blue Dun." —*Darrel Martin*

Greyhounding—a term used to describe the long, shallow leaps of gamefish fighting an angler's hook; the resemblance is allegedly to a fleet-footed greyhound bounding after the rabbit. Large saltwater species, in particular marlin and sailfish, often "greyhound" spectacularly, in a procession of sometimes six or more jumps that may cover a 90-degree arc of the horizon. Of freshwater flyrod species, salmon are most likely to greyhound; trout, bass and so on are more "vertical" fighters.

Grip—The grip is where the rod is held. Flyrod grips are nearly always made of cork, which is glued to the end of the rod butt above the reel seat in one-inch rings and then turned to shape with rasps and sandpaper on a lathe. Preformed grips are available from rod-building supply houses.

A century ago rod grips were made of solid wood, rattan, rubber or celluloid—straight, fluted or ribbed. The American rod-making genius Hiram Leonard was apparently the first to use cork; his "ladies' rod," introduced in the 1890s, offered cork for its softer feel and lighter weight. Within the decade, nearly everyone followed suit and cork has been the grip of choice ever since. Some companies experiment with grips made of Hypalon or other soft synthetics, which have been accepted on trolling rods, but fly fishers are tradition-minded. As high-grade cork (double AA, with few voids and with wavy lines on its surface) becomes scarcer, however, it may be inevitable that a fly rod made of graphite and epoxy will someday come with a man-made handle—perhaps one that molds itself to the angler's hand, just as some ski-boot liners flow around the foot.

While a few rod manufacturers develop proprietary styles—such as the Orvis Co.'s "Superfine," on some of its top-end light-line rods—most flyrod grips are simply torpedo- or cigar-shaped. There are, however, at least four other grip styles in general use: The full Wells and half Wells (once popular on heavy-duty rods, for salmon or saltwater), the hammer style and the elegant Ritz, named for the legendary French hotelier and fly fisher Charles Ritz.

Anglers and rod designers tried for decades to unlock the "secrets" of grip design vs. hand size vs. type of fly-fishing and fly-casting, but to no end. There is no secret, no formula that will prescribe the "correct" grip. Some people who focus on the thumb as the driving force behind the forward cast prefer a Wells or Ritz grip because of the surface it provides. Then again others, attaching the same importance to the thumb in casting, prefer a cigar-type grip that drops away . . . . Still others, intent on providing the heel of the hand with something to push against in casting, sing the praises of the full Wells- or hammer-style grip.

Even custom-fitted grips are not necessarily the answer. For some time Orvis offered a personalized grip on its select line of Wes Jordan cane rods: The company would grind hollows into the side/top of the corks just where the owner's thumb and palm fell. It's effective and comfortable, but during a long day on the water many anglers like to vary their hand position on the rod, and this custom grip—just like finger cutouts on a knife handle—tends to force the hand into one position.

(Note that this exactly what's wanted in fitting a custom gun stock: A shotgun should always automatically fit the gunner's body the same way, to shoot to the same point of impact. But fly-casting is not so exacting.)

Palm spread, finger length, web space, flexibility and strength vary infinitely. Just what is the proper grip comes down to balancing off personal casting style, preference, comfort and simply what an angler has become accustomed to. Most rod grips from most rod makers are perfectly suitable for most anglers. Still, fly fishers with unusually large or small hands will benefit by having their rod grips beefed up or slimmed down; too fine a grip can lead to hand cramps, too fat a grip is wearying, and in both cases some rod control is sacrificed. Grips should also be long enough, which sometimes is a matter of balancing rod proportions against human need. Short, delicate rods look misshapen with large grips, but less than six inches of cork is impractical for any sort of casting and fishing.

Grip Check—See Winding Check.

Grizzly—In fly-tying, a hackle feather that is barred black and white (or simply light and dark). The alternating bars of color don't run across the quill at right angles but rather in a V-shape, with the point of the V at the quill, like chevrons. Grizzly hackle is also known as barred rock or Plymouth rock hackle.

Guard Hair—The longest and coarsest fibers in a fur pelt, which together form a protective coating over the softer, thicker underfur. Certain fly patterns may call for tails of guard hair, for example, or specify that the long guard hairs be discarded and only the underfur be used for dubbing (see).

Guide—Someone who takes people fishing for pay. Professional guides often must serve an apprenticeship, be sponsored by an outfitter, and/or pass some kind of certification process. See also Line Guide.

Gut—The "gut" referred to in old angling texts—gut leaders and so on—has nothing to do with intestines; it is the strong, coarse thread with which the silkworm spins its cocoon.

Gyro Hook—A now-obsolete type of fly hook that had a tiny steel point sticking straight up from its shank about a third of the way back from the eye. The intent was to provide a vertical post around which to wrap a palmered parachute hackle (see). It was also known as an "aero" hook.

Fly-Rod Grips

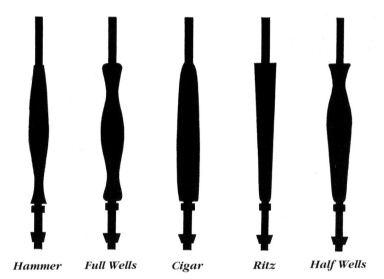

Hammer   **Full Wells**   **Cigar**   **Ritz**   **Half Wells**

Hackle—Fly-tying feathers, from any species of bird. Fly-tying texts from the early 19th Century spelled it "heckle." See also Genetic Hackle.

Hackle Guard—In fly-tying, a small disc of plastic or even cardboard that can be slipped over a hook to protect a hackle from another tying operation. See Fly-Tying Tools.

Hackle Guard

Hackle Pliers—A tool used to grip the tip of a hackle feather in order to wind it around a hook. See Fly-Tying Tools.

Haig-Brown, Roderick—The dean of western fishing writers, Haig-Brown was born in 1908 and died in 1976. As perhaps the most respected of all North American fishing writers, Haig-Brown was the exception to the unwritten rule that "Atlantic salmon inspire the greatest writing," for the steelhead and the Pacific salmons were "his" fish.

While most angling writers are known only to angling readers, he was held in high regard by literary critics, professors of English and New York book publishers, who admired his simple, straightforward prose. Fishermen loved the way he evoked the feelings and pleasures of their sport, yet they also knew to pay attention to his technical advice—for, like all outdoor writers, he loved to pass on what he had learned, whether it was how to tie the Steelhead Bee pattern (*Fisherman's Fall*) or how to cover fast water with a dry fly (*Fisherman's Summer*). Haig-Brown was also an ardent, outspoken and effective conservationist.

Roderick Haig-Brown was born in Sussex, England, in 1908. His first book, *Silver*, was published in England in 1931 (and for the first time in North America by Lyons & Burford in 1990); it chronicles the life of an Atlantic salmon in the British Isles. Although written for juveniles, it was a clear signal that a major new talent had arrived, and the book is still as fresh and worthy as the day it was written. Haig-Brown visited North America in 1926 and then in 1932 relocated permanently to Canada, where at first he scratched out a living as a hunter and a trapper, a guide for tour groups, a logger and even a prizefighter, writing all the while. With his wife, Ann, he settled for good on the banks of the beautiful Campbell River in British Columbia, where they raised their family and where he wrote most of his many books, articles and essays. His daughter, Valerie Haig-Brown, who has taken on the role of curator of her father's works and library, lives there now.

After service in the Canadian Army in World War II, he became a magistrate and then a judge of the Provincial Court. The University of British Columbia awarded him an honorary LL.D. in 1952 and from 1969 to 1972 he served as Chancellor of the University of Victoria. In 1978, two years after his death, a stretch of the Adams River—a key salmon-spawning tributary of the Fraser River—was dedicated to him in memory of his lifelong dedication to salmon and his decades of leadership in fisheries restoration and conservation.

Haig-Brown published some 25 books. Among the most important are: *Silver: The Life Story of an Atlantic Salmon* (1931), *The Western Angler* (1939), *Return to the River* (1941), *A River Never Sleeps* (1946), *Fisherman's Spring* (1951), *Fisherman's Summer* (1959), *A Primer of Fly Fishing* (1964), *Fisherman's Fall* (1964).

This is the conclusion of *A River Never Sleeps*, which follows the life of an angler through a 12-month cycle, and which has been called the finest angling book of all:

"I still don't know why I fish or why other men fish, except that we like it and it makes us think and feel. But I do know that if it were not for the strong, quick life of rivers, for their sparkle in the sunshine, for the cold grayness of them under rain and the feel of them about my legs as I set my feet hard down on rocks or sand or gravel, I should fish less often. A river is never quite silent; it can never, of its very nature, be quite still;

it is never quite the same from one day to the next. It has its own life and its own beauty, and the creatures it nourishes are alive and beautiful also. Perhaps fishing is, for me, only an excuse to be near rivers. If so, I'm glad I thought of it."

Hair Stacker—A short section of tube with one end closed off, used in fly-tying to even up a clump of hair that is to be tied into a fly pattern. The hair is clipped off and put in the tube; a couple of gentle raps against the table top and the ends are neatly aligned. See Fly-Tying Tools.

Hairwing—A fly tied primarily with hair, or fur, as opposed to one made of hackle (called a featherwing, see); usually used to describe Atlantic-salmon patterns. Commonly the hairs are bucktail, squirrel tail or moose mane.

Hairwing—a black-and-white Bomber fly (tied by Darrel Martin) with wing, tail, hackling and body all made of hair.

Half-Frame Reel—A half- (or open-) frame fly reel is one in which the outer rim of the spool is exposed, unprotected by a frame rail. This feature is usually found only on more expensive light- to medium-duty reels; it both reduces weight and allows "palming" the outer spool rim, for fingertip braking. (Note, however, that so-called palming rims are also available on many full-frame reels; the spool rim simply extends out and over the frame.) Heavy wooden Nottingham reels from 18th-Century England were half-frame types, but the modern version was developed by Lee Wulff, probably early in the 1960s. It is reported that the prototypes were made to Lee's order by Stan Bogdan, and then later The Orvis Company put the design into production as its CFO series.

Half-Hitch Tool—In fly-tying, an ungainly looking wire-form tool used to spin half-hitches in the tying thread around the head of a fly to finish it off. Another kind of half-hitch tool is a tapered tube that lets several wraps of thread slide off onto the head of the fly. Half-hitches can be tied easily with fingers alone, but the tool helps produce smoother wraps. See Fly-Tying Tools.

Halteres—vestigial wings; on midges (see), *Diptera*, halteres are the knobby appendages that appear behind the wings.

Harling—A method of fishing that is especially common and effective on Scandinavia's very large and turbulent Atlantic-salmon rivers, where conventional casting—much less wading—may be impractical; essentially trolling, it can be done with flies, prawns or lures (which are legal in European salmon fishing). With a guide at the oars of a small skiff, the angler simply lets a hundred yards or so of line—sinking or floating, depending upon conditions—stream out behind in the current. As the boat drops downstream with its bow to the current, the guide maneuvers back and forth to swim his client's lure through holes and passages where fish lie or travel. The angler's sole contribution comes when a fish is hooked and must be played.

The classic Norwegian harling skiff is a beautifully varnished lapstrake-built wooden boat with pleasing curves and a rounded bottom. The prow may be pointed or squared off, and the square stern may have a harling board attached, with notches for several rods.

Hatch—The emergence of an insect on a trout stream, as when the nymph (see) of a species rises to the top of the water, splits its skin and metamorphoses into a winged, air-breathing adult. Fish begin to feed actively as the nymphs congregate; topwater feeding climaxes as the actual hatch takes place, for the adult insects must dry and harden their wings and bodies before they can fly away. This is the pinnacle of the dryfly angler's sport, and it calls into sharp focus every skill from fly-tying ("matching the hatch") to casting, presentation and streamcraft. See Mayfly.

Haywire Twist—The strongest loop connection for tying solid wire (a shock tippet for barracuda or shark, for example) to a fly, and it is very easy to make. See Knots.

Head Cement—A lacquer-like liquid applied to the head of a finished fly to lock the tying thread in place and protect it from abrasion and wear. See Fly-Tying Tools.

Herl—The individual barb of a feather, usually from a peacock's tail or an ostrich plume. A length of peacock herl may be wound around a hook shank to make the body of certain fly patterns such as the Leadwing Coachman.

Hewitt, Edward Ringwood—1866-1957, the "acknowledged master" of Eastern fly-fishing in the 1930s; the resident sage of the New York Angler's Club; and a free-thinking innovator who often broke with hallowed fly-fishing tradition. Hewitt studied trout and salmon intensely for much of his life and he wrote at least nine angling books. He had a famous fishing camp (he called it a "club") in the Catskills—on a stretch of the Neversink that was drowned when the Neversink Reservoir was created—that most of the angling luminaries of the day made pilgrimage to. He allowed his "club members" to fish there, for trout he'd raised and studied, for a fee. In *Rod & Reel* (November/December 1983) Lee Wulff recalled Hewitt's unique expertise:

"On some evenings, he would watch his club members fail to catch trout although the fish were rising steadily. At the last moment, Hewitt would pick up his rod, walk down to the pool and proceed, in short order, to take a few trout. When asked how he did it, he explained, 'There are several species of aquatic insects rising out there. You've been matching the larger ones, which are easier to see and match. The trout don't like those insects. They're bitter. Instead, they are taking these very small, dark insects, which are sweet and they like them.'

"To the query, "How do you know?' Hewitt replied, 'I tasted them.'"

He is best known now as the originator of the Bivisible (see) and the Spider (see) dryfly patterns, which were both startlingly innovative in their day, and as one of the first proponents of small—#16 and #18—fly hooks. He also may have been the first angler to intentionally "skate" a dry fly (his own Spider performed beautifully this way) across the water, breaking with the dead-drift dryfly tradition again. He developed a unique way to darken silkworm-gut leaders with photographic chemicals so that fish couldn't see them so easily. And he invented what soon came to be called "Hewitt dams"—extended wooden structures placed in a stream that aerated the water passing over them and also provided cover for fish.

Hippers—Hip boots, whether stockingfoot or bootfoot (see).

HMH Vise—The renowned and classic fly-tying vise designed by salmon-fly dresser Bill Hunter, founder—along with his wife, Simone—of Hunter's Angling Supplies, New Boston, New Hampshire. Late in the 1970s, the HMH Premium became the first vise to sell for more than $100 retail. Hunter reportedly produced 341 of this model himself (made to order by a local machine shop), and a decade later these original vises were trading at more than ten times that price. Hunter soon licensed the production to API (see), which continues to make the vises. HMH, while it conjures up regal associations (like "HRH"), stands for "Hunter's Mad House."

Homer Rhode Loop Knot—Streamer fishermen sometimes want a connection that lets the fly swing freely on the tippet, for a more lively action. The Homer Rhode Loop provides that action, but at a price—it is a weak knot and should be tied only in fairly stout tippet material. The Uni-Knot made the Rhode Loop somewhat obsolete (a Uni-Knot loop is not only stronger, it also slides closed when a fish strikes, for a better connection still), but many people still use it. See Knots.

Hook—Like clubs and knives, fishhooks were among man's earliest tools. The historian of the venerable O. Mustad and Son hook-making company, Hans Jørgen Hurum, writes that the earliest hooks were probably made of wood, sections of branch with sharpened, often fire-hardened, twigs protruding at backward angles. Coastal Alaskan natives caught huge halibut with wooden hooks that were reinforced with lashings of sinew and often carved like miniature totem poles, with fanciful heads and faces. Other "natural" fish hooks included the beaks and claws of birds of prey; carved sections of bone, tusk, tooth, horn and shell; and even the hard, strong, hooked leg of *Eurycantha latro*, an enormous insect found in New Guinea (the joint of the upper leg, with the protruding chitin spur, can be more an an inch and a half long).

Such hooks have a dimension to them that steel does not: They often float, or at least don't sink with the lifeless behavior of drawn steel, and they may exude a faint natural scent. For centuries, burbot fishermen in Sweden have sworn by hooks carved from juniper branches; the oil, they claim, attracts the fish. (Such hooks are lures, not just the means by which the fish is snagged and held.)

Iron, bronze and copper hooks led finally, in the Middle Ages, to high-quality steel—the best hooks, asserted "The Treatyse of Fysshynge wyth an Angle," in the 1496 *Boke of St. Albans*, were to be made from needles. (The modern versions of these two products, both relying upon high-quality wire, grew up together.) Steel fishhooks as

HMV Vise—the pedestal-base, standard model.

we know them probably were first produced, by hand, some time in the 1300s. The idea of lashing feathers—as well as perhaps impaling bits of food—onto a hook was already at least a thousand years old by then, if not much older.

(The idea of carving a representation of a baitfish to act as a lure—with a hook attached—or a decoy—to attract fish within reach of a net or spear—may be as old. Hurum's *A History of the Fish Hook* includes a sketch of a fish-shaped "lure" from the Middle Ages. It has a drilled eye at the head and a multi-pointed forged-iron gang hook sprouting out of its blunt tail.)

Like much fly-fishing tackle, today's hooks got their start in England. Around 1650 a man named Charles Kirby developed an effective heat-treating process for steel hooks and London's needle manufacturers expanded into the hook business. The city was destroyed in the Great Fire of 1666 but by the turn of the century the industry had re-grouped in Worcestershire, in a small town called Redditch whose needle makers had built water-powered machine tools. The name of the town was given to the hook-sizing system that eventually grew up there: The Redditch Scale was an attempt at standardization that dictates, for example, that a #10 fishhook be nine-sixteenths of an inch long. However the Scale apparently never took hook gape into account and the differences between hook sizes are uneven and disproportional—a #12 is not 20 percent smaller than a #10. Furthermore, not even the English adhere to their own scale, for two "#10" hooks can differ in length by as much as a quarter of an inch, depending on the type of hook.

Hook manufacturing spread around the world from Redditch. The English hook industry, largely represented by Partridge, is still there (and still making hooks with much hand labor, while their competitors in France, Scandinavia, the USA and Japan have installed highly automated machinery).

In 1877 O. Mustad and Son began producing fishhooks in Norway. In order to compete in a world market so dominated by the British hook makers, Mustad was forced to adopt much of the same nomenclature and a similar—but not identical—size scale. English experts, hired by Mustad to put the plant on line, also transplanted their hook-making terms and traditions. Eventually, as Mustad established itself and its machine-made hooks earned a reputation for uniformity, the company's own size scale evolved, but it is no more logical than Redditch's.

In 1910 VMC—Veillard Migeon et Cie.—began to manufacture hooks also, in Alsace-Lorraine, France. VMC had been making wire and related goods since 1796 (and the Migeon part of the company dates back to 1648). Despite the ubiquity of the Redditch Scale, the French developed their unique sizing system, which is as imprecise as any other.

In the 1930s an American fly tier named Andrew McGill realized that the pending European war would cut off his supplies of fishhooks. He set out to make his own, and today the Wright & McGill Eagle Claw plant in Denver also competes worldwide. Eagle Claw hooks, however, are generally sized according to the Mustad scale, with some variations.

Fishhooks were produced in the Far East prior to World War II, but the conflict interrupted or shut down most hook manufacturers there and in Europe, leaving the field essentially to Mustad and Wright & McGill. As the latter took advantage of the enormous boom in lure-fishing in the 1950s and '60s and ignored the fly-tying market, Mustad became the hook of choice for several generations of North American fly fishers. But their dominance was abruptly challenged in the middle 1980s by excellent fly hooks from Japan. Professional and amateur fly tiers alike quickly came to appreciate not only the uniformly high quality of these hooks but also their logical design. Many were chemically sharpened—by using an acid bath to fine down the points—and carried fine barbs and unusually well-formed eyes.

Hook lengths, in the Redditch Scale or any other, are indicated by numbers between 1 and 28, and the gap (or gape) between the shank and point changes with length. What, if anything, these numbers were originally based upon has been lost in time— and every hook manufacturer's size scale is different. Equally mysterious is the practice of designating extra large hooks by adding /0 after a size number. These "aught" hooks increase in size as the number goes up, while hooks without the /0 suffix decrease in size as the numbers get bigger. Few, if any, manufacturers still make smaller hooks in odd-numbered sizes but they still make large hooks in #1/0 and so on. Until a rational hook-sizing system is adopted internationally, fly tiers will have to continue to

Extra-long or short shank, heavy- or fine-wire hooks are listed as X-sizes above or below the normal. A 1X-Long hook has the same shank length as the standard hook one size-number larger. If the hook is not made in an odd-numbered size, a 1XL #10 would be as long as a #8 but with the gape of a #10. A 1X-Short hook corresponds in shank length to the next smaller size hook of that pattern. Similarly, wire diameters can vary: A 3X-Fine #10 is made of the same wire as a #16 (same hook type, in even sizes only). A 1X-Stout has the wire diameter of the next larger hook.

Hook Keeper—The small wire ring or loop, usually just above the grip of a fly rod, through which the angler is meant to hook his fly when he has reeled the line up and is moving from one pool to another or taking a break. Unfortunately, the hook keeper is also usually near the balance point of the rod, and thus many an angler has accidentally stuck himself while carrying a rigged rod in hand. Rod makers insist on putting keepers on their products because they hate to see anglers jabbing the hook into the cork grip instead (and also because many fishermen simply expect to see one on a fly rod, particularly an expensive rod). Most experienced fly fishers, however, have learned to loop the leader around the bottom of the reel and hook the fly to the stripping guide. Not only does that keep the fly safely away from their hands, it almost always means the entire length of the leader will be beyond the rod's tiptop (see). That in turn does away with having to shake the leader-line connection out of the tiptop for the next cast, and it also means no sharp kink will be formed in the butt of the leader, where it bent around the tiptop.

Hook Sharpening—All but the smallest dryfly hooks, the largest custom-made big-game hooks, or some of the new-generation chemically sharpened hooks need sharpening right out of the box. And even those that were properly tipped at the factory have been dulled by shipping and handling, corrosion, bumping around in a fly box or simply catching fish—or brush, rocks, fingers, etc. Research by hook makers indicates that a dull hook requires two to three times as much force to set as a sharp hook does. Furthermore, it is not only the point of the hook that must be sharp—the tip of the point makes the initial puncture; the rest, including the barb (or the hump where the barb was flattened), must follow along with minimal resistance.

Several years ago, Berkley and Company's Paul Johnson looked into needle design. (Needles and fishhooks have been related since the 17th Century—see Hook.) He learned that a point known as a sidecut spatula ellipsoid was found to provide superior penetration and minimal tissue damage in delicate eye surgery. Field and lab tests proved its efficiency in fishhooks as well. The drawing shows the sidecut spatula shape, as dressed with a fine jeweler's file and 180-grit emery paper. The cutting edge of the ellipsoid runs around the point; in cross-section, the edges are perpendicular to the bend of the hook and taper off into the wire near the barb.

Very small hooks, or hooks with very fine points (such as many Japanese fly hooks have) can be almost impossible to sharpen; use a fine grit and stroke the hook gently on its side in the direction away from the point.

Big-game fishermen often prefer a triangular (in cross-section) point, roughed in with a file and then finished with an oilstone or tool hone. The apex of the triangle is a knife edge that runs from the tip of the point up to the tip of the barb. The other two edges are honed as well. This makes a very strong point that cuts in three directions and helps to insure that the barb seats properly. It is said that in certain conditions such a hook can eventually cut itself free, but many professionals put their trust in it.

Hoop Strength—The ability of a hollow fly rod section to keep its walls and its cross-sectional shape (the "hoop") intact while the rod is being flexed, in casting or fighting a fish. Without sufficient hoop strength, the rod blank would collapse under load. See Rod Action.

Howell Process, The—Named for its inventor, Gary Howell, the patented Howell Process is a method of laying down filaments into a tubular fishing-rod section. It was first used with glass fiber and then adapted to graphite, but it is much less common than the wrapped-mandrel construction method (see Graphite Rod Manufacturing), which is simpler, less expensive and produces a rod blank of equal or higher quality. Howell Process rods are similarly hollow and made with mandrels, but it takes two steps: First the mandrel is spiral-wrapped with resin-dipped fibers running at a high

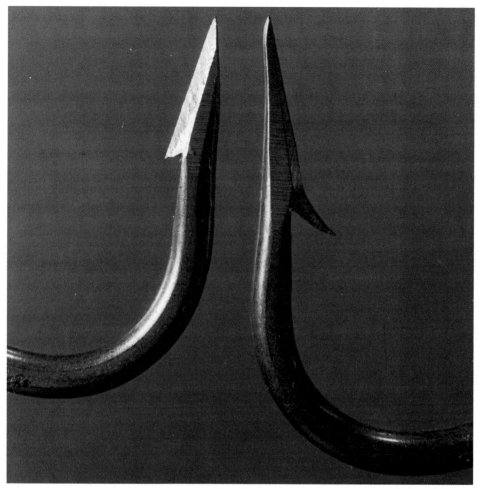

***Hook Sharpening—on the right, a factory hook; on the left, a barbless hook that
has been sharpened to a triangular knife edge.***

angle around its circumference (for hoop strength—see). Then, for beam strength, an
outer layer of fibers is laid down longitudinally over the first wrap, parallel to the long
axis of the blank. A die travels up the blank as the fibers are applied, to shape the outer
wall, and then (as with conventional construction) the assembly is wrapped with
special cellophane tape. In the curing oven the tape shrinks, to squeeze out excess
resin and improve the fiber-to-resin ratio, and the remaining resin then hardens to bind
the fibers together. Howell Process rods usually have solid tips because the inner fibers
can't bend far enough to wrap around the tiny circumference of the mandrel there.

A complex variation of the Howell Process is a method of weaving fibers around a mandrel by feeding the fibers from heads that move helically around and along the mandrel.

Huchen—*Hucho hucho* is a primitive, and now rare, generally landlocked salmonid native to much of northern Europe and Asia; it is closely related to another *hucho*, the taimen (and both are closely related to the various charrs.) Huchen are native as far east as Japan—where they are called *ito*, and prized by anglers—and west to the Danube River. They were once a popular stocking species in Europe; early in the 20th Century huchen were introduced into England's River Thames. It was thought they might replace the Atlantic salmon that could no longer tolerate London's pollution, but huchen were unable to prosper there either at that time.

Huchen are generally spring-spawning river fish and, except in Japan and perhaps Korea, are not anadromous. Yet even without the benefit of migrating to large bodies of water (with their larger populations of shrimp, herring or other baitfish), huchen can grow at a rate of up to four pounds per year, according to British fisheries biologist David Marlborough. There are reliable, if now old, reports of huchen of more than 60 pounds, and Japanese fisheries scientists write of huchen up to two meters, or 80 inches, long—fish that must have weighed more than 100 pounds. Such large specimens are rare today, as more and more of central Asia and Siberia has been penetrated and developed, for huchen (and taimen too) were an important food species to the local people, although by reputation they are not good table fare.

Huchen and taimen are colored like greenish-gray brown trout, but with a slimmer, torpedo-like shape and a larger head, and taimen have distinctly reddish fins. Their bellies are usually white or silvery. Both *Hucho*s are formidable predators, powerful and aggressive, with mouths full of sharp teeth. They became household words among avid fly fishers in the late 1980s, when the Iron Curtain came down and Western anglers began to fish the rivers of northern Russia and Siberia.

Humpback Salmon—Known also as pinks, humpback salmon (*Oncorhynchus gorbuscha*) are a relatively small (generally three to five pounds), somewhat slab-sided anadromous species. They are one of the five species of Pacific salmon native to North America; like the other four, humpback salmon die after their first spawn. At sea they are a bright silver color with black spots on their backs and tails, like all salmon. As they enter their spawning streams, at about two years of age, they turn pink with olive-brown streaks and splotches. Spawning males develop grotesquely humped backs and almost beak-like jaws. They are not accepted as "real" gamefish, but humpies still manage to give the angler a decent thrash on rod and reel. In addition, their pink, delicate meat makes them excellent table fare when they are fresh from the ocean,

Humpback Salmon, western Alaska.

especially for river campers who need a break from Spam.

Though not as desirable as coho or sockeye salmon, pinks are a valuable commercial catch. In season, they are especially plentiful in the coastal rivers of Alaska and British Columbia, and they occur as far south as northern California and as far east as the MacKenzie River watershed in the Northwest Territories. There are now small runs of humpback salmon in a few Great Lakes tributaries and the species has even been transplanted to Labrador and Newfoundland, from which they are slowly spreading. In 1926 humpback salmon were introduced into the Dennys River in Maine, to augment a threatened run of Atlantic salmon; according to reports, several generations of fish returned to spawn but then they disappeared.

In Asia, pink salmon occur naturally in drainages of the Sea of Japan and the Bering and Okhotsk seas. Like chum salmon, pinks enter fresh water to begin their spawning run in late summer, so sometimes they are locally known as fall salmon. See Pacific Salmon, Salmon.

IGFA—The International Game Fish Association; see.

IGFA Records—The oldest standing all-tackle record (also the oldest freshwater mark) is a four-pound, three-ounce yellow perch caught in 1865 by a Dr. C.C. Abbott at Bordentown, New Jersey. The oldest saltwater record is a 221-pound Pacific sailfish caught by Carl Stewart in 1947 off Santa Cruz Island, Ecuador.

A 27-pound, three-ounce brown trout taken by Joe Butler in April 1978 out of Flaming Gorge, Utah, on a 12-lb tippet is the oldest freshwater fly-fishing record. Stu Apte's 58-pound dolphin, caught at Piñas Bay, Panama, in 1964, is the longest-standing saltwater flyrod mark. The white shark of 2,664 pounds landed by Alf Dean at Ceduna, South Australia, in 1959 ranks as both the heaviest all-tackle record and the 135-pound line-class record. (A year later, Dean brought in a 2,344-pound white shark on 80-pound line for the second-largest saltwater line-class record.) The largest IGFA-certified freshwater catch is a 468-pound sturgeon, which was taken on 80-pound line by Joey Pallotta, at Benicia, California, in 1983.

The surge in popularity of fly-fishing, especially in salt water, is reflected in the growth of IGFA's flyrod records. In the past two years, 51 new saltwater fly records were recognized, of a total of 231; there are still, however, almost 200 tippet classes vacant. All the white shark classes, for example, are open, as are broadbill swordfish—and the 1-, 2- and 4kg slots on tautog. In 1981 flyrod-record tippet classes were standardized at: 1kg/2-lb, 2kg/4-lb, 4kg/8-lb, 6kg/12-lb and 8kg/16-lb. And on April Fool's Day 1991, the Association officially ratified a 10kg/20-pound tippet class, a move welcomed by billfish, tuna and shark anglers. See also Big-Game Fishing, International Game Fishing Association.

Imago—The adult, sexually mature stage of an insect's (here referring to a mayfly or certain other aquatic insects) life; also known as a spinner.

Impoundment Striper—A landlocked striped bass that has acclimated to fresh water. See Striped Bass.

Impregnated Rod—A split-cane rod blank that has been soaked in some sort of resin, or made from bamboo that has been so treated. The process has been around in one form or another since before World War II, and at times it has sparked controversy among rod experts. Some held that it made a rod "soggy" and heavy; others pointed to the protection it provided a delicate and valuable bamboo rod. Today, of the major cane-rod manufacturers—Orvis, Thomas & Thomas, Winston and others—only Orvis impregnates all its bamboo rods; the others offer it as an option.

According to Hoagy Carmichael, in *A Master's Guide to Building a Bamboo Rod* (Nick Lyons Books, 1977), rod craftsman Everett Garrison experimented with impregnation in 1934 and '35; he'd heard of experiments at the US Forest Products Laboratories that indicated wood could be protected from decay by forcing resins to infiltrate the grain. Garrison said his main interest was "to equalize the quality of the cane for rod-building. Some of these stalks would have their fibres pretty well separated and I thought that the fact that they didn't have the hardness or the stiffness was due to the lack of a good bond between the fibres." Impregnation might improve a weak bond, Garrison reasoned, as it might repair severe bruises in a section of cane. (Good, rod-quality bamboo has always been rare; anything that might save a few culms from the scrap heap was worth investigating.) He was disappointed, however: ". . . I don't think there is anything to be gained for bamboo rods by impregnation. You have a heavier rod and a harder rod, depending on the resinous matter they are impregnated with. Impregnation cannot make good bamboo out of poor quality cane; good cane must be selected if one wants a good rod. What [impregnation] will often do is hide unwanted glue lines and imperfections in the bamboo."

Garrison was looking for the wrong benefit. A few years after he gave up on the process, Wes Jordan (see), the renowned rod designer at Orvis, began his own experiments with impregnation. Rather than improve substandard cane, he wanted to protect good cane by giving it a finish that penetrated below the surface. The varnishes of the day chipped, cracked or peeled, exposing the bamboo to rot. According to Paul Schullery's company history, *The Orvis Story* (1980), around 1940 Jordan enlisted the aid of the Bakelite Company; its chemists soaked bamboo strips in their resin and returned them to Orvis, where Jordan tried to glue them into rod sections. The problems seemed insurmountable—the glues wouldn't bond to the plastic resin and the cane developed a mottled look. Jordan soldiered on. Eventually he learned to flame-temper the rough-sawn bamboo culms, which drove out any moisture (and also darkened the bamboo). Then he split and milled the cane into segments and glued them together, not with the old hide glue but with a phenolic resin-based adhesive. And these assembled sections he immersed in a heated tank of Bakelite phenolic resin, and then dried them in an oven. The result was a bamboo rod section whose pores were truly impregnated, filled with resin to well below the surface. Moisture or salt could not enter; there was no varnish to cause problems; extremes of temperature could not harm the bamboo; and the lustrous finish could easily be renewed, even after decades of use, simply by buffing the rod on a cloth wheel. Wes Jordan applied for a patent in 1946; it was granted, and assigned to Orvis, on December 15, 1950. Advertisements at the time showed Jordan pouring boiling water from a tea kettle onto an impregnated rod section lying on a block of ice. The new technology was cautiously added to the product line to test customer acceptance. When no problems arose, Orvis went fully impregnated in 1954 and has been ever since.

Improved Blood Knot—A modification of the blood knot used to join monofilament lines of unusually different thicknesses—12-pound-test to 60-pound, for example. The end of the thin line is simply doubled over and the knot is then tied as usual, making about twice as many wraps with the doubled line as with the heavier line. See Knots.

Improved Clinch Knot—The basic knot used to tie flies to tippets; the tag end is extended through the loop at the hook eye and then passed back under itself (between the twisted part of the knot and the tag end). This is probably the most common of all fishing knots, and unfortunately one of the weakest as well. See Knots.

IM-6—A brand name for rod-grade graphite with a high Modulus of Elasticity, or stiffness. IM-6 has a Modulus of 39 to 42 million PSI. In comparison, low-Modulus graphite has a Modulus, or E, of about 32 to 34 million PSI; and some rods are said to be made of graphite with a Modulus of 47 to 50 million PSI. See Graphite, also Rod Action.

Instar—A period in the lifecycle of an aquatic insect between moults, or stages.

Intermediate Line—A versatile fly line designed for neutral buoyancy, with a density close to 1, the density of water. In shallow water they are often favored for tarpon, bonefish, steelhead and Atlantic salmon, spooky species that may demand long, careful casts. Float-tube fishermen use them with great success over shallow weedbeds too. See Fly Line.

International Game Fish Association, The—The IGFA is the recognized world-wide record-keeper for sport fishermen, but it is more, too, as evidenced by its bylaws: ". . . to encourage the study of game fishes for the sake of whatever pleasure, information, or benefit it may provide; to keep the sport of game fishing ethical, and to make its rules acceptable to the majority of anglers; to encourage this sport both as a recreation and as a potential source of scientific data; to place such data at the disposal of as many human beings as possible; and to keep an attested and up-to-date chart of world record catches."

The International Game Fish Association has never charged a fee for any services, and relies only on donations and memberships. IGFA is the only body serving all anglers throughout the world.

Until 1939, when the Association was founded, there was no universal code of ethics to guide anglers in their pursuits. Some rules pertaining to gentlemanly and sporting conduct in marine game-fishing were in effect at certain respected fishing clubs, but they varied from one to the next. To quote the contemporary angler/writer Philip Wylie, ". . . good competition requires precise rules, but ocean fishing was full of quirks and inequities. It was somewhat the way you'd find football if you put a squad of 11 men on the field and learned that the opposing team played with 15 men—but nothing could be done about it."

The IGFA did something about it—namely, succeeded in establishing the universally accepted standards for granting world fishing records. The idea of a worldwide association of marine anglers had been brewing for some time in England, Australia and the United States. The first steps in this direction were taken in the late 1930s by members of the British Tunny Club, who hoped to establish a headquarters in England to formulate rules for ethical angling. The threat of war, however, interrupted their plans.

At the same time, Michael Lerner, a renowned pioneer of angling in the United States, was organizing a fishing expedition to Australia and New Zealand in conjunction with the American Museum of Natural History, in New York. Lerner had heard something of the British Tunny Club's plans, and when he arrived in Australia he immediately looked up one of that country's finest anglers, Clive Firth, to discuss the idea with him.

It was Firth's suggestion that Americans should devise and administer the rules for records. The Australian noted a long-standing tendency of the colonies and the mother country to quarrel about everything, even fishing, and Firth, aware of the saltwater angling feats of Californians, Floridians, Long Islanders and others, felt that England and her dominions would accept American judgment as sporting and impartial.

Firth was President of the GFAA, the Game Fish Association of Australia, and in mid-1938 this body resolved to establish a uniform set of angling rules that would be binding on all the Australian states.

When Lerner and members of his Australia-New Zealand expedition returned to the US, they contacted outstanding anglers, fishing clubs and tackle makers to solicit their opinions about an international association of marine angling clubs. The response was such that on June 7, 1939, the International Game Fish Association was formally launched at a meeting at the American Museum of Natural History. Present were Lerner, Dr. William King Gregory (who became the first president of the Association), the well-known writer and sportsman Van Campen Heilner, and Francesca LaMonte, the Museum's associate curator of fishes and science leader of several Lerner expeditions.

The new officers immediately began to establish angling guidelines and requirements for world-record catches. Records of a sort had been noted jointly by *Field & Stream* Magazine and the Museum for 18 years. According to the minutes of the first IGFA meeting in June, 1939: "Miss LaMonte reported that she had talked with Mr. Dan Holland, the fishing editor of *Field & Stream* . . . , and that Mr. Holland was in full accord with and enthusiastic about the idea of the association." Thus it was that a new system of world record-keeping, to specific angling rules and regulations, was launched.

Another immediate task was to notify scientific institutions and fishing clubs throughout the world about the IGFA. Within six months, the group had two associated scientific institutions, 10 member clubs and 12 overseas representatives. Firth of Australia was elected IGFA's first overseas representative, and others were chosen in Nigeria, New Zealand, Bermuda, the Bahamas, Chile, Costa Rica, the Canal Zone, Cuba, Hawaii, Mexico and Puerto Rico. Among the first associated clubs were the Catalina Tuna Club, the Miami Beach Rod and Reel Club, the Cape Breton Big Game Anglers' Association, the Long Island Tuna Club, The Atlantic City Tuna Club, the Freeport Tuna Club, and the Liverpool and Wedgeport divisions of the Lunenburg Tuna Club. By 1948 the numbers had grown to 10 institutions, 80 member clubs, and IGFA representatives in 41 regions of the globe.

As news of the IGFA spread, many noted sportsmen and scientists were drawn to it. Among the early officers were fisherman and novelist Ernest Hemingway, a vice-president from 1940 until his death in 1962; Philip Wylie, elected field representative in 1941 and a vice-president in 1948; B. Davis Crowninshield, who became an officer in 1948; and Charles M. Breder, Jr., who served as chairman of the Committee on Scientific Activities.

The early days were spent devising angling rules and reviewing data on large fish caught before IGFA was born. The first official rules and the first official world records were published in 1943. That original records chart listed 39 eligible saltwater species. Braided linen lines were used in those days, and the IGFA recognized line classes of 6, 9, 15, 24, 39 and 54 threads.

Noted were 19 thread-class (the forerunner to today's line class) records and 38 all-tackle marks. Only the yellowfin tuna all-tackle category was vacant. (The 54-thread class was later dropped and two all-tackle records set on this line were deleted.) There were some notable achievements on that first list: Mrs. Keith Spalding's 105-pound bluefin tuna on 9-thread line in 1922; a 177-pound, 8-ounce Pacific sailfish taken on 24-thread line in 1927 by C.F. Underhill; and John Stuart Martin's 821-pound bluefin tuna on 15-thread line.

From the beginning, it was decided to keep separate records for men and women, which remains in effect today for saltwater line-class records. It has been suggested that the records be combined, but there was too much precedent involved and there are too many marks that were firmly established over decades. When fly-fishing and freshwater records were added, in the '70s, the separation was dropped, and in those categories men and women compete equally.

As IGFA's reputation grew, so did the correspondence and visitors from all over the world. Miss LaMonte, who served as the Association secretary for many years and as a trustee until her retirement in 1978, wrote: "The Museum already had a space crisis in general, and when the IGFA took on two more employees, they had to be housed in an office lent to us by the Department of Herpetology. Later, that department found itself in a similar need for space [and] there was no more room at the Museum. Finally, it was decided, after nearly 20 years at the Museum, to move the headquarters to Florida. Mike provided the offices . . . and it remained in them at the Alfred I. DuPont Building in Miami until a very well known angler, William K. Carpenter, was nominated President by Mike . . . ." Carpenter became President in 1960 and moved IGFA headquarters to Fort Lauderdale in 1967.

The subject of freshwater records came up as early as August 2, 1940, at the fourth official IGFA meeting. According to the minutes of that meeting: "The matter of freshwater record catches was brought before the committee and the committee voted to do nothing about such records until the mechanism for dealing with our present records is perfected." As the years passed, it became clear there was no such thing as a "perfected" records system; maintaining sporting angling rules proved to be an ongoing process, and IGFA still constantly reviews and revises its regulations, in keeping with changes in angling methods and equipment.

Though others had been compiling records for freshwater fishing and fly-fishing, none earned the international recognition that IGFA's saltwater program had. By the late '70s, there was pressure to make IGFA the world's center of record-keeping for all types of recreational fishing.

In March 1978, *Field & Stream*, which had been marking top freshwater catches for 68 years, officially turned its record-keeping responsibilities and historical data over to IGFA. A few months later, the Saltwater Fly Rodders of America, International, did the same. They felt their records, and the sport of fly-fishing, would get more international participation and interest as part of a larger and more diverse organization. Officer Dick Ream put it this way : "IGFA's established and expanding worldwide contacts in compiling and maintaining saltwater records and their recent move to freshwater areas make them the logical recipient of the ISFA fresh- and saltwater files."

IGFA President Elwood Harry and other experts immediately got to work establishing rules for freshwater and fly-fishing, reviewing past records, and adding new species to the record listings. Their goal was to establish freshwater and fly programs to parallel the system already in effect for saltwater line-class and all-tackle catches, and they launched a worldwide survey for comments and suggestions. In 1979, freshwater all-tackle and saltwater flyrod records and requirements were published for the first time in the annual IGFA book. In 1980 came an expanded program of new line-class and flyrod records for fresh water, and a search for the species most favored by anglers throughout the world.

From the first, angling rules and regulations were kept as simple as possible, though constantly updated. Today they are adopted by most angling clubs and tournaments worldwide. They are the standards for all line classes, and throughout the years they have also been a guideline for manufacturers of fishing lines.

In 1949 the thread-line classes were recalibrated to pounds-test. From that day on, all line samples (which must be submitted with record applications) have been tested for strength. IGFA presently keeps records for 157 species in up to 10 line and six fly-tippet classes for both fresh and salt water. There are also all-tackle records, for the heaviest of all species whether or not they are considered for line-class or tippet records; the records in this category now cover 376 species.

Years ago, prophets predicted that IGFA records would soon plateau off at unbeatable weights, and the keeping of records would come to a halt. But during 1985, 694 records were granted. In 1986 the total was 619, and 1987 saw 519 records issued. With the improvement in all types of tackle and techniques, the exploration of new waters, the addition of the 10kg/20-lb tippet class in fly-fishing, and the spread of the IGFA "gospel" throughout the world, record-keeping has constantly increased.

Record-keeping has helped bridge the gap between anglers and the scientific community. For more than 50 years, IGFA has kept every record application and its supporting data. Today, this vast bank of information is helping develop and maintain the history of angling. It helps settle questions of taxonomy, helps establish common names for species, and helps the anglers of the world learn the scientific names of their species.

IGFA files also hold tens of thousands of fish photographs, more than 8,000 angling books, and thousands of angling periodicals. New works enter this International Library of Fishes as they appear, and IGFA commissions dealers to find out-of-print books. There is also a large collection of fishing films and videotapes. There are even fish stamps and fish scales (in the old days, a scale was required with each record application), as well as angling memorabilia, fish mounts, rods, reels, lures and flies, and correspondence from the great names of fishing. The data is now being categorized and cross-referenced by computer.

In the early 1970s, Elwood Harry, the IGFA's new president, proposed that the organization be opened to individual public membership, to broaden the base for funding, and to unite international anglers directly for better awareness of the threats to fisheries.

Legislation and conservation programs were becoming essential to preserve the oceans. The IGFA, under the leadership of Mike Carpenter and Elwood Harry, began to move into a new role, that of making the recreational angler a force in marine fishery management.

In March 1973, IGFA was re-chartered as a broadly based, non-profit, tax-exempt group with responsibilities for educational, scientific and charitable contributions. Donations to IGFA became tax-deductible. Within a few months, more than 2,500 anglers had joined. At the time, club memberships were over 900, and there were nearly 100 IGFA representatives in more than 65 of the world's countries and territories. No longer was a large offshore boat and expensive equipment necessary to enjoy saltwater fishing; hundreds of thousands of people were now fishing near-shore waters in small outboards.

A new breed of angler meant changes in record-keeping procedures. Late in the '70s, record categories were expanded to include a 6-pound line class, and IGFA began to add more of the smaller coastal fishes to its list of species. This gave inshore anglers, not just deepwater fishermen, more shots at international records, and the rules were no less stringent.

The need for standards in fishing gear also prompted IGFA to forge closer ties with tackle manufacturers. As the metric system became universally accepted, for example, metric line classes had to be established to comply with international technology. In 1976, IGFA established a liaison with AFTMA, the American Fishing Tackle Manufacturers Association, to keep IGFA tackle regulations within the realistic abilities of the industry. Thus, when metric line classes for world records were announced by IGFA in September 1976, they were sanctioned by manufacturers in the US and abroad alike.

In 1978, IGFA's annual rules-and-records list grew from 88 pages to a 240-page book. For the first time, illustrations and detailed descriptions were provided for all major marine game fishes, along with articles on fishing methods, a summary of tag-and-release programs, a guide to fishing knots and splices, and plenty more. The following year, the book, now called *World Record Game Fishes*, was expanded to include freshwater species.

Opening the IGFA to active individual membership also offered advantages in gamefish research. The reports of the widespread new members became essential to assessing certain fish stocks for conservation. The IGFA could now relay to its anglers (and they to others) the need for—and then the results of—tagging and data-collecting programs, and teach them how to take part. In 1984 the Association organized the first World Angling Conference, in France, where groups from around the globe discussed problems and proposed solutions, and it made fishermen aware of the challenges that must be met. The conference established on-going relationships and collaborations between anglers, scientists and writers. Other world conferences are planned.

Individual membership in the IGFA costs $20 per year ($30 US other countries), and entitles the holder to a copy of the annual book *World Record Game Fishes* and a year of the quarterly newsletter *The International Angler*, with conservation items and news of tournaments and notable catches from around the world. Members also receive supplementary papers, news releases and cards, patches and decals. Membership is not a requisite for setting a record.

To join or to get a record application form (with instructions), contact the IGFA at 3000 East Las Olas Boulevard, Ft. Lauderdale, FL 33316; 305-467-0161. —*Ray Crawford*

Jock Scott—Possibly the most famous of all Atlantic-salmon flies, and one of the most apocryphal as well. Legend has it that the first fly was tied with strands of Lady John Scott's famous red-gold hair. A "booklet" called *Collection of 'Wroth Silver,'* by one R.T. Simpson and dated 1884, includes the following: "Lady John [née Alicia Anne Spottiswoode] at the time of her marriage (1836) was a noted beauty, and had glorious Titian hair, from a strand of which on one occasion a salmon fly was made, now celebrated among fishermen under the name of 'Jock Scott' fly . . . ." There is no indication of what part of the fly the hair was used in.

The fly was named for Lord John Scott's gillie, Jock Scott (reportedly no relation), who invented it for his master, apparently while aboard ship en route from Scotland to Norway's salmon rivers. In Sir Herbert Maxwell's book *Salmon and Sea Trout* (1898) there is a caption under a photograph of the fly, which reads: "The original 'Jock Scott' dressed by Jock Scott 1845 when on his way to Norway in the service of Lord John Scott." However, no less an authority than the late Col. Joseph Bates, author of *The Art of the Atlantic Salmon Fly* (1987) and other works, refutes this, quoting an obituary of Jock Scott, written by a friend of Lord Scott's, that appeared in the British sporting paper *The Field* in 1893: "It was while acting as fisherman to Lord Scott at Mackerston in 1850 that he set himself to devise something new and taking; the Jock Scott was the result and, on trying it himself, he was so pleased with it that he gave a pattern to the late Mr. Forrest, fishing tackle maker, Kelso, who one day, I think at Bemmirride, after trying a lot of flies in vain, put it on with such marked success that he thereupon named it after the inventor and, as 'Jock Scott,' it will remain while salmon swim in the Tweed."

"Jock Scott" was also the pen name of Donald Rudd, author of *Greased Line Fishing* (see).

The classic Jock Scott pattern is dressed with hackles from no fewer than 18 birds: swan, teal, grey mallard, gamecock and "barred summer duck"; peacock and peahen (from Sri Lanka, then called Ceylon); Chinese golden pheasant; Madagascar guinea hen; toucan, macaw and blue chatterer (from Central or South America); North American turkey; bustard and black ostrich (Africa); and Indian crow, florican and jungle cock from India. Other materials include yellow silk (or Titian hair), black silk, and both narrow and broad strands of silver tinsel.

Jordan, Wes—The rod designer who, following in the footsteps of Yankee business-men/inventors Hiram Leonard and Charles Orvis, helped The Orvis Company survive the lean years of the 1940s and who supervised and continually improved every aspect of the production of their fine split-cane rods until about 1970. He also invented and patented (1946) the first successful method of impregnating a bamboo rod to protect it against the elements (see Impregnated Rod).

Jordan was born in Massachusetts in 1894 and went to work in the tackle industry in 1919 with the Cross Rod Company, in Lynn. There he learned the production end of the rod business inside and out; he built rod-making machinery, earned a patent on a reel seat, and built bamboo rods of up to 12 strips. Around 1930 the South Bend Bait Co. bought Cross and Jordan relocated with it to South Bend, Indiana, for about 10 years. Not long after he returned to Lynn in 1940, Duckie (Dudley C.) Corkran, who then owned the Orvis Company, recruited him to come to Manchester, Vermont, to take over rod production there.

Jordan was, according to Orvis historian Paul Schullery, "both his own best field-tester and customer"—he was an avid lifelong angler (and hunter) and an exceptional fly caster. In honor of his accomplishments and his widening fame, in 1966 Orvis launched a line of top-grade bamboo fly rods called the Wes Jordan series. When the author worked in the Orvis rod factory in the early 1970s, Jordan's famous two-ton milling machine was in regular use, annually turning out thousands of triangular-section bamboo strips, each precisely machined to within a thousandth of an inch. Jordan himself, retired then, a slight, dapper man who usually wore a suit and a fedora hat, liked to visit unannounced, perch on a workbench and spin yarns for an hour or two at a time. He died in 1975 at the age of 81. His son, Bob, worked for Orvis for many years also, grading and preparing raw bamboo for production.

Wes Jordan in the Orvis rod shop, demonstrating the parabolic bend of one of his heavy-duty three-piece bamboo rods.

King Salmon—Western Alaska: a 50-pound male in spawning colors.

Keel Hook—An unusual bent-shank fly hook developed by Michigan Orvis-Shop owner Dick Pobst in the 1970s. When it is dressed as a fly, the keel hook floats upside-down—that is, with its point up instead of down. The idea is to reduce snagging weeds, by keeping the point up off the water's surface a bit or by shrouding the point in the wings or hackle of the fly. The down hook shank resembles a ship's keel. See Hook.

Kelt—A Black Salmon; see.

Killick—An anchor; the term is used on the Atlantic salmon rivers of the Canadian Maritime provinces, which are commonly fished in "drops," or stages, from square-ended wood-and-canvas canoes.

King Salmon—The largest, least plentiful and most valuable, for market and for sport, of the Pacific salmon (see) is the chinook, or king salmon, *Oncorhynchus tshawytscha*. The average fish weighs about 20 pounds but individuals may exceed 100 pounds and five feet in length. Anglers who fish southwest Alaska's coastal streams in the early summer can often take sea-bright 40-pounders on fly tackle. However taking the larger fish, in the big fast-flowing rivers they seem to prefer, is usually a chore left to big spinning outfits or two-handed fly rods. In many regions kings are among the first Pacific salmon to migrate in from the sea, usually arriving in fresh water between January (in southern California) and June (in Alaska). Like the other species of Pacific salmon, kings are distributed throughout the northern Pacific Basin and up into the Bering Sea and they are found on the Asian as well as the American coasts. At sea, king salmon are bright silver with dark green to black backs and a scattering of irregular black spots on their upper flanks. After they've been in their spawning streams for anywhere from a few days to a few weeks they quickly turn a dark red color; the males develop enormous, toothy kypes. A large pair of spawning king salmon can look like tarpon that were caught in some mysterious nuclear accident.

In British Columbia king salmon may be called tyee. Some Native American tribes know the fish as quinnat, a name that stuck when these salmon were successfully transplanted to the South Island of New Zealand. Kings have also been established in southern Chile. The most successful transplant has been to the Great Lakes, where small (by Alaskan standards) runs of fish up to 25 pounds or so have established lucrative sport fisheries in many lakeshore towns.

Kirby Hook—An old hook style, credited to English hook-maker Charles Kirby, with a somewhat squared-off bend and a point that is offset, or Kirbed, to one side. When seen from above, the point angles away from the line of the hook shank. The intent

Keel Hooks

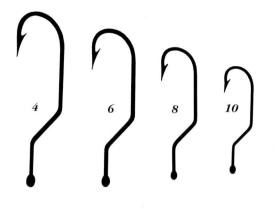

4 6 8 10

Kirby Hooks

4

11

18

was probably to make a hook that twists in a fish's mouth, for better hooking, but the design also provides a small hook with a slightly larger effective gape. See Hook.

Knots—To many fly fishers, a good knot is a thing of beauty and a comfort to the mind. Like a well-tied fly, a solid, craftsmanlike knot, one that is appropriate for the task and tied properly, is a solid indication of the angler's all-around expertise. Furthermore, knots signal not only their tier's abilities but also their own—a knot that is tied wrong almost invariably looks wrong too, even to someone who may not know exactly how to tie it. Hand a fly fisher a rigged-up leader, and he or she will look at the knots even before tugging on them, to look for symmetry, smoothness, lack of bulk, and closely clipped tag ends. A good knot is critical to fishing success; a poor knot is the proverbial weak link in the chain.

Fly-fishing knots are usually tied in nylon monofilament (see), which is relatively stiff and slippery. If mono is too stiff, or if retains its spool coils, dip it in warm water or stretch it between your hands (carefully) or pull it through a folded square of rubber or leather. Do the latter with caution as well; it's easy to generate enough friction to "burn" the nylon and possibly weaken it.

Allow plenty of line to work with, and form the knot carefully. Lubricate the line, preferably by dipping the loose knot in water. (Some salivas chemically attack nylon.) Then, evenly and gently, draw the knot together by pulling the proper end(s). Barrel-type knots, with many winds of line, sometimes need to be nudged into place with a fingernail. If all still looks good at this stage, tighten the knot down by pulling firmly and evenly on the standing parts. (The standing part of a line is the working or main part, as opposed to the tag end.) Apply as much pressure as the line will take, with pliers or gloves if necessary. With pliers, grip only tag ends that will be trimmed off; or use them to hold swivels or large hooks. To tighten a stout monofilament loop, pass it over the smooth, closed jaws of the pliers, or over the rubber-coated grip, and then pull. Thin mono can easily cut skin.

If the knot looks lumpy or otherwise misshapen, cut it off and start over. When the knot look right, test it again by applying all the load the line can take. (Don't give a sudden jerk.) If it passes the test, trim the tag ends off about two line thicknesses away from the knot. Don't trim a new knot absolutely flush; many knots fail when a closely cut tag slips into the turns under pressure. Heavy, well-ground sidecut or endcut clippers work best on monofilament. Don't burn line through, or try to "set" a knot by partly melting it; high heat will only weaken the line. (Only the Goddard knot requires heat; see.)

As braided lines and monofilaments become ever stronger for their diameter, they become more forgiving of less-than-perfect knots. New splicing methods involving braided-mono sleeves have made a number of knots simply obsolete. And cyanoacrylate "super" glues (see) frosted the cake: Nearly any clumsy, ineptly tied knot can be made more or less fail-safe simply by "locking" it with a dab of such glue—the glue binds the individual parts of a knot together, preventing the slippage that usually causes a knot to fail. Glue can even do away with the need for certain knots altogether.

Knots are often rated at "70%" or "95%" of the line's breaking strength. Often those figures are only indications of relative effectiveness, for knots tied by human hands are subject to variation. In 1980, Paul Johnson, a Berkley employee, took electronic testing equipment to an Outdoor Writers of America conference and invited everyone to tie their favorite knots for the machine—again and again. Fifty-three writers tied and tested 265 knots in line that tested at 12.5 pounds breaking strength.

The strongest knot tested was the so-called Trilene Knot, publicized (if perhaps not invented) by Berkley and named for its then-premium monofilament. (It is sometimes known as the two-times-around knot too.) It achieved an overall average break strength of 11.6 pounds, or about 93% of the line strength. Next came the Palomar knot, at about 86%. The improved clinch knot, probably the most popular fishing knot is use, was the weakest: It broke at an average nine pounds, or 72%. The average spread between a writer's weakest and strongest Trilene knots was 2.9 pounds. Some writers, however, were able to achieve strength variances as low as 0.3 pounds.

Perfection Loop
A slightly tricky but virtually fail-safe loop knot for monofilament. In fly-fishing it shows up most often in the loop-to-loop connections between a leader butt permanently attached to a fly line and the leader itself.

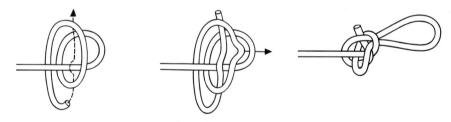

Surgeon's Knot
A very strong, ridiculously easy way to tie two lines (or, in an operating room, ligatures) together, and it successfully joins even monofilaments of different thicknesses. It is nothing more (or less) than a double overhand knot, and it can be tied quickly and securely even in finger-numbing cold or a pitching boat. Simply lay the two lines together with an overlap of several inches; tie a loose overhand knot and then, still holding the two strands parallel and together, pass them through the overhand knot

a second time. Lubricate the knot and pull all four lines firmly apart. If there's any trick to the surgeon's knot at all, it lies in keeping the two lines lying neatly against each other throughout the various twists and turns.

Saltwater anglers use the surgeon's knot mostly to tie shock tippets into their leaders; all anglers use it whenever they've forgotten whatever other knot they were trying to tie in the first place. The surgeon's knot leaves a notable lump in the line even after the tags are trimmed closely.

Surgeon's Loop

A simple, strong loop often used as part of a saltwater leader system or to create a dropper loop. Double over a few inches of the tag end of the monofilament and tie an overhand knot in it. Don't tighten it but instead just pass the loop through the overhand knot again. Lubricate the knot and carefully draw it tight.

The surgeon's loop, like the surgeon's knot, can be used for a variety of emergency fixes when the "right" knot is in a reference book at home, but it too leaves a lump in the line that does not always run smoothly through the guides.

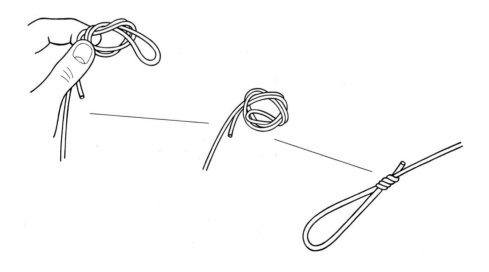

Improved Clinch Knot

Probably the most common of all fishing knots, and also one of the weakest. The tag end is put through the loop at the hook eye and then passed back under itself (between the twisted part of the knot and the tag end).

Trilene Knot

Also known as the two-times-around knot, this could in fact be called the improved, improved clinch knot. It is perhaps the best way to attach fly to tippet for all but big-game fishing. After passing the tippet through the hook eye, bend it around and pass it through again, forming a complete loop; pinch this between thumb and forefinger and then wrap the tag end of the tippet around the standing part (three to five times, depending upon thickness) and bring it back to the eye. There are now two loops at the hook eye; pass the tag through both, immobilize it, lubricate and carefully draw it tight by pulling on the hook and the standing part of the tippet. Trim away the excess tag. Unlike other forms of the clinch knot, this one—properly tied in unscarred mono on a hook eye free of burrs—will virtually never fail; the tippet will break first.

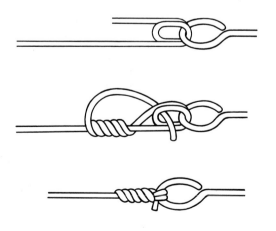

Goddard Knot

A variant of the nail knot, which is used on monocore fly lines. The coating of the fly line is stripped away for an inch or so at the tip, and then the end of the tip is melted into a ball with a match. The nail knot is tied around the fly line above the ball, which acts a stopper to prevent it from sliding off. (In a conventional coating-over-braid fly line, the nail knot bites deeply into the fly line for a good hold.)

Blood Knot

One of the most useful knots not just in fly-fishing but in any fishing that uses monofilament lines, the blood knot is also one of the more difficult to master. It joins monofilament together smoothly and—at least if tied properly—it maintains 90%+ of the unknotted line's breaking strength. Thanks to its streamlined shape (the tag ends can be trimmed close to the body of the knot), it casts well and if need be can be drawn through the line guides of the rod fairly well. Since it relies upon coils of line sliding together, the blood knot is well suited to slippery mono. In addition, the blood knot is unusual in that it can fasten together monofilaments of very different diameters. The sections of a multi-piece tapered leader—that is, a leader that is not one length of mono that has been chemically tapered—are tied together with blood knots. Even fly fishers who use one-piece leaders have to learn the blood knot, however—either that, or change the entire leader when it's time for a new tippet.

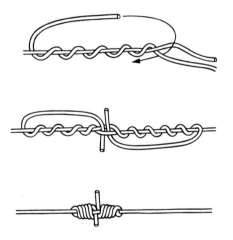

The blood knot requires some care and concentration, especially when joining, say, 6X to 3X, but in time the movements become second nature. The problem comes in winding up to six or seven turns of fine, springy, nearly invisible nylon around another piece of mono, then keeping all that stable while doing the same with the other length, then interlocking the two tag ends properly in the middle of all those wraps and drawing the whole thing up into a smooth, compact barrel shape. And finally, many a harried trout fisher—with dusk falling, a hatch boiling at his feet, fingers trembling and eyes crossing from the effort—has driven his or her blood pressure skyward at the *dénouement* by tremblingly trimming the wrong piece of mono with his clippers and having to start over.

Guides and other experts seem to be able to do it in the dark or while their attention is on a feeding fish, but for decades inventors have been producing no end of mechanical devices to help us cope with the blood knot. Some of them actually work. One thing the gadgets don't do, however, is help tighten the knot—a critical step in any connection but especially for the blood knot: The wraps must be lubricated first and then drawn up smoothly and unhesitatingly by pulling on the two standing sections.

To tie together monos of vastly different diameters—a 50-lb.-test shock tippet to a 12-lb. leader section, for example—the *improved* blood knot can be used.

Improved Blood Knot

A modification of the blood knot used to join monofilament lines of unusually different thicknesses—12-lb.-test to 60-lb., for example. The end of the thin line is simply doubled over and the knot is then tied as usual, making about twice as many wraps with the doubled line as with the heavier line.

Nail Knot

A strong, reasonably smooth connection in which the end of the leader makes several turns around the tip of the fly line.

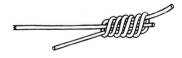

185

Bimini Twist

Sometimes also called the 20-times-around knot or the double-line loop, the Bimini Twist is most often used to create the loop that forms the long doubled-over part of a big-game trolling rig. In fly-fishing, it may used to make the six- to eight-inch loop in the end of the backing to which a smaller eye loop in a fly line is connected (although in reality a blind splice [see] is a better and easier connection to make in hollow-braided lines, be they backing or flyline core). Saltwater fly fishers also use the Bimini Twist in leader constructions that call for a doubled-over section. The Twist is not nearly as complicated or as difficult to tie as many people think, and tying it well is as satisfying as tying a good fly. However, better (that is, stronger for their thickness) monofilaments, other knots, and even superstrong cyanoacrylate glues (see) have left the Bimini Twist all but obsolete for even big-game fly-fishing.

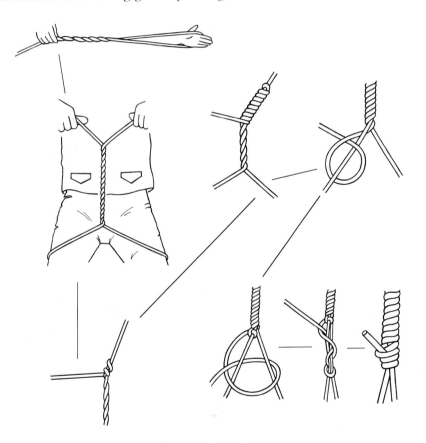

Needle Knot

A slightly stronger version of the nail knot, in which the butt of the leader goes right into the core of the fly line and then out through its side before wrapping around it.

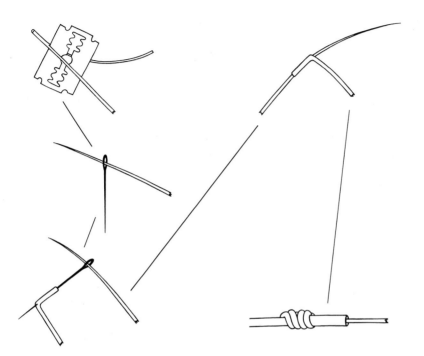

Haywire Twist

The strongest loop connection for tying solid wire (a shock tippet for barracuda or shark, for example) to a fly. Thread the tag end of the wire through the hook eye and bend it back against the standing part in a narrow loop. Cross the doubled wires and twist them between thumb and forefinger so that they wind evenly around each other in an X shape (like tying off a garbage bag with a wire twist). Make four of these X wraps and then bend the remaining tag end out at a right angle to the standing part of the wire. Now, without bending the standing wire at all, wrap the tag end four times around it, at 90°, in neat parallel coils. To trim the knot, hold it in one hand and flex the tag end back and forth until the metal fatigues and the wire breaks. (Don't just snip it off with sidecut pliers; that will leave a meathook that you may regret later.)

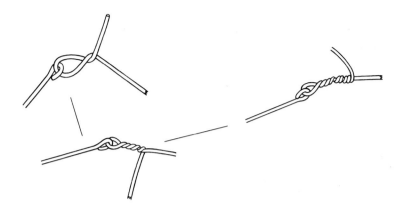

Uni-Knot

The name comes from "universal knot," which is what fishing writer Vic Dunaway set out to create. And in fact the uni-knot can be used or adapted to meet just about every fishing need in both fresh and salt water, from tying backing to the spool arbor to attaching a fly to the tippet. It is a snell-type knot, which relies on the friction of several wraps of line around itself, but unlike other similar knots it can be left loose—to let a fly swim more freely, for example—without giving up any of its strength. It is a good connection for large saltwater streamers on heavy shock tippet: Make three turns, tighten the barrel of the knot, and close the loop down almost onto the hook eye; when a fish strikes, the loop will slide closed, for a better fish-fighting connection.

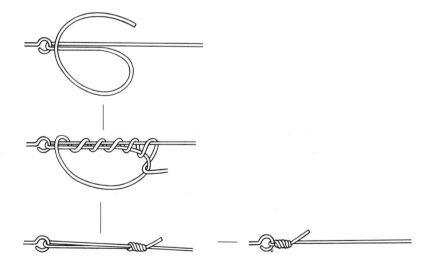

Homer Rhode Loop Knot

Streamer fishermen sometimes want a connection that lets the fly swing freely on the tippet, for a more lively action. The Homer Rhode Loop provides that action, but at a price—it is a weak knot and should be tied only in fairly stout tippet material. The Uni-Knot made the Rhode Loop somewhat obsolete (a Uni-Knot loop is not only stronger, it also slides closed when a fish strikes, for a better connection still), but many people still use it.

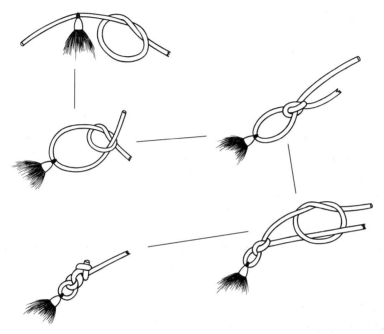

Palomar Knot

An excellent, very strong, easy-to-tie connection between hook (or swivel) and line that doesn't require the finger-twisting or needle-threading movements of the clinch knot. Simply double a few inches of the end of the line or tippet over, pass this loop through the hook eye, and tie an ordinary overhand knot in it—but don't tighten it. Instead, slip the loop over the back end of the hook and then, holding the hook bend in one hand, draw up the knot by pulling both ends of the line with the other hand. Make sure the line loop slides past the hook eye before final tightening. Trim the tag end neatly.

The Palomar knot is not commonly used by fly fishers, possibly because the dressing of many flies interferes somewhat with passing the tippet loop over the entire hook. But it can be done, and it's a worthy connection.

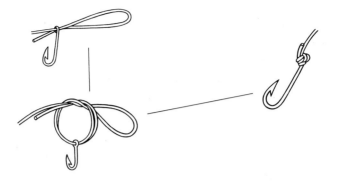

Albright Knot

Named for Captain Jimmy Albright, the dean of Florida Keys fishing guides, this is an excellent connector for monofilament lines of highly unequal diameter—which, in fly-fishing, usually means tying heavy saltwater shock tippets (see) to much lighter class tippets (also see). Often the end of the class tippet is doubled over with a Bimini Twist loop, and the double strands are used to tie the Albright knot to the shock-tippet section. This is a painstaking, very strong connection that most anglers prefer to tie up ahead of time, at home, not in a rocking boat; any difficulties lie not so much in the various wraps as in tightening the various tags and standing parts smoothly and correctly. Because the tag end of the thicker line has to be doubled over, the Albright knot leaves a good-size lump in the line, but it can be trimmed smooth and it leaves both lines pulling along a common axis.

The Albright knot is also a good, if perhaps overly complicated, way to tie a leader butt to the tip of a fly line, and it can even serve to attach monofilament to a wire loop.

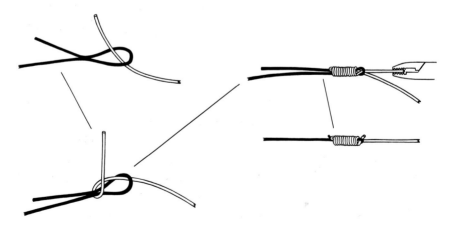

Turle Knot

A slightly awkward knot to tie, but it offers a special advantage to anglers who fish flies with down-turned eyes: The line grabs the hook and emerges from the eye in such a way that it makes a straight-line pull on the hook. An ordinary clinch knot, in comparison, grips the outermost lip of the eye, which on a down-eye hook results in an offset pull that tends to stand a retrieved fly such as a streamer on its nose.

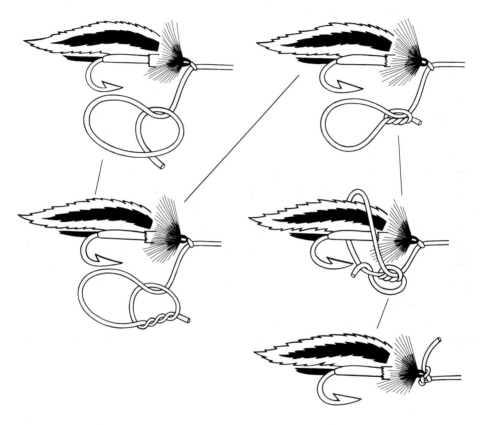

Arbor Knot

A slip knot often used to attach backing to the arbor of a reel spool. Tie an overhand in the tag end of the backing; pass the backing around the arbor and bring it out again between the same frame pillars. Now tie the tag end in a overhand knot around the standing part of the line and draw it closed but not tight. Pull on the standing part of the line and this overhand knot will slide down against the spool arbor. Keep pulling until the first overhand knot slides down against the second one and jams there as a stopper. The grip on the arbor should be enough to let you begin to wind line onto the reel.

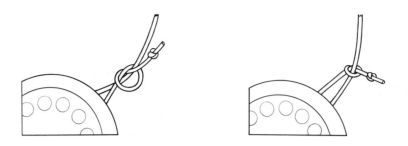

Knot Books

Fisherman's Knots and Nets, by Raoul Graumont & Elmer Wenstrom. Cornell Maritime Press (Centreville, MD) 1948; 6th printing 1980. A definitive work for the commercial fisherman as well as the angler.

Practical Fishing Knots, by Lefty Kreh & Mark Sosin. Nick Lyons Books/Winchester Press (New York City/Piscataway, NJ) 1972.

Fly Fishing in Salt Water, Revised Edition, by Lefty Kreh. Nick Lyons Books/ Winchester Press, 1986.

Fly Fisher's Rigging Kit

These tools will suffice for nearly all fly-fishing knots and other connections with monofilament, fly line, backing, braided leaders and even wire. For saltwater work with wire, some experienced anglers would add a pair of crimping pliers, appropriate sleeves, and a pair of work gloves.

1. Cyanoacrylate glue such as Zap-A-Gap, Hot Stuff Super T or CA+.

2. Aquaseal or similar liquid rubber coating and thinner.

3. Acetone to strip fly-line coatings.

4. High-quality needlenose pliers.

5. Locking hemostats (a valuable third hand).

6. High-quality leader snips.

7. Razor knife (a good one is the Olfa brand, which has snap-off blades).

8. Needles in assorted sizes for needle knots, nail knots and eye splices. Look for tapestry needles with large eyes that will accept fly-line cores. Sharp points aren't necessary.

9. Butane cigarette lighter.

10. Small spool of 30-lb. Dacron backing.

11. Fly-tying bobbin loaded with a good grade of size-A white cotton thread or bonded (smooth finish) Kevlar thread.

12. Several small nails (to heat-set braided leader butts).

13. Squares of wax paper (to keep glue off fingers).

All these items can be carried conveniently in a zippered leather or Cordura fly wallet.

Kokanee—The landlocked form of the sockeye salmon, *Oncorhynchus nerka*, sometimes also known as silver trout. As with landlocked (Atlantic) salmon, the two strains are identical but the freshwater version tends to be smaller than fish that have matured at sea, where food may be more plentiful and water temperature more ideal for converting food to biomass. (A large sockeye is 12 pounds; a large kokanee is four pounds.) Kokanee have been stocked as far east as Maine and as far south as Utah but their natural range is the same as the sockeye's—along the northern Pacific coasts from the Klamath watershed of California nearly to Point Barrow, Alaska, and, on the western side, from northern Japan to the Anadyr watershed of Siberia.

Kype—A growth on the end of the lower jaw of a trout or salmon, especially the males; it makes the jaw seem to curve upward like a hook. The kype becomes particularly large on older fish and during spawning, and a smaller kype may appear on the upper jaw as well. In extreme cases it actually prevents the fish from closing its mouth and it can make hooking the fish difficult—the fly simply slides out of the gap between the fish's jaws.

Kype—An Alaskan male silver (coho) salmon in full spawning dress and with a kype so enlarged that the fly hook could easily pass through its mouth.

Lake Trout—Lake trout are deep-dwelling members of the charr family, *Salvelinus namaycush*, generally unspectacular in color or behavior, with only their size to recommend them to sport fishermen. Of all North American salmonids, the lake trout is regularly outgrown only by the Pacific chinook (king) salmon. In the Great Lakes, where these trout were an important commercial fish before the sea lampreys were introduced and drastically diminished the population in the 1960s, netters occasionally reported lake trout of 100 pounds or more, but a rod-and-reel fish of half that size is rare today even in the big lakes of the Northwest Territories. Lake trout are widely distributed across most of Canada (where they're sometimes called gray trout), even well up into the Arctic islands, and from the coast of the mainland Maritime Provinces west into Alaska to Bristol Bay (the regional name there is mackinaw). In the Lower 48, lake trout occur naturally only from northern New England (in Maine they're called togue) and upstate New York to the Great Lakes region. Lake trout have been transplanted, however, as far west and south as northern California.

Lake trout demand cold, clean water and they generally inhabit deep, well-oxygenated lakes with good smelt populations. They are the premier gamefish of the tremendous lakes of the Canadian shield—Great Bear, Great Slave, Athabaska and others—and anglers come from around the world to troll and cast for these huge, somewhat ponderous, wilderness predators. Catch-and-release fishing is equally critical even in these remote waters, for research has shown that a 60-pound lake trout from these frigid lakes is about 60 years old.

In warmer climates, lake trout escape midsummer temperatures by living at depths of a hundred feet or more. They spawn in the fall, by simply broadcasting their ova across a rocky bottom; the eggs that slip between the stones and out of reach of predators, survive to hatch. Lakers can often be taken on conventional fly tackle in the spring, soon after ice-out, when the upper layers of the water column are still cold and the fish feed near the surface.

Lancewood—An exotic hardwood shipped to England from Cuba and the British West Indies in the late 1800s. Relatively light and whippy, it was used chiefly in building carriages, but it often found its way into flyrod tip sections too. Lancewood is lighter in color and weight than greenheart and not as strong.

Landing Net—In fly-fishing, a mesh bag on a frame used to scoop a hooked fish out of the water. Special catch-and-release nets have extra-shallow bags made of soft, molded material; such a net doesn't bend a fish in half or score its skin with rough knots. Keeping a fish in the net to remove the hook is less harmful than picking it up by hand, and reviving a tired fish is just a matter of dipping the net into the current until the fish can swim out by itself.

Landlocked Salmon—A landlocked salmon is an Atlantic salmon that is unable to go to sea because of physical barriers—a dam, for example—or because it lives in a closed watershed. Therefore it has learned to substitute a clear, cold lake for the ocean, in which to mature, and then in the summer or fall the "landlock" swims up into a tributary stream to spawn. Biologically and physically it is the same as its sea-run relative. In eastern Canada the landlocked salmon is called *ouananiche*.

The original landlocked salmon were undoubtedly cut off from the Atlantic Ocean by some glacial accident. After the last glacier retreated from northeastern North America, 6,000 to 10,000 years ago, these freshwater salmon were established from Labrador and Newfoundland to Maine and as far inland as Lake Ontario. Overfishing, pollution, dams and habitat destruction eventually shrank the range of the landlock to Maine and eastern Canada. Fortunately, Maine began to propagate the species for sale in 1868, and virtually all the landlocked salmon that have been transplanted around the USA and in the rest of the world—to more than two dozen other states and countries—were Sebago fish. In America, Sebago descendants are found throughout the Northeast into Michigan; elsewhere, they thrive in Patagonia—southern Argentina and Chile—where currently the biggest landlocks in the world are found.

Bowing to scientific evidence, the International Game Fish Association (see) removed the separate category for landlocked salmon in its record books, combining it instead with the Atlantic salmon. Because the sea-run variety is inevitably larger, this meant that the 22-lb 8-oz landlock caught in Sebago Lake in 1907 had to be disqualified as an Atlantic-salmon record. To the passionate landlocked-salmon fishermen of New England, this was a blow to their pride—they would have to regard their fish as nothing more than a scaled-down Atlantic. But like the sea-run race, the landlocked variety is a strong and fast gamefish, though a five-pounder is uncommon.

Largemouth Bass—Probably the most sought-after freshwater gamefish in North America, *Micropterus salmoides*, one of the so-called black basses (the other is the smallmouth—see), is a voracious predator that feeds on everything from ducklings to its own offspring. Large largemouth bass have even been seen attacking birds sitting on branches lying over the water. The species lives in warm (or at least not cold) still waters and can grow to impressive size. (The current all-tackle world record is a 22-lb., 4-oz. fish caught in Georgia in 1932.) Lab tests have proven the bass to be the smartest—that is, the most able to learn—of freshwater fish. The enormous proliferation of bass lures is due in part to this ability: Largemouth bass quickly learn to avoid lures they have encountered before, and catching trophy bass on heavily fished lakes is a true test of angling skill and inventiveness. However, even small largemouth bass are great sport on fly tackle; they attack bass bugs, poppers, sliders and other topwater attractor patterns with what looks undeniably like enthusiasm.

Largemouth bass are block-bodied, heavily shouldered fish with prominent lower jaws and a two-part dorsal fin. In color they range from green to nearly black backs over white bellies with a dark, irregular lateral line separating the two. When its mouth is closed, the point of the fish's jaw extends behind its eye (while a smallmouth bass's does not). Largemouths are nest-building fish that spawn in the spring and guard their nests and fry aggressively.

Because of active breeding and stocking programs, largemouth bass are now found in every state of the US, in Cuba, Mexico and Central America, and throughout much of Canada and Europe. Although they thrive in the cool lakes of Maine, Michigan, Oregon and the rest of the northern tier, largemouth bass grow larger the farther south they go, where conditions encourage year-round feeding. The next world-record largemouth—which could bring its captor enormous rewards from promotion-minded tackle manufacturers—will probably be caught in Texas or Florida, where bass are a major industry.

Lateral Line—A row of sensory cells that extends down each side of a fish, from the tip of the gill plates to the tail. The lateral line functions as a hypersensitive "ear" that picks up low- to intermediate-frequency vibrations in the water and lets the fish triangulate their point of origin. Thus it lets the predator home in on a disturbance that might be a struggling item of food, and it also can warn the prey of the approach of a fish higher on the food chain. In many fish, the meat near the lateral line is darker than the rest of the fillet.

Leader—The connector between fly line and fly, made of nylon monofilament. Since the fly line itself is thick and highly visible, even at its tip, knotting the fly directly to it is neither possible nor desirable—the fly would hit the water too hard, the fish would see the line, and the fly could not swim freely and naturally in or on the water. The leader, which normally tapers from line to fly, solves (or at least mitigates) all those problems.

Leaders are produced commercially in a great variety of thicknesses and lengths for every conceivable type of fly-fishing. Dedicated anglers often tie their own leaders, as they do their own flies, and the skills so gained often help them custom-tailor leaders on the spot for unusual fishing situations.

The best connector for leader sections, which are usually of different thicknesses, is the blood knot. A leader is commonly attached to the fly line with a nail knot. Some fly lines are available with short lengths of looped monofilament already attached; the fisherman only has to tie a loop (turle or surgeon's) in the leader and hook the two together. That makes changing leaders simple. (See Knots for examples.) And more and more anglers are using braided sleeves to connect line and leader in an arrangement like a Chinese finger trap.

A leader for wary trout in slow, clear water can be 15 feet long and taper from a butt diameter of 0.019"-0.025" down to a 7X (that is, 0.004"—see X-Sizes) tippet. A big-game leader for tarpon or billfish might be only one third as long and include a class tippet rated at 20-lb-test and a shock tippet of 100-lb material.

Also available commercially are leaders that sink, for wet flies. These are usually of braided construction (see) and contain lead or tungsten inserts. See also Breakaway Leader, One-Piece Leader, Tippet.

Left-Hand Wind—The term refers to a fly reel that has been set up to be cranked with the left hand, while the right hand holds the rod. Since most people are naturally right-handed, and since fly-casting is more difficult that just working a reel handle, learning to use a left-hand-wind reel is a distinct advantage to a right-handed angler: Between casting and fishing, he or she doesn't have to switch the rod from hand to hand. Furthermore, since the right arm too is often stronger or more coordinated than the left, this puts the dominant arm in charge of the rod while playing a fish, too.

Anyone who is even slightly ambidextrous can, and should, learn to crank left-handed very quickly. Others can teach themselves with only a bit more effort. Some expert saltwater fly fishers maintain than winding line with the dominant right hand is the only way to keep up with the long lengths of slack line that a fast-swimming ocean fish can leave behind at a moment's notice. Like the "controversy" over anti-reverse vs. direct-drive reels, this is a topic of never-ending debate among the pedantic; the "answer" is to do what works best for you, based on experience.

On buying a fly reel, the angler should ask it to be set up for left- or right-hand wind, to make sure that the line (or the backing, if they are to be spooled on by the seller) is wound on in the right direction and also so that the drag or the overrun protector (see) are set to work in the correct direction of rotation. See also Right-Hand Wind.

Lenok—A still-unclassified Siberian/Asian salmonid, of the family *Brachymystax*, that is being caught by increasing numbers of American and European anglers who are traveling to Russia since the fall of the USSR to fish for Atlantic salmon. Many rivers hold two distinct kinds of lenok: the blunt-nose variety, sometimes called the leopard lenok, which has a trout-like mouth; and the sharp-nose variety, most often called *limba*, whose lower jaw is underslung so that it nearly resembles a bottom-feeder. Both fish reach five pounds or more; both are typically grayish-brown, sometimes with hues of red or olive, and are covered with black spots. The limba usually has rosy blotches on its flanks. American and Russian fisheries biologists disagree on whether sharp- and blunt-nosed are separate species; Russian scientists report that intermediate forms exist, which indicate that the two can interbreed successfully and which indicates that the two are simply varieties of the same species. A final determination, and official classification, awaits DNA and tissue studies.

Leonard, Hiram Lewis—The most important of all American rod makers, and perhaps of all rod makers, H.L. Leonard was born in Sebec, Maine, on June 23, 1831. He died at home, in comfortable circumstances, in Central Valley, New York, on January 30, 1907. Leonard left behind a famous rod company that prospered at least until 1964, when a fire all but wiped out the manufacturing shop. By then the company had long since passed completely to members of the Mills family, which had acquired an interest in H.L. Leonard in 1878. But in the mid-1970s the company was sold again and then twice more, once belonging for several years to giant Johnson's Wax. The new owners all seemed bent on creating another Orvis, trading on the sterling reputation of Leonard himself (and the highly skilled rod makers whom he taught and employed) to sell upmarket angling, shooting and country-life accessories by mail. However, mismanagement or misfortune or both took a deadly toll: In April 1985 the Internal Revenue Service shut H.L. Leonard down, reportedly for nonpayment of various taxes; two months later the company's assets had been auctioned off, but by then all that was left was some vintage machinery, materials, a few rod components, and a grand old name.

The man who made the name grand was himself something of a prodigy, for he seemed to excel at whatever he devoted his attention to. When he was still very small his family left Maine for New York State and then Pennsylvania; his father, Lewis, was a renowned maker of oars. After high school Hiram Leonard taught himself civil engineering and went to work for a coal company in Pennsylvania. But his health deteriorated, which forced him to leave mining, and he moved back to Maine when he was about 20. Based in Bangor, over the next decade Leonard became a highly skilled gunsmith, hunter, fisherman, canoeist, fur buyer, trader, woods traveler and eventually sporting-goods merchant who was known and respected throughout northern Maine and then all of New England and eastern Canada.

Henry Thoreau wrote, in his book *The Maine Woods*, of meeting Hiram Leonard in a stagecoach bound toward Mount Katahdin: "He had a fair white complexion, as if he had always lived in the shade, and with his quiet manners might have passed for a divinity student who had seen something of the world." This description was all the more unusual for Leonard's company on the trip, a group of his men prepared for a six-week journey through the wilderness and all so heavily armed that, "If you looked inside this coach you would have thought that we were prepared to run the gauntlet of a band of robbers . . . ." In surprise Thoreau went on to note that Leonard, with his "gentlemanly address and faultless toilet," seemed to be the "chief white hunter of Maine" and added that in the spring he'd saved a stage driver and two passengers on this road from drowning in the Piscataquis River—which earned him the right to ride the coaches at no charge.

In 1858 Leonard moved into Bangor to settle down after marrying Elizabeth Head. They soon had a daughter, Cora, but the onset of more respiratory problems drove Leonard and his family back into the woods for "the cure." Not for another 10 years could he live in town for any length of time, but finally he was able to open a gunsmithing business on Bangor's Main Street.

The fishing-rod business began by accident. Tackle historian Martin Keane, in his *Classic Rods and Rodmakers* (1976), wrote that around 1870 Leonard built himself a fly rod in his spare time. Two friends, one the Fish Commissioner of Maine, were so impressed with it that they asked Leonard to build rods for them. Another friend sent a Leonard rod—these had solid ash butts and lancewood tips—to Bradford & Anthony, the prominent sporting-goods dealer in Boston. (Today the store is called Stoddard's and it is the oldest continuously operating fly shop in the US; see Dame, Stoddard.) The store asked him if he could also build split-cane rods. He said he'd do better than the rods Bradford & Anthony showed him. Keane quotes a 1905 letter in which Leonard says he was unimpressed with those first rods he saw, which were of four-strip construction, and that he invented six-strip rods as improvements. Although six-strip bamboo rods (see Cane Rod Building) had been made elsewhere at least a decade earlier, it is possible that Leonard didn't know of them and therefore believed he had invented modern six-strip cane rods.

He certainly could have, for he was a brilliant, inventive, painstaking, demanding engineer and craftsman. Around 1871 Leonard moved into a larger building and began to concentrate on making fishing rods. He and his burgeoning company went on to dominate the tackle market like no other. These early rods, beside being made of Calcutta cane, were not hexagonal; they were planed round. In 1875 Leonard was awarded a patent for his waterproof ferrule, an important if subtle advancement that could greatly extend the life of a heavily fished rod. Three years later he developed the modern serrated ferrule, which could fit onto (and also seal the end of) a hexagonal-section rod. Within a few more years his company was no longer rounding off the corners of its rods but leaving those strong outer fibers in place to contribute to the rod action. As Leonard continually refined and re-refined the tapers of his rods, he also sought ways not only to boost production (back orders were apparently always a problem) but also to make his rods always more consistent in their quality and action. The answer to both concerns was his world-famous beveler, which was developed in the late 1870s. See Milling Machine.

As demand continued to outstrip production, Leonard took on a partner named Kidder, who soon sold his interest to William Mills & Son, the tackle dealer in New York City. Mills persuaded Leonard to move the factory closer to the store, to cut down on shipping and improve order fulfillment. They chose Central Valley, New York, and in 1881 the two partners built what Keane calls "the most modern rod-building facility in the nation." And with that, Bangor was eclipsed as the rod-building capital of the US, if not the world, for Leonard brought a number of his Maine craftsmen with him and set about hiring and training others. Central Valley became to bamboo rod-building what Redditch, England, was to hook-making or, later, Detroit to automobiles.

Leonard Reel—See Raised-Pillar Reel.

Level Line—A type of fly line that has no changes in its diameter, no bulky casting head or tapered sections; although it has a plastic coating over a braided core, as most fly lines do, it is level, or constant, in its thickness from one end to the other. See Fly Line.

Lie—The position a fish holds in the water, usually for feeding; its "home." A stream trout's lie is determined by the pecking order in that stretch of water: The largest, strongest, most predatory trout takes the best—i.e. most productive—station, where the mix of food, cover and cool,oxygenated water is most beneficial. A trout's lie may determine, to some extent, how fast and/or how large it will grow, or can grow. Leaving aside the need for cover—shade and protection from other predators—the ideal lie is one that requires the fish to expend little energy to stay in place, yet positions the fish alongside a current lane that brings food close by. In moving water, trout holding in their lies face upstream, to see what the current will bring; for shelter from the current, they will hover in the lee of a rock or a downed tree, or in an undercut embankment. At certain times trout leave their lies to cruise their stretch of river in a more active hunt for food.

Limerick Hook—An old Irish hook design that is characterized by a gradual transition from hook shank to bend, followed by a much more sharply bent transition from bend to point. Most streamer hooks are Limerick types. Because of the abrupt decrease in the bend radius, Limerick hooks are inherently somewhat weak and in the larger sizes should be made of relatively heavy wire. See Hook.

Limerick Hooks

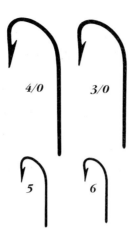

4/0   3/0

5   6

Line—When fly fishers speak of "lining" a fish, they mean they have spooked the fish by letting it see the line (or the leader) before it had a chance to take the fly. A lined fish may leave its feeding station or change its course, or it may show no outward sign of having been spooked except a new unwillingness to investigate the fly. Even unsophisticated wilderness fish may react badly to being lined, for nearly all shallow-water fish are nervous about threats from above. Lining can take place on the water, if the final presentation cast happens to drop the line (instead of the tippet and fly) over the fish by mistake, or it may happen during false-casting, if the fish spots and reacts to the line when it's still in the air. Strongly colored lines can show up very clearly against sky or wooded banks, and a wet fly line may sparkle briefly when sunlight catches it a certain way in the air.

Bonefish in shallow water are particularly susceptible to being lined either way, for the tropical sun often not only highlights a line in the air, it also casts a strong line shadow on the flat that the fish is slowly feeding across. Trout holding in the current are no less sensitive to being lined, and part of the skill in taking such fish lies in learning to cast just far enough to present the fly but not so far that the line intrudes into the picture.

To avoid lining a fish in the air, false-cast short and then shoot the final cast with precision. Or false-cast in a slightly different direction, changing angle only on the final cast to lay the fly down where it should go. Stream fishermen sometimes move above (up-current of) a wary trout and make a downstream presentation (see), so the fly is the first thing to float into the trout's view, with leader and line out of sight behind it—

which presents its own problems and challenges.

Line Dressing—A treatment applied to fly line to clean it and to restore at least some of its casting finish and even its ability to float. Most fly line coatings—the part that gives the line its particular taper and weight—are some form of polyvinyl chloride (PVC) and they do wear out over time and use. The ultraviolet portion of sunlight attacks plastic; sweat, sun oil, bug dope, fish slime, salt, outboard-motor gas and oil, natural tannin and pollutants eventually affect fly lines as well. (The chemical known as Deet in many insect repellents dissolves plastic on contact.) Line coatings deteriorate mechanically too—they dry out and crack with age or they are abraded by sloppy casting over gravel surfaces or just by being stepped on. A good line dressing can slow the deterioration and keep a line casting smoothly, but only if it's used often. Some line dressings are applied with a rag, others come in impregnated pads that the line is drawn through. Periodically, rumors sweep the fly-fishing world of one or another automotive or household cleaner that works miracles on fly lines, but simply cleaning and refurbishing a line often is probably more important than what it's done with.

Until microballoons came along, fly lines had to be dressed in order to float. The "grease" Arthur Wood used in the 1920s to dress his silk line (see Greased-Line Fishing) was red-stag fat. See also Fly Line.

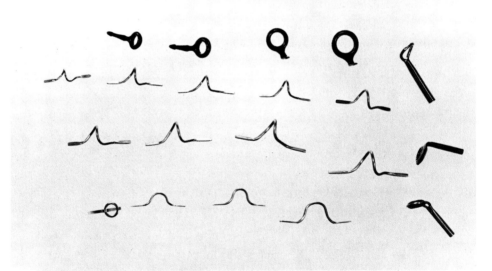

Line Guides— At the top are ring guides; the others are snake guides, with (right) tiptops and (lower left) a ring-type hook keeper.

Line Guide—One of the rings attached to a fishing rod to keep the line close to the rod sections, so the angler can take advantage of the casting and fish-fighting characteristics built into the rod. Too many line guides on a rod add unnecessary weight and stiffness; too few guides let the line slap uncontrollably in casting and don't spread the load properly along the rod. Ring guides are full circles in a wire frame (often with an insert of some hard, smooth material); most of the guides on a fly rod are snake guides, twists of steel wire that do not make a complete circle. The stripping guide on a fly rod—the lowest of the guides, just above the reel—is, however, a ring guide. Guides are usually attached to fly rods by wraps of thread that are then varnished for strength. The part of the line guide that sits directly on the rod is called the foot. See Single-Foot Guide, Snake Guide, Stripping Guide.

Line Winder—A device, usually powered by a reversible electric motor and mounted on a tabletop or a large plate, for spooling line on or off reels. The essential elements include a spindle to hold a bulk spool of line, some kind of universal mount to clamp a variety of reels in place, a drive socket for the reel crank, a counter to measure the line being spooled, and a series of eyes or rollers to guide the line as it flows. Often a foot pedal serves as a variable-speed control, so the operator can feed line accurately and under proper tension. For a fly shop or guide service, a line winder saves hundreds of hours of hand labor in a season. Some line winders can also be used to test reel drags under high load and RPM.

Long-Belly Line—A variant of the basic weight-forward fly line with a longer front taper and belly that comes close to being the front half of a double-taper line. See Fly Line.

Long-Line Release—A tongue-in-cheek euphemism for a lost fish, one that escaped the hook while there was still a long line on the water. In the catch-and-release era, when mortality (see) studies began to indicate that handling fish (particularly delicate salmonids) could do more injury than hooking them, the term "long-line release" was elevated to pseudo-scientific jargon to dismiss the loss of fish as intentional, meant to avoid damaging the fish by bringing it to hand.

Which is not to say that it is of recent vintage. In his story "North Umpqua Steelhead," which appeared in the September 1936 issue of *Sports Afield*, best-selling author and world-class fly fisherman Zane Grey summed up his party's catch on the river: 64 steelhead of between five and 12 pounds caught and kept; countless others let go out of hand or by "long line release."

Line Winder—set up with a fly reel (right), a yardage counter (center) and a bulk spool of backing. The black box houses a reversible electric motor, controlled by a foot-pedal rheostat.

Long-Lining—A phrase used in different regions for a variety of angling methods that involve . . . long lengths of line. In Canada's Maritime provinces, for example, fishermen sometimes catch spring salmon by long-lining; that is, by letting 100 yards or so of sinking line hang off an anchored skiff. As the angler retrieves slowly, the current sweeps the fly back and forth.

Commercial long-lining is an altogether different matter. This is high-seas hook-and-line fishing on an incredible scale. Fishing lines sometimes dozens of miles long are floated in the sea, with thousands of short lines hanging from them, each dangling a baited hook. Automated machinery on the fishing boat baits, sets and then retrieves the lines, and even removes and strips the fish. Compared to the "walls of death"—miles of gill nets that stop everything that swims into them—long-lines are relatively discriminatory. By adjusting hook size, bait, depth and location, the boat can concentrate on certain species; and when a hook is filled, no other fish can be destroyed by it.

Low-Water Fly—A small, simply dressed variant of any fly pattern. Unlike the full-size version, it is more effective in low, clear, slow-moving water. The distinction between normal and low-water flies is most important in fishing for Atlantic salmon, where a

---

low-water pattern is a small fly tied on a large hook. To balance the smaller dressing, low-water hooks are generally made of a finer wire and have a slightly longer shank than a standard hook of that number; the gape, however, will be the same. The reduced bulk of the dressing is more appropriate for the water conditions, yet the fly has all the holding power of a large hook. In addition, the longer shank helps take finicky, short-striking fish.

Although salmon do not feed while spawning, low-water flies may suggest the smaller insects found in salmon rivers in late summer, when water levels are often low. The normal large flies, which appeal to salmon earlier in the season, may imitate the shrimp, baitfish and other larger food they were recently feeding on in the sea.

Loop-to-Loop—a simple means of joining two lines.

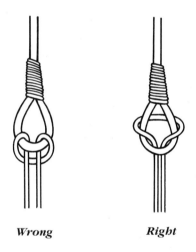

Wrong   **Right**

Mandrel—The steel bar around which raw graphite or fiberglass cloth (or "pre-preg"—see) is wrapped in order to form a fishing-rod blank. To get the particular casting action and fishing characteristics that are wanted in a certain rod, the mandrel has to be precisely tapered and perfectly round in cross-section. (The thickness and orientation of the sheets of fibers that are wrapped around it must also be exactly controlled.) Generally, a different mandrel—or set of mandrels, butt and tip, for two-piece rods—has to be machined for each rod model in a manufacturer's line.

At the butt end, a mandrel has a slot or hole by which it can be hung, tip down, in a curing oven, where the thermosetting epoxy that binds the graphite or fiberglass together hardens. Then the resultant tube has to pulled off the mandrel, usually by some sort of hydraulic stripper. So, to keep the scrap rate low, the surface of the mandrel has to be polished smooth. Over time, as the mandrel is used, the surface of the steel becomes "seasoned," like a good omelette pan.

Marabou—In fly-tying, a long, fluffy feather originally from the African marabou stork; the modern substitute is an equally fluffy immature turkey feather. Because of its delicacy, marabou tied into a fly undulates with the slightest motion or whisper of current and it makes the fly seems to "breathe" in the water.

Marbury, Mary Orvis, 1856-1914—She was the first (of four—the others were boys) child of Charles F. Orvis and Laura Walker Orvis, of Manchester, Vermont. The year she was born, her father founded the company that still bears the family name and that is still based in Manchester. The success of the company is due in no small part to Mary's efforts as a fly tier, businesswoman, author and editor. Mary wed a John Marbury in 1877, but the marriage didn't "take"; the two separated and their only child died young.

In the Victorian era, fly-fishing became popular as a "refined" way to fish, and the modern merchandising triangle of manufacturer/retailer, publisher and consumer was established. It functioned just as it does today—small companies make tackle, the sporting press writes about it, and consumers read and buy. Charles Orvis knew how to play this game; He also knew that fishing flies were in short supply, late in the 19th Century—at least the sort of flies that were, first, effective on trout and other gamefish, and second, recognized by anglers in general. Exotic materials for tying fliers—from polar bear hair to macaw plumes—were available, and in a great flurry of activity every region of America was busily developing its own fly patterns and its own names for flies that anglers in other watersheds might know as something entirely different.

Into the breach stepped daughter Mary. To assure her dad of a reliable source of flies tied to consistent standards, in 1876 she took over the company's commercial fly production. She had earlier shown considerable interest in fly-tying, so much that

Charles had hired an expert fly "dresser" to come to Vermont from New York City to teach her all he knew. Mary's half-dozen tiers, all young women, worked upstairs in a white clapboard building on Union Street that still belongs to The Orvis Company. At the time there were larger fly factories in America, but from this small one would come not only very fine flies but also the beginnings of the standardization that brought order to fly-pattern chaos.

Mary Orvis is best known for her book *Favorite Flies and Their Histories*. It was the first of many about flies to be published in America, and it began to take shape around 1890. Mary wrote to anglers around the country ("in the localities affording the finest fishing") soliciting information on their favorite flies and how they were made and fished. The resulting book was published in 1892. It was so well received that, according to Schullery & Hogan's *The Orvis Story*, it went through at least nine printings by 1896—a fishing best-seller by any standard. To date, *Favorite Flies* has been reprinted only twice since then—in 1955 by the Charles T. Branford Co. of Boston, and by The Wellfleet Press, Secaucus, NJ, in 1988.

Mary's efforts as compiler and editor resulted in publishable responses from more than 200 fly fishermen in 38 states, detailing almost 300 flies. At last there was a definitive encyclopedia of American (as opposed to British) patterns, accompanied by fascinating and expert advice on their use.

When Mary Orvis died, in 1914, the *Fishing Gazette* headlined her obituary this way: "The Most Famous But One Female Angling Author." As much as anything said or written about her in her lifetime, it signaled the place she would occupy in sportfishing. For the *most* famous of female angling authors would be none other than the mysterious Dame Juliana Berners (see), who reputedly wrote "The Treatyse of Fysshnge wyth an Angle," a chapter in *The Boke of St. Albans*, which appeared in 1496.

Matching the Hatch—The purist dryfly angler's holy grail is to be able to put on the water an exact imitation (color, size, silhouette, stance, behavior) of whatever species of aquatic insect is emerging from its shuck at a particular moment; in other words, to match the hatch. The intent being, of course, to lure the trout that come to the surface to feed on the naturals into taking the artificial. No one knows how long fly fishers have talked of "matching the hatch," but angler-author Ernest Schwiebert popularized the phrase when he used it as the title of his seminal first book, published in 1955.

Mayfly—The mayfly is the archetypal "fly" around which fly-fishing evolved, an insect celebrated for centuries in prose and poem. In North America there are at least 500 species of mayfly—of the order *Ephemeroptera*, which is derived from the Greek *ephemeros*, meaning "lasting a day," hence the old name "dayfly"—and many of these

Mayfly—a large green drake.

and others are found on trout streams throughout the rest of the world as well. The dozen fly patterns that the apocryphal Dame Juliana Berners (see) lists in the "Treatyse of Fysshynge wyth an Angle" are mostly mayfly imitations, and the hundreds (if not thousands) of angling authors who followed her into publishing history also chose to place the mayfly top-center on their lists.

While mayflies are not the trout's most plentiful food—the midges (see) most likely claim that honor, at least in numbers, if not in mass—they may be the most notable. Mayflies are so-called "upwing" insects; these finely veined appendages, arranged symmetrically in two pairs, large and small, rise from the insects' shoulders. The arched thorax, ahead of the insect's tapering, segmented abdomen, sits up on three pairs of articulated legs. The three long, fine tails are balanced by a distinct head at the other end, crowned with a large pair of compound eyes. The impression is of a graceful, fragile creature, poised and alert—as quintessential an insect as the trout is a fish. Literature through the ages is peppered with references to mayflies sailing like little ships down their streams, and homespun philosophers have for centuries used the mayfly's brief lifespan as a metaphor for brave futility. Mayflies are warm-weather insects; in temperate climates the hatches typically begin in the spring—hence the name. From the fly fisher's perspective, their size ranges from a #24 hook (the

Tricorythodes, or simply Trico, mayfly, which may be only three millimeters long) to a long-shank #6 (*Litobrancha recurvata*, the Green Drake—formerly classified as *Hexagenia recurvata*—which may reach 40 millimeters).

Their lives as air-breathing fliers are short—a few days at most—but in fact mayflies live far longer than that underwater, as nymphs, before they hatch into adults at the water's surface. Some species live as long as three years, others only three or four months; the average is about a year. The four major stages of the mayfly's life are: egg, nymph (larva), dun (subimago) and spinner (imago). The nymph is at least as important to the fly fisher as the two air-dwelling stages, and mayfly nymphs can be divided into four main groups, each with their own characteristic shapes, sizes, behavior and habitat: crawlers (*Ephemerellidae, Leptophlebiidae, Tricorythidae, Caenidae*); clingers (*Heptageniidae*); burrowers (*Ephemeridae, Potamanthidae, Polymitarcyidae*); and swimmers (*Baetidae*). As the moment of hatching approaches, the nymphs leave the underwater cover that has protected them throughout their lives and prepare to swim or float to the surface. They are increasingly vulnerable to trout at this stage, and the predation peaks as the hatch actually takes place. While a few mayfly species hatch at the stream bottom and rise to the air as a fully formed dun, others crawl onto the stones at the stream's edge and emerge in relative safety. Most species, however, swim or float to the top and hatch there, struggling sometimes for minutes to split their nymphal cases, emerge, unfold and dry their wings, and finally fly away.

This is the classic "hatch" that dryfly anglers anticipate. While it is going on, trout feed heavily on the ascending nymphs, the struggling molters, and the newly formed duns resting on the water. The flies are also picked off by birds, frogs, dragonflies, salamanders, bats and other hunters. Probably because of the quantities of food suddenly available, the trout usually become extremely selective, keying closely on the color, size, silhouette and behavior of the natural insects. The fly fisher trying the match the hatch may meet with frustration: His or her artificials may not be close enough to the real thing; or there may be so many flies on the water that a skillful imitation simply doesn't stand out and, like thousands of the real insects, is repeatedly overlooked by cruising fish who have too much to choose from. (This can happen with any kind of aquatic insect, not just mayflies.)

The survivors–and there are many—extend and harden their new wings and bodies and fly off the water, ascending gracefully into the trees at the stream's edge. For the next 24 to 48 hours the mayflies congregate on the underside of leaves and undergo yet another transformation, from dun/subimago to spinner/imago. Like spawning Pacific salmon, their digestive organs atrophy and their sexual organs mature. They moult once more, re-emerging—with difficulty, for their final set of wings are large and fragile—as ethereal-looking spinners, sexually mature adults. They leave their cast-off dun shucks behind in the vegetation and both males and females swarm over the stream in their mating flight. After copulation the males deposit their eggs in the water. Some simply eject their ova streams in the air; other species land on the surface to do this; and still others swim beneath the surface to deposit their eggs. Finally, spent and exhausted, the spinners fall to the water. Those that are not eaten by fish die naturally.

McClane, A.J.—Albert Jules McClane, born in 1922 in Brooklyn, New York, was for decades the best-known fishing writer in North America and a true expert angler; perhaps no one was as well versed in so many aspects of sport fishing as he was. In 1947 he joined the staff of *Field & Stream* Magazine and he held various positions there until his death. He also wrote more than 20 books, most about fishing (of all kinds) and about fish and game cooking. McClane managed to be a specialist in several different fields at once: His first book, published in 1953, was *The Practical Fly Fisherman.* Arnold Gingrich, founding editor of *Esquire* and a bona fide fly-fishing celebrity himself, called it "the most comprehensive and useful single volume on all forms of freshwater fly-fishing." Yet at the same time McClane established himself as an expert in spin-fishing as well, and his influence and advice helped that form of angling grow to mammoth proportions in the 1950s and '60s. His skill and knowledge in the kitchen led to consulting jobs with restaurants, hotels and airlines and eventually to *The Encyclopedia of Fish Cookery,* published in 1977. His final book, *A Taste of the Wild—A Compendium of Modern American Game Cookery,* was published by Dutton in December 1991, the month he died.

McClane was one of the very few so-called outdoor writers who ever became wealthy from his writing. His best-selling work, the one that irrevocably (and deservedly) made his name and his fortune, first appeared in 1965 and was updated in 1974: *McClane's New Standard Fishing Encyclopedia and International Angling Guide,* the 1,156-page reference work (from Holt Rinehart Winston) without which no fishing library is complete. As of the author's death, sales stood at nearly a million copies.

McClane's position at *Field & Stream* enabled him to travel and fish all over the world, eventually reaching some 140 countries. He consulted with a number of governments about aspects of their sport fisheries, and this may have led to the persistent rumor that he was "on the payroll at the CIA." Perhaps living in plush Palm Beach, near Florida's expatriate Cuban community, helped this rumor along as well.

McClane never succumbed to star fever, however. An anecdote from his final year shows that his sense of humor stayed fresh to the end: Early in 1991 a fishing magazine, reacting to a rumor, rushed into print with a full-length obituary for McClane—and then retreated with acute embarrassment when it was discovered that he was still very much alive. In fact, McClane enjoyed this immensely, despite the fact that shortly afterward he was diagnosed with terminal intestinal cancer. In late April Lee Wulff (see) died suddenly. McClane called publisher Nick Lyons for confirmation: "Tell me," he asked Lyons, "is Lee really dead? Or is he dead like I'm dead?"

McClane died a few days before Christmas '91, but not of the cancer that was supposed to kill him that summer; it was congestive heart failure. He was 69 years old.

McKenzie Boat—The quintessential fly-fishing river boat, named after the McKenzie River in Oregon. It is similar to the high-sided, hard-chined, deeply rockered dories in which codfishermen braved the North Atlantic for centuries, but the design evolved on its own. On most trout rivers it is overkill—an inexpensive tin jonboat would be as seaworthy—but the McKenzie design is highly maneuverable, holds a great deal of gear, and provides first-class accommodations for a fly caster in both bow and stern. Half a dozen or more companies make these boats, out of wood, fiberglass or aluminum, but few use the term "McKenzie," preferring instead to call them drift boats.

In the 1920s wooden "pole boats" were used on the McKenzie, the Umpqua and other northwestern rivers. According to Keith Steele, of Leaburg, Oregon, who began building river boats in 1950, the next step was the "Rapid Roberts," a square-ended river dory that had one fault: "You had to hit a wave at an angle—if you got it straight on, you'd take an awful jolt." And then, shortly after World War II, when plywood became available, the modern McKenzie boat arrived. The first one was made by Springfield, Oregon, boat builder Woody Hindman. The design has changed little since then; river runners say it will "survive any water that a man has the courage to tackle—so long as he doesn't make a mistake." See Drift Boat.

Medalist—A simple fly reel made by the Pflueger Company (or at least under the Pflueger name) since about 1925. Its significance in American fly-fishing is due to the enormous quantities in which it has been made, to its low price, and not least to the wide range of sizes in which it was offered. For generations of Americans, Medalists were their first fly reel. And until Scientific Anglers introduced its System reels in the mid-1980s, those who wanted to try fly-fishing in the ocean without first spending a lot of money for a purpose-built saltwater fly reel were limited to the large Medalist 1498—the only inexpensive fly reel around that could pack 200 yards of backing and a heavy fly line. In the late 1970s and early '80s, several companies offered aftermarket parts aimed at improving the big Medalists' performance—balanced one-piece spools, for example, that would run smoothly at high RPM; bronze drag components that wouldn't wear out as fast as the stock plastic items; and so on. Because the Medalist

Medalists—Pflueger's influential fly reel.

carries only a click drag, some saltwater fly fishers cut away part of the reel sideplate so they could apply pressure to the exposed spool rim with their fingers. (Dragging your fingers on the other side of the spool, the one that was already exposed, put them in the way of the crank handle.) These modifications, worthy in and of themselves, succeeded largely in pushing owners' expectations beyond reality. No matter how equipped, a Medalist usually could not take more than a few bonefish or tarpon without needing repairs. More than one angling writer noted that converting Medalists this way served only to "make a lousy $100 reel out of what had been a perfectly decent $30 reel."

According to reel authority John Orrelle, the first Medalists cost about $6 in 1928, when three sizes were available. That was not a low price then; Pflueger's most popular fly-fishing models sold for only a dollar, and the company offered stamped bait-fishing reels ("Sold in Gross Lots Only," announced Pflueger's catalogs) at 10¢ apiece. Today, adjusted for inflation, the price of Medalists is far less—almost comparable to those "dime reels." In the 1980s, when imports from the Orient took over the North American general-fishing tackle market, production of the Pflueger Medalist went offshore. The appearance of the Medalist hasn't changed in decades, although certain parts are not interchangeable between manufacturing generations.

Mend—To move a fly line laterally on the water, by flipping or lifting it with the rod in such a way that the fly itself is not disturbed. Mending is the most useful technique for controlling the fly while it is swimming, and it applies equally to dryfly and wetfly fishing, to drag-free floats and retrieves under tension. It is also a good way to keep the line away from obstacles in the water.

In a classic across-stream wetfly presentation, mending the line upstream will slow the fly down; mending downstream will speed it up, by increasing the pull of the current on the line. Mending is a important element in greased-line fishing (see). And when fishing a dry fly, since midstream currents often move faster than the water at the edges, an upstream mend will keep the fly floating naturally by the bank longer. A reach cast (see) is a mend made in the air before the line settles to the water.

Midges—Tiny, two-winged aquatic insects, part of the order *Diptera* (which means "two wings" and also harbors thousands of other insects, from deerflies to gnats), that resemble undersize mosquitoes. In the United Kingdom, the larger midges are sometimes called buzzers; in North America they are gnats. In sheer numbers, if not perhaps in mass or volume, midges (and their larvae and pupae) are the most important insect in a trout's intake. Midges are the most common of all aquatic insects and they flourish in a wide range of waters, moving and still, warm and cold; furthermore, individual species of midges may hatch twice a year—or more. In many trout waters, even in temperate latitudes, midge hatches occur somewhere virtually every day all year-round.

Midges go through a full three-stage underwater life cycle—egg, pupa, larva—and then swim to the surface to hatch as flying adults. Trout rarely feed actively on the air-breathing adults, which would be tied on size #18 to $28 hooks, unless the flies have been clumped together by wind or current. Once airborne, the adults soon collect in mating swarms above the water. Then the females fly down to deposit their eggs on the surface; both sexes die within hours after mating. There is no significant spinner fall for fish to feed on.

Midge larvae look like segmented worms up to half an inch long; they propel themselves through the water with inchworm-like contortions. Some kinds rise to the surface of ponds at night, and trout actively cruise the zone to feed. Imitating the behavior of the larvae with artificial flies is too difficult to be worthwhile.

According to *Dave Whitlock's Guide to Matching Aquatic Trout Foods* (1981), stomach samples indicate that trout eat some 50 midge pupa for every adult. The pupae, then, are the most important stage for fly fishers. Seen next to a larva and an adult midge, the pupa is clearly an intermediate step: it has the segmented, worm-like body of the former but in it can be seen the thicker, nascent head and thorax of the fly-to-be, as well as the swelling that hides the folded wings and legs. To hatch, midge pupae rise from the bottom and float in or just below the water's surface; the skin splits along the back and the adult struggles out. At this point the insects are most vulnerable to fish, and most interesting to anglers matching the hatch. Trout are said to be "midging" when they feed in smooth, easy, shallow rises that seem to extend along the surface; they're inhaling midge pupae in large numbers.

Midge Fishing—A term loosely applied by many anglers to fly-fishing with unusually small imitations. It is in fact a misnomer; see Midge, above.

Milling Machine—Also known as a power beveler, the milling machine has a special place in the history of flyrod manufacturing. A milling machine cuts a long, precisely tapered triangular-section segment out of a raw splint of bamboo. Six of these segments are then glued together into a bamboo rod (hence "split cane"). Before the milling machine, bamboo segments had to be cut and planed to shape by hand. When rod maker Hiram L. Leonard (see) invented the power beveler, around 1876, it turned the rod business around, for suddenly it became possible to manufacture dozens, hundreds, thousands of identical segments in what seemed almost no time, and to within repeatable tolerances of a few ten-thousandths of an inch. It was a milestone not unlike Henry Ford's assembly line or Eli Whitney's standardized rifle parts.

Leonard was well aware of the significance of what he had invented. His production milling machine, made of wood, was installed in a special locked room at the factory, in Bangor, Maine, and even trusted employees were reportedly threatened with instant dismissal should they enter. But word got out, inevitably, and other machines appeared, in the hands of competitors. The history of one of them is worth following, for it illustrates how past and present are woven together in cane-rod making:

Rod craftsman Walt Carpenter today uses a beveler that was made in 1890, for Fred E. Thomas, Eustis Edwards and Loman Hawes. They were ex-H.L. Leonard Company people (Hawes was a nephew of Hiram Leonard himself) who went into partnership for themselves in the Catskill Mountains. This was after Leonard had moved from Maine to Central Valley, New York. In its early years the machine made the now-classic Kosmic rods sold by A.G. Spaulding in New York City.

When Hawes died in 1891, a young man named Edward Payne came aboard, and the company moved out of the Catskills to Brooklyn. (Payne had been a partner of

Francis Philbrook, inventor of the raised-pillar reel; he went on to become one of the finest American rod makers.) F.E. Thomas, however, quit and went north again, to Brewer, Maine, where he installed a commercial laundry in the basement below his own rod shop. Back in Brooklyn, however, in 1898, Kosmic production stopped; Eustis Edwards temporarily gave up the tackle business to travel the West as a photographer, while Ed Payne moved the beveler out to Highland Mills and set up the to-be-renowned E.F. Payne Rod Manufactory.

In the mid-1920s, the machine was shipped up to Brewer; Ed Payne had sold it back to Thomas (and Edwards, who'd returned from his adventures and rejoined his friend in Maine). Those two then relocated a few miles down the Penobscot River, in Bangor, where the beveler stayed until their F.E. Thomas Company went out of business in 1958. Then a rod maker named Sam (Clarence H.) Carlson brought the beveler to Hampden, Connecticut, where he made his own well-known four-sided "quadrate" rods. Carlson sold the beveler in 1973 to young Walt Carpenter—who happened to be the last rod maker employed at Payne when that firm went out of business in 1978. (Jim Payne, son of Edward and a master rod maker himself, had died 10 years before.) That year Carpenter went into business for himself and moved to Chester, New York, finally bringing the Thomas beveler full circle. The machine is still cutting cane after more than a century; the only difference is that it is driven by modern electric motors instead of overhead drive belts and it is fitted with modern cutters.

The demand for split-cane rods has dwindled to where mass production isn't needed. Nor is it even good merchandising, in the eyes of some craftsmen—they say their clients want a fully handmade product, and they dismiss milling machines as too "industrial." The very few makers who produce significant numbers of cane rods still use milling machines, of course, and their rods are, dollar for dollar, as fine as anyone's. The "secret" lies in knowing how to use the machine properly.

Modulus of Elasticity—See Rod Action.

Moe Flies—An acronym for "Mother of Epoxy"—see.

Monocore—A type of fly line with a core of braided nylon monofilament instead of braided Dacron. The first commercial monocore fly line was a neutral-density Scientific Anglers tarpon line that made its debut in 1988. With its a clear tapered coating over a clear core, it was relatively invisible to the fish in the water. It also felt somewhat stiff and "snakey" in hand, so it was promptly dubbed the "slime line." It performed its design task—casting large tarpon flies quickly and accurately—very well, but it had a short performance life; two or three large fish could stretch the line permanently out

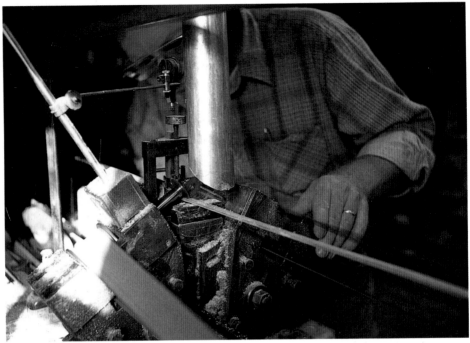

Milling Machine—The Thomas, Edwards & Hawes beveler, as modified by Walt Carpenter.

of shape. In the rarified atmosphere of world-class tarpon fishing, however, these shortcomings weighed little against the chance for a better shot at a 150-pound-plus fish.

Monofilament—A single strand of translucent nylon, made in different thicknesses, tensile strengths, colors and flexibilities, which is used as fishing line, leader and tippet material, and occasionally (when braided) as the core of tapered fly lines. From the fly-fishing perspective, monofilament is almost colorless, highly resistant to abrasion and shock, limp enough to cast flies yet strong enough to land fish, and it absorbs so little water that it can be spooled onto a reel and put away wet. The invention of monofilament, however, had to wait for the invention of a moldable superpolymer called nylon. That occurred in the laboratories of E.I. Du Pont de Nemours & Company. Nylon was the first completely synthetic fiber, and (company records indicate) it was first shown to corporate officials in 1935, by Dr. Wallace C. Carothers. By then the project had consumed seven years and $27 million in research and development. Commercial adaptation of nylon took two more years. On September 21, 1938, Du Pont publicly announced its "new silk." The first stockings woven from the new fiber created a sensation at the 1939 World's Fair in New York, but in that same year Du Pont began experimenting with monofilament fishing line and leaders. World War II interrupted the sporting-goods business and may have helped name the new substance, which became very important to the war effort: Rumor has it that "nylon" is an acronym for "Now you look out, Nippon."

In 1953 world-class angler Joe Brooks, writing in *Du Pont Magazine*, called monofilament "the greatest weapon ever invented for taking gamefish." Continual refinement has improved monofilament greatly since then. The chemical formulation of monofilament can be varied almost infinitely. The differences between brands of mono are the result of special blends of nylon monomers, heated, extruded, cooled, and drawn according to secret methods to obtain each manufacturer's preferred combination of tensile strength, knotting ease, stretch, flexibility, abrasion resistance, color and price.

Monofilament is so successful as fishing line because it is thin, strong, and nearly invisible; but another important factor is its stretchiness, which absorbs the shocks of fighting a fish—or tugging a fly out of a tree. A fresh (no nicks or knots) 30-inch 3X tippet may stretch to 40 inches before it fails. However, the last four inches or so of this stretch is permanent deformation, which does not disappear if the load were relaxed at, for example, 39 inches; the tippet has been damaged. Curiously, it may have an even greater breaking strength after being stretched beyond its elastic limit—but its ability to absorb shocks is much less and the tippet will break more easily on a strong fish.

(Too much stretch is as useless as too little. Setting the hook in a fish becomes progressively more difficult the farther away the fish is because the line simply stretches too much.)

Monofilament can absorb up to about 10 percent of its weight in water, which weakens the line, makes it swell and leaves it more elastic. The result is a decrease in the breaking strength of some 10 to 15 percent. (Returning monofilament to its normal three or four percent moisture content would take hours in an oven or many days in a tackle closet.) Some line companies compensate for this by labelling as "10-pound-test" monofilament that actually breaks at, say, 15 pounds—which has led to some ridiculous advertising claims along the lines of "The strongest 10-pound-test line you can buy!" It has also caused countless disappointments among anglers who submitted large fish catches to the IGFA (see) for certification as world records in a particular line class. The IGFA demands a portion of the actual line used to take the fish, to test for actual breaking strength. A line that tests too high disqualifies the catch.

The ultraviolet portion of sunlight also eventually weakens monofilament, and permanently. However the greatest danger to mono is surface damage. In manufacture, a tough skin forms over the nylon filament. Nicks, cuts, or abrasions immediately weaken the line at that point. Damaged sections should be cut away. Similarly, casting knots (see Wind Knot) weaken monofilament by as much as 50 percent or more; nylon tied in a simple overhand knot will cut itself long before its unknotted breaking load is reached. And a wind-knotted tippet loses about half its ability to stretch before failure. Thicker monofilament is less susceptible to such damage simply because there is more of it to wear or cut through. Check leaders often and thoroughly, and replace them if there is any reason to suspect damage.

Mortality—It is a modern irony that no one worries more about the death of a fish than the fisherman. Intent on maintaining the mythical balance of nature, desirous of leaving a fish alive as—in the words of Lee Wulff—a gift to another angler, unwilling to kill purely for pleasure . . . whatever the motive, never have so many fish of all kinds been caught and then so gently released again. However, whether these fish will survive the next hour and the next day is a question that all anglers have to ask themselves. All indications are that as anglers learn more about *how* to let their fish go, instead of merely *why* to, the mortality rate of caught-and-released fish is decreasing. (For information on the mechanics of unhooking and freeing fish, see Catch-and-Release.) Despite the occasional injuries caused by rough handling of a caught fish, the greatest killer of released fish is careless removal of the hook. It has been well established that single hooks produce a lower mortality rate than gang or treble hooks. The reason, however, is not simply because single hooks leave fewer puncture wounds; it's because single hooks (especially those whose barbs have been pinched down with pliers) are so much easier to remove without causing serious damage.

In 1979 an issue of *The Progressive Fish-Culturist*, a technical quarterly published by the US Fish and Wildlife Service, presented the results of a three-year hooking-mortality study supervised by Maine fisheries biologist Kendall Warner. Large numbers of landlocked salmon in two hatcheries were hooked and carefully released, using single-hook lures, treble-hook lures, flies and worms. The average mortality rates among the released fish were: single hook, 4.6%; treble hook 6%; flies, 4.1%; worms (the fish were not allowed to take them deeply), 5.7%.

Then 106 salmon were hooked deeply on worms; 56 were released by cutting the line and leaving the hook in place; 50 were released after the hook was removed. Of those fish, 90% died. Among the fish released with the hook still in, 57% died.

Among the first set of test salmon, of those fish that did die, 43.5% were hooked in the gills; 24% were hooked in the esophagus; 8.1% in the roof of the mouth; 8.1% in the jaws; 9.7% in the tongue; and 6.7% in the eye.

After hook-related injuries, sheer exhaustion is probably the second most important killer of released fish. It leaves a fish weakened and therefore easier prey for its predators. Some South Florida guides say that a large tarpon, no matter how carefully revived after its all-or-nothing battle, needs up to eight hours of recovery to be able to flee sharks the way it should. Exhaustion can also kill directly, and without the lactic-acid buildup and oxygen debt once thought to be the culprits. According to writer John Reubens (who himself credits Robert Carline, editor of the *North American Journal of Fisheries Management*), a fish that has been hooked, fought and brought to hand undergoes many changes in blood and body chemistry, which brings on stress that may be related to the clinical shock that injured humans slip into. Reubens, writing in *Fly Rod & Reel* (April '92), concludes with: "All fish tire faster and show more ill effects from being played in warmer (65° - 70°) rather than cooler water. At these temperatures, as determined by experiment, a safe limit for playing trout of 13.5 to 18.5 inches, be they wild or hatchery, seems to be five minutes. In 50° water, add two minutes." These figures support the old rule of thumb—a minute per pound to land a fish.

Mother of Epoxy Fly—Also known as the Moe fly, it was developed in the late 1980s by Florida Keys guide Harry Spear as a highly durable imitation of the crabs that permit and bonefish feed on. It proved very effective and the pattern was kept a secret for nearly a year, presumably to give its few users, all professional flats guides, an edge in getting their clients into fish.

Spear created his first resin-body Moe flies by molding lumps of five-minute epoxy to shape in a bowl of vegetable oil or liquid soap, to keep the quick-setting glue from sticking to his fingers. A later variant of the Moe was developed by Jack Montague, another Floridian; he dripped puddles of melted glue from a glue gun onto wax paper and laid a hook into each. When the glue cooled he cut it to an arrowhead shape with sidecut pliers, then dunked it into hot water to make the plastic flow just enough for the final shaping and smoothing. Since then, dozens or hundreds of variations have been created and Moe flies are now available with everything from embedded glitter dust to weed guards.

Epoxy stands up to saltwater gamefish far better than hair and hackle, and the shape of the body can be fine-tuned to create a crab that swims just right. Even the density can be adjusted by adding lead shot to the mix before it sets up.

According to saltwater angler Lefty Kreh, the forerunner of the Moe appeared in the late 1960s. It was based on the fast-sinking, diamond-shaped jigs made by Nickelure in Florida for permit; they were dressed with feathers and had an eye on one end and a hook on the other. Lee Cuddy, who owned a tackle shop in Coral Gables, persuaded Nickelure to mold a few of these jigs out of pink and tan plastic instead of lead, for fly-fishing, but they proved too light to behave properly in the water.

Mudding—A term used to describe bonefish feeding for crabs. A fish moves across a sandy flat with its head down, rooting in the bottom and thus creating a characteristic plume of "mud" that hangs in the water. A large, closely packed school of bones can throw enough sediment into suspension to cloud the entire flat. Experienced flats fishermen can spot telltale "mud" from a long way off.

Another, less common meaning is the intentional stirring up of the stream bed by a wading fisherman who wants to kick organisms into the current and thereby stimulate trout to feed more actively. It is possible to bring feeding trout up the plume of disturbed bottom sediments right to one's waders—and so this practice isn't regarded as entirely sporting.

Multi-Piece Rod—Strictly speaking, nearly every fly rod is a multi-piece rod since, for convenience in storing, transporting and manufacturing them, so few are one-piece. But it has become convention to regard a multi-piece rod as one that is three sections or more. (The usual fly rod being a two-piece.) Until the early 1980s, these were often called pack rods, the main market for multi-piece rods being hikers who wanted something to fish with in camp. Pack rods were usually fiberglass, usually not of top quality. Often they were also combination rods, "fly-spin" models that could, according to the maker, be used either way. In fact they were usually too stiff to cast a fly well, largely because they had three or more ferrules. When the fly-fishing-travel market suddenly began to boom, in the early '80s, rod designers turned to making multi-piece rods that could travel as carry-on baggage to Alaska or New Zealand but that gave away no fishing performance in the bargain. Thanks to research, better materials and manufacturing technologies, and eventually even computer-aided design, they succeeded admirably. To accompany this move up-market, the name "pack rod" gave way to "travel rod."

A rod with more ferrules was no longer automatically either too stiff or exceedingly expensive. More ferrules simply meant more convenience, not less performance. Today, more and more anglers buy multi-piece rods as a matter of course, and rod companies have greatly expanded their multi-piece lines. Even heavy-duty #12 tarpon rods and #14 big-game rods are now available in three-piece construction.

Multi-piece rods will always be somewhat more expensive than comparable two-piece models. Beyond the materials and labor involved in making and fitting more ferrules, there is also the expense of creating a separate mandrel (see) for each section of rod. And simply cutting an existing two-piece rod into more pieces won't do it because adding ferrules changes the characteristics of the blank. To get the same action, compensations have to be made.

Note that until graphite became the material of choice for fly rods, around 1975, it was common for split-cane fly rods to be made in three pieces. But that was less a matter of convenience than it was of the relative scarcity of long strips of high-quality bamboo.

Nevertheless, true multi-piece rods precede graphite by a century or more. So-called valise rods of six or more sections were made as specials for wealthy sportsmen (and to show off the skill of the builder). Occasionally they were called Sunday rods—they could be hidden in the buggy or even under a coat; as soon as the service ended, it was off to the stream.

The most common travel rod construction today is four- or five-piece, but there are eight-piece rods as well, that truly fit an attaché case. And don't confuse these with the cheap telescoping rods sold by novelty catalog houses. See Ferrule.

Multiplying Reel—As opposed to a single-action reel. A gear-driven fly reel whose spool turns more than once for every revolution of the crank handle. The benefit is that it lets the angler pick line up quickly, a boon when a fish turns and swims toward the fisherman. The disadvantages are that such reels rarely have interchangeable spools, and a high gear ratio in a direct-drive (see) multiplying reel means that the handle will turn at tremendous speeds when a powerful fish strips line out. Many anglers regard multiplying reels as inherently fragile or trouble-prone, but that is not necessarily the case, especially when the gear ratios are less than 2:1. See also Fly Reel, Saltwater Reel.

NAFTA—The North American Fly Tackle Trade Association; see.

Nail Knot—A strong, reasonably smooth connection in which the end of the leader makes several turns around the tip of the fly line. See Knots.

Needle Knot—A slightly stronger version of the nail knot, in which the butt of the leader is inserted into the core of the fly line and then out through its side before wrapping around it. See Knots.

Neoprene—A synthetic rubber that dates back to World War II. Like nylon and several other man-made substances, it was developed as a a strategic material in response to the Axis seizure of various natural resources, in this case the Japanese takeover of Malaysia, where most of the world's natural rubber was produced. Neoprene earned an honorable place in stream fishing in the late 1970s, when the first neoprene waders appeared on the market.

Strictly speaking, neoprene waders (and gaiters, hippers, etc.) are made of closed-cell neoprene foam—synthetic rubber that has been shot through with air bubbles. The result is the thick, stretchy, light, comfortable and slightly buoyant material that anglers have come to love. The insulation value of neoprene foam is relatively high, and these waders are particularly favored by coldwater fishermen. (Waterfowlers often find them a boon too.)

Unlike divers' wet suits or surfers' body suits, neoprene waders need not cling tightly and they should be fairly easy to slip on and off. Thus the rubber itself is usually faced on one side or both with a nylon fabric (which is also stretchy) that slides more easily over skin or clothing. Neoprene is available in a wide range of thicknesses; waders are usually made of two-, three-, four- or five-millimeter material. Top-line waders, custom-made or off the shelf, may use several thicknesses in each pair—extra layers in seat and knees, for example, where abrasion is high; less in the uppers, where heat buildup is often a nuisance.

Also unlike wet suits, neoprene waders are constructed to be watertight, and this places an extra burden upon the manufacturer. Despite great advances in materials—and neoprene is one of the most significant of these—modern fishing waders still share at least one big problem with the heavy rubberized-canvas waders of pre-WWII: Leaks are all too common. Neoprene, at least, is easy to patch. And even leaky neoprene waders provide warmth, thanks to the insulation value and relatively close fit of the stretchy, thick rubber.

Neoprene waders will eventually wear out, first in areas of high compression—such as underfoot—and then in the crotch or knees, where the material may be repeatedly flexed and compressed; the rubber itself is abraded or the air bubbles within slowly collapse. See also Waders.

Net Keeper—The clasp or other device used to attach a landing net to a fishing vest or shoulder bag. A net must be stored out of the way for wading, casting or playing a fish, but it should be instantly accessible thereafter. Net keepers are of two kinds: the harness-clip type, which can be opened with one hand to remove the net from its D-ring; and the retractor, which is just an oversize version of the pin-on "zinger" that anglers hang their clippers and other small gadgets from. The perfect net keeper—one that holds with absolute reliability and convenience until the net is needed, when it lets go just as reliably and conveniently—has yet to be invented, and the search keeps a number of gadgeteers perpetually busy.

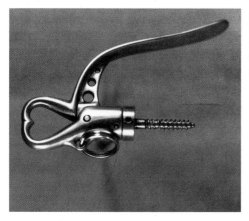

Net Keeper—a harness-type: The threaded shank screws into the net handle; squeezing the finger lever opens the catch to the left. The split ring is for a lanyard.

Nickel Silver—Also called German silver, nickel silver is an alloy of copper, zinc and nickel in proportions of roughly 3:1:1. There is no silver in nickel silver.

Nickel silver is notably malleable and ductile, fairly strong, relatively easy to machine, inert and unaffected by exposure to water or air. Today it is commonly used in food-service and hospital equipment, tableware, costume jewelry and so on. In addition, nickel silver has been established since at least 1900 as the ideal ferrule material for split-cane fishing rods. That is, it offers the best mix of strength, flexibility and weight for the job. Some rod makers stipulate an alloy with 18% nickel content. Fine ferrules such as the Super Z (see) are machined from drawn tubes of nickel silver.

According to tackle historian Jim Brown, Chinese metalsmiths were producing the alloy, which they called *pai-t'ung*, as early as 200 BC, and its composition was set in the West by 1776. The name German silver was prevalent before the 1850s.

Node—In a culm, or stalk, of bamboo (see) a node is the wall between two of the hollow cells. Externally, a node shows up as a distinctly swelled ring around the culm; on the inside, there is a thin diaphragm of pith that goes completely across the inner diameter. How the nodes are dealt with is a major element of building a split-cane fly rod. See Bamboo, Cane Rod Building.

North American Fly Tackle Trade Association, The—The trade organization for makers and sellers of fly-fishing equipment, clothing and accessories (as opposed to AFTMA, the more broadly based American Fishing Tackle Manufacturers Association; see). The idea for such a professional self-help group got its first public airing at a meeting of exhibitors at the first Fly Tackle Dealer Show, in Hershey, Pennsylvania, in September 1987. The meeting was called and then chaired by the author, editor of *Fly Tackle Dealer* Magazine and producer of the show.

The name NAFTA (at first, the more literal NAFTTA) was not formally adopted for another two years or so. In the meantime, half a dozen importers of flies, following in part the impetus generated by that meeting, banded together to lobby the US Customs Service and the Internal Revenue Service over matters of import duties and related taxes. Their success—federal agencies who would not speak to the individual companies proved eager to assist a group with an official-sounding alphabet-soup name, which was made up of exactly those same companies—helped prompt the formation of NAFTA, which, as its name implies, is not restricted to fly makers or importers.

Nottingham Reel—The English fisherman's old wooden "centre-pin" reel. Although it has been used for every sort of fishing, including wire-line trolling, its design and resemblance to a modern fly reel makes it particularly interesting to fly-tackle collectors. As a type, the reel originated in Nottingham, England, in the 1700s. So many were made, well into the 20th Century, that they are a staple at tackle auctions and swap meets. Nottinghams, with their brass or even silver fittings and their double crank handles of wood or bone, are big, bulky and heavy, but undeniably handsome. The wooden spool generally turns on a brass or iron spindle and is often held in place against its wooden backplate by a simple wingnut. Some reels have U-shaped wire line guides. Being wood, backplate and spool were liable to swell or warp when wet, and it's impossible to keep varnish on two surfaces that rub against each other. Later Nottingham reels were stiffened with brass straps across the backplate, and these "star-back" reels can be very attractive—and reasonably priced—additions to any collection.

Though they were used for many kinds of fishing, and hung both above and below the rod, Nottinghams were precursors of the modern fly reel. The design evolved to click-type check and drag mechanisms and pillar-frame, center-spindle reels. There is a strong mechanical resemblance to today's half-frame, exposed-rim fly reels such as the classic Orvis CFO.

Nottingham reels.

Nymph—The immature water-dwelling stage of an aquatic insect's life cycle; also an artificial fly meant to imitate such an insect. Some nymphs crawl the bottom of a stream, others seem to swim freely; some live in the substrate (that is, under the rocks on the bottom) and others inhabit underwater vegetation. When it is time to emerge as mature winged insects, some nymphs—such as the huge western salmonflies—crawl to the edge of the water where they can metamorphose more or less undisturbed and then fly away. (Newly formed salmonflies are shaky fliers, however, and they often settle onto the water in their first attempts, and that's when fish predation takes its toll.) Other nymphs, mayflies and caddis, for example, simply float or swim to the surface and hatch—or try to hatch—there. The struggle out of the nymphal shuck may take some minutes and then the new insect must unfurl its wings and let them dry and stiffen in the air before it can fly up into the trees. Meanwhile the insect is floating with the current and may pass over dozens or hundreds of trout, whitefish, smallmouth bass, grayling, etc., all of which feed actively on insects. This is the "hatch" (see) that fly fishers seek to "match" with their emerger and dryfly patterns.

A hatch is a short-lived phenomenon, however, and so is the mature insect's life in the air. As nymphs, however, most insect species live for several months or a year in the water. It is estimated, then, that 90 percent of a trout's diet is nymphs, taken underwater—which should prompt all fly fishers to learn to fish artificial nymphs effectively. See also Mayfly.

One Fly Competition, The Jackson Hole—An annual two-day invitational fly-fishing contest held each September since 1987 on the Snake River between the town of Jackson, Wyoming, and Jackson Lake, in Teton National Park. Anglers fish from drift boats with a guide/referee at the oars, and earn points based on the number and size of the fish, usually cutthroat trout, they catch (and release—points are lost for dead or injured fish). The twist is that each fisherman can compete with only one fly each day, which must be registered with an official every morning. When, or if, the fly is lost, the angler may of course tie on another fly and keep on fishing, but not for points. Normally aggressive, skilled fly fishers find themselves being very cautious as they cast toward brushy banks, and only the foolhardy or overconfident fish with light tippets or weighted flies.

The event is based loosely on the famous One-Shot Antelope Hunt that takes place nearby every year. Similar fly-fishing contests have sprung up too, the best known of which is probably the Tallahassee Two-Fly, in Florida.

The One-Fly is always attended by dinners, parties, barbecues and other socializing. Any funds left over from the entry fees go to stream improvement. There is another fund-raising aspect too: Proceeds from the annual silent auction go to the family of Peter Crosby, a guide who drowned in the first event.

One-Piece Leader—A tapered leader that is continuous; one length of monofilament, as opposed to several strands of different thicknesses that are knotted together. Such leaders are made by drawing the mono through an acid bath to reduce its diameter from butt to tip (usually in steps, not in a truly continuous taper). The advantages are strength—even well-tied blood knots are weaknesses—and smooth construction; aquatic weed can hang up on knots, and occasionally small fish even strike at the knots. There are no real disadvantages beyond those shared by any commercially made leader, namely that poor construction—in this case, the wrong taper—will affect performance. See Leader.

Open-Frame Reel—see Half-Frame Reel.

Orvis, Charles Frederick—1831-1915. Founder in 1856 of The Orvis Company, in Manchester, Vermont, which today is North America's and perhaps the world's best-known vendor of fly-fishing tackle. Although early Orvis bamboo or lancewood rods are not avidly collected, in his day Charles Orvis produced fly rods that rivalled the best from Hiram Leonard (see). Orvis also invented the modern fly reel (see below) and his daughter, Mary Orvis Marbury (see), made significant contributions to fly-tying and to angling literature herself.

In 1883, with A. Nelson Cheney, Charles Orvis co-edited *Fishing with the Fly; Sketches by Lovers of the Art, with Illustrations of Standard Flies*, a collection of angling articles by 24 well-known fly fishers illustrated with color plates of 149 trout, salmon and bass flies. Four editions were printed and the Wellfleet Press published a reprint in 1989.

Orvis 1874 Reel—The Orvis Company's Trout Reel, patented on May 12, 1874, built upon certain trends of its day to finally, firmly and apparently for all time set the design standard for modern fly reels. Unlike some contemporary fly reels, which were wide enough to resemble bait reels, it was almost exaggeratedly narrow, and both frame and spool were radically drilled, to dry the line and prevent mildewing. It sat vertically on the rod and soon boasted a click mechanism. Eventually it was offered in various spool widths—and thus capacities—and with a plain or counterbalanced, S-shaped crank handle. (While Orvis rods have always been built at the shop in Vermont, Charles Orvis hired the Manhattan Brass and Manufacturing Co. of New York City to make his reels.) Furthermore, by the turn of the century, the Orvis was being made of aluminum, which is still the material of choice for fly reels today. Earlier models were nickel-plated brass or nickel silver, also known as German silver. Light but strong, aluminum had previously been virtually a precious metal; but as breakthroughs came in refining bauxite, the cost of aluminum dropped significantly. After 1900, aluminum became increasingly common in fishing reels, and this, like the patent date of hard rubber, can serve as a quick yardstick for dating a reel. (Curiously, however, the Orvis patent describes a reel made of hard rubber—although Orvis added that he did "not wish to be confined to this material, as the reel may be made of metal throughout." To date, no hard-rubber prototype has yet turned up. Nor have any of the "Heavy Gold Plate" models offered in 1876 for $10.)

At a quick glance, an 1874 Orvis is nearly indistinguishable from a modern trout reel, except perhaps for its bright, potentially trout-spooking finish and its fitted walnut box. American fly fishers took the reel to heart immediately. It sold well for some 40 years (it was discontinued in 1920) and, as much as any other item, helped make Orvis a household name among anglers. See also Billinghurst Reel, Fowler Reel, Fly Reel.

Otolith—A hard calcium body in the inner ear of a vertebrate animal. Its significance to fisheries is that in the 1970s, scientists—chief among them Dr. Robert Bachmann, a biologist at the University of Pennsylvania—discovered that a fish's age could be found much more accurately by dissection of one of its otoliths than by counting growth rings on its scales. Aging a wild fish is necessary to gauge its growth and reproductive rate, which in turn is critical to setting regulations to preserve the species.

Orvis 1874 Reel—the standard-bearer for all modern trout reels.

Overrun Check—Also known as an Overrun Protector. It is a simple brake mechanism in a fly reel that prevents the spool from turning too freely, or overrunning, when the angler yanks line out. Without it, a too-enthusiastic tug can instantly create a bird's-nest tangle of line like the messy backlash of an old-style, level-wind casting reel. In many simple fly reels, the overrun check also serves as a low-grade drag, since it will put a little pressure on a running fish. In other reels, it's necessary to set the drag to a certain minimum level to prevent the spool from overrunning. See also Clicker, Sprocket & Pawl.

Ouananiche—The term used in Maritime Canada and northern Maine for landlocked salmon; see.

Pacific Salmon—A spawned-out, dying chum, or dog, salmon.

Pacific Salmon—In North America, the five species of salmon found along the Pacific coast, from Monterey, California, to the Bering Strait. All are members of the genus *Oncorhynchus*. Like *Salmo salar* in the Atlantic, these salmon migrate every summer from the sea into freshwater rivers and streams to spawn. Unlike the Atlantic fish, these salmon do not necessarily return only to the rivers they were born in; nor can they survive their spawning. After rapidly changing from the silver they wear at sea to various unearthly shades of red and olive or dark green, and developing incredibly hooked kypes and (some species) deeply humped backs, every one of the millions of these species dies in its river. Like Atlantic salmon, these species stop feeding entirely upon entering fresh water; unlike Atlantics, however, their digestive organs atrophy completely as all their energy is diverted into reproduction. The entire ecology of northwestern North America depends, directly and indirectly, upon these enormous runs of migrating salmon. Alive and then in death, the fish and their eggs feed everything from insects to grizzly bears. They are also an extremely valuable part of North America's commercial fishing industry—valuable not only in dollars but also because, nearly alone among major wild fisheries, they appear to be flourishing. Alaska's commercial fishermen are now perhaps the most regulated and watched on earth, and these runs of salmon among the most closely monitored.

Because they tolerate a wider range of water conditions than Atlantic salmon and because they spawn freely in rivers other than their natal streams, Pacific salmon have been transplanted around the world. Californian chinook salmon were established in New Zealand (where they are called quinnat); and in 1967 coho salmon were released into the Great Lakes, where they have flourished and spread even farther east. Attempts to move Pacific salmon into Atlantic watersheds date much further back that that, however; the eminent fisheries scientist Livingston Stone, when he was deputy US Fish Commissioner, went to California in 1872 to collect chinook eggs for eastern waters. They were meant to replace the rapidly disappearing stocks of Atlantic salmon, but fortunately they did not adapt.

(The steelhead was reclassified in 1989 as an *Oncorhynchus*, a Pacific salmon, so strictly speaking there are six species in North America. Few fishermen recognize the change, though, which was purely taxonomic; under their new name, steelhead did not suddenly begin to die after spawning. And in the western Pacific there is a sixth—or seventh—salmon called the cherry salmon, an important gamefish in Japan.)

Each of these five salmons has at least two names, depending on region and who is speaking of them, and some exist in landlocked varieties that also have different names. The largest, least plentiful, and most valuable (for market and for sport) is the chinook, or king salmon. The other four are the coho, or silver salmon; the chum, or dog salmon; the humpback, or pink salmon; and the red, or sockeye salmon. Together they are the largest and most important link in the food chain of the entire Pacific Northwest. See entries for these species; also Salmon, Spawning.

Pack Rod—A fishing rod that breaks down into many sections to fit into a backpack; often a "fly-spin combo." See Multi-Piece Rod.

Pale Morning Dun—The most important aquatic insect in the Yellowstone Park region, the PMD hatches almost continually and in great numbers beginning in May and lasting into September. Trout feed heavily on all stages of the insect's lifecycle, from nymph through spinner, and the dun hatches may last for hours. The Pale Morning Dun is actually two species of mayfly: *Ephemerella infrequens* and *E. inermis*, which look and act alike and differ only in size—*infrequens* typically is dressed on #14 to #16 hooks and *inermis* on #18 and #20. The duns may vary a great deal in color but they are basically yellow and may range up and down the spectrum from greenish to a dark brown. They do generally hatch in the morning, too—after the chill has left the air and before the heat of midday.

Palmer—A method of winding hackle feathers "sideways" around a hook in such a

Pale Morning Dun—an imitation tied by Darrel Martin.

Palmer—the barbs of the feather wound around the book support and float the fly.

way that the barbs of the feather fan apart and form a continuous collar around the shank. Palmered hackle is a basic ingredient of most conventional dryfly patterns; the flaring hackle tips support the fly on the water or in the surface film and they may also trap air bubbles for extra flotation. The deerhair bodies of such high-floating patterns as the Humpy or the various frogs and mice are also palmered—twisted or spun around the hook in such a way that the individual hairs stand up vertically, like the barbs of the feather. Since deerhair is itself hollow, these flies float especially well. See also Catskill Patterns, Fly-Tying, Parachute Fly.

Palming Rim—The edge of the spool of a fly reel that has been left bare (that is, uncovered by the reel frame) so that the angler can brake a fish's run by applying drag with his or her palm—or, as is usually the case, fingers. Some simple fly reels have only an overrun check (see) and a palming rim, and in the hands of skilled anglers have taken very large fish. Other reels offer a bare rim in addition to a more significant internal drag. In that case, the mechanical drag can be set to some safe level that falls below the tensile strength of the terminal tackle and the final, fish-beating drag can be applied (and instantly varied as needed) by hand.

Although exposed-spool reels have existed for more than a century, it took Lee

Wulff's perspicacity to popularize the design, by pointing out its benefits, in the modern era. For a time, in the 1970s, before the saltwater market had expanded to offer moderately priced reels with adequate drags, Lefty Kreh and other experts were converting big Pflueger Medalist reels (which had line capacity but no real drag) into "poor man's Fin-Nors" by cutting away part of the sideplates to expose the spools for palming.

(This led to a brief boomlet in precisely machined and balanced accessory spools for Medalists, and then even bronze drag components—see Medalist.)

Palming rims demand a certain level of skill, and on very powerful fish they can lead to skin burns or abrasions, but they are an extremely useful design evolution. See also Drag.

Palomar Knot—An excellent, very strong, easy-to-tie connection between hook (or swivel) and line that doesn't require the finger-twisting or needle-threading movements of the various kinds of clinch knot. The Palomar knot is not commonly used by fly fishers, possibly because the dressing of many flies interferes somewhat with passing the tippet loop over the entire hook. But it can be done, and it is a worthy connection. See Knots.

Panfish—A colloquial term for a group of "sub-gamefish," species small enough for the pan. Taken from farm ponds and freshwater lakes across North America, these include yellow and white perch, bluegill and other sunfish, rock bass, crappie and bullhead or hornpout. Almost every angler who learns to fish as a small boy or girl begins with panfish, usually taken first on a live worm dangled below a bobber; then, as advancing age brings spending money, on lures and spinning tackle; and finally, with the onset of maturity, on fly tackle—when other species aren't cooperating, when the angler wants to relive his childhood, or when he's teaching the next generation the joys of topwater fly-fishing. Bluegills especially are entertaining on ultra-light fly rods and small popping bugs; they can be "cheeked" (as opposed to filleted) and pan-fried or easily released.

Parabolic Action—Another term for progressive action, which describes the behavior of a fly rod that bends at its tip under light pressure and then flexes progressively farther down into the butt section as more and more load is applied, in fishing or in casting. See Rod Action.

Parachute Fly—A type of dry fly that has its hackle palmered horizontally around the stem of the upright hair wing (or something else—see Gyro Hook) instead of vertically

***Parachute Fly**—this mayfly imitation, by Harry Ranger, is tied with the hook upside-down, so the parachute hackle rests directly on the water.*

around the hook shank. The effect is of a parachute, gently lowering the fly to the water—and always right side up, which is not necessarily the case with conventional "fuzzball" dry flies dressed on small hooks. A less obvious but no less real benefit is that parachute hackle does not obscure the body of the fly, which can be important in situations where "matching the hatch" properly means imitating the silhouette of a natural insect's thorax/abdomen.

Parr—A young salmonid, specifically an Atlantic salmon between the alevin and smolt stages. Parr are usually some five to eight inches long and have distinct dark bars running vertically down their sides. They are a freshwater stage of the salmon's lifecycle and they feed actively, often taking small flies meant for trout. Early in the 1800s controversy arose among naturalists in England, who were split on whether parr were an immature salmon or a separate species entirely. And if they were indeed salmon, did they become smolts and then migrate to sea in their second or third year? To settle the matter, a pair of Scots named Shaw and Young bred salmon in wooden pens and documented the parr stage. They also learned that some smolts from the same year-class went to sea in their second summer and some in their third. See also Atlantic Salmon.

Pelagic—Referring to fish such as marlin, sailfish and tuna that live in the open ocean, as opposed to near-shore, flats-dwelling or reef species.

Perfect Bend—A type of hook with a symmetrically rounded bend. See Hook.

Perfection Loop—A slightly tricky but virtually fail-safe loop knot for monofilament. In fly-fishing it shows up most often in the loop-to-loop connections between a leader butt permanently attached to a fly line and the leader itself. See Knots.

Permit—*Trachinotus falcatus,* a member of the pompano family, the permit is the most challenging of all flyrod gamefish, at least of those under 100 pounds. On the Atlantic coast of North America it can be found as far north as new England, but for angling purposes it is a tropical fish, found on the coral flats and in the blue holes of the Florida Keys and the Gulf of Mexico. Permit feed much as bonefish (see) do, rooting head-down in the marl for crabs, sea urchins, various crustaceans and other forage, but usually in smaller numbers and without stirring up as much mud. As they grow, permit become more solitary. Also like bonefish, permit are a brilliant chrome-silver, perfectly camouflaged for their habitat; their fins and tail are dark, however, and tailing permit are easy to spot. Often they are very wary and will almost literally disappear at the first hint of pursuit.

Modern crab patterns (see Mother of Epoxy Fly) have made permit hookups on flies fairly common now, but bringing the fish to hand is another matter. Permit are very fast and powerful swimmers with deep slab sides, which they use in the water like sea anchors. Pound for pound, they are much stronger than bonefish and they are capable of long, unstoppable runs. A permit will stand on its head to cut the leader on coral; its mouth is so hard that even a well-sharpened hook penetrates with difficulty; and its shellcracker jaws can crush a hook. The angler must maintain constant tension so the fish can't spit the hook and he must also keep the fish's head up so it can't roll to take the leader in its teeth.

The first permit taken on a fly is attributed to master angler Joe Brooks; it weighed 12 pounds 8 ounces and was caught near Content Key, in Florida, in May 1951. Currently the largest permit recorded by the IGFA (see) on a fly is a 41-pound 8-ounce fish taken near Key West, Florida, by Del Brown on March 13, 1986.

Personal Watercraft—A term that entered fly-fishing in the early 1990s, when the gap between float tubes and "real" boats—skiffs, rafts and canoes—began to fill up with an assortment of odd one- and two-person aquatic conveyances. These fit no existing categories and could only be called water*craft.* Many of these devices are partly or

Personal Watercraft—This is a K-2 Drifter.

completely inflatable, although a few rely on pontoons of Styrofoam. Many require the user to wear waders. Some have built-in seats; more elaborate types have rigid alloy frames that hold swivel seats, coolers, even small electric or gas motors—although the most common form of propulsion by far is foot fins, to leave the hands free for fishing. Like a float tube, the most basic kinds are safe only in still water, but larger craft, designed with some directional stability and strength, can be used to run rivers. The common denominators among personal watercraft generally include: portability (some by backpack, others by car); a relatively low profile on the water (for stalking fish—or game); room for no more than two persons and usually only one, plus perhaps fishing/camping gear; and a high degree of innovation in their design. Many are produced by small companies that don't need to tool up for runs of thousands of units in order to make a profit. And many companies offer equally innovative accessories for personal watercraft—ultralight plastic anchors, different kinds of foot paddles, add-on trolling-motor platforms, air pumps and even a pressurized, refillable gas cartridge to make short work of inflating pontoons. See also Float Tube.

Philbrook & Payne—Francis J. Philbrook and Edward F. Payne, who together patented (in 1877) and manufactured the famous raised-pillar fly reel that the H.L. Leonard Rod Company sold for many years. Philbrook was a renowned gunsmith;

Payne went on to become a master's master rod builder. See Raised-Pillar Reel.

Pike, Northern—*Esox lucius*, the waterwolf, is one of the finest and least appreciated freshwater flyrod gamefish. Its name comes from the fish's resemblance to the slim and deadly blade of the eponymous medieval weapon. Its feeding habits do nothing to dispel that image either; like barracuda, pike are extremely efficient and skilled predators. They lie in ambush and take their food (mostly other fish but also ducklings and swimming mice) by running it down in a short, fierce sprint. Pike often hunt by sight and their eyes are mounted on the top front of their heads, which provides binocular vision and a keen ability to judge distance and relative motion of their prey. And when the visibility is poor, pike hunt with what may be the best vibration-sensing system known to fisheries science. Instead of simple lateral lines (see) of receptors, or neuromasts, pike have a series of neuromasts all over each flank, each in a pit at the leading edge of a scale. Furthermore, these sensors are calibrated to provide horizontal and vertical "bearings" on the source of the vibration in the water, which lets them home in quickly on live food.

Pike vary from a dark olive to a golden green; they are nearly black on top and creamy below, with rows of oval dark blotches along their flanks—perfect camouflage for shallow, weedy, still waters. Pike, especially large fish, are sometimes found in moving water as well, such as the quieter stretches of some of the trout streams of Labrador and Alaska. They also flourish in the brackish waters of the Baltic Sea, where they grow huge on the abundant herring.

Early European angling literature contains many incredible pike stories, and the biggest pike still occur in northern Europe, where 50-pounders are verified almost every year (but there are reports of 70-pound Amur pike in Mongolia). Few North American northerns exceed 25 pounds, but given the pike's long body, such a fish leaves an impression of great size and strength. Originally found in the Americas only north of about 60 degrees latitude, pike made their way into New England in the 19th Century and have since been transplanted throughout the Midwest and as far south as North Carolina. (The pike's panfish cousin, the chain pickerel, *Esox niger*, occurs naturally almost everywhere east of the Mississippi drainage.)

Pike readily strike streamers and occasionally poppers. Beginning with the attack on the fly, their fight is spectacular if sometimes short-lived. Pike migrate with the seasons from the weedy shallows to rocky depths and sometimes well up into feeder streams. They are early-spring spawners; in lakes they often move into the flooded shorelines right after ice-out, where they can be seen finning and tailing in the warmer shallows. The State of Vermont for many years had a short spring hunting season for mating pike; "anglers" could take pike by shooting into the water near their heads, to stun them.

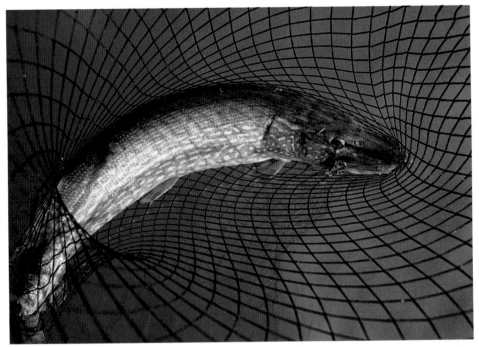

Northern Pike—Esox lucius with a large streamer fly in its mouth.

Pile Cast—A form of slack-line cast; see.

Pillars—The cross-pieces that connect the backplate of a fly reel to the outer rim; only a full-frame reel (see) has pillars, which may be integral with the frame or separate pieces fastened to it. If a reel has a line guide built in, it is often attached to one or more of the pillars. Or the pillars themselves are smoothly finished so they don't abrade line as the angler strips it off the reel. A half-frame, exposed-spool reel has no pillars. The Philbrook & Payne reel (see) patented in 1877 had raised pillars. See also Fly Reel.

Pink Salmon—*Oncorhynchus gorbuscha*, one of the five species of Pacific salmon native to North America; see Humpback Salmon.

Pin-On Reel—A small retractor device consisting of a lightweight spring-loaded chain or cable and a clip or safety-pin back. It holds a leader clipper, tippet straightener, forceps or other gadget (sometimes called "danglies") on the angler's vest, out of the way but instantly accessible; the cable may stretch two feet or so, to let the tool be used, and then it disappears back into the reel. The Simms Company, of Jackson Hole, Wyoming, makes an unusual retractor that is a length of tightly coiled wire that springs back into a small tube. Also known as a zinger.

Poacher Button—See Clicker.

Popper—A type of surface fly with a blunt or concave face that produces a popping, gurgling noise when the angler twitches the fly through the water. Poppers have solid or semi-solid bodies commonly made of cork or balsawood or tightly packed deerhair, and tails of hackle or hair. Some also have rubber or hair legs, and many have painted eyes. All sorts of crazy color schemes have been tried, but the most popular colors, year in and year out, are combinations of red and white or green, black or white. Poppers make excellent imitations of frogs or injured forage fish. A small popper body may be the size of a pencil eraser; a large one as big around as a golf ball.

Poppers are commonly used on warmwater lakes and about everywhere in the ocean except on the coral flats. (Occasionally they may be used to considerable effect on trout streams, too.) Surface-feeding predators—from bluegills, largemouth bass and northern pike to bluefish and stripers to sailfish and marlin—will take poppers very aggressively.

Pre-formed popper blanks are available from fly-tying supply companies; most are already slotted for the hook. Hook manufacturers, in turn, offer special popper hooks with a bend in the shank that keeps the popper body upright on it. See also Slider.

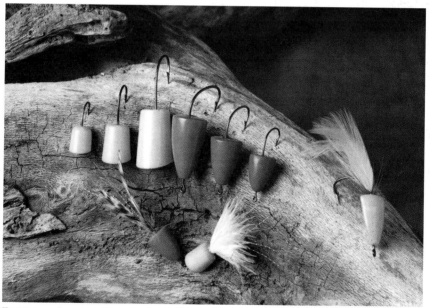

Popper—An assortment of pre-formed popper (and slider) bodies.

Portageur Canoe, on Labrador's Minipi watershed.

Portageur Canoe—"Portageur" in French means "one who carries" (portages). The canoe is a large, beamy, broad-bottomed craft, nearly always made of wood and canvas and square-ended; a freight canoe. In Canada's Maritime Provinces, portageur canoes are used to fish the Atlantic salmon rivers. Unlike the drift boats of the Intermountain West, which have an oarsman in the middle and two anglers, portageur canoes are fished with one angler, who sits in the middle, and two guides. The stern man is senior; he poles the boat between "drops," or fishing stages, and the bowman handles the anchor, called a killick. If the canoe is being used for something other than fishing, it may have a small outboard motor attached.

Power Snap or **Power Stroke**—The short acceleration just after the forward or back cast has begun that loads the rod in fly-casting. See Fly-Casting.

Pre-Preg—The graphite cloth from which rod blanks are made, which has been "pre-impregnated" with resin. See Graphite Rod manufacturing.

Presentation Cast—The final cast, when the fly is allowed to drop to the water, to be "presented" to the fish. The presentation cast puts a premium on casting and line-handling skill, especially in dryfly fishing, for it determines to a great degree how lifelike the fly will appear on the water. The first presentation cast over a lie or to a visible fish is particularly important—like making a "first impression" on a blind date, it often determines whether the outing will be successful. In the 1890s Frederic Halford, in his *Hints on Dry-Fly Fishing*, wrote: ". . . the first throw with a new fly should accordingly be made with the greatest care, as the most likely one to tempt the fish, and also because at each subsequent cast the probability of his suspicions being aroused by some slight mistake is ever increasing." See Drag-Free Float.

Priest—A small club used to deliver the "last rites" to a fish that will not be released. A sharp rap on the back of the head crushes the fish's spinal column and kills it. The term comes from British salmon-fishing history. In keeping with the upper-class traditions of that sport, a priest was often handsomely made of brass or wood (often inlet with lead), well balanced, and might have a knurled or wrapped grip and a lanyard. In old-world Atlantic salmon fisheries where no-kill regulations have not been imposed, it is still considered proper to ask, "How many salmon did you kill?", not "How many salmon did you catch?"

Progressive Action—A term that describes the behavior of a fly rod that bends at its tip under light pressure and then flexes progressively farther down into the butt section as more and more load is applied, in fishing or in casting. See Rod Action.

Put-and-Take—A somewhat cynical colloquialism for fisheries created by stocking; a hatchery puts the fish into the water and anglers converge afterward to take them out again. The concept of bolstering failing fisheries by adding tank-raised fish, which began in the US at about the time of the Civil War (the Eastern brook trout was one of the first fish to decline and thus to be "hatcherified" in North America, and Maine-stock brookies have been shipped almost all over the world), is coming under increasing attack as anglers learn more about the reasons and the consequences. Before the impact of less-obvious forms of pollution were understood, it was accepted by most sportsmen that as their numbers grew, nature could not keep up with the demand for fish and that state and federal hatcheries were only "helping out." Then, as water pollution became both better understood and more widespread and varied in character, this logic began to be twisted and then perverted. Professional hatchery biologists and managers undertook to breed strains of gamefish that would resist the pollution. Some anglers, naturalists and other biologists saw the enormous irony in this and began to demand that the water be cleaned up rather than the fish degraded. Pursuing *this* logic, they point out that in many cases there is no need for hatcheries—

in clean water and with both sport and commercial fishing regulated wisely, the native species can invariably reproduce and thrive on its own.

Too many fishermen are still ignorant of the ecology of their waters and still fish only for a body count. To satisfy these legions, often comprised of unskilled fishermen who complain that "there aren't as many fish in the river as when I was a boy," some hatcheries breed albino fish to release along with the normal hatchery product; the intent is to provide fish that anyone can spot in the water, as proof that "the state is doing its job."

Poorly conceived put-and-take programs have also introduced exotic—that is, non-indigenous—fish species into thousands of waters around North America. Sometimes this brought about great improvements in sport fishing; perhaps even the most devout salmonid purist would agree that the introduction of brown trout into the US in 1886 turned out "OK" (although educated fly fishers would campaign against such a plan today). More often, however, the exotics failed or suppressed the native species and forever altered the ecology of those watersheds.

As modern sensibilities prevail, ridding small watersheds of their implanted exotics and re-introducing the indigenes leads to some situations that are fairly ironic themselves. For instance in the late 1980s, to rehabilitate the greenback cutthroat in its native streams and lakes in the Colorado Rockies required that the exotic—but by then well-established and accepted—brook trout be eradicated. The State urged anglers to kill all the brookies they caught. Fishermen, inculcated with the need for catch-and-release (see), refused. Then state fisheries biologists began to poison off the brook trout, which led to a minor uproar. Everyone settled down when full explanations were made, and Colorado's greenback program is succeeding.

Some hatcheries are now being converted from generic-fish factories to breeding stations where biologists seek to re-create original strains of trout, salmon or steelhead destined for degraded watersheds that will be restored. As public understanding and acceptance grows, this "higher use" of facilities and manpower will spread.

Quadrate—A split-bamboo fly rod with four sides, that is, of four-strip construction. Until six-strip rods became the rule in the 1880s, most rods were laminated of four pieces of Calcutta cane, and the corners were planed or sanded down. The best-known modern "quad" rods were built by Sam (Clarence W.) Carlson, in Hamden, Connecticut, but many other significant rod craftsmen have built or experimented with four-strip rods also. See Cane Rod Building.

Quill—In fly-tying the word has three distinct meanings: it can be the stem of a feather; it can refer to a fly wing made of sections of barbs, cut from a feather and married together; or it may be a stripped herl from a peacock tail feather.

Quill—A Ginger Quill (tied by Darrel Martin), characterized by its body, a hackle quill stripped of its barbs and wound around the hook.

Raft—As used in fly-fishing, inflatable rafts are found on generally the same waters inhabited by drift, or McKenzie, boats (see), but there are important differences. Such rafts are long-wearing, highly portable and storable (for a 13- to 16-foot boat, that is), draw very little water and ultimately are very safe. Rafts, however, give up a great deal in maneuverability over skiffs. An inflatable river raft has a flexible bottom, which sometimes seems to create suction between it and the water. In addition, such rafts lack keels, rudders and hard chines to "grip" the water. Thus they have little directional stability, do not answer well to their oars (except to spin), and prefer to be swept along with the current rather than move over, across or against it. Rafts are well suited to shallow, riffley rivers. Where hard-bottom boats scrape and bang along, a raft may just scoot across, suffering no damage and making nearly no noise if it does touch the bottom. A raft is also an excellent choice for the opposite extreme—heavy rapids that demand flexibility, great buoyancy and shock absorption under the worst conditions (though these are hardly ideal fly-fishing conditions, of course). A McKenzie boat with 150 pounds of river inside loses much of its vaunted maneuverability, and then may break up on the next rock.

Any raft is trailerable, but fishing-size inflatables can easily be collapsed at day's end, rolled up—their seats, rowing frames, coolers and any other hard fittings removed—and stowed in the back of a utility vehicle or lashed atop a motor home. A small air compressor that runs off the vehicle's electrical system can re-inflate it in a minutes.

While McKenzie boats have built-in knee braces in the bow and sometimes the stern, so that passengers may cast standing up, for better reach and control, rafts with their low freeboard can only be fished from a sitting position. The basic seats are inflated tubes; however, accessory folding swivel chairs can often be added, for a more comfortable trip. See also Avon.

Rainbow Trout—In June 1988 the Committee on Names of Fishes, of the American Society of Icthyologists & Herpetologists, determined that the North American rainbow trout (and all the other trout of western North America and the northern Pacific drainage), long classified as *Salmo* (genus) *gairdneri* (species), should instead be known as a *mykiss*. *Mykiss* is the Asian rainbow trout, found on Siberia's Kamchatka Peninsula, which faces Alaska across the Bering Sea; the species name was adopted for both since the two fish are biologically identical and *mykiss* predates *gairdneri*. Going further, however, the committee addressed the genus of the fish, which brought up the question: Is the steelhead (see) an anadromous rainbow? Or is the rainbow a landlocked steelhead? Because of evolutionary similarities based upon the fossil record, the scientists settled upon the latter, which rendered the rainbow trout (and its sea-run form, the steelhead) not trout but salmon, a Pacific salmon—*Oncorhynchus*

Rainbow trout—A heavily spotted, well-marked Alaskan "leopard" rainbow.

mykiss. The new classification hasn't entered popular use, however, and perhaps it never will; the rainbow will always be regarded as a trout by anglers.

In light of its qualities as a leaping, hard-fighting, predatory gamefish plus the fact that it is indigenous to North America, the rainbow trout, and not the transplanted brown, perhaps better deserves the title of America's premier freshwater gamefish.

Rainbows are western trout who were moved east in North America, as well as all over the rest of the world, to Europe, Africa, South America, New Zealand, Australia and Japan. Unlike the brook trout, rainbows established themselves well in many of those places, and have become as popular there as the immigrant brown trout have in America. Unlike most other salmonids, wild rainbows generally spawn in the spring. They also cross-breed readily with other species (to the detriment of cutthroat trout in many Rocky Mountain watersheds), and of all the trouts they accept the widest range of water temperatures and quality. This made the rainbow the ideal of fish-culturists and has led to many hybrids and artificial sub-subspecies and hatchery experiments. The non-fishing public who see trout only on a plate, garnished and stuffed, might recognize the rainbow; most frozen supermarket trout are rainbows.

The trout is named for the slash of color that decorates its flanks. This may be a wide band of brilliant pink, a pale rosy line, or simply an irregular boundary between zones of spots on the fish's back and sides. The rest of the fish may be deep green above, fading through yellow to a white belly, patterned with irregular black specks, or—particularly near salt water—blazing silver with hardly any spots at all. Rainbows can show remarkable variation from one river or lake to another, not simply from region to region and season to season, and there are dozens of different non-migratory strains. Among the better known of these subspecies are the redband trout of the Columbia River Basin and the Kamloops trout of British Columbia. Some rainbows migrate readily to open water such as lakes or even the sea, others remain resident in their rivers year-round. And the potential for tremendous growth is there too: Canadian fisheries biologists reportedly netted a Kamloops-strain rainbow of more than 52 pounds in Jewell Lake in British Columbia.

Raised-Pillar Reel—A raised-pillar reel is one in which the posts, or pillars, that connect the two sideplates are mounted outside the rims of the sideplates. This increases the line capacity of the spool without a significant increase in the overall diameter or weight of the reel. The design is little used today as most smaller fly reels are now of the half-frame, exposed-spool type, which is lighter and more compact yet.

The original raised-pillar fly reel, sold as the H.L. Leonard Patent Click Reel, received a US patent on June 12, 1877, in the name of Francis J. Philbrook, a noted Maine gunsmith, reel maker and later rod builder. Philbrook assigned the rights to Hiram Leonard (see), whose company sold the reel for nearly a century. Hiram Leonard's rod company could have manufactured the reel itself, but instead bought them for resale. From 1877 until about 1900, the makers were Philbrook and his partner, Edward F. Payne, who went on to become a brilliant rod craftsman himself. (Like Leonard at the time, the two lived in Bangor, Maine; the arrangement may have been part of the patent assignment agreement.) Collectors today sometimes refer to raised-pillar Leonard reels from this era as Philbrook & Paynes, from the Philbrook & Payne Rod and Reel manufacturing Company, formed in 1878. Around the turn of the century Julius Vom Hofe took over production of the reels, which did not cease until World War II.

Raised-pillar Leonard reels were made in many sizes, from tiny trout models only 21/8 inches in diameter to 41/2-inch salmon reels. All are distinctive collector's items, yet still excellent fishing tools. A few very early examples have brought record prices at auction.

Reach Cast—A form of slack-line cast; see.

Redd—A fish's nest, nearly always made by the female, who swims on her side at the bottom and flaps her tail to clear a shallow depression in the substrate before

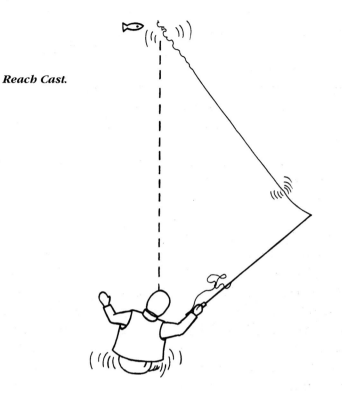

Reach Cast.

Raised-Pillar Reel—An early Philbrook & Payne raised-pillar trout reel.

Redfish.

*Reel Seat—A heavy-duty
full-metal, up-locking reel seat
on a tarpon rod.*

depositing her ova in it. (The archaic popular use of the word was as a verb—to "redd" meaning to clean or tidy up, or arrange neatly.)

Redditch Scale—The British system of sizing fishhooks. See Hook.

Redfish—Also known as red drum, red horse and channel bass, *Sciaenops ocellatus* seems to have a split personality: In the Carolinas channel bass grow to 30 pounds and more and are a favorite with surf casters; in the Florida Keys and along the coast of the Gulf of Mexico, five- to 10-pound redfish are increasingly popular with fly casters on the flats. The species is found only along the East Coast of North America, occurring only rarely north of Long Island. In the early 1980s redfish were severely overharvested in the Gulf of Mexico; the demand was apparently spurred by Cajun chef Paul Prudhomme's trendy blackened redfish entrée. Strict regulations and controlled fishing brought the species back within a few years.

Red Salmon—See Sockeye Salmon.

Reel Seat—That part of the butt of a rod to which the reel is fastened, or seated. On a single-handed fly rod the reel seat is attached below the handgrip. The simplest type of reel seat, often found on light fly rods, is the sliding-band type: an alloy ring slips over each end of the foot of the reel to clamp it against the barrel, or insert, of the seat. A medium-duty fly rod usually has a screw-locking reel seat: One end of the reel foot fits into a hood—a stamped or cut-out alloy band—at the end of the reel seat; the other end is held by a threaded ring that screws down over it. A heavy-duty saltwater fly rod may be fitted with an all-metal, double-locking reel seat, which has a second threaded ring to be screwed down on top of the first ring in order to jam it securely (the vibration of a long battle or even just a long boat ride has been known to unscrew a reel seat).

For proper rod action and strength, the end of the rod blank must extend all the way down through the grip and well into the reel seat. Heavy-duty reel seats often have accessory fighting butts (see), special extensions that fit into the end of the seat—after removing the butt cap—to provide extra leverage in fighting big fish.

Replica Mount—An entirely artificial reproduction of a fish, usually made of some sort of cast resin; also known as a catch-and-release mount. Replica mounts may simply be ordered by the inch (or the foot) from supply houses. The best examples, however, are created to order and mimic a particular fish as closely as careful measurements and color photographs taken in the field will allow, right down to hand-painting a trout's spots and molding in a kype or a humpback or other physical features. The result is that the fish can be released back into the water, to spawn or be caught (and perhaps released) again, and the angler has his or her trophy too. See also Skin Mount.

Retractor—See Zinger.

Riffling Hitch—Also known as the Portland Creek hitch, for the place where it originated, the hitch is a way of tying on a wet fly in such a way that the fly can skim, or riffle, across a river's surface. This produces a noticeable wake, which often seems to attract fish, and it keeps the fly up on top, where it—and a strike—can easily be seen. A hitched fly is fished down- and across-stream and it relies on the current pulling against the line and leader to make it work. No one can say why fish strike a wet fly that skates across the current in such an unusual way, but then no one can say just why spawning salmon or steelhead strike any fly. The riffling hitch has been proven effective on Atlantic salmon and steelhead rivers throughout the world, but it is rarely used. The hitch will also provoke strikes from trout and smallmouth bass when conventional retrieves fail, but it is almost never used by anglers who haven't seen it in action on a salmon river.

To hitch a fly, attach it to the tippet with the usual knot and then throw two half-hitches in the monofilament just behind the head of the fly. That way the tippet comes off the shank of the hook at an angle. The tippet should be adjusted to make the fly skim the water with its point facing downstream. If the current is flowing to the left, the tippet should come off the left side of the fly (looking at it from above and holding it with the head pointed away); if the water flows left to right, the tippet should come off the right side of the fly. The half-hitches may weaken a modern nylon tippet slightly, but on relatively heavy salmon or steelhead tackle this is a moot point.

Lee Wulff (see) was the first to tell the world about the riffling hitch, which he preferred to call the Portland Creek hitch in honor of its inventors. In the late 1940s and early '50s he ran a salmon camp on Portland Creek in northwestern Newfoundland, and he found the local fishermen using this unusual knot, which in their accent they called the "rivveling" hitch. Wulff scoffed at it until he saw salmon strike at his leader knots when drag made them cut wakes in the water. He switched over and immediately began to take many more fish. Years later he said that although the hitch produced strikes for him on virtually all salmon water, nowhere was it as effective as on Portland Creek. Did it work so well because the locals used it there for years and "taught" it to "their" salmon?

The hitch developed, Wulff reported, out of frustration—with flies, not with salmon. Years before, the locals were using old, obsolete gut-eyed salmon flies given to them by officers of the British Royal Navy. The gut had aged and weakened, and people lost fish and flies when these snelled eyes broke. However, one inventive angler not only

Riffling Hitch.

tied his tippet to such a fly, he also took a couple of half-hitches behind its head, to make sure it wouldn't break off. He kept his fly and he also caught significantly more fish with the unusual fly behavior brought on by this "insurance" knot.

Right-Hand Wind—A fly reel that is set up to be cranked with the right hand, while the left hand holds the rod. This is desirable for many anglers since most fly fishers are, like most people, naturally right-handed. However, for that same reason, most of these anglers then have to switch the rod over into their right hands in order to be able to cast. Although this quickly becomes second nature, on the face of it this is a time-wasteful and inefficient procedure, and occasionally quick-striking fish are lost in this moment of changeover.

On buying a fly reel, the angler should ask it to be set up for right- or left-hand wind, to make sure that the line (or the backing, if they are to be spooled on by the seller) is wound on in the right direction and also so that the drag or the overrun protector (see) are set to work in the correct direction of rotation. See also Left-Hand Wind.

Rocket Taper—A variant of the weight-forward fly line with an especially short, steeply tapered tip and a bulky belly, or casting head. The taper was designed for saltwater-flats use; with its heavy head, it could "rocket" a fly out to a feeding bonefish or passing tarpon with minimal false-casting. See Fly Line.

Rod Action—One of the distinguishing highlights of the sport of fly-fishing is the endless search for the "perfect" fly rod, a rod long enough to provide line control and casting accuracy yet short enough for easy handling; delicate enough to present small flies at short range yet powerful enough to cast the entire fly line with a big popper; soft enough to cushion a fine tippet yet stiff enough to out-muscle a strong fish; and that can be cast all day long with an easy, comfortable rhythm. No such fly rod exists, of course, any more than one golf club can play every lie on every hole exactly right. The best fly fishers can hope for is one rod within a certain range of line weights that

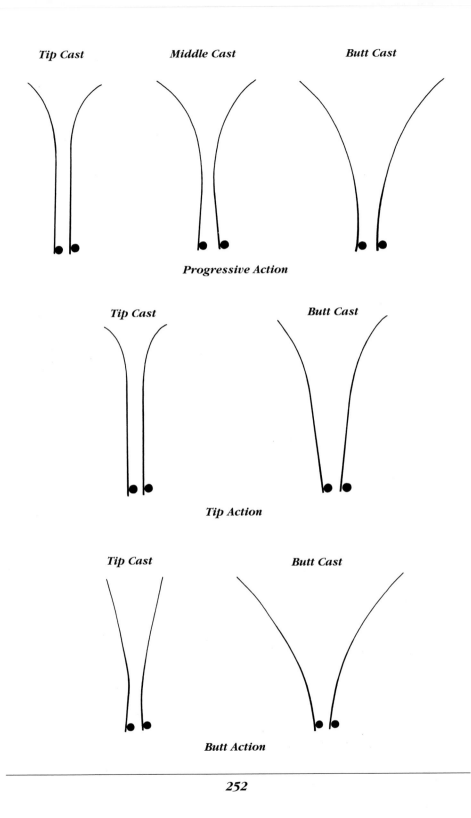

Tip Cast   Middle Cast   Butt Cast

Progressive Action

Tip Cast   Butt Cast

Tip Action

Tip Cast   Butt Cast

Butt Action

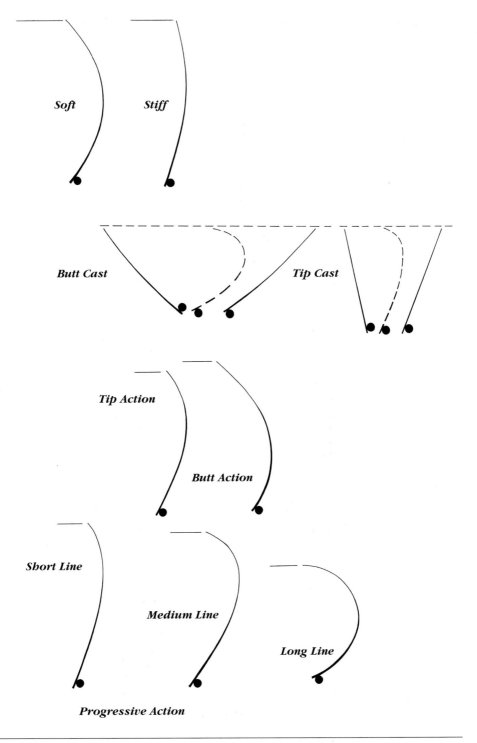

Soft

Stiff

Butt Cast

Tip Cast

Tip Action

Butt Action

Short Line

Medium Line

Long Line

Progressive Action

can handle most of these duties—a salmon rod, for example, or a trout rod or a bass rod or a saltwater rod. But as anglers grow increasingly skilled and sophisticated, they find themselves dividing these categories even further: into light, medium and heavy salmon; Eastern and Western trout rods, or brush rods and float-tube rods; tarpon rods, billfish rods, etc., etc. Today one can buy fly rods rated for line weights #1 through #15, in lengths that step by six-inch increments from about 6 to 16 feet, in one piece or in as many as seven or eight sections. And within each specific class—9-foot, two-piece for 6-weight line, for example—each rod manufacturer's offering(s) vary from the others' in flex, feel and "action."

To complicate matters further, there is no standard language to describe flyrod action, the way a fly rod handles and casts; instead, rod designers, manufacturers, casting teachers and fly fishers rely on a hodge-podge of inaccurate and misleading terms.

In fact, however, a fly rod is a simple tool. It can be defined in simple terms and those terms can be related to fishing and casting needs. Fly-casting authority Mel Krieger writes:

Let us use the words butt and tip to describe the parts of a fly rod, and the words stiff and soft to describe a fly rod's resistance to bending.

Some use fast and slow to mean stiff and soft; I don't, because "fast" has come to mean not only a stiff rod but one with a tip action. Similarly, a "slow" rod is now thought to be one with a bendy, butt-action feel. Rod action, the way a rod bends, can be defined in terms of where this action takes place; e.g. a "tip-action" rod bends mostly at the tip, a "butt-action" rod at the butt of the rod. All rod actions fall between the extremes of tip action and butt action, and stiff and soft.

As we consider the relationship of rod action to fly-fishing and casting, we find that all the variations of action and stiffness, however subtle they might be from one rod to another, are simple combinations of these simple descriptions.

One highly desirable compromise, or combination of these two basic actions is called progressive action. This begins with tip action and works progressively down the rod to butt action as the load increases. (The load is the weight of the line outside the tiptop, as well as the leader and fly, and/or the amount of power applied by the caster—both of which make the rod bend.)

The most significant aspect of rod action is in its relationship to fly-casting. The efficiency of making long or short casts relates directly to the stiffness of the rod. A stiffer rod will, in general, cast a longer line because it allows the caster to develop more line speed. (This additional speed is also helpful on windy days and often has advantages in fly presentation.) On the other hand, a shot cast can be made more comfortably with a rod soft enough to bend easily under the load of the shorter line.

Some anglers like to get as close to their quarry as possible, often making casts of only 10 or 15 feet. Others, spotting a fish at 30 feet, will back up so that they can make a 60-foot presentation. And there are also fly-fishing situations that in themselves demand long or short casts—large rivers and lakes versus small streams, for example.

In addition to considering this fishing style, when choosing a fly rod factor in personal preferences: the slow, easy, full casting stroke of a soft rod versus the more forceful, narrower stroke of a stiffer rod. (Note that experienced anglers often underweight or overweight a particular rod by changing the line to make the rod feel stiffer or softer. A fly rod rated for a 6-weight line is effectively stiffer with a lighter 5-weight, and feels relatively softer—it bends more—with a heavier 7-weight line. Note also that rod manufacturers are not always consistent in rating their rods for line sizes. Be sure to try any new rod with more than one line.)

Now consider rod action in terms of where—butt or tip or inbetween—a rod bends in relation to a casting stroke. I've mentioned butt-action rods and tip-action rods. Now let's consider a butt fly-casting stroke versus a tip cast. The butt cast is a wide-arc casting stroke that requires a full bend in the rod (in order to maintain the straight-line path of the rod tip that's needed for good casting—see diagram). It is generally much easier to obtain that full bend in a fly rod that has a butt action, and those who prefer to cast this way will do well with such a rod. Similarly, those who like to fire the line off the tip of the rod, using a narrow casting stroke, will do better with a tip-action rod.

Most of the better fly rods available today utilize some version of progressive action, with varying degrees of emphasis on tip and butt. While a good progressive action actually enhances both the tip and butt casting stroke, it is ideal for the angler who uses a wide variety of casting strokes in his or her fishing. A tip-action rod in which the butt is too stiff to use when it's needed—or a butt-action rod in which the tip is too stiff—are limiting.

My personal evaluation of a fly rod's action is based on the way it handles all the fly-casting strokes. My choice is a progressive rod that is nicely balanced between tip and butt action. It is a rod sensitive enough to let me feel the tip working while casting a short line with a tip-action stroke. And as I lengthen line and increase power, the rod must comfortably cast off its middle without the tip giving up entirely or the butt beginning to "hinge." During both these casts, the butt section should be stiff enough to stay intact, with no feeling of any appreciable bend. As I apply more power still, then I want to feel the rod bend well down into the butt section. In this butt cast, I'd like the bend to progress through the rod from tip to butt with no feeling of inconsistency or hinging. Such a beautifully balanced progressive-action rod casts smoothly and well from a butt cast to a tip cast, from leader-only range to the full fly line.

Every fly rod has an action that can be described with some combination of the labels tip-action, butt-action, stiff and soft. While there are variations within these terms, there's nothing mystical or mysterious about rod action.

Evaluating Flyrod Action

Whenever possible, get some help from a good fly shop, one that has a variety of fly rods available. The basic, approximate determinations of length and line weight will depend mostly on the type of fishing you will do with the rod. Once that's set, take the time to cast different rods with different lines.

We've all seen people standing in front of a rod rack in a shop, new fly rod in hand, waggling it around. It's likely they don't know what they're looking for. But a good wiggle will tell us a great deal, and will help select a few rods to take outside and actually cast. The wiggle is second only to real casting and fishing in communicating rod action.

Assemble a fly rod, without a line. Hold the rod out in front of you and, using a very short stroke, whump the tip—just the tip. Lock your wrist and use a decided start-stop motion, gently. This tip cast is a flicking, flipping motion. Only the top two feet or so of the rod should bend appreciably. Note that it is necessary to move your hand only a few inches to make this stroke.

Now, using a slightly more emphatic whump and a wider arc, force the rod to load and unload down into its middle. Finally, a wider casting stroke and even more force, to load the rod into the butt—right down into the handle. The whole rod, butt through tip, should be bending.

Wiggling the rod horizontally lets you see the type of bend you're putting into it; you should see and feel the rod working very clearly. The illustrations indicate how different rods behave during the wiggle. —*Mel Krieger*

Rod Designer's Glossary

Damping

The rate at which tip wiggle dies out in a fly rod after casting or mending. Waves in the rod become waves in the line, after all. Damping is affected by 1) the amount of original deflection or bend, 2) the stiffness of the rod, 3) the inertia of the rod tip, and 4) the aerodynamic drag of the tip. This last is important and usually overlooked. Air drag affects a fly rod more than any other outside force, and a very thin tip section may oscillate longer than a thick one simply because it presents less surface to the air (but many other factors are involved as well).

Elasticity

The property that lets a body return to its original shape, after a force that deforms it is removed. Things that are elastic have *elastic limits*—sometimes called the proportional limit—beyond which they cannot be bent without suffering damage. A graphite rod taken to its limit will snap. A cane rod may first take a "set" when its limit is approached; fracture is the next step.

Hoop Strength

The resistance offered by a tube, such as a rod blank, to crushing. Hoop strength is what keeps a loaded rod from suddenly caving inward at some location along its compressed side. Virtually all hollow graphite rods have some fibers (usually fiberglass, sometimes graphite or even Kevlar) wrapped laterally or roving helically along the blank to provide hoop strength. A perfect resin would bind the longitudinal graphite fibers together strongly enough so that this inner wrap isn't needed, but no such glue exists yet.

Modulus of Elasticity

The Modulus, or E, of a material is a constant—one of the physical characteristics that describe a material scientifically, like its density. E is the ratio of stress to deformation; it indicates how far that material will bend under load (so long as the load isn't enough to break the material). Modulus is, then, a measure of stiffness. It is usually expressed in millions of pounds of pressure per square inch. The E values sometimes given in rod manufacturers' catalogs are "pure"; that is, for the fiber alone. But when the fibers are built into a rod blank, within a shell of the epoxy resin that binds them together, the "effective E" drops considerably. The stiffness v. weight of a finished fly rod also depends on many other factors, including ferrules, line guides, finish and fiber direction.

Stress/Strain

These terms are closely related in that the former causes the latter. *Strain* is a measure of deformation in a material caused by outside forces, namely *stress*—anything from a simple push to temperature changes that cause expansion or contraction. For example, we stress and therefore strain a fly rod when we pick line off the water for a back cast.

Tensile Strength

Strain Rate: The resistance offered by a material to tensile stresses—in other words, stretching; a longitudinal pull. Ultimate tensile strength is the force required to break the material divided by the cross-sectional area of the material.

When a fly rod bends, its upper surface is under tension; but the opposite side of the rod is under compression, and so fly rod material must have compressional strength as well as tensile.

Rolling Table—A machine used to wrap a pre-preg "flag" (see) around a rod mandrel (see) under pressure and so without gaps or voids. A rolling table looks like a pair of large ironing boards, one above the other. The operator places a wrapped mandrel on the lower table; when he activates the machine, the upper table moves down onto the mandrel and then the two tables move horizontally in opposite directions, like a pair of hands rolling a bread stick. See Graphite Rod Manufacturing.

Rod Blank—The rod alone, without any of its furnishings such as line guides, grip, hook keeper, etc., but usually with its ferrule in place. An un-ferruled rod blank is just two or more rod sections or segments. Selecting a blank on which to build a rod at home means choosing between graphite, fiberglass, bamboo, or some exotic hybrid such as boron or kevlar with graphite—or even split bamboo over graphite. See Cane Rod Building, Graphite Rod Manufacturing.

Roll Cast—A unique cast that does not require split-second timing, great effort, false-casting (see) or even putting the line up in the air at all, which makes it effective in thick brush or strong wind. The roll cast begins with the line extended on the water and the rod, tip nearly in the water, aligned in the same direction: Raise the rod smoothly (canted slightly so that the line falls to the outside of the rod as it comes off the water) to above eye level so it is tipped slightly past the vertical and the belly of the line hangs behind you. Then sharply power-snap the rod forward and down with the wrist, following through with elbow, shoulder and body, aiming the rod where the cast should go. This forms a loop of line that unrolls crisply across the water, re-extending the line and presenting the fly with minimal fuss.

If the leader or line doesn't unroll but collapses in a heap, you are probably not (1) raising the rod high enough; (2) allowing the line to swing back behind you; or (3) making the power-snap forcefully enough. Moderate angle changes are possible by turning your shoulders and aiming the roll in a different direction. In addition to being quite effective and useful, the roll is perhaps the easiest cast to learn, and many beginning fly fishers have taken their first trout with a roll cast after just a few minutes of instruction. See also Spey Cast.

Roll Pick-Up—A particularly useful move for the upstream dryfly or nymph angler,

Roll Cast

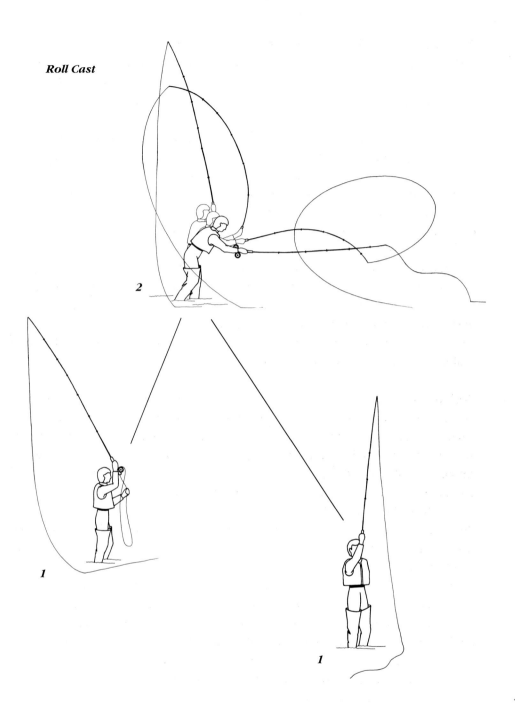

2

1

1

who can't easily make a conventional line pick-up (for a new cast) because of all the slack line created as the fly drifts downstream toward him. Unlike the simple roll cast, timing is important in this case. To make a roll pick-up, begin as for the roll cast (see above; your rod is probably already raised, for line control). But after the forward power-snap, instead of letting the loop unroll across the surface, pick the line up into a back cast as soon as the fly leaves the water. This ensures that the entire length of line is under tension and thus control and helps lead into a strong back cast and then a good forward cast and shoot (see). A roll pick-up and then conventional false-casting lets you cast farther than a roll cast alone.

Rotary Tying—Tying a fly by turning the hook, in the vise, and feeding thread, dubbing, tinsel, yarn, floss, etc. onto it from a stationary bobbin, instead of leaving the hook fixed and winding the material around it. Rotary tying requires a rotary vise, one with a head that can turn like the chuck of a lathe. Some high-production fly manufacturers use rotary vises powered by electric motors and controlled with foot pedals, but usually rotaries have some sort of small wheel or tiller to let the tier spin the jaws by hand. They also have a means to lock the head in one position for conventional tying. Many simple flies with wound bodies can be tied very quickly on a rotary vise. See also Fly-Tying.

Run—To anglers, a "run" is an annual movement of a species of fish, usually on their way to a certain place to spawn (hence "sea-run" for anadromous). Throughout the world there are steelhead runs, salmon runs, alewife runs, shad runs, sea-trout runs, tarpon runs and so on, their timing dictated by the climate and the genetic makeup of the individual species, and possibly modified by the physical characteristics of the waterways.

Running Line—The part of a fly line that lies behind the head; the constant-diameter, relatively thin 50 or 60 feet of coated fly line between the bulkier flyline head and the backing (if any) or the reel spool. Usually the running line is an integral part of a standard 90- or 100-foot fly line, but sometimes a shooting head (see) or some other type of casting head is attached to a separate running line made of level fly line or even a length of monofilament. See also Fly Line.

Sailfish—An increasingly popular target for fly fishers, especially since the IGFA (see) expanded its tippet categories to include 20-pound-test, *Istiophorus platypterus* occurs in tropical and subtropical waters around the world. In Central America they are found on both the Pacific and Atlantic coasts; Costa Rica, for example, is the site of an annual catch-and-release sailfish tournament for fly fishers. Sailfish are elongate, spear-nosed animals with large sickle-shaped tails and faint vertical bars on their sides. Their distinguishing characteristic is the enormous first dorsal fin, the "sail," which the fish uses the way a peacock does its tail. Among offshore trollers sailfish are regarded as a light-tackle species, as they rarely exceed 150 pounds (although there are reports of 200-plus-pound sailfish off northwestern Australia). That makes them a real challenge for fly fishers, however, with their self-imposed tackle limits. It is rare to find sailfish on the surface; usually they are brought within fly-casting range of a boat by towing teasers (see). See Big-Game Fishing, Teaser.

Salmon—Salmon are anadromous fish; they swim up rivers from the sea at certain seasons to lay their eggs. This is the essence of a salmon, what distinguishes it from its close relatives, the trout and charr. Like most of them, the salmon hatches from an egg in a riverbed and passes its juvenile years in fresh water, but then some force as mysterious as the one that originally brought its parents upriver prompts it to swim downstream and out into the ocean. This is the beginning of the salmon's great life-and-death migration. The young smolts mature into salmon at sea, where they can travel freely to feed on herring, eels, capelin and shrimp.

Barring encounters with commercial fishermen (who may not even be looking for them, but may sweep them up as "bycatch" in the pursuit of something else) or with sharks, big cod and a few other predators, life is unhindered out in the open ocean—there is room and food for all. The fish may gain a pound a month. But in two or three years, or five or six in some individuals, an age-old need draws the salmon out of the relatively safe ocean and sets them upon a journey few will survive. The need to spawn, to reproduce the species and keep the cycle going, urges the salmon toward shore. Biological research indicates they navigate according to oceanic currents, the earth's magnetic field, and perhaps even by the positions of the stars.

In coastal waters, relying on a sense of smell/taste far keener than any scientific instrument, salmon home in on minute traces of fresh river water mingling with the sea. When the fish enter the estuaries their troubles begin: The seals increase. Smaller fishing boats find the salmon easily and set their nets. And along the shore may lie elaborate stake nets, weirs, fish wheels and other traps. Then in the river mouths the bottom shoals rapidly and even hungry birds can now reach the fish, though only an injured salmon can fall prey to a bird at this stage. The surviving salmon pass up into

Sailfish—a fly-caught (and released) fish from the Pacific side of Costa Rica.

the still-narrower confines of their rivers and streams. In settled Europe, they are finally relatively safe again, except from man. In much of North America, arctic Scandinavia and Russia, the natural predation begins in earnest: otters, mink, fisher cats; ospreys and eagles. In Alaska and Canada, the grizzlies have been waiting for the salmon to appear ever since they emerged from their winter dens. And man—angler, native subsistence hunter or poacher—is there too, with his dip nets, spears, lures, bait and flies.

At the risk of anthropomorphizing, it is no wonder then that the salmon—grown large and strong in the open sea, now hemmed in by streambanks; forced to thread swift currents and negotiate rapids, rocks and shallows; unable to eat; and diverted from the spawning imperative by predators of every sort—becomes a famous battler for freedom. The saltwater wanderer becomes a freshwater gamefish without peer.

At least for a few weeks: When salmon enter fresh water, their bodies change rapidly. The emphasis shifts from eating/digesting to reproduction, from self-preservation to species preservation. Most salmon are a bright silver color when they arrive from the ocean. Within days, sometimes hours, their appearance begins to change dramatically. Atlantic salmon simply stop eating and grow darker; their qualities as a gamefish never deteriorate beyond a certain point. Pacific salmon, however, turn incredible shades of

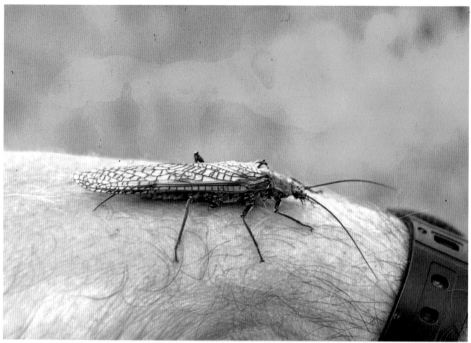

Salmonfly.

red or leprous green-grey. All Pacific salmon die after their first spawn, and their physiologies change far more than the Atlantic salmon's: the males develop exaggerated, luridly toothed kypes, or hooked jaws; some grow humped backs; their digestive organs atrophy completely; their fins wear away to tatters on the rocks they must swim over; and within two or three months of entering the river, flesh and muscle have degraded noticeably as well. The fish are swimming a race between the need to spawn and the inevitability of death. In a few more days, a Pacific salmon stream may look like the victim of toxic shock: thousands of salmon carcasses lining the gravel bars, thousands more littering the bottom, and a stench of rot beginning to fill the air. Within a few weeks, however, all that's left are the clean-picked bones. The salmon have played out their critical part in the regional ecology.

See Atlantic Salmon, Pacific Salmon, Chinook Salmon, Chum Salmon, Humpback Salmon, King Salmon, Landlocked Salmon, Sockeye Salmon.

Salmonfly—A species of stonefly, the salmonfly, *Pteronarcys californica*, is the largest aquatic insect in the North American fly fisher's pantheon. The air-breathing duns, amber and orange, and the mature nymphs, which range from deep brown to black, both may be nearly three inches long. The wingspan of the adult may be four inches. The salmonfly is most common on trout streams of the Intermountain West, where in June, July or sometimes August (depending upon weather) the nymphs, two to four years old, crawl ashore to hatch. After the metamorphosis the adults dry and harden their double pair of wings and attempt to set off, leaving the safety of the bank often to be blown out over the water, where they crash and struggle. Few survive the dunking. At the peak of the emergence, the insects may be thick enough to create a traffic hazard on nearby roads; the trout may feed so heavily that they are uninterested in food for several days. As they go, the salmonflies leave behind them boulders, streambanks, bushes and bridge abutments covered with their empty husks. Less than a week later, after mating with the males, the females leave the trees and swarm above the stream, often fluttering on the water's surface to release their eggs.

Salmon Reel—A fly reel intended for salmon or similar fish, such as large steelhead or sea-trout. Less obviously, a "salmon" reel is often one that is designed to evoke the classic fly reels (see Vom Hofe) of the heyday of Atlantic-salmon fishing, the early decades of the 20th Century. Salmon reels of that time were often enormous by modern standards—as much as five inches or more in diameter and weighing up to a pound and a half (the better to counterbalance a heavy, two-handed bamboo rod that might be 18 feet long). That sort of salmon reel would have, for example, solid black ebonite sideplates and a polished S-shaped crank handle. By contrast, a "steelhead" reel, though mechanically comparable in its ability to fight 10- to 50-pound stream fish, would be a more modern-looking, ventilated-spool design. See also Fly Reel.

Salter—The sea-run form of the brook trout, *Salvelinus fontinalis*, of the northeast coast of North America. Wherever riverine brook trout occur near a saltwater estuary, some of those fish will become salters, but exactly why is not known. It may be a response to overcrowding, it may simply be a case of certain individuals following their food farther and farther out into the sea. (All salmonids adapt easily to salt water.) Along with their riverine cousins, salters declined sharply in the 19th Century when heedless industrialization spread through New England. Salter populations have never truly rebounded the way the brook trout has inland; there are a few still, in little-known but locally prized Cape Cod streams, for example, but in much of southern New England the brook trout has been supplanted by brown trout that are more tolerant of the prevailing stream conditions. And it seems the salter name is now slowly being transferred over to the browns of those streams that have gone out to sea.

Saltwater Reel—A fly reel intended, unsurprisingly, for use on the world's oceans. Though saltwater reels are generally large (that is, of high capacity) and strongly built (often, but not exclusively, machined from bar stock) and thus expensive, the only real criteria in some experts' minds for a saltwater fly reel is that it be somehow proofed against salt corrosion, that it carry some sort of effective drag, and that the spool run smoothly at high RPM. As skills increase and as tippet materials continue to improve, more and more anglers are going after bonefish, barracuda, school stripers, bluefish, weakfish, sea trout, redfish and so on with what their fathers would have called trout reels.

But as anglers progress to large bass, tarpon, sharks, small tuna and billfish, the saltwater fly reel truly comes into its own. Whereas to the small-stream trout fisherman the reel is the least critical piece of gear, to the saltwater big-game angler the reel is of paramount importance. A fish that swims at 12 miles per hour (many saltwater species can sprint much faster than that) is moving at just over 17.5 feet per second. If this fish is peeling line off a three-inch-diameter spool, it will revolve at 1,345 RPM. Were the reel fitted with 200 yards of backing and a 30-yard fly line, and if 40 feet of that line (plus a short leader) were already in the water, the fish would take the rest of the line—all 640 feet— in only 36 seconds. And when the spool/line diameter is down to *one* inch, the reel would be humming along at slightly more than 4,000 RPM.

If the spool is unbalanced—if it lacks a counterweight opposite the crank handle, on a direct-drive (see) model—wobble and vibration can make the rod almost impossible to hold and may even unscrew the reelseat lock rings. If the spool and its spindle are not well made, or if the bearings (sleeve, ball or roller type) are poor or dirty or dry, the reel may simply seize up.

Few, if any, large saltwater fly reels are anything but single-action. That is, one turn of the handle equals one turn of the spool. Gearing that would let the angler bring in more line per turn would also spin the spool that much faster when the fish is running. A clutch to disengage the gear train would be possible, but most big-game fly fishers would regard this as mechanically too complex and thus prone to failure.

If this fish were not only fast—a bonefish, say—but large—a tarpon, perhaps—the saltwater reel should ideally have a high-quality internal, or mechanical, drag (see) to hinder it in its attempt to strip off all that line. In addition, an exposed palming rim (see) would help the angler fine-tune the pressure on the running fish. And finally, if the quarry were a deepwater species, such as tuna or billfish, the reel—now truly a big-game model—should have tremendous line capacity. Five hundred yards is no longer uncommon. See also Fly Reel.

Sans Noeud—Literally, "without node." The French phrase was adopted by Tom Dorsey, rod designer and builder at the Thomas & Thomas rod company, as the name of one of his special limited-edition split-cane rods. The Sans Noeud series was a run of 20 7 1/2-foot, two-piece, five-weight rods built in 1981. The nodes, where the cell walls had been in the whole culm, were cut out of the bamboo strips and the resulting segments were spliced together in long, overlapping "darts." Like all of Dorsey's specials, the Sans Noeud has the unique look and special trappings of a true collector's item, yet the rod is a first-rate fishing tool.

S-Cast—A form of slack-line cast; see.

Scrim—In rod manufacturing, scrim is the thin, woven layer of material that serves as a backing for the fiber "cloth," or pre-preg (see). With graphite, the scrim is usually fiberglass, and it is simply rolled onto a rod mandrel (see) with the graphite layers. In fact, the scrim serves a critically important function: It adds the hoop strength that the epoxy and the longitudinal graphite fibers can't provide; without hoop strength the rod blank would collapse under load.

Note then that many—probably most—"graphite" rods contain a small amount of fiberglass. There are other ways to provide hoop strength, however, that don't necessarily require fiberglass, and a reputable rod company that claims its products are "100 percent graphite" may well be telling the truth (except for the resin fraction, of course). See also Graphite Rod Manufacturing.

Scuds—Often called freshwater shrimp, these are in fact members of the order *Amphipoda* (true shrimp are *Decapoda*). There are terrestrial as well as aquatic species—and marine as well as freshwater types too—and they are important forage for trout and other gamefish.

Sea-Run—See Anadromous.

Sea-Trout—The anadromous, or sea-run form of the brown trout, *Salmo trutta*. In Europe, where it is analogous to the North American steelhead, the sea-run rainbow trout, the sea-trout is highly prized as a gamefish. In Europe at least, sea-trout are long-lived; British angling authority Hugh Falkus writes of individuals who have returned to fresh water to spawn well over a dozen times (while perhaps one percent of Atlantic salmon survive to spawn five times). Unlike Atlantic salmon, sea-trout are relatively casual where their natal rivers are concerned—they will enter and spawn in any clean, accessible stream, tending simply to follow each other and the currents and to avoid obstacles. Wherever riverine brown trout occur near a saltwater estuary, some of those fish will become sea-trout, but the genetic, hereditary or environmental trigger that brings this on is not known. It may be a response to overcrowding, it may simply be

*Sea-Trout—a large hen fish in pre-spawn colors from Tierra del Fuego's
Rio Grande.*

a case of certain individuals following their food farther and farther out into the sea.
(All salmonids adapt easily to salt water.) These fish tend to grow larger faster than their
stream-bound siblings and they take on the silvery sheen of a salmon, but most are
not true sea-trout; their marine foraging can hardly be called a migration.

Sea-run browns occur all along the coast of northeastern North America. Around
1960 true British sea-trout were planted in some estuaries on the Connecticut shore,
and these fish slowly spread. Most of those that are caught are probably mistaken for
salmon. In the Old World small (up to about five pounds) sea-trout are widespread
in the British Isles. In Norway and Sweden, however, sea-trout grow as large as salmon,
often exceeding 10 pounds. Sea-trout are far easier to transplant than Atlantic salmon,
and they have been well established in the Southern Hemisphere, where salmon
stockings have always failed (the water is simply too warm). In the 1920s British sea-
trout were stocked in the Rio Grande on the east coast of Tierra del Fuego; in the 1950s
they were released into a small stream in the Falkland Islands. Both strains have
flourished to the point that these are probably the finest sea-trout fisheries on earth
at the moment. Fish of 15 pounds or more are caught (and released) often.

Seatrout, Spotted—A popular flyrod gamefish along the southern Atlantic Coast of

North American, the spotted seatrout (*Cynoscion nebulosus*) or speckled trout is often confused with its close relative the weakfish (*Cynoscion regalis*) and some anglers seem to use the names interchangeably. The seatrout is most common in the shallow bays and estuaries of the Carolinas, Florida and Texas, and it can be taken on shrimp and mullet flies while sight-fishing from a skiff poled along the margins or across the flats.

The spotted seatrout has a silvery belly and flanks and darkens to blue-gray on its back; the fins may be a greenish-yellow. (And, save for the double dorsal fin, its silhouette is trout-like.) It is often heavily marked with round black spot, which help differentiate it from the weakfish: Seatrout spots extend up onto the second dorsal fin and the tail. In addition, seatrout are often brighter and more vividly marked (often a characteristic of tropical and semi-tropical fish) than the more northern weakfish. Seatrout spawn in the spring, close inshore where the young can reach cover in the eelgrass and other marine vegetation. Spotted seatrout average about four pounds and rarely grow bigger than 10 pounds.

Sedge Fly—Another name for caddis; see.

Shad—The anadromous American shad, *Alosa sapidissima,* is native to the East Coast of North America. The fish resembles an overgrown herring but in the past it was sometimes called the poor man's Atlantic salmon. Today, of course, excellent Canadian salmon water is available to all; and even well-to-do anglers know not to discount the humble shad as a gamefish. In the spring, when the shadbush blooms, the spawning runs begin in Atlantic Coastal rivers from Florida to Labrador. American shad—also called white shad and common shad—commonly weigh two to five pounds but many reach eight pounds and a few henfish hit double digits. The shad is a slab-sided, sea-bright fish with a deeply forked tail, a single dorsal fin and a row of black spots extending back from its gills.

In 1871 Fish culturist Seth Green brought the first American shad to the West Coast. He planted shad fry in the Sacramento River, and today there are shad runs from Baja California to Alaska; shad have reportedly even crossed the Bering Strait and are now spawning in the rivers of the Kamchatka Peninsula. Northern shad typically spawn more than once, and willingly enter rivers other than their birthplace, so this is a dependably plentiful fishery.

The top shad rivers on the East Coast are the Delaware, the Connecticut and the Hudson; there are small commercial netting operations on all three. On both coasts there are shad festivals, offering lessons in de-boning and filleting the fish, and planked shad and shad-roe dishes. When the runs are peaking, fishermen often line up elbow-to-elbow along the shore, below Enfield Dam, for example, on the Connecticut, casting lead-head shad darts to the thousands of fish milling around trying to pass upriver. Shad have soft mouths and broad, powerful sides that they use effectively in the strong current.

The smaller hickory shad, *Alosa mediocris*, with its jutting lower jaw, is more plentiful along the southern Atlantic Coast; although it does reach New England, the heaviest runs occur south of the Chesapeake Bay. Hickory shad are game fighters, but they are smaller than American shad, usually only two pounds or so.

Shank—The long, generally straight, upper section of a fishhook, between the eye and the bend, to which the fly dressing is attached. See Hook.

Shock Tippet—A short section of heavy monofilament or wire used on large or toothy fish to protect the lighter class tippet. See Tippet.

Shock Tippet—Saltwater streamers with wire tippets already attached

Shoot—To shoot line is to let it be pulled out through the guides by the force of the cast. Casters may shoot line on both the back cast and the forward cast, while false-casting or on the final, presentation cast. A strong, controlled shoot is critical to good distance casting. See also Double Haul.

Shooting-Head Line—A specialized composite fly line that has a heavy casting section, or head, attached to a running line that may be level fly line or a length of monofilament. The head itself is usually about 30 feet long (though there are mini-heads of only 10 feet); it may float or sink, and it usually has small loops on both ends, to attach the running line and the leader butt. See Fly Line.

Shuck— The cast-off, empty husk left behind when an insect moults, or passes from one stage of its lifecycle to the next.

Sidemount Reel—While most fly reels project vertically from the rod, a sidemount reel is literally just that: The foot is attached to one side of the reel, instead of along the bottom, and it fastens the reel to the rod horizontally. In casting, gravity dictates that a sidemount reel hang downward, just like a conventional reel. But to wind line in, the angler rotates the rod 90 degrees to one side to bring the crank handle within reach.

Today the sidemount design persists only in a few automatic (see) fly reels, with finger levers set to take up line without having to turn the rod. In the latter half of the 1800s, however, sidemount fly reels were very popular in North America, beginning with the historically significant Billinghurst "birdcage" reel (see), patented in 1859. Because the center of mass of a sidemount reel is closer to the rod centerline, it makes a more streamlined package; but the vertically mounted reel, on a rod that need not be rotated for the reel to come into play, is a more stable "platform" with which to fight a strong fish. Charles Orvis' 1874-patent reel (see), which set the standard for freshwater fly reels, also helped drive the sidemount style off stage.

Sideplate—The "cheeks" of a fly reel, which enclose the spool. Many light- or medium-duty reels, whether they have full cage-type frames or half frames (see), have only one sideplate; the outer flange of the spool is exposed. (This reduces weight and manufacturing costs and also makes it easier to change spools.) A single sideplate is often called a backplate. Heavy-duty reels usually have two sideplates in order to provide support for both ends of the spindle. The sideplates are often where drag knobs or clicker buttons are mounted. See Fly Reel.

Sight-Fishing—Casting to visible fish, the most exciting and often nerve-wracking form of fly-fishing. Watching a cruising predator turn, approach, inspect the fly and then decide whether to eat it—all of which may happen in half an eyeblink or in seconds that seem like hours—can give even an experienced angler a nasty case of hair trigger or the shakes. (One of the hardest things to learn in fly-fishing is to give a striking fish enough time to get the fly in its mouth before reacting.) Sight-fishing is often called "hunting with a fly rod"—stalking the prey with rod instead of shotgun, perhaps with a guide in place of a bird dog—and it puts the same great emphasis on careful approach and skill. Thus sight-fishing is not only exciting but also the best of all ways to sharpen fly-fishing skills, for the results of every move—from stepping into the water to casting to the presentation and strike—can be seen and assessed immediately. The opposite of sight-fishing is blind-casting.

Silicon Carbide—A synthetic "mineral" compound of silicon and carbon that is nearly as hard as diamond; it is used to provide a smooth, non-abrasive and long-wearing surface in line guides.

Silk Line—For about 100 years before synthetic fly lines took over the sport, in the 1950s and '60s, fly fishers used lines made of strands of silk braided together. (And before that, fly lines were, like leaders, made of braided horsetail.) The tapers were created by adding or subtracting individual fibers. If not thoroughly dried after each use, a silk line would rot; it would sink if it wasn't dressed ("greased") properly; and even if it was it would sink soon enough anyway. To try to help them float and repel water, manufacturers tried hollow-braided silk lines and experimented with enamel coatings, but to no avail; the enamel cracked and water infiltrated.

A few purists, however, have never given them up, and a handful of companies continue to produce silk lines for them. A silk fly line has a supple feel and, because it is solid, it has a thin diameter for its weight. Modern silicone-based dressings extend the life of the silk as well. A modern intermediate-weight synthetic line (see) handles and performs somewhat like a silk line. See Fly Line.

Silver Salmon—*Oncorhynchus kisutch*, one of the five species of Pacific salmon that spawn in the coastal rivers of northwestern North America. Although it is much smaller than the chinook, or king salmon, the silver, or coho salmon is generally regarded as a superior gamefish by fly fishers. Its reputation as a hard-fighting, spectacular leaper—and the ease with which it can be transplanted—led to its successful introduction into the Great Lakes in 1967 and then, accidentally and by plan, into other North American waters as far east as Lake Champlain. Coho are now found even in a few coastal New

Silver Salmon—A southwest-Alaska fish just beginning to develop its spawning colors.

England rivers. (The State of New Jersey has been trying to plant coho in the lower Delaware River since the early 1980s. Most fishermen, however, are aghast at the idea, for the Delaware, especially in its upper reaches, is perhaps the finest wild-trout river system in the eastern US. The coho could displace the trout, disrupt their spawning patterns and perhaps introduce new diseases.) Coho have also been released in southern Patagonia.

Although they are anadromous, coho are not thought to be wide-ranging fish; tagging studies indicate they tend to remain near their home rivers and do not roam the ocean basins as widely as chinook or Atlantic salmon do—a fact that also makes them a favorite of transplant-minded biologists.

An indication of how well they flourish as exotics may be that the current IGFA all-

Silver Salmon—A large Alaskan male in full spawning dress and kype.

tackle record coho is a 33-pound, 4-ounce fish that was taken New York's Salmon River, a Great Lakes tributary, in 1989. In their native waters—from California's Monterey Bay to Point Hope, Alaska, and along the Russian and Japanese coasts— coho rarely exceed 12 to 15 pounds.

Silver salmon are, in fact; in the estuaries or newly arrived in fresh water, silvers are handsome, chrome-sided fish with greeny-black backs and a scattering of black spots on their fins and backs. Depending on latitude, they enter rivers in mid- to late summer and have spawned and died by February. Spawning silvers darken noticeably and may develop rainbow trout-like slashes of red on their flanks, and the males grow spectacularly hooked kypes. Along with attracting considerable sportfishing revenue into their areas, silver salmon are also valuable commercially.

Single-Action Reel—A fly reel in which one turn of the crank handle produces one revolution of the spool. Thus such a reel lacks the gear train that drives a multiplying reel, which many fly fishers distrust as inherently fragile or trouble-prone. See also Multiplying Reel.

Single-Foot Guide—A kind of line guide (see) with a full ring and only one foot; that

---

is, one point of attachment to the rod. The ring, usually with an insert of carbide or other hard, smooth material, is cantilevered out from the foot. Compared to conventional bridge-type ring guides, single-foot guides are lighter and they do not stiffen the rod's flexural profile as much. Some custom builders offer them on big-water fly rods, for a presumed gain in casting range.

Single Haul—In fly-casting, a single haul is a pull made by the line hand just as the rod hand begins to power-snap the next cast forward, be it a false cast or the presentation cast, when the fly will be sent on its way. The haul accelerates the line to a higher speed so it makes a tighter loop that can travel farther or punch through the wind better. *Double*-hauling means to pull the line on both back and forward false casts; single-hauling is pulling only on the forward cast.

The rod propels the line forward; the caster hauls by pulling sharply on the line in his hand at the same time (instead of just holding it until it's time to let go for the final shoot). The line moves through the guides while the guides themselves are moving with the rod. The length of the haul varies from six inches on a medium cast to as much as four feet on an all-out heave across a coral flat or a competition casting pool. See also Double Haul, Fly-Casting.

Sinking Line—A fly line that sinks along its full length; also called a full-sinking line (as opposed to a sinking-tip). Sinking lines let the angler go deep with the fly, down to where gamefish feed most often. To do so, these lines come in a great variety of sink rates, from about one foot per second to as much as 10 feet per second. See Fly Line.

Sinking-Tip Line—Sometimes also called a dual-density line, the sinking-tip is just what the name implies: a short (usually 10 to 30 feet) section of sinking line ahead of a floating belly and running line. See Fly Line.

Skamania—A summer-run strain of steelhead; migratory rainbow trout that move into their spawning streams from May through September instead of in the fall and winter. Skamania (and other summer steelhead, from the Rogue, Siletz and Umpqua rivers of Oregon) have been successfully introduced into the Great Lakes in order to provide warm-weather steelhead fishing.

Skater—A type of high-floating dry fly meant to "skate" across the water (a technique that can be devastating on Atlantic salmon that seem to refuse everything else). Like spider patterns (see), skaters have bushy, overlong hackles, but these are palmered parachute style—that is, wound on top of the hook shank like helicopter rotors (or a parachute). Since they need no "rudder" to sit upright on the water, skaters lack tails and they may be somewhat overdressed, for better flotation. It is possible that Edward R. Hewitt (see), developer of the Bivisible and the Spider, was the first to intentionally skate a dry fly for trout.

Skin Mount—The classical taxidermist's replica of an animal; that is, the actual skin of the animal, which has been removed, preserved and then stretched over a lifesize form that has been arranged in an allegedly lifelike pose. A skin mount is a particularly labor-intensive effort even for a fish (despite the fact that most gamefish are far smaller than most game animals) because inevitably a mounted fish skin must be painted to match its original colors. A fish that is to be "stuffed" first has to be skinned, very completely and carefully. This should be done as soon as possible, virtually on the spot, but sometimes the fish has to be frozen first. Then the skin is folded or rolled up and put in a container (a coffee can, for example) with some sort of preservative such as alcohol. The taxidermist is then faced with reconstructing the fish from a wad of slimy, tissue-thin, fragile, colorless material; the fins and tail may or may not be in the coffee can too. Little wonder that a professional skin mount of a trout or salmon could cost four or five times as much as the fine split-cane rod the fish was caught on.

The impracticality of this approach to preserving one's cake became unbearable first in big-game fishing, and so it became common even decades ago to "mount" large billfish and the like by attaching the real spear and maybe the dorsal fin to a synthetic replica of like size. It quickly became possible to order fish "mounts" of many saltwater species by the inch. This freed fishermen from messy, time-consuming and extremely expensive real skin mounts (and of course also from the tiresomely literal truth).

However, as the catch-and-release ethic (see) began to take hold, more and more anglers, particularly fly fishers, began to see that with this method they could have their cake and eat it too—that is, they could release a trophy fish to swim away *and* also have a "mount" made to keep the memory fresh at home. Skin-mount taxidermists began to be replaced by sculptors who, with molds and resins and paints and their own considerable artistic skills, could reproduce a customer's fish just from measurements and color photographs. Some of these artists also arrange the fish in a lifelike setting—posing it, for example, over a gravelly bottom just like its real habitat. Today, a high-quality replica mount (see) is usually more realistic looking than even the best skin mounts, and the hand-painted man-made fish requires no maintenance except dusting; the colors don't fade (unless it's kept in the sun), there's no skin to peel or crack, and the fins don't get brittle with age. The price, however, for a high-quality replica is the same or higher.

Slack-Line Cast—A cast that leaves slack in the line and leader when the fly hits the water; that is, instead of lying straight on the water, the line and/or leader starts out in S-curves. A slack-line cast is very useful in moving water when fishing across-current or straight downstream, when the dry fly or nymph has to drift naturally through a lie that can't be reached from below with an upstream presentation. Any slack-line cast is only as good as the tippet between leader and fly; a tippet that is too short or too thick or too stiff will drag its fly no matter how much slack line has been created. There are several ways to introduce slack into the line:

The **bounce cast** is a normal, straight-on presentation cast that is just a bit overpowered. Keeping the rod tip slightly high, let the line and leader unroll completely in the air above the water and then grip the rod tightly—or even pull it back a few inches—so that the unfurled line stretches out tight and then rebounds, or "bounces" back, a few feet before landing.

The **wiggle cast** or **S-cast** takes slightly more practice but it is also easy and effective; some anglers find it more controllable than the bounce cast. Again, start with a normal, straight-on presentation, aimed slightly above the water. But as the final cast is unrolling forward, shake the rod tip back and forth horizontally. Since the line faithfully follows every move of the rod tip, these wiggles will be translated into the line as it falls to the water—in a graceful series of S-curves. Wiggling early in the forward cast leaves the curves out near the leader; waiting a bit introduces curves closer to the rod.

The **pile cast** concentrates the slack in the tippet, the leader and perhaps the last few feet of the line. Aim the presentation cast even higher than for the preceding slack-line casts; then, as it unrolls, quickly lower the rod tip. The end of the line and the leader will collapse in a "pile" on the water, leaving you in direct control of most of the line while the fly drifts freely for those few critical feet, its progress unhindered by the supple coils of nearly invisible tippet.

The **reach cast** is an easy cross-current presentation that extends the drift time of the fly by a critical few feet or seconds before the line must be mended or the fly begins to drag. As the final forward cast unrolls in the air, simply "reach" with the rod tip to the right or the left; the fly will arrive on target but there will be a large bow in the line between rod and fly. When there is fast water flowing between angler and fly, a reach cast made to the up-current side will let the fly and the line move in tandem.

With all slack-line casts you will have to experiment a bit first to learn to reach the target. You will use more line than if you cast directly to the lie, since the slack uses extra line. The S-cast usually creates the most slack, and you may wish to shoot a few feet of line during the "wiggle" to help compensate. See also Fly-Casting.

Sleeve Ferrule—A type of ferrule commonly used in graphite fly rods, so called because a sleeve (also graphite) attached to the bottom of the tip section simply slides over the top of its mating butt section. The other most common joint in graphite rods is the spigot ferrule (see). See Ferrule.

Slider—A type of topwater fly that has a solid head (of molded plastic, carved balsa wood, rubber or even tightly spun deer hair) and usually a hackle tail, which may represent frog's legs or a baitfish's body. It is called a slider because it slips through the water with relatively little commotion; thus, unlike a popper (see) with its concave face, a slider has a streamlined bullet-shaped head. Sliders are usually used on bass in lakes or on saltwater species such as bluefish or striped bass. Sliders can be tied on just about any long-shank hook; there is no need for a bent-shank popper hook because sliders, lacking the action of a popper, don't need to ride with one particular side upward in the water.

Slime—On a fish, the coating of mucus that protects its skin. Animals that live in the air have an outer covering composed of layers of dead, hardened tissue. But because they live in a liquid medium, fish have a skin that is alive—that is, made up of living cells. The slime exuded by these cells serves as a lubricant to reduce friction in swimming, as a physical and chemical barrier against parasites, and also as a means to maintain internal liquid balances. To protect this mucus coating, fish that are to be released should be handled as little as possible, preferably not at all. Wet your hands thoroughly before lifting a fish from the water, and handle it as gently as possible. Experienced anglers who wear a cotton glove or a bandanna or a section of a nylon stocking over their hands to hold fish do so not to protect the slime but to provide a better grip without having to squeeze the fish. See Catch-and-Release.

Slip Strike—A delayed strike (see) sometimes used where fish take a sunken fly slowly and deliberately. On certain Atlantic-salmon rivers, for example, where anglers cast streamers across the current and let them swing downstream, they may let a loop of line—a foot or less, usually—hang between the reel and the forefinger of the rod hand, which loosely clamps the line. Often the first indication that a fish is mouthing the fly comes when the dangling loop of line magically disappears; when the slack is gone and the line comes tight to the reel, the salmon will have turned, with the fly in its mouth, and it's time to strike by raising the rod tip. A hair-trigger response at the first tug of the fish would simply pull the fly from its mouth. Some salmon guides, introducing trout fishermen to salmon on these rivers, show their anglers how to rig a slip strike and then tell them to watch the birds, the scenery, other fishermen, anything but the line—so the salmon can hook themselves without interference.

Delayed strikes, on wet or dry flies, often have local names: the Hail-Mary strike, the Wait-a-Bit strike and so on. Alternately, some British ghillies tell their sports to chant deliberately "God save the Queen!" before raising the rod tip.

Slut—In Newfoundland and Labrador fishing lodges, a camp pot for boiling tea or coffee.

Smallmouth Bass—The smallmouth, *Micropterus dolomieui*, one of the so-called black basses, is a popular freshwater gamefish. It is common in cool, clear, well-oxygenated water, in rocky-bottom streams or lakes. In its habitat, diet and behavior it more resembles a trout than it does its boisterous relative the largemouth bass. The two basses can be hard to distinguish in some areas, but the smallmouth's jaw does not extend back past its eye and its dorsal fin, though it has two lobes, isn't split as deeply as the largemouth's. Smallmouth bass are usually somewhere between bronze and olive green in color, with darker vertical barring on their flanks. Particularly in moving water, they are slimmer and more streamlined than largemouth bass, and a five-pounder is a large fish. Smallmouths build nests and spawn in the spring, when the water temperature reaches the 60s.

Smallmouth bass are wary diners and often as difficult to catch, on any tackle, as a brown trout of similar age and experience. Smallmouths have been important to New World fly-fishing for more than a century. According to the American Museum of Fly Fishing, the first known reference to fishing for smallmouths with floating flies was a letter in the December 4, 1873, issue of *Forest and Stream*. It was credited to an F.L. King, of Rochester, New York, who wrote of fishing in the Genesee River and "Canandaigua outlet" (still prime smallmouth water). Not only does this precede Theodore Gordon, regarded far and wide as the "father of American dryfly-fishing," it isn't even about trout, the dryfly purist's trophy.

Smut—Any of a variety of small insects. According to fly-tying historian Darrel Martin, the term is descended from Old English and is probably related to smudge and soot, a small black particle.

Smutting—The action of a trout rising to a small insect; characteristically, a slow, gentle rise that causes little disturbance on the water.

Snake Guide—A type of line guide used on fly rods, between the tiptop (see) at one end and the stripping guide (see) at the other. Snake guides are one-piece stainless-steel steel wire (non-reflective matte finishes are also available) and have flattened ends, or feet, that are trapped under the winding thread that holds them in place. The name comes from a loose resemblance to a snake undulating across the ground, but in fact snake guides look more like badly twisted inchworms moving up the rod blank.

Sneck—A style of fishhook with a squared-off bend, the purpose being to make a hook with the longest-possible shank for its gape. The square bend meant the shank was fully as long as the entire hook. The sharp bend, however, was a notorious weak spot and the design has become obsolete.

Snelled Hook—Snelling is a very strong method of attaching a line to a bare hook. However, both ends of the line have to be free in order to tie the knot, which is why snelled bait hooks always come with a length of leader (the snell) attached; it's impossible to snell a hook to a line when the other end is already attached to the reel. Antique (or reproduction) loop-eye flies have been snelled and the dressing applied over the wrapped end of the snell.

Snook—One of the easiest of all fish to recognize, the tropical snook, *Centropomus undecimalis,* has a prominent black line that runs laterally from its upper gills to the fork in its tail. Its silhouette is something midway between a pike and a striped bass, but it has tall twin dorsal fins and a protruding lower jaw. Its flanks and belly are silver; its back may be any color from a brown-bronze to bluish-green. The edges of its gill covers are sharp and serrated, which many inexperienced fishermen learn the hard way. Snook occur on both the Atlantic and Pacific sides of Central America, from Florida along the Gulf Coast south to Brazil and from Baja California to northern Peru. An active predator and a spectacular gamefish, it is a shallow-water, inshore species that prefers to lie in the cover of mangrove roots, dock pilings and bridges, and it swims far up into estuaries, streams and canals, sometimes even above the brackish water. Snook feed on crabs and shellfish and the myriad free-swimming baitfish of warm waters. Most individuals caught in Florida or along the Gulf Coast weigh six to 10 pounds but snook of more than 30 pounds are taken annually. They are an ideal, if difficult flyrod gamefish—wary yet aggressive and powerful, darting from cover to strike a fly, then turning instantly to saw the leader against roots or concrete.

Sockeye Salmon—The sockeye, or red or kokanee, salmon (*Oncorhynchus nerka*) is the most plentiful in the American Northwest. Found from San Francisco on up the coast to Alaska's Bristol Bay, it is the Pacific salmon most likely to show up in a can. It is no trophy even when fresh, but it can be spurred into striking a hook. The sockeye's chief benefit to sport fishermen—and to hunters, netters, conservationists, and anyone else interested in preserving the Northwestern ecology—is the sheer size of the sockeye's annual spawning run. The millions of fish and the billions of their eggs are a critically important food source for many gamefish and for other animals ranging from insects up through birds and foxes to the coastal grizzlies. See also Pacific Salmon.

Soft-Hackled Fly—A type of simple wingless and tail-less wet fly fished on a floating line. Most soft-hackled flies have basic floss (yellow, green or orange predominate) or dubbed bodies and, at the head, a few sparse wraps of partridge or woodcock hackle. Unlike stiff dryfly hackle, this feathered collar hangs almost limply from the hook and in the water it pulsates along the body in a lifelike way. At least one soft-hackled pattern, the Donne fly, appears in the "Treatyse of Fysshynge wyth an Angle," in the second edition of *The Boke of St. Albans*, published in 1496. G.E.M. Skues, the English pioneer of nymph fishing, in his book, *The Way of a Trout with a Fly* (1921), called them Yorkshire hackles and wrote: "What these flies really represent cannot always certainly be predicated. Doubtless the hackles in some cases suggest the wings and legs of hatched-out insects, drowning or drowned and tumbled by the current, and in others they suggest some nondescript, struggling subaqueous creature. In either case the mobility suggests life."

Sylvester Nemes, through his book *The Soft-Hackled Fly* (Chatham Press, 1975) and various magazine articles, popularized the pattern in North America. He pointed out the similarity between the colorful floss-body soft-hackles and caddis pupae. In the US the soft-hackled fly also became known as a "flymph" and in fact it does look like a cross between a dry fly and a nymph. Nemes says he first saw soft-hackled flies in rod maker Paul H. Young's tackle shop in Detroit in about 1960; Young called them P.H.Y. Partridge Spiders and in his catalog described them thus: "Fished like a nymph. This is one of the best all around wet flies I ever used. Fish down and across stream, and take trout. Hackles lay back along the hook when wet, and crawl or work in the current."

South Fork Boat—A type of drift boat designed by Paul Bruun, a fly-fishing guide and business consultant, journalist and entrepreneur based in Jackson Hole, Wyoming. Named for the South Fork of the Snake River, the skiff looks much like a jonboat: It has a blunt bow and stern and lacks the extreme rocker of a conventional dory-type McKenzie boat (see). It is also shorter and more compact. The boat is thus easier to row in flat water and, with its low profile, isn't blown around by the wind as much. (The tradeoff is that it is not as stable and dry in white water.) The South Fork, in nearby Idaho, is generally wider, less rough and more open than the Snake in Wyoming, below Jackson Lake.

Sparse Grey Hackle—The *nom de plume* of Alfred W. Miller, 1892-1983, best known to anglers for his book *Fishless Days*, published by the Angler's Club of New York in 1954 and then re-issued in 1970 by Nick Lyons Books (now Lyons & Burford, NY) as *Fishless Days, Angling Nights*. His most important contribution to fly-fishing, however, was probably the great help and encouragement he was to the masters of his age— LaBranche, Hewitt, Atherton and others. Miller's pen name dates from his early days, when he wrote strong conservation articles in defense of the Beaverkill. In "real" life, Sparse Grey Hackle was a Wall Street reporter with a reputation as a sharp storyteller whose yarns went back to his service with General Pershing chasing Pancho Villa into Mexico. His wife, known as Lady Beaverkill, who was perhaps even more renowned as a fly fisher, died in July 1992 at the age of 91.

Spawning—The act of laying and fertilizing eggs, which for most fish requires relatively shallow water; thus the spawning migrations or "runs" of many open-water species. It is an uncomfortable irony of fly-fishing—with its ethics of catch-and-release and leaving the ecosystem unharmed—that many gamefish may be intercepted and taken on flies only when they are at some stage of their spawning cycle.

Nearly all trout and salmon, whether they live in the sea or in lakes, must spawn in moving water, which helps bury (and protect) the eggs, aerates the covered nest, and probably helps control the water temperature as well. In spring, summer or fall— depending upon the species, the climate and other environmental factors—sexually mature fish enter a tributary and begin their spawning run, or migration. Particularly on the Pacific coast of North America, the run may cover hundreds or even thousands of miles and take very large fish into shallow headwaters streams that are barely wider than the fish are long. The female selects a section of streambed where the current (and thus the gravel) is right and begins to dig her redds, or nests: She turns onto her side in the shallow water and flaps at the bottom with her tail, which frees the gravel; the current helps her move this loosened gravel downstream. When the hole is deep enough—from four or five inches to a foot or more and anywhere from a foot to a yard in diameter, depending on the size of the fish—the female presses her length down into it and expresses her ova. The male doesn't help dig; his job is to chase intruders away. He then joins the hen in the nest and fertilizes the eggs with milt. (Sometimes the male is so engrossed in fending off competitors that he misses his moment, and an observant smaller male darts in and takes his place at the crucial moment.)

With the eggs deposited, the female moves to a new site just upstream and begins again. This time the gravel she displaces drifts downstream in the current and covers up the first redd. The cycle continues for a day or a week. Generally, the male will stay to protect the redds for a while, but in very cold water incubation may take as long as five months.

Lake-dwelling brook trout or lake trout may spawn in still water, leaving their ova on the bottom near upwelling springs, if possible. The female brook trout digs a redd in the usual way but, without currents to help her, she has to cover the nest by pushing gravel back into it from the edges with her anal fin. The lake trout is a more casual parent: The hen simply broadcasts her eggs over a suitable stretch of lake bottom, apparently relying on gravity to sink enough of them into the interstices in the substrate to protect them from predation.

The great salmon spawning runs of the northern Pacific spark a feeding frenzy that carries the whole ecosystem through virtually its entire year. Loose salmon eggs—dropped prematurely by gravid females or washed out of uncovered redds—feed the multitudes of rainbow trout, grayling, arctic charr and Dolly Varden that follow the pods of salmon upstream. In Alaskan rivers where current and bottom conditions are right, by September certain pools may be littered with hundreds of thousands of loose buckshot-size eggs, each a bright orange-red.

Freshwater bass, smallmouth and largemouth alike, also dig redds with tail and fins, but it is the male that does the work. He entices a female in to lay her eggs and then fertilizes them; she leaves (or he chases her off) and, in sequence, several other hens may use the nest, their ova fertilized by the same male. The male guards the redd for the 10 days or so it takes the eggs to hatch, and he even stays to guard the fry for a few days; they stay in or near the redd long enough to eat the yolk sac completely.

Spawning Run—A "run" begins when anadromous fish leave the sea or lake where they have matured and swim up into rivers to dig redds and deposit their eggs. The annual salmon runs along the northern Atlantic and Pacific coasts of North America are some of the most spectacular natural phenomena on earth—millions of fish, some very large indeed, making their way singlemindedly upstream (sometimes more than 1,000 miles) to reproduce their species and, in most cases, to die. Pacific salmon quickly turn some shade of red when their run begins, and in coastal Alaska and British Columbia the fish arrive in such numbers that they often turn entire sections of river an unearthly bright red. See also Atlantic Salmon, Pacific Salmon, Salmon, Spawning.

Speckled Trout—Another name for the spotted seatrout; see.

Spentwing—Used to describe a dry fly tied in imitation of a fallen mayfly spinner (see); that is, with its large, gossamer wings spread flat on the water like the exhausted, spent insect.

Spey Cast—The Spey cast is a British development that lets a fly fisher with a two-handed rod work a long line effectively when there is no backcast room. It is an airborne roll cast that relies on the enormous leverage of a two-handed rod (see) and the drag of the line on the water. With a short line streaming away downcurrent at the end of its swing, the caster raises the rod tip and swings it up, over and behind his upstream shoulder. Then he power-snaps the rod into a forward cast out across the current. The line in the air moves back behind the caster only a few feet; the forward cast creates a loop that unrolls forward in the air, pulling line off the water and through the caster's fingers as it goes.

For real distance, there's the double Spey, which is difficult to describe on paper and looks almost magical in the act. The caster begins as for the single Spey but makes his first rod movement up and over his off shoulder, then swings the rod tip around overhead in a figure-eight before power-snapping it forward from his right shoulder. The line shoots emphatically, and experts can reach well over 100 feet with a double Spey.

These casts are impossible with a conventional single-handed rod, and even some two-handed rods can't perform them well; what's needed is an old-style long rod with a soft, progressive action that quickly gets the entire rod blank involved.

Spey Flies—Atlantic salmon patterns that originated on Scotland's River Spey. They are typically large and have a characteristic humpback wing and heron hackles palmered down along the body; the long fibers of the heron hackle pulsate and "breathe" enticingly in the water. On their home river they were intended to be used in the high water of winter or early spring.

Spider—A type of fluffy looking dry fly, originated by Edward R. Hewitt (see) around 1930, whose palmered hackles are unusually long for its hook. The fly rides high in the surface film or can be skated across the surface, and it offers a wispy, suggestive silhouette to the fish. To float well with their insubstantial hackling, Hewitt tied his spiders on hooks that were unusually small for that day—size #16 to #18—and to keep them balanced upright on the water gave them similarly wispy tails. See also Skater.

Spigot Ferrule—Along with the sleeve ferrule (see), this is the most common type of joint found on modern graphite fly rods. The "spigot" is a thin, solid plug of graphite that protrudes from the bottom of the tip section of a rod and fits into a cavity in the top of the mating butt section. Spigot ferrules are technically more complicated than sleeve ferrules, but with proper engineering and construction, they make a smooth, strong and potentially less air-resistant joint. See also Ferrule.

Spindle—The "axle" of a fly reel; the arbor, or shaft on which the spool turns. See Fly Reel.

Spinner—Also known as the imago, the spinner is the sexually mature form of the adult fly, the stage that follows the dun (see), or subimago. After depositing their eggs, spinners congregate in clouds above the stream and then fall exhausted into the water to die. Such a "spinner fall" can provoke trout to feed as actively as a hatch.

Splake—A fertile hybrid salmonid (a charr, since both are *Salvelinus*) that is the product of a lake trout-brook trout cross. Such an interbreeding would be highly unlikely in nature, but splake were developed in the 1950s in order to create a trout with the size of the laker and the brookie's ability to live in streams. At the time biologists feared for the long-term survival of the lake trout in the Great Lakes because of the lamprey infestation; the splake was seen as the laker's eventual replacement, at least in that watershed. Lamprey control was successful, however, and splake were never well established. Today, when many hatcheries and fisheries biologists and anglers are far more interested in restoring original strains and species of trout, things like the splake sound like a bad joke.

Splice—To join two lines by weaving them together in some way. The version used in rigging fly-fishing lines is a blind splice—"blind" because the line disappears inside itself, with no apparent beginning or end. The blind splice works only on hollow lines; fortunately, most Dacron backings and fly lines are of hollow-braided construction (the vinyl coating that gives a fly line its taper and weight is applied over this core). These braided, hollow "tubes" constrict when they're stretched, grasping anything inside with great strength. A blind splice between fly line and backing, for instance, where one has been inserted into the other, is stronger than either of the lines alone and is as smooth and flexible as a line with no knot. To anyone who has ever had a rod stripped by a powerful fish when a backing knot hung up on a guide, that is as important a benefit as strength alone.

The following techniques were developed by rigging expert Bill Hunter (who also designed the HMH vise—see). He points out that a blind splice is easier to make than some knots; all that's needed is a bottle of acetone, or nail-polish remover, a homemade splicing needle (a foot of .010" music wire crimped in half, into a sharp V), a tube of super glue, small scissors and a bodkin, or dubbing needle.

(Soaking a section of fly line in acetone for a few minutes removes the vinyl coating, to expose the braided core. The coating then simply peels off. Acetone is volatile— keep the bottle covered as much as possible; do this in a vented area; and keep flame away. Backing, of course, doesn't need to be stripped.)

There are two main uses for the blind splice. One is the loop splice, where a line loops back on itself to create an eye. This is the best way to make loop-to-loop joints, which are the best quick-change connectors between backing and fly line, leader and fly line, and shooting heads or lead-core sections and running lines.

The other is the basic blind splice, which can be used to make permanent connections between backing and fly line, or between any hollow-braided lines.

The technique is the same for both. The homemade splicing needle is the key to getting one line inside the other: To make a loop, first insert the needle into one section of line—use the bodkin to start the entry hole if necessary—and thread it up through the center of the line and then out through the sidewall again.

(For a small loop at the end of a fly line, to join backing or a leader, you need to thread only half an inch or so; a six-inch loop in the end of the backing—big enough to pass an entire spool of fly line through—requires three or four inches.)

Then simply trap the tag end of the line in the eye of the splicing needle and pull it back through the threaded part and out. To get the end through the hole in the side of the line, it may be necessary to fray the braid with the scissors for about half an inch at the very tip and then trim away a third to half of the fibers, to make it small enough to start through.

Now you can adjust the length of the loop by pulling the tag end. When you've got the right length, shorten the loop slightly and put a small drop of glue (for insurance) on the tag end near the core and quickly pull the glued spot just into the core. It should set almost instantly. Then push the standing part of the loop up slightly and cut off the extra tag end. Pull on the loop and the tag will slip out of sight into the core.

Some rigging experts recommend a follow-up drop of glue on the hole where the tag disappeared; on a fly line, the hole should be right next to the end of the vinyl coating, so the glue not only reinforces the splice, it also seals the rest of the fly line against water.

A short loop at the tip of a fly line, to attach a leader, can be coated with Aqua-Seal (the wader-repair adhesive) so that the connection doesn't "hinge" during casting.

The basic blind splice is really a double splice—backing into the fly line and fly line (the stripped core) into the backing, for a nearly bulletproof permanent connection between the two.

First push the splicing needle into the flyline core right at the edge of the vinyl coating and down the hollow core for three inches, and then push the needle out through the side of the line. Trap the end of the backing in the splicing needle and pull it into and then out of the fly line with the backing attached.

Now you have to insert fly line into the backing: Three inches from where it disappears into the flyline core, push the splicing needle into the backing and down its center toward the fly line. Just where it goes into the fly line, push the needle out through the side of the backing. Put the tip of the flyline core into the needle and pull it through the backing.

To complete the splice, trim the ends of each of the two lines and bury them inside the other. The final "knot" is as smooth and strong as a line connection can be.

Split-cane—Referring to fishing-rod blanks made of separate strips of bamboo laminated together into a strong, flexible whole. See Bamboo, Cane Rod Building.

Spool—That part of a fly reel that holds the line. See Fly Reel.

Sport Fishing Institute, The—An offshoot of AFTMA, the American Fishing Tackle manufacturers Association; see.

Spring Salmon—An Atlantic salmon that has survived the previous spring or summer run, the subsequent spawn, and the following winter. See Black Salmon.

Sproat Bend—One of the most common types of hook used in fly-tying, the sproat has a mildly angular bend that does not compromise the hook's strength while offering

more "bite" than a round perfect-bend hook. See Hook.

Sprocket & Pawl—The most common and probably the oldest type of internal drag in a fly reel. It is also one of the least effective; in fact, even an adjustable sprocket & pawl mechanism is little more than an overrun check (see). Still, as a true drag, it is entirely adequate for smaller fish, which often aren't played "off the reel" anyway. Even on larger reels meant for stronger fish, this type of drag is common because the angler is expected to supply extra braking and control via a palming rim (see).

The pawl is a triangular metal "tooth" that pivots on a stud inside the reel frame. One of its points meshes with the sprocket, a kind of gear that is pressed onto the spool arbor, and the flat side of the pawl opposite that point has a leaf spring pressing against it. As the spool (and the sprocket) turns, the pawl has to bump from one indent in the sprocket to the next, which slows the spool down a bit and also makes a clicking sound. The spring, since it pushes the pawl against the sprocket, determines just how much the spool is retarded (and how loud the click is). The spring is also a shock absorber that cushions the transition from dead stop to a whirring run.

The composition of the parts is important because this is a high-wear design; on the other hand, the machinery is dirt-simple and requires only the occasional "wipe and squirt" maintenance. Spare parts are inexpensive.

A sprocket & pawl meant as a true drag (as opposed to an overrun check) is usually adjustable—a button on the reel backplate lets the angler vary the spring pressure on the pawl. Nevertheless, in practical terms, the mechanism can exert only relatively little spool braking because of its inherent design limitations. Another limit—a flaw, in fact—is that most sprocket & pawl drags can be made to "float" at high speeds. That is, the pawl doesn't get enough time to fully engage each notch of the sprocket because the spool is turning too fast. Sometimes the spring is overcome entirely and the pawl simply flops over on its side and no longer meshes with the sprocket at all. This happens particularly when a strong fish puts on a sudden spurt, and the acceleration of the spool just kicks the pawl over. The tangle that may happen when a reel suddenly free-spools can be truly impressive.

Many such sprocket drags have dual pawl-and-spring setups, one on each side of the arbor. Normally only one is engaged—which one depends on whether the reel is being used left- or right-handed—and the other is pivoted out of the way and held there by its spring. Thus some spare parts are always at hand. Also, the drag pressure can be doubled simply by engaging the second pawl. Obviously, this means anticipating the need and field-stripping the reel, and in many cases the minimum drag is then too high for comfortable fishing (stripping line becomes inconvenient). However, it's sometimes a valuable option.

SSS—An abbreviation used by tackle companies, particularly reel makers, to denote gear heavy enough for "Salmon, Steelhead or Saltwater." It probably originated in the Orvis catalog. The term is slipping out of favor now, as manufacturers continue to expand their product lines—what might have been a single "SSS" reel in 1975 could today be four models: a light salmon/steelhead, a medium salmon/steelhead, a bonefish reel and a tarpon model, all available in either direct-drive or anti-reverse.

Standing Part—The working or main part of a line, as opposed to the tag end, in which a knot—to fly or backing or reel—is tied. See Knots.

Steelhead—*Oncorhynchus mykiss* (formerly *Salmo gairdneri*); the anadromous, or migratory, variety of the rainbow trout. Like Atlantic salmon, their alter ego on the east coast of North America, steelhead are prized gamefish, often difficult to bring to the fly and then spectacular battlers on rod and line. The name derives from the steelhead's shiny metallic color—and its strength—but as spawning approaches, steelhead darken and develop the rainbow's characteristic red swash along their flanks. As do landlocked rainbows, steelhead adapt relatively easily to new waters and they too have been transplanted across North America. Stocking has been particularly successful in the Great Lakes, where annual steelhead runs into many tributary rivers and streams have become major attractions. Many smaller runs occur as far east as Lake Champlain and even (in very small numbers) along the New England coast. The steelhead's natural range is from southern California to the Gulf of Alaska. There is a very tiny, well-tended but nevertheless threatened run of steelhead into Malibu Creek near Los Angeles; the panhandle and islands of southeast Alaska harbor many strong runs of steelhead. The best-known steelhead, however, are those of Oregon, Washington and British

Steelhead—a sea-bright British Columbia fish.

Columbia. They have attracted visiting anglers since Zane Grey first fished for them on the Rogue River in Oregon in 1922 and then wrote of his experiences. (Incidentally, that was when, and how, Grey became an ardent fly fisherman.)

Like rainbows, most steelhead are fall or winter spawners; however there are many strains, native to certain rivers, that spawn or at least run in the spring or summer. Steelheading is often portrayed as grim winter sport, a battle of numb fingers and feet against iced-up tackle and freezing water, but the reality is different. One of the most famous of steelhead streams is Oregon's Deschutes, a desert river that offers excellent summer fishing.

Across America, a typical steelhead weighs six to 10 pounds. However, much larger individuals—up to 35 pounds or more—are taken and usually released every year in their native range, especially in mainland British Columbia. Ironically, while transplanted steelhead are managed and protected as valuable resources, the native runs are still threatened, notably by interception at sea—by commercial fishermen who profess to be netting salmon—and by interference with their spawning streams. This runs the full gamut from water diversions for agriculture or power generation to clearcutting that raises the silt and temperature levels of the water.

In June 1988 the Committee on Names of Fishes, of the American Society of Icthyologists & Herpetologists, determined that the North American rainbow trout, long classified as *Salmo* (genus) *gairdneri* (species), should instead be known as a *mykiss*. *Mykiss* is the Asian rainbow trout, found on Siberia's Kamchatka Peninsula, which faces Alaska across the Bering Sea; the species name was adopted for both since the two fish are biologically identical and, as a classification, *mykiss* predates *gairdneri*. Going further, however, the committee addressed the genus of the fish, which brought up the question: Is the steelhead an anadromous rainbow? Or is the rainbow a landlocked steelhead? The scientists settled upon the latter, which instantly rendered the rainbow trout and the steelhead no longer trout but salmon—a Pacific salmon, and thus *Oncorhynchus mykiss*.

Steelhead Fly—A type of featherwing wet fly developed on the west coast of North America for steelhead, the anadromous rainbow trout. Steelhead flies evolved from, and are still closely related to, Atlantic salmon patterns. They are tied on the same kind of hook and in silhouette and general appearance are quite similar. However steelhead-fly dressings are non-traditional, including unique colors and materials (often brightly dyed synthetics) that Atlantic-salmon fly tiers—who typically follow established "recipes" and strive to duplicate vintage British patterns—would not. Many steelhead flies also go un-named, except perhaps by the anglers who created them for their own use.

Steelhead patterns emerged as a separate "discipline" in the 1970s when the late Syd Glasso and a few other Northwestern tiers began to attract national attention for their unique creations. As recognizable steelhead patterns began to emerge, they were often named for their rivers: the Skykomish Sunrise, the Rogue Red Ant, the Umpqua Special. Despite their wild colors, many steelhead patterns are notably simple. The current trend, however, is away from simplicity and towards flies that showcase the tier's art rather than the angler's need.

Steeple Cast—A change-of-plane cast sometimes used when a strong breeze is coming from directly behind. Make the back cast sidearm and low to the water, to try to cut through the wind, then, on the final forward cast, raise the rod to semi-sidearm or full overhead position and throw the presentation cast at a steep angle upward; the wind will carry it along to some degree. The chief disadvantage of the steeple cast is that it is virtually uncontrolled and often inaccurate.

Stockingfoot Waders—Chest- or waist-high waders with stocking feet; that is, without attached boots. They must be worn with special wading shoes (see). These shoes (or boots) provide traction and warmth and they cushion and protect the foot, but wading shoes need not be waterproof; the stockingfoot waders worn inside them keep the foot dry. Stockingfoot waders are usually made of neoprene, latex or urethane-coated nylon. The first two materials are stretchy and waders made of the third are usually cut very full, so stockingfoot waders are invariably more comfortable and easier to maneuver in than conventional canvas-type bootfoot waders. And in addition, wading shoes are more comfortable and provide better foot support than clumsy, loose-fitting one-piece bootfoot waders. The only disadvantage to stockingfoot waders is that they are more cumbersome to put on and take off; but fly fishers who spend hours at a time in moving water, often on rocky bottoms where footing may be precarious, usually prefer them. The Goodyear India Rubber Glove Manufacturing Co. ("rubber goods of every description") was producing latex stockingfoot waders—then called wading pants—in the 1880s.

Stonefly—There are an estimated 400-plus species of stonefly, of the order *Plecoptera*, in North America, and they form an important part of the ecology of many trout streams, especially in the west. Although some are less than half an inch long, many stoneflies are large—the salmonfly (see) is often nearly three inches long—and they may hatch in swarms too thick to see through. The lifecycle of a stonefly is much like a mayfly's; after anywhere from about one to four years (depending on size) the nymphs crawl ashore to hatch in relative safety on land. After molting from their

Stonefly—The newly emerged insect and its cast-off shuck, on the banks of Wyoming's Snake River.

nymphal forms the adults dry and harden their wings and then try to fly away into the trees. Most stoneflies are clumsy in the air, however, and a breeze can push the insects over the water, where they fall in—and fall victim to cruising fish. Most species of stonefly have four wings arranged in two pairs, which fold back across each other over the abdomen; long, forward-thrusting antennae; and two shorter tails. The wings are generally prominently veined. Some smaller species—the so-called Little Yellow Stonefly, *Isoperla* or *Alloperla*—are bright yellow, but most North American stoneflies vary from gray through brown to amber.

Stream Cleats—A device that fits onto wading shoes or the boots of a pair of waders to improve traction. Some stream cleats resemble tire chains; others are entire soles studded with metal, which fit over a boot like rubber overshoes or strap on like hiking sandals. In freestone streams most anglers are well served by felt-soled waders; but on boulder or ledge bottoms, especially in heavy current or where algae grows thickly, metal cleats provide a much better "bite" and far safer footing.

To generalize: chain-type cleats (which are also sold to mail carriers and others who spend time on icy sidewalks) are inexpensive, offer all-around utility and take up very little room in a vest pocket; they are meant to cope with unusual, short-term needs. Anglers who daily encounter treacherous footing should look for a more heavy-duty solution. The sandal- or overshoe-type cleats have steel spikes, screw heads or even sections of aluminum channel on the bottom, and these generally provide the best traction over very slippery ground. Look for a sole sturdy enough to hold the inserts, a good distribution of inserts across the bottom of the foot, replaceable inserts, and uppers that won't come off the wader too easily.

There are some drawbacks: Especially aggressive cleats may protrude so far that walking in them takes getting used to. Some cleats may pick up mud in impressive quantities; and anything attached to a boot—especially the sandal- or chain-type cleats—offers a place for sticks or brush to become entangled.

Some companies will outfit their felt-sole waders with metal studs as an option. These may require some break-in—the studs are recessed into the sole slightly, to allow for compaction of the felt around them—but they are effective (although less so than the most aggressive cleats), always present, and they greatly extend the life of the felt sole. Also available are wading shoes (for stockingfoot uppers) with carbide-tipped steel cleats already set into their felt soles.

Streamer—A type of wet fly that is generally meant to imitate a forage fish. The elongate, streamlined shape is created with hackle feathers tied on an extra-long-shank hook. Saltwater streamers, however, meant for billfish or other big game, may be eight inches long and tied on tandem hooks connected by a short length of heavy mono or cable.

A similar fly tied with a hair wing or tail is called a bucktail. To carry out the imitation successfully, streamers and bucktails both should be fished actively—retrieved through the water or cast down or across the stream on a tight line to "swim" in the current.

Stream Reclamation—To anglers, the act of improving a stream so that it will support some kind of a natural fishery. Strictly speaking, this means restoring water to its former "wild" condition by repairing damage done by run-off pollution, agriculture, over-use or nearby development—but, according to operators who do this commercially, it may also mean improving the habitat in an already healthy stream so that it may support more aquatic life.

The former is a popular long-term project among local fishing clubs, who rally around a damaged stream and turn its restoration into a valuable community effort. The latter is often commissioned by landowners who fish or who sell their fishing rights and who want to improve the carrying capacity of their stream. This generally means mechanical repairs: putting a backhoe into the streambed in order to dig out silted pockets or mats of brush, adding tree trunks at strategic locations to break the current and create pools, planting riparian vegetation for cover, fencing a stream against cattle and so on. The best stream-reclamation consultants are part biologist, part hydrologist, part landscape architect and part legal expert; they work with, not against, natural forces, and they do so within local, state and federal wetlands regulations.

Strike—The "take" of a fish, or the response of the angler; a fish strikes the fly and the fisherman strikes back. As in life, timing is everything on the strike: Small fish in fast water usually require an instantaneous response; larger fish in slower water may hook themselves and require no response (see Slip Strike).

If the present trend towards protecting animal rights continues, anglers may find themselves fishing for the strike alone, not with barbless hooks but with hookless flies. And in the Florida Keys, guides are forever yelling "Strike! Strike!" at their tarpon fishermen, to get them to drive the hook home in the fish's hard mouth. (And this brings to mind the definition of fishing as a string with a jerk on both ends.)

Strike Indicator—A piece of brightly colored yarn or foam used in nymph-fishing. It is attached to the leader above the fly (exactly how far up depends mostly on how deep the fly is working in the water), where it serves exactly like a kid's bobber—when a fish takes the subsurface nymph, which the angler can't see, the indicator twitches to signal him to set the hook. A yarn indicator can be tied in with a slipknot that then just pulls out afterward. (If the knot is above the tippet or if the tippet is not too fine, the knot generally won't compromise the strength of the leader too much.) The yarn can be dressed with fly flotant to keep it riding high.

Foam indicators often have some sort of adhesive backing that is meant to stick them to the leader; sometimes it works.

One of the oldest, best and most versatile of strike indicators is the classic two-fly dropper rig (see), with a nymph at the leader tip and a high-visibility dry fly above it as the dropper. One or the other will take fish, and the dry fly acts as the nymph's "bobber."

Striped Bass—*Morone saxatilis*, the striper, is one of the most important saltwater gamefish of North America. Originally endemic to the Atlantic Coast from Prince Edward Island to Florida and the Gulf Coast states, it was transplanted to California late in the 19th Century and it spread successfully along the Pacific Coast up into Washington. Stripers are handsome, silvery, well-proportioned fish with seven or eight prominent black stripes running horizontally parallel to the lateral line from gills to tail. These fish are omnivorous predators and first-rate gamefish, whether caught by night-casting in the beach surf or stalking the grassy estuaries with streamer flies or poppers. Both anadromous and migratory, striped bass spawn in the spring, entering the estuaries of major rivers and swimming well upstream into brackish water or even farther, above the tidal influence to fresh water. The average fly-caught striper weighs

Striped Bass.

less than 20 pounds, but fish of 60 pounds or more are fairly plentiful. East-Coast striper populations crashed in the 1980s under relentless pressure from commercial rod-and-line fishing, sport fishing and degradation of their inland spawning habitat. A concerted effort among government agencies and private anglers brought about a swift and dramatic turnaround within five years.

Taking a cue from the spawning behavior of the sea-run striped bass and from the existence of more-or-less nonmigratory strains of striper that live in New York's St. Lawrence and Louisiana's Lake Ponchartrain systems, biologists began landlocking striper bass in fresh water in the late 1960s. The experiment was such a success—the bass acclimated easily and still reach their normal saltwater size as well—that now more than half our states have such "impoundment" stripers.

Stripping Basket—A large, open, smooth-sided container, often plastic, into which fly line is stripped on the retrieve. It is usually worn on a belt at the caster's waist, but it may be free-standing on a boat deck as well. A stripping basket prevents the line from washing away in a strong current or tangling in rocks or brush on the ground and keeps it close at hand for the next cast. When fishing from a skiff in tropical conditions, where fly lines may go limp in the heat, a block of ice in a plastic trash barrel/stripping basket helps keep the line handling better; the fresh meltwater also washes some of the salt off the line.

Stripping Guide—The bottom-most guide on a fly rod, situated usually two feet or so above the reel. Unlike the other guides on a fly rod, which are called snake guides (see), the stripping guide is a ring type and it usually has an insert of some hard, smooth material such as carbide to let the line flow easily. The stripping guide is where the angle of the line changes, from the reel or the caster's hand to where it flows parallel to the rod; thus the stripping guide carries more load than the snake guides, which only direct the line. To further share the load, some heavy-duty fly rods have two stripping guides, the upper one slightly smaller. See Line Guide.

Subimago— The subimago, or dun, is an adult stage in the life of a mayfly or certain other aquatic insects when the insect develops the ability to fly but not yet to reproduce; it comes after the nymph and before the imago, the sexually mature state of its life. See also Mayfly.

Substrate—In an angling context, the bottom of a river, lake or other natural body of water. The term is usually used by fly tiers or entomologists who are referring to where most aquatic insects live.

Sunday Rod—An obsolete term for a fishing rod that breaks down into many small sections. It was a "Sunday" rod because it could be tucked into the pocket of one's best suit and then put to immediate use after church let out. Alternately, the fine tackle retailer Abbey & Imbrie, in its 1912 catalog, offered a "Sunday Special" as part of its series of "Suit Case Fishing Rods"—a five-piece rod short enough to hide in a pants leg when you were going to the stream instead of to church. (Fifteen years earlier, the company had offered "Bicycle Rods"—five-piece rods, of lancewood or split bamboo, in canvas cases meant to "fit between the frames of any bicycle.") See Multi-Piece Rod.

Super Z Ferrule—The modern standard in machined ferrules used on split-bamboo rods. The patented Super Z design is an improvement over the so-called Swiss ferrule (see); it provides both great strength and a slim profile when the male and female sections are joined. Previously, the male ferrule was "stepped down"—reduced in diameter—at the shoulder, to slide into the female. This weakened the male ferrule exactly where maximum bending stresses would concentrate. Furthermore, to fit into the ferrule and then up into the slide (the part of the male captured within the female), the split-cane rod section itself had to be turned down in two steps; the second reduction in particular removed most of the strong outer fibers of the bamboo, which left the ferrule carrying virtually the entire load of casting or fish-fighting. The Super Z required only one cut into the diameter of the rod sections (and a small one, at that) and no step-down in the male slide. Instead of the male shrinking to fit into the female sleeve, the sleeve grew slightly to accept the full diameter of the male slide.

The Super Z was put into production in 1948 by its inventor, Lou Feierabend, of Pearl River, New Jersey. The "Z" of the name is an engineering value, the Section Modulus, or strength factor, of a tube; Feierabend called it the "Super Z" because his design offered significantly more tube strength than other ferrules. One of Feierabend's first customers was premier cane-rod maker Everett Garrison, who had been dissatisfied with other ferrules. In his book, *A Master's Guide to Building a Bamboo Fly Rod* (with Hoagy Carmichael; Nick Lyons Books, 1977), Garrison wrote: "The Super Z ferrule was the only ferrule ever marketed that was, from an engineering standpoint, stronger than the rod section itself. The ferrule allowed for 'continuous action' through the rod sections. It had a stiffness which was transferred back and forward but nothing bent between the ends of the ferrule."

Surface Film—The air-water interface at the surface of a body of water; the nearly microscopic zone where small flies ride not on top of the water but *in* the top of the water.

Surface Stone Fly—An Atlantic-salmon dry fly invented by the late Lee Wulff (see) in about 1950. The original pattern had a wing and tail of either hackle or hair tied on a cigar-shaped yellow plastic body molded to a streamer hook. It rides half-sunken in the water, like a drowned insect, and it can be difficult to float. Wulff recommended casting it sidearm, so it wouldn't have far to fall to the water. More than once Wulff called it his "secret weapon" and noted that other anglers thought it was either a gag or a red herring to draw attention away from the *real* "killer" fly with which he took salmon when no one else could. The modern version of it—still available from Royal Wulff Products, the company founded by Lee and his wife, Joan—is much the same except that a tiny knob has been added to the top of the plastic body, to wind a parachute hackle around.

Synthetic flies are usually regarded as a "modern" development. However Wulff, a lifelong iconoclast and innovator, founded the Lee Form-A-Lure Company in 1951 to manufacture a series of synthetic streamer flies and lures. They were advertised to be more durable than conventional flies not only because of what they were made of but also because of how they were made: Instead of being lashed on with thread, the dressings—synthetic or natural fibers—were literally welded into the plastic bodies. A drop of solvent melted the plastic long enough for the material to be wrapped or pressed into it. Sparkles, eyes and other effects could be added the same way. Form-A-Lure was wiped out by a flood in 1955 but its products had failed to storm the market anyway. Wulff himself continued to make and fish plastic-body flies, of which the Surface Stone Fly is the best known and probably the most successful.

Some 30 years later, Wulff revived the idea as a commercial venture, this time under the trade name "Flies of the Future." He offered four basic plastic bodies, on hooks as small as #18 and large enough for tarpon. The fly bodies are made on simple pneumatic injection machines using molds Wulff carved himself, with a dentist's drill. The polystyrene bodies are of neutral density; the flies float or sink depending on how they are dressed. A wide variety of patterns can be "tied" on these hooks. They offer at least two distinct advantages: They are extremely easy and quick to tie; and they are virtually indestructible.

Surgeon's Knot—This is a very strong, ridiculously easy way to tie two lines together, and it successfully joins even monofilaments of different thicknesses. Saltwater anglers use the surgeon's knot mostly to tie shock tippets into their leaders; all anglers use it whenever they've forgotten whatever other knot they were trying to tie in the first place. The surgeon's knot leaves a notable lump in the line even after the tags are trimmed closely. See Knots.

Surgeon's Loop—A simple, strong loop often used as part of a saltwater leader system or to create a dropper loop. The surgeon's loop, like the surgeon's knot (above), can be used for a variety of emergency fixes when the "right" knot is in a reference book at home, but it too leaves a lump in the line that does not always run smoothly through the guides. See Knots.

Swiss Ferrule—A type of machined rod ferrule made with no step-down in the diameter of the male or female section; the forerunner of the Super Z ferrule (see).

Tag End—The end of a line in which a knot is tied. It also refers to the short piece of excess line that is left over (sticking out of the knot) when the knot has been tightened down. The opposite of the standing part of the line. See Knots.

Tailer—A handle with a noose on the end, to slip over the tail of a fish to drag it ashore or into a boat. The advantage over a landing net is that, for large fish, a tailer is smaller and easier to carry. However, tailers only work well on stiff-tailed fish such as Atlantic salmon; otherwise the loop may slip off. Salmon tailers are often handsomely made and have some kind of release mechanism that holds the loop—usually steel cable— open until it has been slipped over the fish, then lets the angler or guide pull it tight. For generations a tailer was as much a part of the Atlantic-salmon angler's gear as a priest (see), but as no-kill salmon fishing spreads around the world, both devices are rapidly disappearing. The abrasion and stress of a loop drawn tight around the fish's caudal peduncle—its "wrist"—often shortens a salmon's life even if it is then released.

Some anglers tail salmon by hand, which can be effective and harmless if done properly. (Harmless to the fish, that is; 20 pounds or so of fighting salmon can be quite a handful.) Do not squeeze tightly; just enough to immobilize the fish in the water. And don't raise a fish that will be released out of the water by the tail—its own body weight may separate the vertebrae. (Also be aware of the fish's protective coating of slime; see.)

In the oceans, fish are usually landed or boated with gaffs, although a loop of rope thrown around the tail is sometimes used to immobilize a fish for measurement—and the few sport fishermen who still kill sharks often do so by dragging them backward by the tail behind the boat, which rapidly causes death by drowning.

Tailing—The act of using a tailer on a fish, or seizing it by the "wrist" above the tail to land it (see Tailer). Also a way that some fish signal their feeding: Bonefish or permit grazing across a shallow flat with their heads down, rooting in the sand or mud for food, often have the upper lobe of their tails above the surface of the water. Such "tailing" fish are usually easier to spot. Sometimes anglers squat down to scan a flat at water level; that makes the tails, waving gently in the air, more visible against the horizon. Virtually any gamefish that enters shallow water may be "tailing" at some time.

Tailing Loop—A casting fault in which the line and the leader cross or collide while the forward or back cast is unrolling in the air. The cause may be a severely unbalanced line-leader-fly combination, but it is usually caused by poor technique, especially a too-narrow casting arc or power applied too early in the cast, which bends the rod tip too soon and creates a dip in the line path. Tailing loops are the most common cause of so-called "wind" knots—which thus should be called casting knots.

Taimen—Like its relative the huchen (see), the taimen is a large landlocked Eurasian salmonid of the genus *Hucho*, closely related to the charrs. Biologically, huchen and taimen seem to differ only in their gillrakers, but taimen grow larger and are the more restricted and northerly of the two. In Russia taimen are said to be distributed from approximately the Volga River in the east to the Amur River in the west, which amounts to most of Siberia and northern Mongolia. (Huchen, by contrast, are native as far east as Japan and are distributed farther south.)

Taimen are spring-spawning, apparently non-migratory river fish. Yet even without the benefit of migrating to large bodies of water where there are concentrations of shrimp, herring or other baitfish, taimen can grow at a rate of up to four pounds per year, according to British fisheries biologist David Marlborough. There is a reliable report of a taimen netted in the Kotui River in 1943 that weighed 231 pounds and was 84 inches long. Such giants must be rare today, as more and more of Siberia has been penetrated and developed, for huchen and taimen both are important food species to the local people.

Few Westerners have caught or even seen these fish, especially taimen, which were slipping into angling folklore when the Soviet Union began to open up in the late 1980s. Those few who have done so report taking fish up to about 65 pounds (laboratory study showed that fish to be about 50 years old) and one angler hooked a taimen before witnesses that, after clearing the water several times and breaking off, was estimated to be six feet long. Others spoke of seeing very large fish rise from deep pools to follow their flies before turning away.

Taimen are colored like dark brown trout, but with a slimmer, rounder and more torpedo-like shape and distinctly reddish fins. They are formidable predators, powerful and aggressive, with mouths full of large, sharp teeth. They have been seen engulfing swimming ducks and muskrats, and taimen whose stomachs have been opened commonly contain large grayling and salmon of five or six pounds.

Tailwater/Tailwater Fishery—A "tailwater" comes out of the bottom of a dam; it is the flow that is released to maintain the river below. In some cases—the Green River in Utah and the Bighorn in Montana, for example—tailwater trout fisheries are among the most spectacularly successful in North America, because the water makeup and temperature is exactly right for supporting the trout ecosystem. Furthermore the outflow from these dams stays, within a few degrees, the same year-round and, without summer highs or winter lows to depress their feeding, the fish grow larger faster. In addition, the impoundment upstream of the dam also acts as a settling pond, so these tailwater rivers also tend to be clear of sediments.

Not all tailwaters make prolific fisheries; a number of factors and conditions have to come together in just the right combination. In many instances artificial dams have destroyed top-quality stream fisheries and drowned miles of wildlife habitat and scenic valley, perhaps replacing them with a stillwater fishery of some sort and a lake for recreation. Few dams are being built in North America today, but any new or re-licensed dam operator should be required to maintain a certain downstream flow level, to support fish and other wildlife properly, and the dam itself should be equipped with outflows that can take water off at different levels, to get the optimum temperatures to support the fishery.

Tarpon—*Megalops atlanticus*, the tarpon, is often called the fly fisher's ideal big-game fish. It grows to great size, often eats flies willingly, fights the hook with incredible energy and abandon, and, at least in Florida, passes through warm, shallow waters where flies are most effective and where it can easily be seen by anglers in skiffs. The tarpon is also an impressively beautiful fish—a primitive, chrome-plated missile covered with large, hard scales. In the Florida Keys, tarpon routinely exceed 100 pounds and six feet in length; 150 is not rare. The IGFA world record for a fly rod is 188 pounds, and the all-tackle record is 283 pounds—a fish taken in Venezuela's Lake Maracaibo. Very large tarpon have also been found in coastal South American and African waters, but these are relatively deepwater fisheries where the fish are not sighted first. Baby tarpon of up to about 30 pounds are common in Florida's rivermouths, canals and salt ponds.

Tarpon can inhale air directly by rolling on the surface, a unique ability that lets them enter stagnant backwaters where the small fish are safer from predation. In the spring tarpon appear in the Keys, after migrating from South America, to spawn in shallow estuaries. Anglers by the hundreds also come, to stand on the tiny foredeck of a skiff for hours in the sun, prepared at a moment's notice to launch a huge streamer fly toward a passing fish. Tarpon are difficult to hook because their mouths are unusually bony.

To fight the hook in shallow water, the tarpon has no place to go but sideways or up. A giant tarpon may jump 20 times, as much as 10 feet out of the water. It may run off 300 yards of line and backing, or it may go into the air a rod length from the boat. Tarpon have been known to jump right into a boat—or to be pulled in, by an angler who pulls hard on the fish while it's in the air alongside. Professional fly-fishing guides have learned to treat tarpon as the valuable resource they are, sometimes cradling them in the water for many minutes to revive them after a hard fight, or shepherding them for a time after release to protect them from sharks.

Tarpon—a pod of cruisers; the largest fish is about five feet long.

Taxonomy—The identification and classification of species according to agreed-upon scientific criteria.

Teaser—A hookless bait or lure used to draw a gamefish to within casting distance or sight of a hooked lure. Teasers are common aboard offshore boats hunting sailfish or marlin, where they increase the odds of attracting fish. In addition to several rods or outriggers trolling hooks, the boat usually drags a teaser somewhere between the real lures or baits. The teaser itself may be a string of "birds," winged plastic shapes that flutter and thrash on the surface, creating a helpless-prey commotion that predator fish home in on. When a billfish breaks the surface behind the teaser, the boat's deckhand pulls it aboard and the angler lifts one of the working rods out of its socket and begins to manipulate the real lure toward the fish. Yanking the teaser away often seems to enrage a marlin, and it is very likely to take the next "prey" it sees—hopefully the lure. But sometimes the fish will take the teaser in its mouth and simply refuse to give it up. And sometimes a particularly aggressive, stubborn fish is boated on the teaser alone.

Fly-fishing for marlin or sailfish is much the same except that the fly is not trolled along with the teasers. When the fish rises, the teaser is taken away and the angler casts (or just heaves) his or her fly to the fish. It is all but impossible to fly-cast aboard an offshore boat fitted with trolling rods and outriggers, so big-game fly-fishing is often done from relatively small, center-cockpit type boats or even skiffs.

Tensile Strength—Breaking strength; the greatest load a line or section of leader can take before failing. In fishing, breaking strength is usually expressed in pounds-test: a 12-pound-test leader, for example. Scientifically, the tensile strength of a line is expressed in pounds per square inch of diameter. That 12-lb-test leader could be 0.010″ thick, in which case its tensile strength would be approximately 152,800 PSI—that is, a length of the same monofilament with a one-square-inch cross-section would have a breaking strength of 152,800 pounds. (If nothing else, this should impress us with the phenomenal strength of modern terminal tackle.)

Tiger Trout—A brown trout-brook trout cross, which does not occur in nature. Unlike the splake (lake trout-brook trout) or the brownbow (brown trout-rainbow trout), the tiger trout can be a spectacularly marked hybrid; often the vermiculations of the brook trout cover the entire body of the fish in a unique pattern that looks like a blend of a bowhunter's camouflage with a tiger's stripes.

Tip Action—A term used to describe the behavior of a fly rod that bends mostly at its tip. See Rod Action.

Tippet—the very end, or tip, of a fly-fishing leader (see); usually the thinnest section. Known in the United Kingdom as a "cast." A tippet is often replaced frequently while fishing, as repeated fly changes whittle its length down or as conditions demand larger or smaller flies and thus heavier or lighter (or shorter or longer) tippets. Like the rest of the leader, the tippet is nylon monofilament. Common sizes are 20 to 36 inches and thicknesses of 0.005″ to 0.012″, which have breaking strengths of approximately four to 15 pounds. For best performance, tippets should be matched to the leader, but occasionally spools of tippet monofilament are incorrectly labeled; some anglers check new spools with a micrometer to verify their diameter. There is a further choice, of hard or soft tippets (relatively speaking, of course). The former are sometimes preferred for certain kinds of wet-fly fishing, while a softer, more flexible tippet often helps the angler achieve a realistic, drag-free float with a dry fly.

A class tippet is one that meets IGFA (International Game Fish Association—see) standards for length and breaking strength. In order for a fish to be considered for an IGFA fly-fishing world record, it must have been caught on a class tippet—and the tippet must be submitted as part of the documentation process. As of 1992, the IGFA

Tippet—Spools of tippet mono; two are in a special dispenser that stores tippet material and feeds it conveniently through grommets at the side.

recognized six tippet classes: 2, 4, 8, 12, 16 and 20 pounds.

A shock tippet is an extra length of monofilament added ahead of the class tippet to protect it. A shock tippet may be anything from 30- to 100-lb.-test monofilament, whatever can withstand the rough skin or sharp teeth or gill plates of the intended quarry. (A shock tippet can also be effective in waters where coral grows.) Shock tippets for world records are also regulated by the IGFA. Because of the sometimes great difference in thickness between class and shock tippets, great care must be taken in knotting the two together. Knotting a thick 100-pound shock tippet to a hook can be difficult too. See also Leader, X-Sizes.

Tiptop—The uppermost line guide on a fishing rod.

Tonkin Cane—*Arundinaria amabilis*, the extraordinarily tough and resilient Chinese bamboo that became the craftsman's choice for fine split-cane fishing rods in about 1920. See Bamboo.

Torpedo Taper—Another variant of the weight-forward fly line; see.

Travel Rod—A fishing rod that breaks down into three or more sections to fit into a suitcase or duffle bag. See also Multi-Piece Rod.

Triangle Taper—A type of fly line invented and marketed in the mid-1980s by Lee Wulff. From its relatively fine tip, the line diameter increases continuously for the first 40 feet; at that point, the profile then reverses and the thickness tapers rapidly, in the next eight feet, down to the thin running line (see). The Triangle Taper's continuously increasing diameter means that as the head unrolls in normal casting, thinner line is always being pushed (or pulled, depending on how you look at it) by heavier line. The same is true in roll-casting, where TTs also really shine: heavier line is always pulling lighter line from the water surface. See Fly Line.

Trilene Knot—Also known as the two-times-around knot, this could in truth be called the improved, improved clinch knot. It is perhaps the best way to attach fly to tippet for all but big-game fishing. Unlike other forms of the clinch knot, this one—properly tied in unscarred mono on a hook eye free of burrs—will virtually never fail; the tippet will break first. See Knots.

Trout Reel—A fly reel suitable for trout fishing; that is, relatively light-duty use. A trout reel generally weighs no more than six to eight ounces; holds no more than approximately a 7-weight line and perhaps 100 yards of 20-lb-test backing; and has a rudimentary internal drag, if not simply a palming rim and/or a clicker, or overrun check (see). As the market for fine fly reels began to expand in the 1980s, the unwritten definition of a trout reel began to blur and expand. Many manufacturers now offer trout-*size* fly reels that are engineered like big-game reels, with drag systems all out of proportion to their intended use. Such reels still balance a light trout rod perfectly, yet they also serve as insurance against the day when the angler unexpectedly hooks up with, say, a salmon. And as fly-fishing frontiers expand, anglers are using these powerful reels in places where a true "trout" reel would never have survived—on the bonefish flats, for example. See Fly Reel.

Trout Unlimited—"America's leading coldwater fisheries conservation organization," Trout Unlimited (also known simply as TU) is a national/international not-for-profit group dedicated to preserving and enhancing trout fisheries and fostering a supportive sporting ethic. The membership is divided into some 435 local chapters in six regions, which are supervised by 35 state TU councils and a national staff and board of directors, based in Washington, DC. Present membership is about 70,000 in the United States and 30,000 in affiliated organizations around the world. National TU operations include publishing *Trout*, the quarterly magazine of Trout Unlimited, and major resource programs, such as Embrace-A-Stream, aimed at watershed protection, federal lands management, acid-rain control and even Atlantic salmon restoration. TU also lobbies the Congress and federal agencies and has sent experts and goodwill ambassadors around the world to advise other countries on fisheries and stream conservation.

The national office budget in 1992 was just under $3 million; of that, two-thirds was spent on conservation programs or returned to local chapters and regional councils for their use. Funds are raised from membership dues, the sale of promotional items, and specialized programs such as dedicated bank credit cards. Each region also hosts an annual conclave, a gathering for the membership that is part sportsmen's show and part game fair.

At the grass-roots level, chapters arrange local fund-raising dinners and other events; organize work parties to clear streams damaged by runoff or other accidents; serve as informal water bailiffs; lobby their states for better coldwater-fisheries management; and teach beginners young and old about stream ecology and responsible sport fishing.

The idea for an organization to restore and then protect trout fishing was born in July 1959 at the home of George Griffith, near Michigan's Au Sable River, where a handful of angling conservationists had gathered. Their concern was that the direction of public trout management was "deplorable—ever-increasing numbers of cookie-cutter, legal-sized hatchery trout were being dumped in Michigan streams, to the neglect of healthy habitat and wild populations." A formal declaration of intent was made shortly after, on September 5, at a meeting of 15 people in the American Legion hall in Grayling, Michigan. Along with Griffith, one of the most active proponents was George Mason, then president of American Motors. Dr. Casey Westell Jr., of Filer City, Michigan, was elected president of the new group, which took its name from the highly successful waterfowl conservation organization Ducks Unlimited. At first the intent was simply to focus on one river and then one state, but expansion was inevitable.

Efforts soon paid off at home in Michigan. Within five years the state's Department of Conservation (as it was known then) had been completely reorganized and a new team of more progressive, forward-looking fisheries professionals installed. The enormous "hatchery-catchables" program was replaced with stream improvement, protective fishing regulations, sensible management, and the planting of fingerlings. At the time it was the most modern wild-trout management in North America. As the word spread, concerned angler-conservationists in other states banded together under the Trout Unlimited cause and name too. And eventually a few state groups split off from what had become a national organization in order to pursue their goals their own way. (See CalTrout.)

Trout Unlimited is not a fly-fishing group, but it espouses catch-and-release angling with flies, lures or bait so long as a single hook is used. (See Mortality.) Other planks in its original philosophical platform include the belief that "trout fishing is not just fishing for trout," it is:

- Fishing for sport rather than food, where "the true enjoyment of the sport lies in the challenge, the lore and the battle of wits, not necessarily the full creel."
- The feeling of satisfaction that comes from "limiting your kill instead of killing your limit."
- Communing with nature, where the "chief reward is a refreshed body and a contented soul, where a license is a permit to use, not abuse, to enjoy, not destroy our trout waters."
- Subscribing to the proposition that "what's good for trout is good for trout fishermen, and that managing trout for the trout rather than for the trout fisherman is fundamental to the solution of our trout problems."
- "Appreciating our trout, respecting fellow anglers and giving serious thought to tomorrow."

Today, "managing the resource" has become TU's goal. A recent statement summed up future goals:

"Far too much money is still wasted producing fake fish to satisfy short-term angling demand. Excessive water withdrawals, livestock overgrazing of sensitive riparian zones, siltation from careless logging, stream channelization, acid deposition, dams— these and other habitat-wrecking activities continue to take a frightening toll on the places of wild trout."

The national headquarters of Trout Unlimited is at 800 Follin Lane SE, Suite 250, Vienna, VA 22180-4959.

Tube Fly—A streamer fly whose dressing is tied not on the hook shank but on a tube; the tippet is passed through the tube and tied to a hook, which is then pulled part way up into the tube (which is usually plastic). This technique was developed on the Atlantic-salmon rivers of Europe. Although tubes can be put to very good use on any gamefish that prefers large streamers, they have never caught on in North America. The tube lets the tier create a large, long-bodied fly that is unusually light for its size; and, since the hook is interchangeable, tube flies can be finely tuned for depth by choosing single, double or treble hooks. Very heavy flies can also be made this way, by using tubes made of brass instead of plastic. To dress them, tubes are slid onto a mandrel clamped in the jaws of a conventional vise.

Tup—A "tup" is English country slang for a ram, and Tup's Indispensable is a British fly pattern from the early 1900s that called for body dubbing that contained the yellowish, urine-stained wool from a ram's scrotum. The other ingredients were the

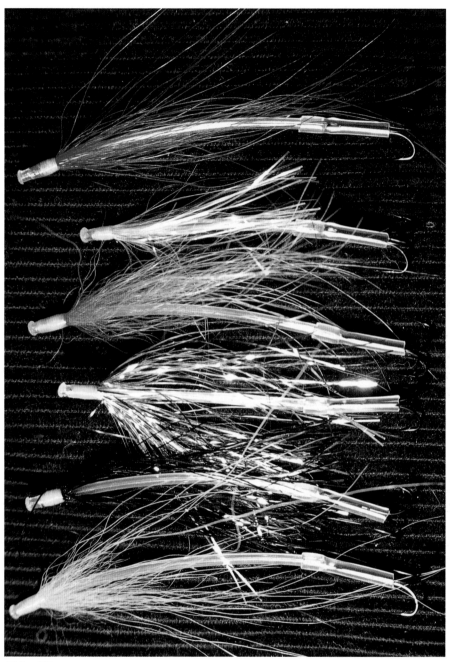

Tube Flies.

"lemon" hair from a spaniel dog, rabbit fur and red mohair. According to fly-tying historian Darrel Martin, the dubbing recipe was kept secret until 1934, when it was published in the *Flyfishers' Club Journal* in England.

Turle Knot—This is a slightly awkward knot to tie, but it offers a special advantage to anglers who still fish flies with down-turned eyes: The line grabs the hook and emerges from the eye in such a way that it makes a straight-line pull on the hook. An ordinary clinch knot, in comparison, grips the outermost lip of the eye, which on a down-eye hook results in an offset pull that tends to stand a retrieved fly such as a streamer on its nose. See Knots.

Twenty-Times-Around Knot—Another name for the Bimini Twist (see); see also Knots.

Two-Handed Rod—An extra-long fly rod meant to be cast and fished with two hands; the reel, still slung below the rod, is between the two grips, like a surf-casting rig. Very common in the United Kingdom and Scandinavia, especially on Atlantic-salmon water, two-handed rods as long as 16 feet are again showing up more and more in North America now as well (particularly on the salmon and steelhead rivers of Oregon, Washington and Alaska). Their great length and power offer distinct advantages in casting, line control, fish-fighting and overall efficiency. The ease with which a two-hander can throw 80 to 120 feet of line—with no more than one or two false casts—makes a long day on big water less of a physical challenge. It also means the angler can simply reach and cover much more water than with a 9- or 10-foot single-handed rod, which is an important consideration to someone who has paid hundreds of thousands of pounds or *kroner* for a beat on a Scottish or Norwegian salmon river. With a roll cast or Spey cast (see), the long rods are also extremely effective in places where there is little or no backcast room. As well, mending the line on the water (or in the air) is very much easier with a longer rod, and the increased leverage of such a rod makes it relatively easier to beat a large fish.

Modern two-handed rods—that is, rods made within the past century, with true casting actions and stand-up ring guides for shooting line—vary from about 11 feet in length to as much as 16. The major North American rod manufacturers all offer a few such models, but most come from England. They are usually made in two or three sections, but if the demand for two-handers continues to build in the USA, where the emphasis is on air travel, it's likely that rod designers will invest the research to put more and stronger ferrules on these rods. The advent of graphite was a huge boon to two-handed fly fishers—the weight of a 16-footer could be cut about in half, to well under a pound, with a concomitant increase in strength too—but as with single-handed rods some purists still prefer split bamboo. Many North American anglers tend to view two-handed rods as somehow unethical, as though they convey an unfair advantage; European big-water fly fishers scoff at Americans' insistence on their "baby" rods, linking it somehow to the cowboy penchant for handguns.

Two-Times-Around Knot—See Trilene Knot.

Tyee—A regional name for king salmon (see) in British Columbia.

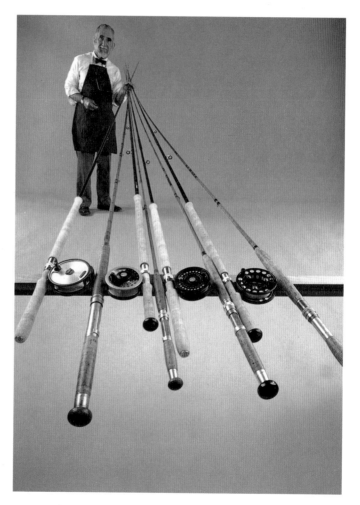

Two-Handed Rods—
An assortment of new
(graphite) and old
(split bamboo)
two-handed fly rods
of 14 to 17 feet length.

Underfur—The short, thick, soft pelt closest to a fur-bearing animal's skin; in fly-tying, it is often used to make flybody dubbing (see). See Guard hair.

Uni-Knot—The name comes from "universal knot," which is what fishing writer Vic Dunaway set out to create. And in fact the uni-knot can be used or adapted to meet just about every fishing need in both fresh and salt water, from tying backing to the spool arbor to attaching a fly to the tippet. It is a snell-type knot, which relies on the friction of several wraps of line around itself, but unlike other similar knots it can be left loose—to let a fly swim more freely, for example—without giving up any of its strength. It is a good connection for large saltwater streamers on heavy shock tippet: Make three turns, tighten the barrel of the knot, and close the loop down almost onto the hook eye; when a fish strikes, the loop will slide closed, for a better fish-fighting connection. See Knots.

Upstream Mend—A way of repositioning a fly line on the water so that it lies above— that is, upstream of—the fly. If the current the fly is riding in is moving slower than the water where the belly of the line lies, an upstream mend will prolong the drag-free float of the fly by delaying the moment when the line outpaces the fly and uses up the slack in the leader. The mend lets the fly stay even with the line, at least briefly.

If the situation is reversed or if the current is the same everywhere along the line and leader, then an upstream mend will make the line drag the fly sooner than otherwise— a situation that is not necessarily bad; Atlantic salmon, for example, sometimes prefer a fast-moving fly that skates across the water.

An upstream mend may be made when the line is on the water—by flicking the line in the right direction with the rod tip—or it can be made while the cast is still in the air, by reaching upstream with the rod to make sure the belly of the line hits the water there. See also Mend.

Upstream Presentation—The classic method of fishing a dry fly: From the water or the shore, casting the fly up-current so that it drifts back down toward the angler. Since stream trout face into the current when holding in their feeding lies, an upstream presentation is a logical approach—the fish can't see the angler behind it. The angler must be careful not to "line" the fish, however; to cast too far upstream of the fish, letting it see the fly line instead of merely the fly on its presumably invisible tippet.

In the old British sphere of influence, "trout fishing" meant fishing a dry fly upstream, period. It took free-thinking Americans such as Lee Wulff to break the bonds of convention and turn fly-fishing into an enjoyable puzzle that intellect and imagination, as well as mere mechanical skill, could solve: If an upstream presentation doesn't work

Valise Rod—A fishing rod that breaks down into sections small enough to fit a valise. The term has been obsolete since at least the advent of graphite as a rod-making material in the early 1970s. See Multi-Piece Rod.

Variant—A fly pattern with unusual proportions; also a hackle feather or cape of more than one color.

Vent-Spool *or* **Ventilated-Spool Reel**—A fly reel with series of holes or other cutouts machined in the flanges of the spool (and often in the sideplates or backplate as well). The holes are functional—they allow the line and backing to dry more quickly and they also lighten a reel appreciably—and often highly decorative as well. Care must be taken in machining the holes; if any burrs are left on the inside of the spool, they may cut or abrade the line. Big-game fly reel spools are left un-drilled, for strength and also to keep the line from bulging out through the holes if it is wound on under tension. The look of a modern fly reel, with its narrow, tall spool decoratively drilled with concentric rings of holes, dates back to the trend-setting Orvis 1874-patent reel (see). At that time, when silk lines were used, the air-drying function of the holes—they are "ventilations," after all—was particularly important.

Ventilated-Spool Reel.

Vest—A staple of modern fly-fishing: a sleeveless, button- or zip-front garment with as many as two dozen (or more) pockets sewn into and onto it, many of them sized and placed for specific items ranging from fly boxes to sunglasses to stream thermometers to rain shells. As the tackle box is to the spinfisherman, the gear vest

Vest—a "shorty" style, for anglers who wade deep.

is to the stream fly fisher. (In a boat there is little reason to wear a vest.)

Difficult as it may be to imagine, before World War II fly fishers, even in North America, did not carry their gear draped about their torsos in multi-pocketed vests. Instead they wore tailored tweed jackets with long sleeves; across their shoulders they might have slung a satchel for their fly boxes and dressings and tools. The very first purpose-made fly-fishing vest appeared in 1932; like so many other effective, liberating angling innovations, it was invented by Lee Wulff (see). Wulff, always an original thinker, sought function and comfort over fashion. He sewed together a garment— possibly based on an upland gunner's vest—with pockets to carry the gear he needed for a day's fly-fishing *while he was fishing.* That is, he could find what he needed without leaving the water, which wasted time and opportunity and sometimes spooked the fish.

Unlike the Wulff patterns (see) and his plastic-bodied flies, Lee's vest seemed to be accepted by anglers rather quickly. It is possible that WWII helped: Not only was the war a cultural watershed—what was unquestioned before 1940 was often fair game after 1945—but hundreds of thousands of returning infantrymen had learned the practicality of stowing their combat gear about their bodies on web belts and chest harnesses and the like.

For decades vests were made of cotton poplin and then of various polyester blends. Around 1980 a Colorado angler, fly shop owner and guide named Chuck Fothergill made waves with a fishing vest that had a thick, soft knit collar, which helped cushion the weight of a heavy load. (He also introduced colors other than olive green and khaki.) Other evolutions, successful and not so successful, followed: safety vests with built-in inflatable flotation chambers; cool, ultralight vests of synthetic mesh fabrics; a water-repellent French-made vest with detachable sleeves for cold weather; and the Simms Ultimate, with its weight-distributing shoulder yoke of stretchy, comfortable neoprene.

Vise—In fly-tying, a clamp for a hook, to hold it by the bend while the fly tier dresses its shank with hair, hackle, tinsel, floss and so on. A tying vise may have a clamp, to grip the edge of a table, or a pedestal, a flat, heavy base that sits on the table top. Vintage vises often had thumb loops, so they could be hand-held, or the standrod was coarsely threaded to be screwed into a tree stump or a wooden bench. Tying vises come in a wide variety of styles and prices, but in general they can be divided into home and travel types. Travel vises fold or disassemble into compact bundles; they are meant to be used in camp or even right at streamside, to match exactly whatever the fish are feeding on. See Fly-Tying Tools.

Vise—A table-clamp model.

Vomerine Teeth—Supplemental teeth located well inside the jaws of some species of fish, on the roof of its mouth. (The vomer is a bone that forms the forward section of the roof of the fish's mouth.) The vomerine teeth are sometimes used to help identify salmonids: True trout, for example, have a complete set of vomerine teeth while charrs usually have only a few teeth on the front of the vomer; brown trout have a well-developed double row of these teeth while Atlantic salmon have only one row, and some of the teeth may be missing.

Vom Hofe—Five male members of this family, over three generations, made an indelible mark on the manufacture and design of bait, trolling and fly reels. Their reign as America's pre-eminent reel designers and builders was firmly established by 1880 or so, but the family businesses, which were in Manhattan, spanned nearly a century, from 1857 and 1940. In that year the Edward Vom Hofe Company was sold to the Ocean City Manufacturing Company and relocated in Philadelphia, still building reels. However the onset of the Second World War, with its shortages of men, materials and machinery, not to mention the decline in recreational activities, spelled the end of the business.

The Vom Hofe family and companies produced, under their own names and for other well-known tackle retailers, the finest fly reels and level-wind saltwater reels yet built; some collectors claim that modern reels have at best equalled the finest Vom Hofes but not surpassed them, in craftsmanship, quality of construction, elegant esthetics or function. Vom Hofes pioneered many advances in reel design and technology and were granted many patents, which added up to reels that were lighter and stronger and simply better than those of their predecessors or competitors. The quintessential Vom Hofe fly reels (built by Edward) so sought-after by collectors have full frames of polished nickel silver, rich black ebonite (hard rubber) sideplates and elegantly curved serpentine crank handles, also polished nickel silver and also set off by black knobs. Each fitting and component, from the knurled drag knob to the sliding clicker button, from the countersunk screw heads to the shouldered pillars, from the oil caps to the bronze bearings, was machined not only with precision but with artistry. The influence of the Vom Hofe family is still strong in American fly reel design: Stanley Bogdan (see) and his "imitators," from Peerless to Winston to Saracione, all pay homage to Vom Hofe, as did Arthur Walker and Otto Zwarg before them and even the venerable English firm of Hardy Bros.

The patriarch of the clan was Frederick Vom Hofe (1806-1885), a Westphalian German, possibly of aristocratic blood, who was a brass artisan. He and his wife, Wilhelmina, eventually had five children, two of whom—Julius (1837-1907) and Edward (1846-1920)—not only entered the family trade but also themselves had sons—Julius Jr. (1871-1939) and Edwin (1878-?)—who joined their fathers' companies. Frederick brought his family to New York City in 1849 and in 1857 went into business making fishing reels. These were heavy ball-handle, level-wind reels made of brass, mostly for salt water. Julius joined the business around 1860, and thereafter the reels were marked "F. Vom Hofe & Son, Maker." In 1867 Edward entered the tackle business on his own, eventually owning a large retail tackle shop and mail-order business and producing his own reels as well. The two companies apparently co-existed peacefully, and Edward sold not only his own reels but his brother's as well. It was Edward who reached the pinnacle of the reel business, combining his inherited talents with what he learned from his brother and father and then developing his own designs based on what he learned as an avid fisherman. Reel historian Jim Brown credits him with being the second angler to land a tarpon of more than 200 pounds, and estimates out that he produced two or three times as many saltwater reels as freshwater. His Florida tarpon trips probably helped him invent the slip-clutch star drag that is still used in trolling reels. In fly reels his "silent tension drag" set the same standard of performance.

Edward also made trout, bass and salmon fly reels that are all highly functional and prized. Many of the model names changed, and they were available in different sizes and with a variety of options, but by the time of his death the fly reel series had expanded to seven basic models: the "Peerless" for trout and bass, with just a click drag; the "Perfection" trout reel, which generally had an adjustable drag; the "Cascapedia," a salmon reel with a clicker; the "Restigouche" salmon reel, with or without an adjustable drag; the "Tobique," a multiplying salmon reel with an adjustable drag; the "Colonel Thompson," also an adjustable-drag salmon multiplier but with an offset crank handle; and the "Griswold," an even stronger version of the Thompson meant for big salmon and tarpon.

Vom Hofe—One of Edward's fine salmon reels.

Wading Shoes—Shoes (or low boots) meant to be worn over stockingfoot waders. Wading shoes are generally available with felt, studded or molded-lug soles. Their function is to provide traction, cushion the foot, and protect the toes and heel from boulders. Wading shoes need not be waterproof; the waders worn inside them keep the foot dry. Generally speaking, wading shoes and stockingfoot uppers are more comfortable and provide better foot support than clumsy, loose-fitting one-piece bootfoot waders; the disadvantage is that they are more cumbersome to put on and take off. Fly fishers who spend hours at a time in moving water, often on rocky bottoms where footing may be precarious, usually prefer wading shoes.

Known for decades as brogues or brogans, wading shoes for a long time were only heavy-duty leather work shoes with felt or studded soles. Even with the best of care the leather, alternately wetted and dried, broke down in fairly short order. In 1980 an American company, Weinbrenner Shoe, introduced the Borger Ultimate, a wading brogue made of a synthetic that looked and felt like real leather but lasted nearly indefinitely, and with no care whatsoever—no careful drying and no greasing. The shoes might eventually break down mechanically—wear through or simply pull apart at the seams—but the material never cracked, split or stiffened. At about the same time the Danner company introduced a wading shoe made of neoprene-impregnated leather, which has also proven itself to be exceptionally durable and comfortable. The Danner product is a true boot, with nine-inch uppers that have unique nylon mesh panels in them, to let water drain away while keeping gravel and sand out.

For a time the "poor man's wading shoe" was the 1950s-vintage canvas sneaker, and wading-wear manufacturers pursued that line of development as well, adding rubber bumper strips and felt soles. The eventual result was the variety of popularly priced Cordura-based shoes now available. Some have zippers or Velcro straps instead of laces.

A third style of shoe came in the 1980s from the Simms company, which adapted a molded plastic Austrian (Koflach) mountaineering boot to wading use. In particularly rocky rivers, this hard-shell boot offers excellent foot protection.

For decades anglers wore thick woolen socks between their shoes and their waders, for comfort and to keep out stream gravel, which could quickly abrade the thin, flexible wader feet. In the late 1970s the neoprene revolution spilled over from diving and surfing into fishing, and anglers began to wear neoprene socks and then, when neoprene waders arrived, neoprene gaiters, or cuffs, with their wading shoes for the same purpose. See also Stockingfoot Waders.

Wading Staff—An invaluable aid to wading anglers when the water gets deep, the bottom slippery or the current powerful. (Falling in is usually not what injures stream fishermen—it's falling onto the rocks in shallow water that causes sprains, fractures and concussions, and breaks fine fly rods.) Wading staffs run the gamut from hastily cut tree branches to fine split-bamboo works of art to lightweight alloy tubes that fold or telescope into belt holsters. The important elements of a functional wading staff include: the strength to stand up to fast water; some sort of relatively non-skid tip; and a means of stowing it away for fishing (a belt lanyard or holster). Whether a staff floats is not very important—pushing it through the current can be difficult whether it is wood or aluminum, and when it is dangling at one's side, the current takes it away, no matter if it sinks or floats.

Wading Shoe—The Simms molded-plastic boot, shown without neoprene gaiters.

Wallop-Breaux—An amendment to the Dingell-Johnson Act (see), the Federal Aid in Sport Fish Restoration Act, passed in 1950. The sponsors were Louisiana Representative John Breaux and Wyoming Senator Malcolm Wallop. It was enacted in 1984 and it expanded the funds available for "sport fish restoration" nationwide to some $200 million annually.

Walton, Izaak—The author of *The Compleat Angler*, first published in 1653. The book is a series of conversations between Walton's three characters, Piscator, Venator and Auceps (Angler, Hunter and Falconer), mostly about fishing with bait for such species as bream, tench, carp, barbel, roach and so on. The book had little to offer fly fishers until Walton's friend Charles Cotton was invited to write "Instructions, How to Angle for a Trout or Grayling in a Clear Stream," a disquisition on fly-fishing, for the fifth edition, published in 1676. The bland dialogue and gentle homilies seem to say less about fishing than about a moderate and contemplative philosophy of life, which may explain why the book became a classic of English literature. As of 1990, no fewer than 456 edition had been published, making *The Compleat Angler* the third most reprinted book in the English language (behind only the Bible and *Pilgrim's Progress*), not to mention one of the books most frequently translated into other languages. In nearly three and a half centuries, Walton—the envy of every struggling outdoor writer—has never been out of print. This incredible longevity has spawned a cottage industry of Walton-collecting and at least three scholarly guides to the editions: *A New Chronicle of The Compleat Angler* (1936) by Peter Oliver; *The Compleat Angler 1653-1967* (1970) by Bernard Horne); and *Izaak Walton: A New Bibliography, 1653-1987* (1989) by Rodolphe L. Coigney.

Weakfish—The name refers to the soft, easily torn tissues of its mouth; the weakfish, *Cynoscion regalis*, is actually a strong and predatory gamefish and, like many flyrod species, an indicator of environmental conditions. Regionally it is also known as squeteague, tide runner or gray trout. Its range encompasses the Atlantic Coast from Florida to New England, the schools moving seasonally south or north to follow warmer temperatures. Except for its double dorsal fins, the weakfish (like its close relative the spotted seatrout) is generally shaped like a trout, with handsome, if subdued, tones of green and blue above silver or bronze; the fins are yellowish. Also like seatrout, weakfish are irregularly spotted on back and sides (but, unlike seatrout, the spots do not extend onto the tail or dorsal). Its projecting lower jaw is distinctly un-troutlike, however, and the upper jaw carries a pair of prominent canine teeth.

Weakfish are opportunists that school up to chase sand eels, herring, menhaden and any other baitfish, and they eat shrimp, crabs and other molluscs as well. In the warmer months they can be found in estuaries and the inshore shallows; when the waters cool down they may go deeper. Weakfish can be caught from piers and jetties; from boats anchored where tidal flow moves food around; by moving slowly alongshore and through coves and rivermouths; and even in the surf. They readily come to the surface to take flies as well. Double-digit-size weakfish were rare in the 1950s and '60s but they seem to be returning as the Atlantic Coast is slowly cleaned up and as saltwater species are managed better; still, three to five pounds is the average in most fisheries.

Webbing—In fly-tying, the thick, fluffy barbules clustered at the base of a feather.

Weight-Forward Line—The weight-forward line has most of its casting weight (and thus its thickest diameter) in the belly, the 30 feet or so just behind the front taper. The rest of the WF profile is relatively fine-diameter running line. Line manufacturers experiment continually with their WF designs, changing the tips and bellies, the length and steepness of the tapers and so on. Bass-bug, "rocket" or saltwater tapers, and shooting-head lines are variations on the basic weight-forward theme. See Fly Line.

Welt—the raised lip soldered onto the end of the female section of a machined rod ferrule. Along with serving as a decorative touch, the welt also reinforces the end of the ferrule sleeve and helps guide the male slide in.

WFFC—The World Fly Fishing Championship; see.

Wheatley—A unique type of metal fly box, made by the Wheatley Company of England since the 19th Century, that has a separate, spring-loaded lid over each dryfly compartment, so they won't blow away in the breeze when the halves of the box are opened. The lids have plastic windows in them (vintage Wheatley windows are celluloid) and each compartment can be opened by itself. Over the decades, Wheatley has manufactured an enormous variety of now-collectible fly boxes, for everything from tiny trout flies to large salmon patterns and in unusual combinations of compartments, clips, springs, panels and even built-in leather wetfly wallets.

Wheatley fly box.

Whip Finisher—A bent-wire tool used to tie a whip-finish onto the head of a completed fly. See Fly-Tying Tools.

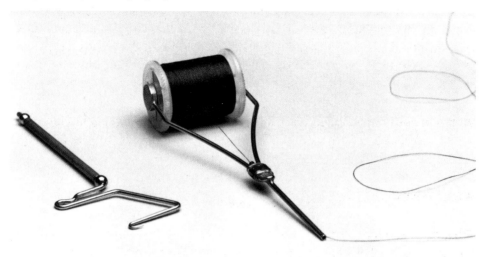

Whip-Finisher—on the left.

Wiggle Cast—A form of slack-line cast; see.

Willow Fly—Another name for the salmonfly; see.

Winding Check—Also known as a grip check, a winding check is a wide ring (or truncated cone) that fits over the base of a rod butt section where it disappears into the top of the grip. Like a molding between wall and ceiling, it serves as a finishing element to dress up the spot where hexagonal cane meets round cork (winding checks are less common on graphite rods). Since it is made of malleable metal, one end of the winding check takes on the shape of the rod and the other stays round; without it, the rod builder would have to fill in the tiny voids in the cork where the flats of the cane emerge from a round hole (and these fill-ins would quickly work loose under the repeated flex of casting). Winding checks may be themselves finished off with a short section of wrapped thread that matches the guide wraps. See Cane Rod Building.

Wind Knot—A knot inadvertently created in a leader or line during casting; the name implies that "the wind did it," but in fact poor casting technique (most often a tailing loop, in which the line and leader cross while the cast unrolls) is usually to blame. They are usually simply overhand knots, but sometimes real bird's-nests can happen.

Casting knots should be undone as soon as they are discovered, for a knot weakens the line or leader (see Monofilament). Also, even if the next fish doesn't snap the knotted leader, the strain of fighting the fish will draw the knot tight and make it much more difficult to untie.

Winds—The fine lashing of thread that holds the line guides on a fishing rod or reinforces a ferrule or even a repair in the rod section. By using colored threads, rod builders make their winds decorative as well as functional, and then several coats of varnish or epoxy bond the thread wraps into super-strong bands.

Wing—In reference to fishing flies, "wing" can be used to describe the swath of feather or hair that extends back from the eye of the hook above and along the shank of a streamer or bucktail. In the water, such a wing actually forms the body of the baitfish that the fly is intended to imitate. In a narrower sense of the word, "wing" refers to the upstanding feather(s) of an classic dry fly (within the palmered hackle) such as the Adams. These wings are suggestive; they create the silhouette of a mayfly riding high in the current, its wings closed above its back. More specifically still, the word refers to the literal wing on an imitation of a mayfly, caddis or any other insect.

The search for proper winging material, that would not only closely imitate the gauzy, finely veined wings of a real insect but that could also stand up to the rigors of fishing, has been going on for more than a century. Today various plastics do the job well. But in the late 19th Century it was discovered that the inner membrane of the scales of the shad, red snapper and several other fish made excellent wings: "Flies made with the wings of this membrane are extremely durable and lifelike in appearance; the wings are too tough to be torn, but in the water become pliable and offer to the fish no resistance." (Mary Orvis Marbury, *Favorite Flies and Their Histories*, 1892). There was a caveat, however: ". . . yet, attractive as they appear, [these wings] have not proved very popular with fishermen, owing chiefly, we think, to a slight rustling noise they make when cast through the air. It is doubtful is this sound is really any serious objection to these flies, but it seems to have been a fault that has prevented their extended use." See also Fly, Fly-Tying.

World Records—See International Game Fish Association.

Wulff Flies—A popular series of relatively bushy dry flies, often used for Atlantic salmon or large trout, characterized by bucktail wings and tails. Lee Wulff designed the first two patterns, the Gray Wulff and the White Wulff, in 1929 or '30, as oversize imitations of the coffin mayfly and the large gray drakes that hatch in the Catskills in

Wulff Flies—a yellow Wulff (tied by Darrel Martin), characteristically busby and hackled and tailed with bucktail instead of feathers.

the early fall. They were the first known dry flies to use animal hair instead of hackle. Unlike the sparsely dressed, slim, English-type dry flies of the day—which, Wulff noted, all looked the same silhouetted against the sky—these were different: buggy and alive-looking. In heavy water and for big fish, the hair dries offered other advantages too. He wrote (in his book *The Atlantic Salmon*, A.S. Barnes and Co., 1958) that the hair wings and tails gave them "extra toughness and durability and finer floating qualities than feather fibers had been able to supply. They floated a heavier body than the other dry flies of that time and were more representative of a class of insect not then well represented [among salmon patterns]. They captured the 'look' of an insect which seems to be the basis of the salmon's rise."

Wulff's own name for the new patterns, which were an immediate hit with trout and then salmon, was the Coffin May and the Ausable Gray. It was Wulff's friend and angling companion Dan Bailey (see) who called it the Gray Wulff, and that was the name that stuck.

Eventually the original two patterns were expanded to include the Brown, Black, Blonde and Grizzly Wulffs, and then finally the Royal Wulff, a Royal Coachman (which had been invented by Mary Orvis Marbury and named by her admiring father, Charles Orvis) done with white bucktail wings and tail. (The Royal Wulff became the logo of the company Lee and his wife, Joan Salvato Wulff, founded to sell their angling products.) According to Wulff himself, the Irresistible was born when the late Kenneth Lockwood substituted clipped deer hair for the blue-gray angora body of the Gray Wulff.

Popular and widespread as the Wulff patterns are today, it took decades for them to be widely accepted. Incredible as it may seem, the "heresy" of using hair in dry flies and of tying such bulky silhouettes put anglers off for years. In a conversation with the author in 1986, Wulff recalled that, back in the 1930s, "No one was interested—they were just too different, didn't look like anybody's idea of a bug. I'd give them away to people, and then a year or so later I'd see them in their fly boxes, untouched. They wouldn't use them."

Wulff, Lee—The most outstanding angler and angling conservationist of the 20th Century. Wulff was born on February 10, 1905, in Valdez, Alaska, where his father had settled after an unsuccessful stint as a Gold Rusher. It proved to be a most symbolic birthplace for a man whose life would revolve around wilderness and wildlife. And Lee Wulff died on April 28, 1991, of a fatal heart attack at age 86 while he was at the controls of his Piper SuperCub—a death no less appropriate than his birthplace had been, for Wulff was in all ways an adventurer who charted his own course. In the years between, he made his mark on virtually every aspect of sport fishing, especially fly-fishing, and almost single-handedly he ushered in an era of wiser use of sport fisheries.

Wulff began to fish almost as soon as he learned to walk; his mother, he said, told of "tiny trout caught on a bent pin, their miniature tails peeking jauntily out of the pants pockets of a very small boy." Later Wulff thought the most exciting way to fish was with a spear, but when he was nine years old he met a fly fisherman and his father bought him fly tackle so he could fish with his new friend. When Wulff was 10 his family moved to Brooklyn, New York, an impossibly exotic place for a kid from Alaska. But he adapted well to the city too, and summers spent on lakes in upstate New York or in nearby Pennsylvania kept his outdoor skills alive. (Throughout his adult life he lived only as far from New York as Keene, New Hampshire. As he made the outdoors his career, he understood that sport fishing was a business and that businesses need large markets. All his life he would work with editors, publishers and producers in New York, and he and his wife, Joan Salvato Wulff, eventually located their fly-fishing school and business in the Catskills, within easy drive of the city.) In his late teens, the family moved to San Diego, where Wulff attended San Diego State University for two years; he finished his college years at Stanford University, graduating as a civil engineer in 1926, but discovered that engineering was not for him. Instead he decided to study art, even spending the year in Paris (1926) that was *de rigueur* with art students. Back

Lee Wulff—1981; bundled against the early-spring chill on New York's Beaverkill.

in New York again, he became a designer for an ad agency (working for a while with the famous designer Norman Bel Geddes) and then, in 1930, moving to Louisville, Kentucky, as the art director for an ad agency. Kentucky made him miss New York State and the Adirondacks; and the Great Depression eventually soured him on business. He moved back to New York and went to work, for $35 per week, as a package designer for DuPont Cellophane. Wulff determined he wanted to "buy his own time back"; he developed a plan: He would become a teacher, writer, lecturer, photographer and eventually film-maker on outdoor topics—and through countless hours of effort he taught himself all those crafts. (Much later, for example, while driving in his car, he would record and listen to himself speak, to hone his diction and cadence for audiences.) It took six years to break away from New York and move upstate, to the banks of the Battenkill. From then on, his life's purpose never wavered.

Despite the move to New York and his artistic and scientific education, Wulff's love for fishing and hunting had never abated, and as a young working man he often visited the trout streams of the Catskills and the Adirondacks. Sometimes he and his friends—some, like Dan Bailey, went on to great fly-fishing stature themselves—would ride the subway out of the city with all their gear for the weekend stuffed into their waders and the waders sitting like headless bodies on the seats between them. When they got off, they carried these strange duffle bags piggyback through the streets. One of Wulff's first fishing businesses, in partnership with Bailey, was a fly-fishing school. The first and only class was held in Wulff's apartment in Greenwich Village. It drew three students—John McDonald, a well-known fishing writer and later editor at *Fortune* magazine; Ray Camp, rod & gun editor of the New York *Times*; and John McCloy, who became a top advisor to FDR.

Wulff's circle widened rapidly; his reputation as an outdoorsman grew and he traveled farther afield to fish and to speak. In 1935, while fly-fishing the Battenkill on the Vermont-New York line, Wulff met another angler, also up from the city for the weekend. His name was Horace Stokes and in 1939 he published Wulff's first two (of eight) books—*Lee Wulff's Handbook of Freshwater Fishing* and *Let's Go Fishing*. In his final magazine column, which appeared in *Fly Rod & Reel* several months after his death, Wulff wrote of the need for streamside courtesy. He referred to this chance meeting—when he impulsively helped a stranger try to catch "his" fish, instead of shooing the intruder away—which would have such beneficial repercussions, as an example of "what seemed like a foolish thing to do [that] turned out to be a blessing." Throughout his decades in the public eye, this tall, craggy, movie-idol-handsome "ultimate outdoorsman" remained approachable, unpretentious, friendly and considerate of others.

In 1936 Wulff caught the biggest bluefin tuna of the season off Nova Scotia, which landed him an invitation to fish on a team (two invitations, in fact—from the US team and the Canadian; he chose Canada because they were the underdogs) in the first International Tuna Tournament at Wedgeport a year later. Team Canada won thanks to Lee's 560-pound fish, an event that also changed his life: A picture of the giant tuna appeared in the New York *Times* and his fame led the Newfoundland Tourist Board to hire Wulff to open up their sport fishing, for tuna and then for trout and salmon. He fished the Province's rivers and caught "thousands of Atlantic salmon" as he evaluated and filmed each stream for the government. At the same time he continually sharpened his skills as an angler and a fly tier and an observer of nature, and he took notes for hundreds of magazine articles. For nine years (1945 to 1954) Lee ran a Atlantic-salmon camp at Portland Creek on Newfoundland's northwest coast. He also helped the US military, which then had a substantial presence in far northeastern Canada, set up R&R fishing camps in the wilderness. In 1957 he discovered the Minipi watershed in Labrador—still, because of the management practices he set up, famous for its enormous brook trout. To move about more easily (and to get guests into Portland Creek) he acquired a bush plane, a Piper Cub—dubbed Yellow Bird—that everyone assured him was too light and underpowered to survive Newfoundland's fierce winds; it was the first small private plane in the territory. But in three weeks he learned to fly and then, to cope with the weather, he began to watch the birds and pattern his own flying after their behavior. He became as expert in the air as he was on the water. After a highly publicized bad-weather flight to rescue a woman in labor, other bush pilots began to emulate him. To stay ahead of the "crowd" he flew always farther north and then across the strait into Labrador until there were no more rivers left to explore.

Wulff was always an independent thinker, a man who automatically questioned the conventional wisdom and who often noted that conventional thinking was upside-down. To debunk the myth that chest waders were death-traps that would drown an angler who fell in, in 1947 Wulff dove off a bridge into the Battenkill in Vermont and then swam easily to shore, proving to the onlookers what he'd know all along: That it was easy to release any air trapped in a pair of waders—and that water inside waders is not one bit heavier than the water outside them.

He could clarify problems and then identify their solutions with an ease that befuddled others: Normal featherwing dry flies won't float in heavy water? See Wulff Flies. Shouldn't tackle be readily accessible while the angler is in the water? See Vest. Shouldn't a fly reel have an instantly and infinitely adjustable drag? See Half-Frame Reel and Palming Rim. Salmon won't strike conventional dries? See Surface Stone Fly. A weight-forward fly line won't roll-cast well or deposit flies gently? See Triangle Taper. A trout can only be approached from the current side? See Upstream Presentation. If fly fishers banded together, wouldn't they gain national clout for conservation? See Federation of Fly Fishers. Shouldn't the heritage of fly-fishing be preserved? See American Museum of Fly Fishing.

Wulff's practical approach to angling even affected the nation's choice of fly rods and how we cast them. In the 1940s and '50s, when Atlantic salmon fishermen were arming themselves with long, heavy rods, Wulff demonstrated that a light, progressive-action (see) rod could do the job very well and with much less effort. His "signature" rods were usually six-footers for 7-weight lines and weighed less than two ounces—split-cane, of course—and many were made for him by Wes Jordan at Orvis. His search for ease and efficiency spilled over into fly-casting, where Wulff applied a loose, full-body style that let him achieve impressive range with these "tiny" fly rods. (Although he fully regarded his short rods as superior fishing tools, he wasn't above an occasional stunt: To emphasize that long rods were not necessarily better, he caught a 10-pound salmon without any rod at all—casting to, hooking and landing the fish with his arm alone.)

Despite—or probably because of—his enormous impact on tackle design, Wulff was largely unsentimental about his gear. It either performed its function or it did not, and if the latter it would be replaced or improved. He was not one to glorify the mellow beauty of bamboo or rhapsodize about the sheen of rare feathers. It was an attitude that developed after he bought a fine new Payne rod for $49 when he was still living in Greenwich Village. He discovered he was afraid of damaging it: "Something had changed. The rod was fishing me, not I the rod." He sold it to a friend for just what he'd paid for it and instead bought a $15 Heddon. "My fishing became a happier thing. I cast with abandon, caught more fish . . . ."

In 1963 Wulff set another precedent, by having the first network-TV hunting show, a CBS Sports Spectacular. Wulff became the fishing and hunting consultant for CBS and more shows followed. Then when ABC launched the *American Sportsman* series, Wulff became one of that program's most highly regarded field producers, eventually winning at least nine Teddy awards for his TV films. With a mandate to explore the planet and a budget to go with it, the *American Sportsman* gave Wulff fantastic opportunities, and he let few go by. It was while on assignment for ABC in Ecuador in 1967 that he caught the his world-record 148-pound striped marlin on 12-pound tippet (and with a five-ounce fiberglass fly rod and a cheap, drag-less clicker reel), which still stands.

The TV show also brought Lee together with his "finest catch of all." In 1966 Kay Starr, from *Wheel of Fortune*, was scheduled to fish for giant tuna with Lee in Newfoundland. She developed a minor illness and cancelled, to Lee's regret; he'd always wanted to meet a national celebrity and Kay was exactly the sort of petite, attractive female he'd wanted for the show, to set off the enormous tuna. Instead ABC sent a last-minute substitute—national casting champion Joan Salvato, who demonstrated tackle for the Garcia Corporation. She caught a 572-pound bluefin for the camera, which looked all the more impressive next to her 122-pound frame, and handled herself with charm, patience, skill and grace. Lee was bowled over by her (and discovered he was grateful to Kay Starr after all); Joan was equally impressed and they were married in 1967.

The stories surrounding Wulff's feats of angling have spread around the world and into the fabric of the sport. On August 17, 1967, for instance, he broke the 50-pound-test world record for bluefin tuna (in Newfoundland's Conception Bay) by boating a 597-pound fish—after fighting it for 13 hours and 25 minutes. And then there was his informal Sixteen-Twenty Club, entry into which seems so difficult that few people even try to take a 20-pound fish on a #16 fly, even though Wulff has written clearly how it can be done. He himself proceeded to go the "club" several steps better, first by taking a 27-pound Atlantic salmon on a #16 and then by seeing how large a fish he could take on a #28 hook. In 1985, after many attempts, using a #28 hook with an oversize Prefontaine skater pattern tied onto the tippet, he caught and boated (and released) an Atlantic salmon of 10 pounds on New Brunswick's Restigouche River. The tippet was 4X, four-pound-test—nearly three times as strong as the hook (which has a gape of only a sixteenth of an inch)—and the fight took 31 minutes. A few seasons later he topped himself again, this time with a 12-pound salmon on a #28. The exploits, which to Wulff were not "exploits" at all, but tests of himself, continued to the end. In March of 1991, a few weeks before his death, Wulff was in Costa Rica, where, at age 86, he took a large sailfish on a dry fly.

The most important concept of present-day sport fishing, and the one that is chiefly responsible, directly and indirectly, for the great improvement in trout and salmon fishing in North America, is the idea of releasing a fish unharmed to spawn and even to be caught and to fight again another day. Much of the credit for publicizing the idea goes to Lee Wulff, who in *Lee Wulff's New Handbook of Freshwater Fishing* (Stokes) wrote, "Game fish are too valuable to be caught only once" and "The fish you release is your gift to another angler and, remember, it may have been someone's similar gift to you." That was in 1939. He went on to preach that gospel at every opportunity, and he had many opportunities—for more than 50 years he was in constant demand as a speaker, film maker and writer on angling. Probably no one has ever reached more outdoors people.

A corollary to catch-and-release was Wulff's advice that if we were to kill any gamefish it should be the small ones, not the large, trophy fish. This flew directly in the face of the "Bambi" school of game management, which applies human values, not biological science, to the predator-prey relationship. The notion of sparing the young, the weak, the small and the female has been around possibly forever, but Wulff pointed out that sparing small fish (or deer or whatever) skewed natural selection their way; eventually, there would only be small fish or deer left. Of minimum-size limits, he wrote, "Someone should have asked: 'If we cut off the head of every American over five feet tall for three generations, what would it do to our basketball teams?'" The fish to release, he said, were the large, strong, healthy super-predators, the individuals who had demonstrated in the clearest possible way that they could survive and prosper.

In his will, Wulff left a sum of money to The Angler's Club of New York, where he had been a member for decades, with instructions that it be used after his passing to "throw a happy party celebrating my long and pleasant stay on earth."

Lee Wulff—his signature fly pattern, the Royal Wulff; this example was tied by Lee himself, without a vise.

X-sizes—The numerical range of thicknesses of the most often-used tippet material, from 0X through 7X. The higher the X-number, the finer the tippet. The key is to remember that the X-size and the tippet diameter add up to .011"—11 thousandths of an inch. Thus a 3X tippet is .008" thick, a 6X tippet measures .005" and so on. These measurements are critical to the proper performance of a tapered leader (see) in fly-casting, for the tippet, the last section of the leader, must deliver the fly to its target yet be invisible to the fish. A thicker tippet is generally a stronger tippet, but the X-scale indicates only relative, not absolute, strength. The march of technology has led to dramatic increases in the tensile strength of nylon monofilament. A 1X (.010") tippet may be rated for for as much as 15 pounds of pull; a 6X (.005") tippet for three pounds—more, in fact, than a #24 hook can sustain before the bend straightens out. As tensile strength increases, diameter can be decreased; some trout anglers now carry 7X tippet and 8X (.003") is available.

The convention of using an "X" code to denote diameter dates back more than two centuries, to the early decades of the watch-making industry in Europe. To resolve differences between metric, English and other measurement systems, jewelers standardized the apertures bored in their draw-plates according to a scale of X-sizes. Seeking standardization also, some anglers eventually began to shave down strands of silkworm gut by pulling them through these draw-plates. The "Rule of 11" used today for springs from the original jeweler's X-scale: a 10X aperture was very close to .001".

Zinger—A little spring-loaded device that pins to a fishing vest and holds small tools such as line clippers. The line or wire or fine chain coiled up inside a zinger generally reaches out about two feet, so the tool need not be detached when it's needed; and when the job is done the wire retracts neatly into the body of the zinger and the tool hangs there until it's needed again. An interesting variation is the zinger (brought to market by the Simms Company) with what looks like extra-tightly wound telephone cord that disappears into a plastic tube. Also known as a pin-on reel.

PHOTO CREDITS

R. Valentine Atkinson, Silvio Calabi, Tim Leary, Darrel Martin, C. Boyd Pfeiffer.

THE AUTHOR

Silvio Calabi is the Editor of *Fly Rod & Reel* Magazine and the author of *Game Fish of North America, The Collector's Guide to Antique Fishing Tackle* and *Trout & Salmon of the World*. He lives with his wife and two children in Camden, Maine.

——ACKNOWLEDGMENTS——

To the memory of Lee Wulff, who tried to teach me to think for myself.

And to a number of persons whose own thoughts have, fortunately, colored mine: John Betts, Tom Dorsey, Bill Hunter, Mel Krieger, Fred Oswalt, Howard Steere, Ted Williams, Harry Wilson, Joan Salvato Wulff.

And to Bill Anderson, Jim Butler, Carol Des Lauriers Cieri, Marcel Dagneau, Allen Fernald, Dave Jackson, Tim Seymour, Sarah Pearse and Kit. What would, or could, I do without you?

Portions of this book have appeared in *Fly Rod & Reel* magazine.